KIM AND JIM

KIM AND JIM

Philby and Angleton:

Friends and Enemies in the Cold War

MICHAEL HOLZMAN

WEIDENFELD & NICOLSON

First published in Great Britain in 2021
by Weidenfeld & Nicolson

Weidenfeld & Nicolson
The Orion Publishing Group Ltd
Carmelite House
50 Victoria Embankment
London, EC4Y 0DZ

An Hachette UK Company

1 3 5 7 9 10 8 6 4 2

A CIP catalogue record for this book
is available from the British Library.

HB ISBN 978 1 4746 1780 2
TPB ISBN 978 1 4746 1781 9
eBook 978 1 4746 1 7833

Typeset by Input Data Services Ltd, Somerset

Printed and bound in Great Britain by Clays Ltd, Elcograf S.p.A.

For Jane

Acknowledgments

Many friends and colleagues have read and commented on parts of the manuscript at various stages of its production. I am particularly grateful to Jeff Hulbert, a superior researcher, and to Shelley Glick, the intrepid reference librarian at the Briarcliff Manor Village Public Library. Jane MacKillop has read the entire manuscript many times, patiently providing criticism, support, and encouragement.

Errors, of course, are my own. I would be grateful to have them brought to my attention so that they might be corrected.

Health warning: Information from secret intelligence organizations and those associated with them are not to be accepted without independent corroboration.

Contents

PROLOGUE:

London, April 1946

The war in Europe had been over for nearly a year. Churchill, the victor, had been thrown out of office by the votes of his own soldiers and sailors. England was exhausted, bankrupt, many of its factories and the centers of its cities destroyed, food rationed, hundreds of thousands of its men still overseas, the economy dependent on the labor of enemy prisoners of war. London, capital of the greatest empire the world had seen, was broken, pockmarked with wild-flower-strewn bomb sites. But the headquarters of the Secret Intelligence Service, MI-6, in Broadway Buildings and across St. James's Park that of its counterintelligence division, Section V, had survived intact. As had the Café Royal in nearby Regent Street, London.

Captain James "Jim" Angleton, chief of counterintelligence for the Mediterranean Theater for the US Army's Strategic Services Unit—the SSU, all that survived of the fabled OSS—had traveled up from Rome seeking advice from his mentor, H. A. R. "Kim" Philby, formerly of Section V, MI-6 counterintelligence. After meetings during office hours, they, and the head of Section V, Lt. Col. Timothy Milne, went to a nearby restaurant for a long dinner.

The Café Royal was a short twenty-minute walk across St. James's Park from the Broadway Buildings, and less than half that distance from Ryder Street where MI-6 had sub-let accommodations to the American counterintelligence staff of OSS. It had been at Ryder Street that the future leaders of the CIA learned their trade. Malcolm Muggeridge described them in his condescending, oft-quoted description: "Ah, those first OSS arrivals in London! How well I remember them, arriving like *jeunes filles en fleur* straight from a finishing school, all fresh and innocent, to start work in our frowsy old intelligence brothel; all too soon they were ravished and corrupted, becoming indistinguishable from seasoned pros who had been in the game for quarter of a century or more." Among the most innocent had been young, passionate, Jim Angleton, rescued from a dismal term in the Harvard Law School by a friendly conspiracy between his father, already a major assigned to OSS, and his old Yale instructor, Norman Pearson, head of X-2. And in this case Muggeridge was right: by that postwar spring Angleton had become professionally indistinguishable from the seasoned pros in MI-6, such as Kim Philby.

After his 1944 induction into counterintelligence tradecraft by Philby in London, Angleton had been posted to Italy, beginning his work there with routine interrogations of people who had been captured trying to cross the lines between the Allied and Axis armies. He then established networks of agents and opened relations with the Italian naval and civilian intelligence organizations. Soon enough he was, in effect, running those organizations insofar as their activities interested him. He developed liaison relations with a dozen or more foreign intelligence organizations, securing access to, and copies of, their files (a collection later to become the foundation of CIA's own "Registry." Angleton would always stress the importance of files and liaisons.) He intervened in Italian politics at the highest levels, seized fascist collaborators at gunpoint from under the noses of partisans, ate well, and from time to time, with traces of remaining innocence, wrote poetry late into the night.

But during that April 1946 lengthy dinner in London he was once more the apprentice, literally outranked by Milne and effectively outranked by Philby, who was a civilian, but arguably the equivalent of a colonel in the British service (as he would later claim to be in the Soviet service as well). Angleton needed advice because President Truman had been cleaning house, abolishing the OSS among many other Roosevelt-era organizations, making it known that he disliked espionage, per se. As a consequence the British secret intelligence organizations did not know what to make of the rump of OSS that was the Strategic Services Unit. Or so they said, gaining a certain advantage in negotiations by emphasizing the question of the SSU's possibly brief survival. The Brits weren't the only ones who claimed to be doubtful of the need to share secrets with what perhaps was a dying organization. The London branches of the other American intelligence agencies, such as the army's G-2, the navy's ONI, the

FBI, were also offering limited cooperation. What was to be done? Angleton turned to his old teacher: Kim Philby.

That dinner conversation no doubt included a tour of the counterintelligence horizon—Italian and Greek struggles between the British-backed monarchists and the communist partisans, the threat to northeastern Italy posed by a Yugoslavia still firmly aligned with the Soviet Union, the futures of Spain and France. There was so much to discuss, so many secrets to share, hint at, regretfully decline to fully reveal. Philby dangled the bait of "certain materials" that would become available to the SSU once it was clearly *the* American counterintelligence interlocutor with Section V. The purpose of the bait, as was made clear to Angleton's superior officer, Colonel William Quinn, in an August 1946 meeting with Sir Stuart Menzies, Chief of MI-6 and, again, Kim Philby, was a merger of MI-6 and the SSU. The British wished to have their American colleagues share the cribs, as it were, in their "frowsy old intelligence brothel." Quinn replied, as apparently Angleton had not, that he preferred to build his own house, while also enjoying access to the favors available in that of Menzies. It would take the full force of Director of Central Intelligence General Walter Bedell Smith to achieve that goal.

The lasting influence of a charismatic teacher is something of a cliché. In this case that influence came with both a positive and negative sign. During the immediate postwar years Angleton and Philby continued from their respective posting and travels that professional intimacy forged in Ryder Street during the war. By 1950 when both were in Washington, Philby, remaining the dominant partner, effectively forged that near-merger of the two services he had proposed in the summer of 1946. And then, in the 1950s and 1960s, one intelligence disaster following another, it became increasingly clear to Angleton that there had been a third partner to the merger, the KGB. He had more and more reasons to reflect on that formative relationship, to wonder to what extent those disasters were "Kim's work."

PREFACE

"The Cold War is over. It is time to discard its stupid stereotypes, which portrayed the people on one side of the barricade as schizophrenics, homosexuals, alcoholics, chiselers and scoundrels, and their opponents as pure saints, committed to moral values."*

When James Angleton died in 1987 and Kim Philby died exactly a year later, the overarching historical narrative seemed firmly in place: in the nearly century-long struggle between communism and capitalism, communism had lost, capitalism had won. Philby, with all his virtues, had chosen the wrong side; Angleton, for all his faults, had been on the right, the ultimately triumphant, side. Things look less certain today. Capitalism has come close to collapse, and in its recovery looks less and less closely allied with democracy. And if the lands of the former Soviet Union are no longer ruled by the Communist Party, virtually all of the East Asian mainland is—shall we say—*managed* by communist parties.

Matters of historical interpretation have become increasingly complicated. That is a good thing. The old certainties created distortions, bending the interpretation of such information we have about the twentieth century so severely as to be useful chiefly as information about the etiology of those certainties and interpretations themselves. We now must gather the used bricks of discredited historical narratives, chip off the mortar of earlier interpretations, and attempt to assemble what remains in ways less predetermined by the conflicting ideologies of their time. Of course, our stories, no doubt, will be determined by ideologies of our own, of our own time, of which we have little conscious awareness.

Further complicating the task at hand, the biographical narratives

---

* Lyubimov, Mikhail. "A Martyr to Dogma." In Philby, Rufina. *The Private Life of Kim Philby*, p. 276.

about Harold Adrian Russell "Kim" Philby and James Jesus Angleton were for the most part created, and kept in place, by their enemies. Angleton and Philby have often been depicted as two-dimensional exemplars of their ideologies: the anti-communist Cold Warrior and the traitorous communist spy. Sometimes they are presented in the psychologizing fashion of the second half of the twentieth century: the paranoid bureaucrat and the duplicitous sociopath addicted to betrayal. Neither should be pinned to their display cards in this way. Although both were alcoholics, as it seemed were an astonishing number of their peers, neither suffered from mental illness on the scale of, say, the first American Secretary of Defense, James Forrestal, with his hallucinations of the Red Army marching across the bridges of the Potomac River.

This study is an attempt to present Philby and Angleton primarily in their roles as secret intelligence professionals, as, perhaps, two of the pre-eminent members of that guild. On the other hand, they had personal lives: parents, friends, spouses, children, and, in Philby's case, an alternate career, that of foreign correspondent. Both had remarkable fathers, Angleton's a self-made man in the mythologized manner of the American frontier, Philby's an important member, then critic of, the colonial service of the Raj. These matters will also be described insofar as they are relevant.

James Angleton and Kim Philby were friends for six years, or so Angleton thought. They were then enemies for the rest of their lives. Both agreed on that. This is the story of their intertwined careers and the effect of those careers on the Cold War.

INTRODUCTION

There are few places on earth more distant from one another than Boise, Idaho, and Ambala, in the Punjab. A hundred years ago Boise was barely a generation from its initial settlement by European-Americans: Mormons moving north from Utah and others moving west, the indigenous peoples having been pushed out by the US Army to make room for the course of Manifest Destiny. Ambala, near Lahore in what is now Pakistan, was then part of the British Indian empire, the Raj. In contrast to raw Boise, Ambala may have seen the armies of Alexander the Great pass by after encountering there a civilization even then perhaps already a thousand years old. And yet, around the year 1950, a few blocks from the White House, the black waiters in the fashionable Washington, D.C., seafood restaurant, Harvey's, every few days brought cocktails, then lunchtime lobsters, to two men with those widely separated origins. James Angleton, who had been born in Boise and was to be buried there, was an important member of the Central Intelligence Agency (CIA). H. A. R. Philby, known as "Kim" since his childhood in Ambala, was a similarly important member of the British Secret Intelligence Service (SIS, often referred to as MI-6). They had known each other for most of a decade, had worked together closely in the past, and were now working together even more closely. They had much to discuss. Their lunches at Harvey's went on late into the afternoons and were often followed (or proceeded) by more formal meetings at the Lutyens-designed British embassy on Massachusetts Avenue on Embassy Row or in the less comfortable offices of the CIA, on the Mall, near the Reflecting Pool. From time to time they would meet after office hours at one or another of the frequent receptions and dinner parties characteristic of the diplomatic-intelligence social circuit they inhabited. They had much in common; many secrets to share; as many to conceal.

As a rule, secret intelligence officers, like diplomats, record each meeting with a foreign official or agent. Angleton's notes of his meetings with Philby are not publicly available. It is said that he burned them. Philby's notes of his meetings with Angleton are also unavailable. Perhaps they reside as yet undisturbed in archives in London and Moscow.

Angleton's position in the very new, still relatively small, quasi-military, American foreign intelligence organization, the Central Intelligence Agency, was as an executive in the division charged with collecting secret information. (Counterintelligence, which would be his métier, was still in the hands of an ex-FBI agent, William K. Harvey.) He had come to the CIA by way of the short-lived Central Intelligence Group and its predecessors, the Strategic Services Unit and the wartime Office of Strategic Services (OSS). Philby, seven years older, held the senior position, serving as liaison in Washington to the CIA, FBI, and the National Security Agency for the Secret Intelligence Service of the British empire. Philby had earlier run the Turkish station for SIS, and before that the section in London that had been established to watch the Soviet Union. During the war he had specialized in counterespionage; Angleton, then a newly commissioned officer in the counterintelligence division, X-2, of the OSS, was tutored and for a time in effect supervised in those matters by Philby. It has been said by a recent observer that Philby was Angleton's "uncle" in counterintelligence matters. Of course Philby had other responsibilities. For fifteen years he had been an agent of the Soviet intelligence services, as he would remain for close to another fifteen years.

The careers of Angleton and Philby, and their relationship, helped shape the covert Cold War. Angleton built the counterintelligence staff of the Central Intelligence Agency, its hundreds of officers dedicated to preventing the penetration of the foreign secret intelligence service of the United States. In this, while he was chief of that staff, as far as is known, they were successful. In addition, Angleton established a worldwide alliance of anti-communist counter-intelligence services and, on the side, as it were, maintained control of intelligence relations with some key countries, such as Israel. During World War II Philby participated in the great secret intelligence triumph of the war, the Double Cross operation, which had penetrated the German Intelligence Service, turning it into a virtual branch of the Allied war effort. He had taught those lessons to

Angleton and his colleagues in the OSS. Simultaneously, in his role as an agent of the Soviet intelligence services, he penetrated first the British, then the American intelligence organizations. That was, for Angleton, when he became aware of it, another lesson Philby taught.

Philby and Angleton were major figures in the Cold War. It is probably an exaggeration to claim that Philby's work for the KGB* defeated the Anglo-American effort in the late 1940s and early 1950s to "roll-back" Soviet power from eastern Europe and areas, such as the Ukraine, of the Soviet Union itself. There were many other factors in play. And yet, without Philby, the Anglo-American-backed rebellions in Albania, Poland, the Baltic states, and the Ukraine might have gained more traction. Their failure was followed by the stasis of the Cold War. Similarly, it was not entirely to Angleton's credit alone that between 1954 and 1974 the operations of the Central Intelligence Agency were not betrayed by Soviet penetrations of its staff,† and that the CIA constructed a worldwide alliance of secret intelligence organizations, but it was largely so.

The usual questions about Philby are those about the cause he served. How could this intelligent, civilized, charming man devote his life to the Moloch of Stalinist Russia? The questions about Angleton are about the effects of his very success. Why did he, why was he allowed to, call into question the loyalty of dozens of his colleagues? How could this similarly intelligent, civilized, personally charming man destroy so many careers?

Those are the wrong questions.

Philby became an agent of the Soviet intelligence services in opposition to fascism and the British empire, for socialism, as he understood it, and against capitalism and imperialism, as he saw them. Angleton was trained in counterespionage techniques—in part by Philby—and was employed for most of his career to apply those techniques. That was his job. As time went by he became increasingly motivated by anti-communism. That, eventually, became his ruling passion, counterintelligence its instrument. Both men had domineering fathers. In each case that is more interesting

---

* "KGB" is used in this book to indicate the civilian intelligence service of the Soviet Union.

† With one, possibly two, exceptions.

than explanatory. There is, as a matter of fact, nothing to explain. The question would not have arisen if Angleton had become, as his father wished, an expatriate businessman in Italy; if Philby had devoted himself to journalism, if they had been private citizens. But they were not private citizens, and that is why they, and their relationship with one another, are of continuing interest.

OSS AND MI-6

If a quite elongated diamond were drawn on the map of England, with one point of the longer axis at Cambridge and the other at Oxford, the shorter axis would be anchored in the north at Bletchley Park and in the south at St. Albans, just outside the London M25 orbital motorway. Not that there was an M25 in 1943. The ancient market town of St. Albans was then sufficiently isolated to serve as an evacuation area, although it, too, had been bombed in the Blitz— lightly, as it were, with three clusters of bomb sites, one especially concentrated off the Hatfield Road, apparently aimed at the then fairly new Beaumont and Verulum state schools' playing fields. The British intelligence services had a predilection for country houses, some great houses, like Blenheim, others merely large houses, like Glenalmond and Bletchley. Glenalmond, an Edwardian mansion, was located three miles away from those strategic playing fields of St. Albans, on King Harry Lane. It housed Section V, counterintelligence, of MI-6, the Secret Intelligence Service. The central registry of MI-6 was nearby at Prae Wood.

The British empire was run on principles of strict economy. The peacetime army, compared to the armies of other European states, was quite small, as was the empire's bureaucracy. The money saved in this way was available for the navy and for the private investments that were, after all, the purpose of the empire. The economical operations of the army and other imperial means of control were made possible in part by intelligence organizations, in other words, spies, notably the Indian Intelligence Service[1] and that devoted to Irish affairs, the Special Irish Branch of the Metropolitan Police of London. The various police and secret intelligence services in India were so omnipresent that during World War II Americans there were warned by their government to regard the country as "a police state."[2] The Special Irish Branch of the Metropolitan Police became known simply as Special Branch as it focused as much on communists and their supposed associates (such as Labour Party government ministers) as on Fenians, in a manifestation of the attitude of some members of the British ruling class that those subjects of the Crown in the British Isles, who were not members of the ruling class, were simply one more subject population. The Security Service, MI-5, and MI-6, secret intelligence organizations that came into existence in the early twentieth century, floated between the uniformed services and the Foreign Office. MI-5, devoted its efforts to matters within the British empire, while the other looked after matters in the rest of the world. There was an official pretense that they did not exist. Their budgets were not included in the official account books, their employees "worked for the government" or, as with SIS staff, "worked for the Foreign Office." MI-5 and MI-6 were quite small until it became clear that a second world war was at hand, at which point they expanded.[3]

The national government of the United States had only had ad hoc experiences of secret foreign intelligence organizations before World War II. There were diplomatic reports, of course, and the army and navy had military intelligence organizations serving military purposes. Beyond that there were the Federal Bureau of Investigation's activities in Latin America, which, from the point of view of the American government, hardly counted as foreign intelligence. The first proper American foreign intelligence organization, the Office of Strategic Services, was an initiative of William Stephenson, head of British Security Coordination, a large imperial propaganda and espionage organization, targeting the United States, with headquarters in New York City. (Stephenson, following the model of Edgar Allan Poe's "The Purloined Letter," had housed his secret organization in the most conspicuous location in mid-twentieth-century America, the Empire State Building.) Stephenson thought it would be useful to the British empire to have, perhaps to control, an American equivalent of MI-6.[4] As explained by a knowledgeable observer, "Short-term considerations suggested that it would be better for the British to get in on the ground floor.

And, by offering all possible help in the early stages, to earn the right to receive in return the intelligence that might be expected to flow from the deployment of the greater resources of the United States. There was also the immediate chance of getting information through United States embassies in countries where Britain was no longer represented, such as Vichy France, the Balkans and even Germany."[5]

President Roosevelt asked William Donovan, a Republican, much-decorated World War I veteran, co-founder of the American Legion and at that point and later a Wall Street lawyer, to lead the effort to create such an organization. This was a fairly typical Roosevelt initiative, at once limiting the scope of Hoover's Federal Bureau of Investigation, co-opting a possible rival politician, bringing under his direct control the collection of potentially valuable information. Donovan went to London to learn how British secret intelligence was organized (and, not incidentally, to assess the prospects for British victory in the war), meeting many of the principals of MI-5 and MI-6. These made the seductive gestures of opening (some of) their secrets to him, seeking by this means to ensure that at that beginning American and British secret intelligence were virtually indivisible; assuming, or hoping, that the former would be an instrument of the latter. As it was, for a time, until those roles, like so many others in Anglo-American relations, reversed.

The new American organization, initiated on 11 July 1941, was made responsible, when in 1944 it was taken from the military and transferred to the Executive Office of the President, for, inter alia, "Coordination of the functions of all intelligence agencies of the Government . . . evaluation, synthesis and dissemination within the Government" of intelligence "in peace and war," collection of information, "subversive operations outside the continental limits of the United States, and "Direct liaison with secret intelligence agencies of foreign governments."[6] OSS became something like a combination of the British MI-6 and the Special Operations Executive (SOE), both collecting information and undertaking subversive operations. It was where the founding group of CIA officials—Dulles, Wisner, Helms, and James Angleton—learned their trade from their British colleagues. Angleton was tutored in his particular specialty in the offices of Section V of MI-6, counterintelligence, which has "a highly specialized target: the enemy's own secret service.

The object is not merely to uncover political, military or other secrets . . . It is rather to build up a detailed picture of the operations, techniques, personnel, structure, and policy of the hostile service. Of course the most desirable information of all is what the enemy knows about oneself and, in a further sophisticated twist, what he knows that one knows about him. If the enemy's secret information about one can be discovered, it is by definition no longer secret, and his knowledge is powerless . . . The ideal objective of counter-espionage is to make the enemy service a docile extension of one's own."[7]

The counterintelligence division of OSS, known as X-2, was established on 1 March 1943. Perhaps its most important achievement was accomplished nearly at once when it was given a copy of the paper "memory" of British secret intelligence. "In return for O.S.S. men and materials, the British now proposed to throw open their legendary . . . archives, that worldwide register of suspects, those precious card catalogs.

With this single breakthrough the O.S.S. was made. One declassified O.S.S. after-action study states: 'Here was a field in which O.S.S. would have otherwise been unable to participate effectively at all. The British provided files, sources for information, operating techniques, trained assistance and facilities which proved indispensable. It would have taken O.S.S. perhaps decades to gain by itself the experience reached in only two years of British tutelage, and to build up the extensive files it was able to copy from British sources.'"[8]

The American theorist of "strategic intelligence," Sherman Kent, underlined the importance of such files: "Acquiring knowledge of personalities is one of the most important jobs of an intelligence organization.

The ideal biographical file would have tens of thousands of names in it, and against each name a very wide variety of data. There must be a wide range of data because there are so many pertinent questions always being asked about people. What sort of man is he? What are his political and economic views? What are all his names and when was he born? Can he speak English? Who are his intimates? What are his weaknesses? How long is he likely to hold his present standing? Where was he in 1937? etc."[9]

OSS eventually obtained similar files from all western European secret intelligence services, as well as from a few others. By the end of the war the American registry included approximately 400,000 names of America's suspected or potential enemies, domestic and foreign.[10] These were passed on to the successor organization, the CIA, where they were—are—augmented and digitized. However, as James Angleton would caution a few years later, even then the lack of a trace did not mean that a suspected spy, for example, was cleared; it meant that there was literally nothing in the files about that person. No one could be *proved* innocent, only not yet proven guilty.

According to the OSS report on its own wartime activities, "It soon became evident that by working in close collaboration with the British, knowledge could be acquired and personnel trained in the highly intricate techniques of counter-espionage manipulation and the control of enemy agents through which knowledge could be gained of the enemy's plans and intentions and the enemy could be deceived as to one's own."[11] The British had an even more intimate relationship in mind. Timothy Milne, a longtime MI-6 official, remembered that although collaboration between MI-6 and what would become its American counterpart began even before the American entry into the war. After Pearl Harbor the head of Section V of MI-6, Felix Cowgill, decided to merge the counterintelligence headquarters of the two organizations: MI-6's Section V and what became OSS's X-2 staff. When the first American X-2 officers arrived in England, they were housed in St. Albans and in huts at Glenalmond. Secret documents were shared between Section V and X2, including ISOS.*[12]

The future head of counterintelligence for the OSS, Norman Pearson, lately and later of the Yale University English Department, and three uniformed officers (and four secretaries), arrived in London toward the end of March 1943. On 15 June 1943, the

---

* Illicit Signals Oliver Strachey: the unit that read 'Abwehr (German Intelligence Service)' messages.

Counter-Intelligence Division of OSS became the Counter-Espionage Branch, X-2. According to an Office of Strategic Services memorandum of 19 May 1944, "The X-2 Branch is primarily concerned with the existence, identity, and methods of enemy espionage, counter-espionage and saboteur agents and protection against them.

> It will, in all cases not imperiling special sources of information, promptly inform the Security Office of evidence of enemy affiliation or association of O.S.S. personnel. It may conduct investigations either on its own initiative or when suggested by the Security Office . . . *The X-2 Branch solely is responsible for coordinating and controlling the operations of double agents.*"[13] [Emphasis added.]

"Double agents": people employed by a secret intelligence agency to spy on an enemy's secret intelligence agency, while being, in fact, the agent of the target organization, were, for counterespionage officials, at the center of their work. Much later, the counterintelligence staff of the Central Intelligence Agency would take its responsibility for internal investigations to heart: some would think too much so; some, that it was too late.

Section V moved on 21 July 1943,[14] to 14 Ryder Street, St. James's, London, across the park from the headquarters of the British Secret Intelligence Service, which were in Broadway, midway between Buckingham Palace and the Houses of Parliament. Ryder Street was not luxurious. The rooms were small and inadequately heated with small coal fires.[15] Nonetheless, it was a good neighborhood: the Ritz a few blocks in one direction; Pall Mall with its clubs a few blocks in another direction, just past Christie's. The then-modern, concrete, Arlington House Apartments, where Guy Burgess's mother lived, was, and is, midway between Ryder Street and the Ritz. The Unicorn pub, a favorite of Section V, was conveniently located between Quaglino's and Wiltons restaurants, barely a block from 14 Ryder Street. Turnbull and Asher, at the corner of Jermyn and Bury Street, have a small black and white photograph of what was left of the buildings across the street after a high explosive bomb had done its work. Three bombs fell at that intersection during the Blitz. Three more bombs fell on Bury Street, just north of Ryder Street, but the Blitz was over by the time Section V took up residence there among those bomb sites, gentlemen's clubs, restaurants, and pubs, leaving only the gaps between the buildings as records of its effects.

X-2 moved into Ryder Street a month after Section V, on 27 August 1943. Its offices were "located on the third (U.S. fourth) floor and consisted of eleven rooms and eight bathrooms.

> There would be space for thirty desks comfortably or forty desks with moderate crowding. The entire collection of rooms could be blocked off from the rest of the building and a passageway cut through to No 14; this job was undertaken by his Majesty's Office of Works in addition to minor repairs necessary as a result of bombs which had fallen nearby . . . the office was not completely established in the new quarters until 15 January 1944."[16]

During official business hours, the head of MI-6, Section V, Felix Cowgill, and his American counterpart, Norman Holmes Pearson, got along well, as each made it his business to ensure.[17] Cowgill's assistant, H. A. R. "Kim" Philby, also made it his business to get along well with Pearson, and most others, including James Angleton.

FATHERS AND SONS

ST. JOHN PHILBY

BRITISH EMPIRE, the name now loosely given to the whole aggregate of territory, the inhabitants of which, under various forms of government, ultimately look to the British crown as the supreme head . . . The land surface of the earth is estimated to extend over about 52,500,000 sq. m. Of this area the British empire occupies nearly one-quarter, extending over an area of about 12,000,000. *Encyclopedia Britannica, Eleventh Edition, 1910.*

The 3 October 1960 edition of *The Times* of London carried an obituary of "Mr. H. St. John B. Philby: Explorer and Arabist." It began: "Mr. H. St. John B. Philby, C.I.E., an explorer of the first rank to whom we owe most of our knowledge of the Arabia of today, died in Beirut on Friday. He was 75." The obituary went on to balance an account of Philby's career and achievements with statements about his difficult character, his "assurance of being always right, especially as against the British Government." It gracefully concluded: "When Philby's eccentricities have been forgotten he will still be remembered for his great work as an explorer.

> The oil prospectors who used his maps and descriptions found them completely accurate. He made large additions to British collections of geological and zoological specimens from Arabia. The British Museum owes to him many new species of birds, including a partridge named after him and a woodpecker named after his wife. He took up the collection and study of early Semitic inscriptions in Arabia, and he claimed to have increased from some 2,000 to over 13,000 the number of known Thamuddic inscriptions . . . Philby married in 1910 Dora, daughter of A. H. Johnston, of the Indian P.W.D. She died in 1957. There were four children."

For most of the forty years before St. John Philby's death, except for a few months in 1955, references in *The Times* to "Philby" were to him, and not to his son Harold Adrian Russell "Kim" Philby.

Harry Saint John Bridger Philby was born into late Imperial colonial society on 3 April 1885 in the town of Badulla, Ceylon (as it was then known), in a mountainous area in the southeast of the island. He was one of four sons of Henry Montague Philby, a coffee planter, and May (Queenie) Duncan, daughter of the commander of the Colombo British garrison.[1] Neither the father's career nor the marriage was a success. When in the late 1890s the coffee plants of the area succumbed to coffee leaf rust, many of the British planters switched to growing tea. Henry Montague did not and lost his farm. May Philby, a more resourceful person, took the children off to live with her parents, who were by then retired and wealthy in London, and thereafter maintained herself and her children by running boarding houses for gentry. Henry and May's son St. John, "Jack," won a scholarship to Westminster School, which he entered in 1898 at the age of thirteen, where he was a success at both games and studies.[2] He would visit and remain loyal to his old school all his life. He won an exhibition in Classics from Westminster School to Trinity College, Cambridge, arriving there in October 1904, where his friends and contemporaries extended from Rupert Brooke and James Strachey to Jawaharlal Nehru. St. John Philby worked hard at his studies, as he always would, while enjoying acting and debate, particularly the latter, as he always would. At the end of his third year, having changed to Modern Languages, he received a first class degree. Given his social class and his father's unfortunate experience in business, Philby's career options came down to two forms of government employment: the army or the civil service. The latter, in turn, offered a choice of the home civil service, the foreign service, or the Indian Civil Service. Unsurprisingly, he chose the last of these.

St. John Philby passed the examination for the Indian Civil Service in 1907. As explained by a nearly contemporaneous article in the *Encyclopedia Britannica*, "Candidates for the civil service of India take the same examination for the 1st class clerkships of the British civil service . . .

The subjects include the language and literature of England, France, Germany, Italy, ancient Greece and Rome, Sanskrit and

Arabic, mathematics (pure and applied), natural science (chemistry, physics, zoology, &c.), history (English, Greek, Roman and general modern), political economy and economic history, mental and moral philosophy, Roman and English law and political science."[3]

Philby did well, as he always did in examinations, especially with languages. As required of those entering the governing caste of the empire, he then spent a salaried year in England, preparing for a final examination in Indian Penal Code and the Code of Criminal Procedure, "Mahommedan" Law, the Indian Evidence Act, and more languages: Hindi and Persian, perhaps Sanskrit. He also passed the compulsory examination in riding. Thus prepared to be a servant of the empire, St. John Philby, age twenty-three, sailed to India in November 1908.[4]

We are familiar with the world of late imperial India, the Raj, from the vast, romanticizing, English-language literature emerging from or describing it: the comfortable life taking place in many-servanted bungalows in the cantonments; the all-important club—no Indians or dogs allowed—the petty intrigues; the "love" affairs; the summer transfers of households from the plains to the incongruous ginger-bread houses of the high mountain town of Simla; the intense male friendships within officialdom, among "our kind." It was part of a world, the British empire, including, formally, informally, loosely, much of Africa and the Pacific, bits of the Americas, aspects of China. However, its heart was the Indian empire, then including not only present-day India, Pakistan, Bangladesh, Ceylon (Sri Lanka) and Burma (Myanmar), but as well, in the Arabian peninsula, Aden (now part of Yemen); Oman ("informally") and the United Arab Emirates: in effect the entire southern and eastern coasts of Arabia. The interior of Arabia was still officially part of the Ottoman empire, which maintained the pilgrimage railroad from Damascus to Mecca, but for most other intents and purposes it was the ungoverned realm of feuding clans and tribes of Bedouin. This westward extension of the Raj would become St. John Philby's home ground.

The overt purpose of the Indian Civil Service was to govern India, to bring the rule of law "to the lesser breeds without the Law" in that vast and varied area. Young "Jack" Philby was first assigned to administer that law in the Jhelum district, Punjab, just southwest of Kashmir. There he learned Urdu and the various requirements of the administration such as finance and judicial procedure. Transferred to Rawalpindi, he put these into practice, learned Punjabi, was highly rated in his work, and repeatedly promoted.[5] He married in 1910 Dora Johnston (slightly déclassée, in the class-obsessed hierarchy of the Indian Civil Service, as her father was only in the Punjab Provincial Engineering Service). Philby's distant cousin, then Lieutenant, later Field Marshal, Bernard Montgomery was best man at their wedding.[6] St. John Philby would continue to accumulate languages, partially in order to increase his income as the government of India offered monetary prizes for good results on language examinations. (While receiving judicial training in Multan, Punjab, Philby learned Baluchi.) Between 1911 and 1915 he earned over 10,000 rupees in this way.[7] In September 1911, after various temporary assignments, the young Philby couple moved to Ambala, between Delhi and Lahore, where St. John Philby served as a revenue assistant, a difficult assignment in the midst of a drought with a famine threatening. There Dora gave birth to a son, on New Year's Day 1912, inevitably, presciently, to be nicknamed "Kim," supposedly because, like Kipling's hero, his first language was not English, but that of his locally recruited Ayah. In 1914 St. John Philby became Deputy and Acting District Commissioner at Lyallpur, halfway between Delhi and Kabul, in the Punjab, then was appointed to the Criminal Investigation Department at Simla, working for the empire's Punjab government.[8] In February 1915, after passing the Urdu language examination in Calcutta with honors, Philby became head of the language board there. With one or two minor hitches, he had made a good start to a career in the service of the administration of the Raj.

The life of the British colonial caste was severely gendered, the men working in the administration of vast populations, playing polo and cricket, drinking, hunting tigers; the women socializing and reproducing. All this while just outside the cantonment gates, the life of India went on as best it could, given the restrictions, taxations, and assorted inequities of colonial rule: the chronic savagery of the empire punctuated by the occasional massacre. St. John Philby, ambitious, gifted, very sure of his own judgments—increasingly as time went on—did not quite fit. Too clever by half, too much given to seeing the "natives'" side of the issues, too often expressive of his own opinions, his career was constantly on the verge of being sidetracked, but in the event, for a time, for nearly a decade, it was not. When the war began in the summer of 1914, St. John Philby was still sufficiently conventional to try to get to the killing fields of the Western Front but was held in post until, on 15 November 1915, he was sent to Basra (now Iraq, then Mesopotamia) and put in charge of the finances of the British administration of areas occupied by the British (Indian) army, as a major in the Political and Secret Department, adding for that purpose Arabic to his language store.[9] As with so many other legends, that of St. John Philby began in Baghdad.

Iraq was then a province—actually three provinces—of the Ottoman empire, which, allied with Germany, was at war with the British empire. In order to protect its Indian possessions from Germany, and to gain additional oil reserves, the British had sent an Indian army to Basra, in the south, and had it march up the Tigris River, aiming for Baghdad. In a legendary exhibition of incompetent generalship, this force, while still short of Baghdad, was thoroughly defeated by a Turkish army at a place called Kut, in April 1916. The commanding English general, Townshend, taken to luxurious captivity in a villa near Istanbul, left his men to die of starvation, disease, and what was called "mistreatment": repeated whippings and rapes. Another Indian army, under a different British general, took Baghdad in March 1917. In October 1916, between the fall of Kut to the Ottomans and that of Baghdad to the British, St. John Philby was promoted to the rank of Revenue Commissioner and made a Commander of the Indian Empire (CIE). In May 1917, he went to Baghdad as personal assistant to the High Commissioner, Sir Percy Cox. While there he became the hero of a story seemingly from the *Arabian Nights*:

> Twice St. John Philby disappeared from base, each time wandering the by-ways of Baghdad disguised as an Arab beggar. Two clever Germans were causing concern to the British forces at this time. One was the famous Wassmuss, who ranged with a band of guerilla fighters throughout Persia, swooping down on oilfields and generally upsetting the British lines of communication between India and Mesopotamia. The other German was Preusser, who claimed to be the master of the Persian Gulf. St. John Philby had to pit his brains against these two clever men. The sequel was inevitable. Preusser was knifed by an Arab one night and died. Wassmuss found a

cordon closing around him in Persia and only escaped by a sensational ride through the night towards the rooftop of the world,
where he took refuge in a Central Asian state. When this work was
finished St. John Philby again disappeared.[10]

The storyteller was the novelist William Makin. When not—
possibly—embarked on Harun al-Rashid adventures, Philby was
sent to Arabia in November 1917, which marked a turning point in
his life.[11]

The Arabian peninsula was at this time part of the "informal"
empire, except those areas, like Aden City, that were overtly held as
colonies. To the north, greater Syria, including Palestine, remained
under the suzerainty of the Ottoman empire. The interior of the
Arabian peninsula was disputed by Arab clans and tribes, their
alliances shifting and rapidly reversing. The empire, informal or
not, in long-practiced fashion, played them one against the other, an
activity complicated in this case by the overlapping responsibilities
of the Indian empire's officers reporting to Delhi and the officers
of the Arab Bureau, headquartered in Cairo. Both wished to use
these tribal warriors to push the Ottoman empire out of the vast
area between the Mediterranean and the Persian Gulf. The rival
tribal leaders, chiefly Ibn Saud (Abdulaziz ibn Abdul Rahman
Ibn Faisal ibn Turki ibn Abdullah ibn Muhammad Al Saud) and
Hussein (Hussein ibn Ali al-Hashimi), each wished to use the British
to become the sole king of the Arabs. The Arab Bureau supported
Hussein of Mecca and his son Faisal: Hashemites; the government
of India supported Ibn Saud, an ally of the fundamentalist Wahabi
sect, but it could just as easily have been the other way around.

St. John Philby, who, despite his putative nocturnal feats of
daring, was unpopular among the representatives of the Raj in
Baghdad—too often asserting his own opinions against those of
his bureaucratic superiors—decided he would rather go exploring
than sit in an office. The expedition in which Philby participated
was intended to persuade Ibn Saud to lessen his hostilities against
the Hashemites, so that the Arab tribes of both western and eastern
Arabia could be used together by the British against the Ottoman
empire. Philby reached Ibn Saud's capital on 30 November 1917. He
found that there were still difficulties between the Hashemite king
and Ibn Saud. This is summed up by a typical comment from St.

John Philby: "Ibn Saud displays consuming jealousy of Sherif [Hussein] whose assumption in correspondence of title of 'King of Arab Countries' galls him to distraction, while at the back of his mind is the suspicion that Sherif's attitude in this connection is based on some secret understanding with us."[12] Philby remained in Arabia for nearly a year, finding his vocation not as a financial control officer in the imperial administration, but as a desert explorer and companion of Ibn Saud, then merely an Arabian chieftain, later, King of (Saudi) Arabia. Philby rapidly adopted Arab ways, food, dress, and manners—useful in winning their cooperation with imperial plans. We have a glimpse of him in this guise during his first journey east to west across Arabia, in pursuit of that elusive alliance between the King of Mecca and Ibn Saud. He had stopped near Mecca, where a British "Arab agent in Taif was to report: 'It was possible to distinguish Philby from the thirty-five Bedouin in his group only by the fact his feet were not quite dirty enough.'"[13]

As World War I was coming to a close, Philby remained in Arabia, beginning to explore the interior of the peninsula, along the way creating the maps for the Royal Geographical Society and amassing those collections that made his name.[14] Then, in London on leave, Philby found himself famous, and, with many months of back pay, prosperous. On 28 April 1919 he was given the honor of reading a paper on "Southern Najd" to the Royal Geographical Society, describing "a journey he took in May and June last year from Riyadh, the Wahhabi capital, to the Southern extremities of the Wahhabi country and back."[15] (He lectured again on that topic for that audience on 3 May 1920.) In June he flew to Arabia on an emergency mission to talk Ibn Saud out of massacring the Hashemites. "Hussein's quarrel with Ibn Saud had been smouldering for months, with repeated border incursions by one side or the other. In late May, a Sherifian army under Abdullah [Hussein's son] had been attacked while sleeping in its tents, and was virtually destroyed."[16] When Philby's aircraft stopped at Suda Bay, in Crete, he was joined by Colonel T. E. Lawrence, who happened to be there also en route to Cairo. Lawrence and Philby reached Cairo on 28 June, where they stayed at the ambassador's residency. Philby soon flew back to London, Lawrence to Paris and the frustrations of the Peace Conference.

Philby's role, as Ibn Saud's minder, involved, among other things, bear-leading him when he was honored with a royal reception in London, on 30 October 1919. *The Times* recorded that "The King, who was accompanied by The Queen and the Princess Mary,

> Received in the Throne Room of the Palace a Mission sent by the Ruler of Najd, consisting of His Excellency's son, Shaikh Faisal ibn Abdul Aziz Ibn Saud, Shaikh Ahmad ibn Thunaiyan Ibn Saud and Shaikh Abdullah al Quasaibi, with Mr. H. St. J. Philby (Mesopotamian Civil Service) in attendance, who acted as Interpreter."[17]

After the royal reception (and an exchange of ceremonial swords by the monarchs), Philby escorted the Saudi party on a tour of the United Kingdom, including a stop at his son Kim's prep school, no doubt thrilling the boys and adding immensely to Kim's prestige. St. John Philby lingered in London, lecturing to the Central Asian Society's Anniversary meeting on 23 June 1920 on the topic of "The Highways of Central Arabia." Towards the end of August, he was sent back to Baghdad with his old supervisor, Sir Percy Cox, to help "restore order" in Mesopotamia, where tribal raiding had become a problem for the imperial administration, despite the comparative novelty of aerial bombardment. Philby became adviser to the Iraqi Minister of the Interior, with a good salary and, overlooking the Tigris, a big house in which he installed Dora and their new daughter, at the center of the local British colonial society.[18]

St. John Philby had been working with T. E. Lawrence to further the cause of Arab independence, which they both advocated, against the grain of Imperial strategy. Things, as usual, got complicated. Lawrence's favorite, Faisal, son of Hussein, struggled in Syria with the French, on the one side, and with more radical Arabs, on the other. Plots followed one another in rather quick succession, and after Cox arranged for a tighter British grip on Iraq, against Philby's opposition, Philby was brought on side by being made Minister of Interior, in his own right, replacing his Arab colleague. He was opposed to this in principle, advocating Arab self-determination and self-rule; in practice, he (and Dora) rejoiced in the power and luxury it brought. It was a short-lived triumph. By October 1921 the Hashemite Faisal, as the candidate of Lawrence and Gertrude Bell, had been installed as King of Iraq, in lieu of his lost Syria. Philby, as an anti-Hashemite, had been fired, and then, by means of a virtual *deus ex machina*, had been named political adviser (Chief British Representative) to another son of Hussein, the Emir Abdullah of the new entity of Transjordan. The "deus," in this case, was T. E. Lawrence, who wrote in a successful recommendation: "Philby is a very powerful and able person . . . We have often thought of him for Trans-Jordan which he would do splendidly if he would play fair. His trouble is an uncertain temper."[19]

To most intents and purposes Philby was now governor of that part of then Mandate Palestine east of the Jordan River. In partnership with the Hashemite Emir, Philby set about creating in the uncertain geographical expression "Transjordan," a state, with a civil service, police force, regular finances, and, perhaps most notably, a British-officered army, which was to become the Arab Legion. The close relationship between the Emir and the imperial government was cemented during a visit by the Emir to London in October 1922, arranged by Philby, by negotiations, ceremonial meals, and a trip to the zoo. The Emir wanted a promise from the imperial administration that Transjordan would achieve the status of an independent, or at least semi-independent, state. The imperial authorities were overtly encouraging, but nothing was concluded during the Emir's time in London. However, as *The Times* put it, "Mr. St. John Philby . . . will remain in London to discuss and settle with the British Government those points of detail which remain to be deposed of,"[20] and communicate such *faits accomplis* to the Emir. In the new year, back in Amman, Philby began the development of the ancient rose-red city of Petra as a tourist destination. Among the first tourists were his wife and son, Kim, who, in the summer of 1923, "arrived [in Amman] agog to see the sights . . ."[21]

After many quarrels with the High Commissioner for Palestine, Herbert Samuel, under whom he served, Philby resigned in April 1924 from his post in Transjordan and went to England on leave for a year, embarking on a round of lectures and book projects. He resigned from the Indian Civil Service itself in May 1925, no doubt to the relief of all concerned.[22] The imperial administration was tired of his "uncertain temper," and he of its policies for both India and the Middle East. He thought, and argued for, a larger, if not the largest, share in the government of India for the Indians themselves, and he, with Lawrence, believed that the empire had double-crossed the Arabs.[23] Philby's resignation did not affect his renown in London as an Arabist. On 16 June 1925 he gave the Royal Asiatic Society's first Burton Memorial Lecture. In the months following he lectured to the Fabian Society on "British Policy in the Middle East, 1879–1926" and on 8 July 1926 lectured to the Central Asian Society, on "The Triumph of the Wahabi" and on the administration of the Wahabi to the Central Asian Society on 19 October 1927.[24]

St. John Philby's life had divided into two parts. In England he was a famous lecturer and writer about Arabian matters; in Arabia, where he lived at first in Jeddah, then in Mecca and Riyadh, he became a companion and adviser to the King, Ibn Saud, and spent as much time as possible exploring the desert, first by camel, later by automobile. He converted to Islam, in the summer of 1930, effectively for business reasons. His biographer comments: "Philby was a celebrity, and his conversion was news abroad; it was immediately reported in the British and Egyptian press."[25] Philby became Resident Director in Arabia of Sharqieh Ltd., an import company, playing a not inconsiderable role in the modernization of the country. (For example, despite the world Depression, which was particularly acute in Arabia, Philby arranged a contract with Marconi for telegraph stations there in 1931.)[26]

But Philby's main interest was in exploration: with the fame it brought and the contributions to science he achieved. His most famous expedition was the crossing of the "Empty Quarter," the Rub' al Khali. Its beginning was signaled by a small item that appeared at the bottom of page 11 of The Times on 24 March 1932 entitled "Mr. Philby's Arabian Journey," with the subtitle "A Scientific Expedition."

> Mr. H. St. J. Philby left Hasa, in North-East Arabia, early in January for the remote oasis of Jabrin, with the intention of crossing the Rub' al Khali from east to west and emerging at some point on the coast of the Hadramaut . . . Good camels have been provided.

On 7 April, readers of The Times were informed that "A telegram was received in London yesterday from Mr. H. St. John Philby stating that he had reached Mecca after a successful expedition." The Rub' al Khali is a sand desert occupying most of the southern part of the Arabian peninsula. Philby's achievement was a noteworthy demonstration of endurance and willpower. After its completion, he went immediately to London, where on 23 May he gave an address to the Royal Geographical Society, entitled "Great Arabian Desert." (The lecture was attended by his wife and son, the latter, "wild with excitement," coming down from Cambridge for the occasion.)[27] On 22 June *Times* readers learned that: "The first of three articles by Mr. H. St. John Philby will be published in *The Times* next Monday.

> The articles describe his crossing early this year of the Rub' al Khali, or Great Southern Desert of Arabia. They will be illustrated by photographs taken by the explorer during his great journey and will include striking pictures of an immense lava field, the meteoric crater of Wabar, the site of an ancient river on which fresh-water shells were found, and the Jurassic cliffs of Wadi Dawasir, which was only reached after a journey of 350 miles across waterless desert."

The first article duly appeared on 27 June; the second on the 28th with a selection of Philby's photographs filling half a page of *The Times* under the heading "Crossing the Rub' Al Khali: Secret of the City of Wabar," the third on the 29th with this introductory note: "In the last of his three articles, which is published in *The Times* to-day, Mr. Philby concludes the description of his remarkable journey through the Great Desert of Southern Arabia. Admirably told there is something in the very air of Arabia that breeds style [a reference to Lawrence and Doughty] it is a fascinating narrative of ninety days of travel in the most inhospitable regions of a barren land."[28] On the 13th the Near and Middle East Association gave a dinner in honor of "Mr. H. St. John Philby" at the Hotel Metropole in London. On the 16th Philby was featured on the evening BBC National Programme. Rudolph Said-Ruete, of the Royal Geographical Society, stated in a letter to *The Times* on 2 July: "Mr. H. St. John Philby's magnificent journey through the Rub' al Khali . . . will rank . . . as one of the most noteworthy ventures of research in Arabia to the present day." Philby continued to be invited to lecture and was feted for the rest of the year: Near and Middle East Association gave a dinner in Philby's honor on 3 July, followed by a lecture with slides by Philby. He again broadcast on the BBC that weekend. Philby lectured to the Royal Asiatic Society on 6 October and two days later was listed in *The*

Times under a schedule of "Lecturers for the Year" at Oxford just after Albert Einstein and J. G. Frazer. St. John Philby was thought of as a hero in the class of Lindbergh or Scott of Antarctica.[29]

St. John Philby's career, his place in British and Middle Eastern society, were instrumental in facilitating his son's journalistic careers and both his entry into MI-6 and his association with the Soviet intelligence services. The father was a famous and influential, if controversial, figure in the British empire and in the Middle East. And he was an anti-imperialist, "agin" the government of the day, at a time when the British empire could be referred to, as justly as Czarist Russia, as a prison-house of nations. He was familiar with the leading members of the ruling class in the countries of the Middle East and was, in effect, the founder of Jordan, while playing a crucial role in the development of Saudi Arabia. He died, it is said, in his son's arms.

JAMES HUGH ANGLETON

James Jesus Angleton was the son of James Hugh Angleton, usually known as Hugh Angleton, a salesman and an adventurer, who alternated between careers in business and the military. While the Philbys, as a family, despite the eccentricities of St. John Philby, were members of the traditional governing class of the British empire, the Angletons were people of the American frontier, always returning to remote Boise, Idaho, ultimately to be buried there. The Angleton family seems to have originated in North Yorkshire, England, some members of the family in the seventeenth and eighteenth centuries emigrating to Virginia and Maryland in what was then British North America. They became part of the westward drift of the European-American population, crossing the Appalachian mountains to Kentucky, then moving on to the Midwest. James William Angleton, a farmer, born in 1865 in Boone County, Kentucky, moved to the central Illinois village of Edinburg, in Christian County (named for an eighteenth-century soldier, not the religion). Christian County, near the geographical center of Illinois, was—and is—nearly entirely agricultural, a vast, flat expanse planted with corn in the north and wheat in the south. A history of the county written in 1901 tells us that: "The life of the early settlers was exceedingly primitive.

Game was abundant; wild honey was used as a substitute for sugar;
wolves were troublesome; prairie fires were frequent; the first mill
(on Bear Creek) could not grind more than 10 bushels of grain per
day, by horse-power. The people hauled their corn to St. Louis to
exchange for groceries."[30]

James William Angleton and his wife Maggie raised nine children—
five sons and four daughters—all but two of whom remained in
rural Illinois as teachers, farmers, housewives, and such. One
became a county supervisor. The two who left Illinois went on west
to Idaho, where one became a road worker. The other was James J.
Angleton's father, James Hugh Angleton, born in 1888 in Sharps-
burg, Christian County, the second child and eldest son of James
William and Maggie Angleton.[31] He attended the public schools
near Taylorsville, Illinois (as opposed to the Westminster School,
London), completing a "work certificate" in 1907, taking a twelve-
week teacher training course in 1909 at Illinois State Normal School
in Charleston, Illinois (rather than Modern Languages, Trinity College), and taught in the Christian County public schools for three
years. Perhaps out of a lack of enthusiasm for a life of teaching in
rural schools, he moved to the western mountain state of Idaho, as
was the tradition in that place and era for ambitious young men:
"*But I reckon I got to light out for the territory ahead of the rest
. . .*" Idaho was thinly populated in the first decades of the twentieth
century, its economy primarily devoted to agriculture and mining,
in roughly equal measure, none of its cities reaching a population
of 10,000. The dominant religion, by far, was that of the Church of
Jesus Christ of the Latter-Day Saints (Mormons). The state's largest
city, Boise, was the site of a candy manufacturing business, Idaho
Candy Company, for which James Hugh Angleton went to work as a
jobbing salesman. He was still in contact with its president, Charles
Adams, a quarter of a century later.

    In late 1915, Francisco "Pancho" Villa, who led the Mexican Divi-
sion of the North, was contending with Venustiano Carranza for the
leadership of the Mexican Revolution. When the United States government recognized Carranza as President of Mexico and took steps
to assist him, Villa began attacks along the border, raiding Nogales,
in Sonora, and, famously, Columbus, in New Mexico. In response, an
American expeditionary force invaded Mexico but failed to capture

Villa and was eventually forced to retreat by Carranza, in one of the usual confusing episodes of the Mexican Revolution. In order to stabilize the border, a large number of United States National Guard troops were called up in 1916, among them those of the Idaho National Guard, to which Angleton belonged. That unit was stationed from July to December 1916 at Camp Stephen J. Little, in Nogales, Arizona, across the border from the Mexican city of the same name.[32] While in Nogales, James Hugh Angleton, then going on twenty-eight, met Carmen Mercedes Moreno, seventeen years old at the time, who had been born in the small town of Suaqui, Sonora, almost three hundred miles south of Nogales. She was the daughter of Jesus Romo Moreno, who, according to a later statement by her husband, owned mines and a store. Carmen Moreno and James Hugh Angleton were married on 10 December 1916.[33] Early in 1917, after the Nogales interlude, Angleton took his wife home to Boise, leaving the Idaho National Guard in April. While the Philbys were to live in a mansion overlooking the Tigris, the Angletons lived in a two-bedroom wooden house in a neighborhood of similar workers' houses in Boise. James Hugh and Carmen Angleton had three children in Idaho: James Jesus almost immediately (9 December 1917, named for his father and maternal grandfather); Hugh Rolla two years later; then Carmen Mercedes.

When the United States entered World War I, James Hugh Angleton spent six months at Camp Pike in Arkansas (1918–19) for Infantry Officers School, graduating as a second lieutenant in the infantry, but did not go to Europe. Back in Boise, he worked for Idaho Candy for five years, selling candy to the owners of stores in the region. He then joined the National Cash Register Company as a sales agent in January 1922, at a salary of $4,000 per year (the equivalent of the average US income in 2017). In the early twentieth century National Cash Register was a technology company, as it would be called today, and one of the era's monopolies. Practically every business came to need cash registers and 90 percent of those were manufactured by National Cash Register. James Hugh Angleton's family legend included stories of mule-back cash register deliveries to isolated frontier towns, and—with the boom and the modernization of the 1920s—a gradual rise through the ranks of the National Cash Register Company, first as sales agent for Southern Idaho and Eastern Oregon, then moving to the Dayton,

Ohio, corporate headquarters in September 1927 as an instructor and a year later as Midwestern regional sales manager. According to a number of the corporation's newsletters from around that time: "J. H. Angleton, the man selected as the manager of the Northern Division, has won success in this business through hard work and study of both of the Company's product and the needs of merchants . . .

> Having had previous selling experience before coming with this Company, Mr. Angleton's first position was that of salesman at Boise, Idaho . . . So successful was he as a cash register salesman that in this same year he was appointed as sales agent at the Boise Agency. As sales agent he was even a greater success than as a salesman. Up until a little over a year ago he operated this agency in a very splendid and profitable manner, building up a fine selling organization . . . His ambition, his desire to get ahead, and his ability to pick and train salesmen were instrumental in his being chosen as one of the Sales School instructors in 1927 and later as an assistant to Mr. East in the Pacific Division . . . When a new Division Manager was needed to fill the vacancy that came as a result of Mr. East's resignation, Mr. Angleton was ready to fill that position."[34]

In Dayton the Angleton family lived in a house twice the size of that which they had left in Boise. It was in the wealthy suburb of Oakwood, then an enclave of National Cash Register executives. A fourth child, Dolores, was born in Dayton. The stock market crash and ensuing Depression strongly affected National Cash Register. Corporate profits reported in March 1931 for 1930 were half those for 1929. By April 1931, with sales improving, James Hugh Angleton had become the company's national sales manager at a salary of $2,100 a month (the equivalent in purchasing power of nearly $400,000 per year today).[35] That December, he became Vice President of Overseas Sales for the company. In 1933 he went to Italy to inspect the National Cash Register operations there, liked what he saw, and—in lieu of a promotion—bought the Italian franchise from the company, moving his family to the grand Liberty-style Palazzo Castiglioni on the Corso Venezia in Milan in December 1933, when his eldest son was sixteen. Despite the stagnant Italian economy, and perhaps because of the support of the fascist state for big business and the restrictions it imposed on unions, James Hugh Angleton's average yearly earnings during the Depression amounted to 700,000 lira, perhaps something more than that number in purchasing power in 2017 dollars.

It was a very long way from Sonora and Boise to the palazzo on the Corso Venezia and all that went with it: the vacations in the Haute-Savoie; meetings with the important people of the fascist zenith; the diplomatic friendship of the American ambassador, William Phillips (who was to be head of OSS in London for the second half of 1942); and the Rotary Club business connections with corporate peers from other American multinationals, including IBM's Thomas Watson.[36] James Hugh Angleton became president of the American Chamber of Commerce in Italy, the center of a network of connections between US and Italian business, on the one hand, and the Italian and US governments on the other. He was probably the best-known American in northern Italy,[37] his appearances at trade fairs and the monthly lunches of the American Chamber of Commerce noted in the *Corriere della Sera*. He traveled widely in France and Central Europe, meeting with National Cash Register colleagues and others; meeting with the German and American military and naval attachés in Rome; keeping track of matters at the boundary between politics and business, and generally exercising some sort of oversight over the European operations of National Cash Register.[38] The busy, athletic, extroverted, quintessentially American father; the polyglot close-knit family around the Mexican mother in the palazzo; the comings and goings of those years (business trips, vacations, Boy Scout Jamborees in Hungary and Scotland) formed a background to James J. Angleton's early life markedly unlike that of many of his American contemporaries.[39] It was, however, converging with the type of life that had been led at the same age by Kim Philby, at least in comparison with the distance from Ambala to Boise. By the mid-1930s their fathers were on more or less equal social footing; the schooling of the sons, comparable; their outlooks similarly cosmopolitan.

YOUNG MEN

KIM PHILBY: JOURNALISM AND ESPIONAGE

In India, Harold Adrian Russell "Kim" Philby learned to speak English soon enough and later decorated it, he recalled, with a stammer "caught" from an admired slightly older boy on the voyage "home" to England. "Home," where he was deposited with his grandmother, was a house in Camberley, Surrey, near the Sandhurst military college. Crossways, as it was called, was a rather ordinary house with the usual small front and larger back garden on a street with similar houses. It was a house full of women: grandmother, great-grandmother, cook, maids, nurse, occasional visiting aunts. In 1919 Kim Philby's parents appeared from "the East," taking him with them to live in town in St. Petersburg Place, near Kensington Gardens, where he went to the school around the corner. At that time he formed an early, characteristic, memory of his father: "I remember he took me through Kensington Gardens to the Royal Geographical Society.

> There, in an upper room he sat me on a stool beside a huge table covered with large sheets of blank paper, ink bottles, pens and a lot of pencils sharpened to the finest point imaginable. My father was drawing a map, and, as far as I could see, an imaginary map at that because he had no Atlas to copy from . . . He was, most probably, filling in the blank spaces in the notorious Empty Quarter, giving reality to what was until them a largely imaginary landscape."[1]

After a year in London, St. John and Dora Philby returned to the East and their son returned to Camberley to what was apparently an innocuous prep school and the typical childhood experiences of a boy of his time and class, chiefly, in his memory, cricket and soccer and collecting butterflies and moths. He followed his father to Westminster School, where he was a King's Scholar, wearing the school's uniform top hat and tails. He collected classical music records (as did his later, much admired, friend, Guy Burgess). He played soccer and cricket and was a fan of the professional soccer team Arsenal. Timothy Milne thought that there was during those school years a good, "adult," relationship between Kim and his father.[2]

At sixteen Kim Philby went on a summer holiday in Spain, the first of many visits to that country, some holidays, some not. In October 1929 he entered Trinity College, Cambridge, following in the footsteps of his father, once more, as was expected.[3] An extraordinarily small percentage of each British generation then attended the two ancient universities of Oxford and Cambridge; that system functioning like a porcelain filter through which penetrated only the pure liqueur of the governing class. Unusually for a Cambridge undergraduate at that time, in the election of 1931 Kim Philby campaigned for Labour, against the "National" party, with a sentimental standard speech: "My friends, the heart of England does not beat in Stately homes and castles. It beats in the factories and farms."[4] It was not enough. Labour did not again form a government until 1945. All through the 1930s Parliamentary democracy in Britain offered no alternative to rule by a "national" party on behalf of plutocracy at home and empire abroad, with a foreign policy based on anti-communism and increasing sympathy for fascism.

Kim Philby shared his father's taste for travel, "rough," by preference. During his first winter at Cambridge, according to Cave Brown, he traveled with one of the Hungarian Szegedi-Szüts brothers, "on Kim's motorcycle to the Black Country industrial towns of central England . . . They lodged with poor industrial families; they ate what the unemployed ate; and they saw for themselves the misery being created by the Great Depression."[5] It was one of the experiences that convinced Philby that, as the organizer of the Jarrow Hunger March put it: "The poverty of the poor is not an accident, a temporary difficulty, a personal fault. It is the permanent state in which the vast majority of the citizens of any capitalist country have to live." During the Easter vacation of 1930, Kim Philby went by motorcycle to Budapest with a college friend, Michael Stewart, then to Nancy, France, at the beginning of August and back through Germany to Budapest with Timothy Milne in the sidecar.[6] The following summer he and Milne walked and hitch-hiked to and through Bosnia, a region then every bit as untouched by modern development as central Arabia.[7] Returning to England, he found a country laid waste by the collapse of the world economy. The machine, which had begun to sputter ten years earlier, had stopped.

In addition to the upper-class students and the working-class servants, at Cambridge in Kim Philby's time there were a few students who were ex-coal miners, one of whom, Harry Dawes, became close to Philby.[8] Dawes, who was "its secretary and prime mover," introduced Philby to the Cambridge University Socialist Society in October 1931.[9] Half a year later a young Cambridge mathematician, David Haden Guest, established a communist group at Cambridge. It included Maurice Cornforth and two or three others, one of whom may have been Guy Burgess. Donald Maclean, who then became the group's Secretary,[10] was soon joined by his school friend James Klugmann. In short order the group had twenty-five members and had openly affiliated with the Communist Party of Great Britain (CPGB). Philby was close to, but not a member of this Communist Party cell. He never carried a British Communist Party card.[11]

Continuing Philby's political education, during the Christmas vacation of 1932, another ex-collier Cambridge student, Jim Lees, arranged for him "to rent (at £3 a week) the Nottingham flat of W. J. H. Sprott, a former Cambridge man who had taken up a lectureship at Nottingham University . . . Later in the same vacation, Lees found Kim lodgings with a real coalminer, Bob Wright . . ."[12] These political explorations did not interfere with Philby's taste for foreign rough travel. That summer he went to Germany, visiting Stuttgart, Berlin, Munich, and Vienna, before going on to Venice, Dubrovnik, Montenegro, Albania, Yugoslavia, Macedonia, and Belgrade. By this time Kim Philby, inheriting his father's facility with languages, spoke French, German, some Hungarian, some Serbo-Croatian, and perhaps some Spanish.[13] While in Berlin, in March 1933, Philby argued with a Nazi in the boarding house where he was staying with his friend Milne. Philby claimed that Nazism was a reactionary attempt to preserve capitalism. He thought that it would lead to war.[14] Many years later, in Moscow, talking about this period of his life, Philby said that he remembered that "It took me a long time to decide to work for the Communists,[15] but the most important period was my last two years at Cambridge . . .

Several factors influenced my decision—inner and external, emotional and rational. The study of Marxism and seeing the Depression in England. Books and lectures and the rise of fascism in Germany. Fascism was one of the deciding factors for me. I was becoming convinced that only the Communism movement could resist it."[16]

Philby had "switched to economics in October 1931 at the very moment when unemployment in Britain was at its peak of 22 per cent [however] . . .

By 1932–3 classical economics seemed to young Cambridge social-ists unbearably irrelevant to the distress around them. The National Government's cuts in unemployment benefits, and particularly the Means Test introduced in November 1931, aroused their violent indignation."[17]

Philby spent an extra year studying with Keynes's disciples, and achieved a II:I. (a very good showing in that field at that time).[18]

Kim Philby left Cambridge in June 1933, and in the autumn returned to Vienna to improve his German for the Foreign Service examination, as he told his father;[19] to work for the Communist Party, as he may have told some of his Cambridge friends. He asked Maurice Dobb for an introduction to the leadership of the Austrian Communist Party. Dobb, given the Austrian Party's then underground status, said he could not put Philby in touch with them directly. Instead, he gave Philby an introduction to the head of the International Organization for Aid to Revolutionaries (IOAR) in Paris. The IOAR, also known as International Red Aid, paid for the legal defense of Communist Party activists.[20] Philby went to Paris. An official of IOAR (perhaps Louis Gibarti)[21] gave him another letter of recommendation, this to the head of the Austrian Commit-tee for Relief from German Fascism in Vienna.[22] Philby continued on to Vienna with this second letter. He had £100 with him, enough to live on for a year in Depression-era Vienna. The Viennese branch of IOAR sent him on to its section in Alsergrund, the ninth district of the city, a university neighborhood. The section was run by a young communist, Elizabeth Kohlmann Friedmann, called Lisl in Vienna, Litzy in London, or, according to Timothy Milne, Lizy.[23] Philby became the treasurer of the district IOAR and was taken by Friedmann as her lover. He was put to work drafting and printing leaflets, raising and distributing money, acting as a courier between Vienna, Prague, and Budapest. All this was much more real than the corner oratory, tea, and conversation style of Cambridge communism.

While Austria itself had a conservative Christian Socialist government, Vienna, "Red Vienna," was governed by Social Democrats with the impatient, critical, cooperation of the usually underground Austrian Communist Party. The city had become a model of progressive government, instituting a variety of social-welfare measures, most notably low-cost workers' housing in large blocks with nearly middle-class amenities, health care, schools, and cooperative features of various kinds. However, the Austrian Chancellor, Engelbert Dollfuss, had authoritarian ambitions, which, shortly after Philby's arrival in Vienna, he fulfilled by dissolving Parliament. On 12 February 1934, one of the Social Democratic party's Republican Defense League shot at a police officer who was demanding admission to the People's House in Linz, the headquarters of the local branch of the Social Democratic Party. He missed, but that was a sufficient excuse for the government to order attacks on Social Democratic locations across Austria. There were mass arrests of the leadership of the Party and of its associated trade unions. The attacks continued for four days, culminating in the famous sieges of the great apartment blocks in Vienna that the Social Democrats had built for the workers and their families. In the classical fashion, that would be repeated in the next decade across Europe, some of the Defense League militants took refuge in the sewers. They held out for a few days.[24]

During the February Uprising, Philby and Friedmann helped with the distribution of supplies, hid fugitives and helped smuggle them out of the city: everything asked of them up to, but not quite including, fighting. According to E. H. Cookridge, Philby helped distribute medicine and food to the wounded who had taken refuge at the Quaker Emma Cadbury's relief center.[25] In his autobiography, Philby described walking through the barricaded streets arm and arm with Friedmann, perhaps on one of these errands, holding his British passport, like an icon in a procession, high above his head.

After the collapse of the Social Democrats, Philby became a courier for the clandestine secretariat of the Revolutionary Socialist Party, which was in touch with the exiled leadership of the Social

Democrats. They were also in contact with the American heiress and psychoanalyst Muriel Gardiner, at whose home meetings were held and materials stored.[26] Gardiner sketched a portrait of Kim Philby as a young communist activist in Vienna in the spring of 1934. He was "an extremely handsome, dark-haired man, probably younger than I, dressed in hiking clothes and boots and carrying a rucksack. He spoke impeccable English, and I felt he must have been educated at an English school." They talked all afternoon about politics, as was inevitable at the time. And then down to business. Philby asked Gardiner if she would be willing to act as a "cut out," taking an envelope containing money, he said, to "a comrade." She agreed. He then gave her a large manila envelope and instructions concerning how to deliver it: place, time, identification phrases, and so forth— the usual tradecraft of the Comintern underground.

Once no longer in the presence of her handsome, intelligent and charming guest, Gardiner had second thoughts: "As the day wore on I became more and more uneasy about the big envelope." She opened it. "In it there were indeed several thousand schillings, but the bulk of the contents was clandestine Communist literature. I felt betrayed and was all the more angry for having so readily succumbed to the charms of a man I knew nothing about." Nonetheless, she delivered the envelope as instructed. Thirty years later she saw "a photograph of Philby as a young man—he was indeed my handsome, charming, trust-inspiring guest of spring, 1934."[27]

The leaders of the February Uprising, socialist and communist alike, were hunted down by the police and right-wing militias, murdered, forced into exile or underground. Again according to E. H. Cookridge, who was there, it was in Vienna that Philby decided to serve the communist anti-fascist effort.[28] Philby and Friedmann married, on 24 February 1934, perhaps so that Friedmann could emigrate to Britain, and in April 1934 they in fact left Vienna for London.[29] Ilse Barea, an Austrian journalist, remembered Hugh Gaitskell (another child of the Raj and a Winchester College old boy), who was at the University of Vienna on a Rockefeller scholarship, telling her how horrified he was to hear of Philby's marriage to "that young communist girl, Alice Friedman."*[30] When they arrived

---

* This implies that while in Vienna Philby maintained connections with the British community in that city as well as working with the Austrian communists.

in London, Kim Philby's mother also did not approve of her new daughter-in-law. "Litzi," Dora wrote to St. John in Jeddah, "was hard, pert and managing . . . You wait till you see her . . . I do hope he gets a job to get him off this bloody communism. He's not quite extreme yet but may become so if he's not got something to occupy his mind."[31] On the other hand, Philby's friend, Milne, found that Lizy was an attractive, lively young woman. He did not believe they married merely to get her out of Vienna.[32]

It seems that once in London, Friedmann continued to occupy herself as she had done in Vienna. According to the barrister Helenus Milmo, an erstwhile colleague who interrogated Philby in 1951, "At the time Philby concedes that he was extremely poor and that he was living on an income of some £3 a week . . .

> Nevertheless, it appears that between 6th March 1934 and 15th April 1934 Lizzie [sic] Philby made no less than three journeys into Czechoslovakia from Vienna on her British passport which she obtained two days after her marriage.* Philby is unable to explain the purpose of any one of these visits. On their return to England, she went to France on 4th September 1934 and entered Spain on the following day. Ten days later she left a French port and on 21st September 1934 she entered Austria where she remained a month. On 8th April 1935 she paid a week's visit to Holland and on 16th August 1935 she arrived in France, entering Spain on the following day. On 3rd April 1936 she entered Austria and a week later went on to Czechoslovakia, returning to Austria again on 22nd April. Between 25th May 1936 and 22nd July 1936, she made a visit by air from this country to Paris and on 22nd July and 28th December 1936 she made further journeys across the channel . . ."[33]

Milmo commented further: "Having regard to this woman's proven connection with the Comintern before her marriage it is difficult if not impossible to resist the conclusion that these trips were made on behalf of and were financed by some Communist or Soviet organization."[34] The visits to Austria would have been quite danger-ous for her, while those to Spain, which were taken with Philby as

---

* The exiled leadership of the Revolutionary Socialists, and perhaps that of the communists as well, were in Brno, Czechoslovakia.

"holidays," occurring during the period of unrest shortly before the Civil War, are particularly intriguing.[35]

Planning at first to take the Civil Service Examination, Philby found that the application required three references, one of which must be from his Cambridge tutor. His tutor in Economics, the then-Keynesian Dennis Robertson, told him that he would feel it necessary to hint in the recommendation that Kim Philby held radical political views. "His father . . . wanted him to fight. [St. John Philby] wrote to Donald Robertson:

'The only serious question is whether Kim definitely intended to be disloyal to the government while in its service. If that was his intention he should not have wasted his time in preparing for the exam . . . Some people may think . . . that *I* was disloyal to the government, but that was never the case. I was in opposition to its policy and always made this clear, and I resigned in order to have freedom to express my views more publicly.'"[36]

But Kim Philby thought it imprudent to be that frank at the beginning of his career and withdrew his application.

Just as his mother feared, at about this time Kim Philby had attempted to join the Communist Party of Great Britain. Philby recalled that "Within a day or two of our arrival, we were at the King Street headquarters of the Communist Party, introducing ourselves to Willie Gallacher and Isobel Brown.

I had never seen Gallacher, but had often heard Isobel Brown from the platform, swaying crowds as effectively as Harry Pollitt, which is saying a lot. There was no question of immediate enlistment. As I explained our position, and gave an account of our past activity in Austria, Gallacher took notes. He then told us, kindly, that he would have to check; there were a lot of strange types emerging from Central Europe those days. As the Austrian party was illegal, it might take some time to get a reply. He suggested that we should return in six weeks."[37]

While the CPGB was, or said it was, following up with Philby's references, there was another intervention. Litzi Philby and her friend Edith Suschitzky Tudor-Hart (who had also married an

Englishman, Alex Tudor-Hart, in Vienna and migrated to London), served as links between British communists, overt and underground, and German and Austrian communists, many of whom were scientists who concealed their communist activities. Edith Tudor-Hart's role as a "linking agent" was particularly crucial. Litzi Philby and Tudor-Hart seem to have decided that Kim Philby needed some career counseling. Tudor-Hart arranged for him to meet "a serious person."[38] As an introduction to the covert life, they took a taxi, switched to a second going in the opposite direction, got on and off cars in the Underground for three or four hours. After this excitement, Philby was handed off to a man sitting on a bench in Regent's Park. This was "Otto," an NKVD "illegal."[39]

Alexander Orlov recalled that "in the early 1930's . . . one of the chiefs of the NKVD intelligence . . . took account of the fact that in capitalistic countries lucrative appointments and quick promotion are usually assured to young men who belong to the upper class, especially the sons of political leaders, high government officials, influential members of parliament, etc.

> To them promotion is almost automatic . . . Accordingly, in the early 1930's NKVD *residenturas* concentrated their energy on recruitment of young men of influential families. The political climate of that period was very favorable for such an undertaking, and the young generation was receptive to libertarian theories and to the sublime ideas of making the world safe from the menace of Fascism and of abolishing the exploitation of man by man . . . when the young men reached the stage when their thinking made them ripe for joining the Communist party, they were told that they could be much more useful to the movement if they stayed away from the party, concealed their political views, and entered the 'revolutionary underground' . . . These young men hardly regarded themselves as spies or intelligence agents. They did not want anything for themselves—least of all money. What they wanted was a purpose in life, and it seemed to them that they had found it. By their mental make-up and outlook they remind one very much of the young Russian Decembrists of the past century, and they brought into the Soviet intelligence the true fervor of new converts and the idealism which their intelligence chiefs had lost long ago."[40]

"Otto" was a pseudonym of Arnold Deutsch, a highly educated Comintern agent. Litzi Philby or Edith Tudor-Hart[41] had told Deutsch that Kim Philby had attempted to join the Communist Party of Great Britain. Deutsch, on that day in Regent's Park, said to Philby: "The Party doesn't play a big part in British life. If you were to sell the *Daily Worker* in working-class neighbourhoods of London that would be a fine thing, of course. But you can help Communism in a much more real and palpable way. You can undertake a real and important job . . . [as] an infiltrator for the Communist anti-fascist movement."[42] Philby agreed to undertake this work. Deutsch then asked him to break off all public connections with known communists. He also asked for a list of possible recruits to join him in underground work with the Comintern, against fascism, for peace, as Philby understood it. He gave Deutsch a list of seven men, including Donald Maclean, Anthony Blunt, and Guy Burgess. Blunt later recalled that he, at least, thought that they were working for the Comintern.[43] In any case, they did not think of themselves as working for Russia. Philby, and the others, did not become secret intelligence agents *for* Russia. They became secret agents *against* British imperialism and fascism abroad and British capitalism at home. That is how they thought of it, both then and later.

According to Milne, providing another indication of Friedmann's dominant role in the relationship—and her other relationships—when in 1935 Kim and "Lizy" moved into a flat near the elder Philbys' house in Acol Road, she made it a social center for central European refugees.[44] (It is quite possible that during the parties there, Milne, unknowing, was one of the only non-communists.) While his wife was establishing herself in the London exile community, Kim Philby joined the Royal Central Asian Society, as a first step in his penetration of right-wing establishment circles—not a very difficult first step, given his father's connections. He elaborated this cover by enrolling in a tutorial in Turki, a Central Asian language, at the School of Oriental Studies. Within two years he had further accomplished an entrée to the more relevant Anglo-German Fellowship through a project for an Anglo-German trade magazine. He attended formal rightist dinners and less formal gatherings; every couple of weeks reporting on conversations and personalities to "Otto." He made contacts in the German embassy in London and was taken by the publisher of the prospective trade magazine to Berlin for at least one week a month: seeking German financial backing, visiting, among others, Ribbentrop himself.[45] These activities were useful in giving Kim Philby a certain reputation and experience, but insufficient to launch a magazine. The project folded.

During 1936 Kim Philby worked rather unenthusiastically for the *Review of Reviews*, which, in any case, also went out of business later that year. Perhaps inspired by his father's example, Philby began to learn Arabic.[46] On 14 July 1936, the English branch of the Anglo-German Fellowship gave a dinner at the Dorchester Hotel in honor of the Duke and Duchess of Brunswick. Lord Mount Temple, chairman of the English branch, presided. Lord Lothian gave a speech advocating negotiations with Germany on a basis of equality. The next day *The Times* listed many of those attending, including R. H. Bruce-Lockhart, diplomat and secret agent; Vice-Admiral Sir Barry Domvile, former Director of Naval Intelligence, who was to be interned during World War II as a Nazi sympathizer; Lord Malcolm Douglas-Hamilton, who the following month would fly a de Havilland plane to Spain for Franco; the Marquess of Londonderry, Lord Privy Seal and Leader of the House of Lords; Ernest Tennant, one of the founders of the Fellowship, and Mr. H. A. R. Philby.

St. John Philby had returned to Arabia in February 1933, and began to work on commission for oil companies seeking concessions in Arabia.[47] In February 1933 he participated in the negotiations on behalf of Ibn Saud. He knew the limitation imposed on Iraq Petroleum, which represented the British interest, to be a maximum down payment of £10,000. Its American rival, Standard Oil, offered £35,000 for the concession and £20,000 was payable in eighteen months plus a yearly rental of £35,000. "Standard Oil's shrewd lawyer, Lloyd Hamilton put Philby on an indefinite retainer of 1,000 dollars a month. There could only be one decision and it went in favour of Standard Oil . . . Philby achieved the political decision he sought to humiliate the British and Ibn Saud achieved the commercial decision that would define the future of his Kingdom."[48] Twelve thousand dollars a year in 1933 had the same purchasing power as $226,000 in 2018—in the United States. In Arabia then it would amount to incalculable riches.

As his commercial affairs prospered, St. John Philby also became yet better known to the public. His account of his journey across the Rub'Al Khali, *The Empty Quarter*, was reviewed in *The Times Literary Supplement* on 25 May 1933; there was a short, favorable review in *The Times* itself on 2 June, and in a listing of "Books for the Holidays" on 28 July, the anonymous *Times* writer called it "An exciting account of a very remarkable achievement." St. John Philby wrote a series of letters to and articles in *The Times* in spring 1934 about Ibn Saud's successful wars extending his domain in the Arabian peninsula. He was in London on 19 July to give a lecture at the Royal Central Asian Society, "Mecca and Medina," and then, back in Arabia, obtained the Ford dealership for the area. St. John and Dora Philby spent the summer of 1935 at lectures, luncheons, dinners, and garden parties in London, St. John Philby writing to *The Times* on 28 May proposing a Chair in Arabic Studies at the University of London as a memorial to his late colleague, "Lawrence of Arabia." Early that autumn, marking a revolution in conditions in Arabia, he and Dora *drove* from London to Jeddah and Riyadh, then straight across Arabia and back. That October, Italy, in violation of Article X of the Covenant of the League of Nations, invaded Ethiopia, using poison gas, airplanes, and machine guns. The next year the Emperor Haile Selassie was living in exile in England and Mussolini, playing Disraeli to the King's Victoria, declared Victor Emmanuel III the Emperor of Abyssinia. Against this background, *The Times,* on 1 April 1936, noted that in an article in the *Fortnightly Review* entitled "The Powers and Raw Materials," "Mr. H. St. J. Philby denies that the great Powers seek new homesteads; what they want is wealth, power, and exploitation of the coloured man." Which brings us back to his son.

The Spanish Civil War began on 17 July 1936. That December, Kim Philby's contacts in the Comintern decided to send him to Spain. The KGB's Moscow Center agreed the following month. He was to attempt to make a name for himself as a journalist, a reputation that might make him attractive to the British secret intelligence service. In addition, he was told to report to Moscow from Spain on troop levels and movements, morale, German and Italian intervention, and so forth. He was given a code and instructed to mail a letter every two weeks to an address in Paris with the coded reports embedded between the lines in what appeared to be an ordinary letter. And he was introduced to an emergency contact in Paris (perhaps Kitty Harris). Philby set about gathering letters of support from his German acquaintances, including Ribbentrop, and vague assurances of interest from various London news publications. Financed by the Comintern, in February 1937 he went to Spain via Lisbon, where he picked up a visa for the area occupied by the Nationalist forces. By this time his marital relationship with Litzy had ended, because of the strain of their respective underground activities and "for other reasons as well."[49] One of those reasons might have been that a communist spouse was not a good fit with his new far-right bona fides. Be that as it may, he maintained a joint bank account with Litzy until 1944, from which she withdrew £40 per month between 1937 and 1940.[50]

Freelancing for the London General Press and other organizations, drawing a stipend from Soviet secret intelligence, hoping, among other things, to place articles in *The Times*,[51] Kim Philby traveled to Seville, then Franco's headquarters. Philby passed the information he gathered from the Nationalists there to Major Alexander Orlov, simultaneously the representative of the NKVD and the Security Adviser to the Republican government of Spain, who met with him from time to time in the seaside French city of Narbonne, near the Spanish border.* Philby also sent information to the Paris Soviet intelligence service residency, with notes in invisible ink between the lines of innocuous postcards.[52] There is a story in his *My Silent War*, set in March 1937, when he was still a freelancer, that Philby, having been arrested in Seville under suspicion of being more curious about Franco's airfields and troop movements than was fitting for a pro-fascist journalist, had been detained and in the process had swallowed the piece of paper containing the codes with which he was communicating with his Comintern contact in Paris. Released, he sent a letter to Paris explaining the situation. He was told to go to Gibraltar to meet a courier who would give him his new codes and more money. The courier, Philby said, was Guy Burgess. It would have been a quick trip for Burgess, as there is no indication in the BBC records of his taking time off from work that month.[53] There

---

* Orlov defected to Ohio in 1938, but, perhaps as a consequence of his bargain with Stalin ("I won't talk; you won't murder me"), he did not reveal that Philby was a Soviet agent.

is another story about the courier. During his third MI-5 interrogation after the Burgess/Maclean disappearance "Philby mentioned a visit made by his first wife to Gibraltar before April 1937 for the purpose of begging him to re-establish a joint household . . . Note: (a) Philby had never before suggested that the desire to separate was not mutual, (b) the visit to Gibraltar, in fact, occurred in June 1937 after Philby had obtained a permanent post in Spain."[54]

You pays your money and you takes your choice.

In the first week of May 1937, Kim Philby's sister Diana was presented at court to King George and Queen Mary, beginning her debutante season, perhaps confirming the Soviet intelligence service's belief that Kim Philby was an aristocrat. It was at that point Kim Philby's father and the old school tie came into play. St. John Philby's biographer tells us that "In the summer of 1937, [St. John] Philby called on the Deputy-Editor of *The Times*, Robin Barrington-Ward, about some articles of his own, and at the same time put the Old Westminster school network to good use. According to Barrington-Ward's diary for 20 May 1937:

> Philby lunched with me. I suggested (after a talk with G.D. [the Editor, Geoffrey Dawson] and Deakin [the Foreign Editor] yesterday) that his son, also an Old Westminster, should become our special correspondent with Franco's force in Spain. He jumped at it . . . His son duly came to see me. He looks good. We fixed him up."[55]

"He looks good. We fixed him up."

Kim Philby was accredited by *The Times* to Franco's headquarters along with a recommendation from the German embassy in London, which described him as "an ardent supporter of fascist ideas." He spent several weeks at *The Times* in London, meeting people and learning how things were done there. Litzy and Timothy Milne gave him a farewell party. Milne invited friends from advertising, Litzy's guests included her "Mitteleuropa" friends.[56] It must have been an interesting party. It was also a farewell to Kim Philby's first marriage. He and Litzy went their separate ways, he to Spain, she to Paris. However, during the next few years she did meet Philby "in hotels in Biarritz or Perpignan, and even in Gibraltar, where he gave her information that she then carried to her control officer in

Paris," for whom she traveled to other cities, on other missions, as well. "That's why she had taken an apartment in Paris and lived there on his salary from *The Times*. It was simply easier to make contact in France." She had a luxurious apartment in Paris and a place in the country, gave lavish parties, danced, and had love affairs. Looking back, long afterward, from the security of a certain eminence in the German Democratic Republic, she saw this period as the most pleasurable of her life.[57]

Kim Philby, now "Our Special Correspondent" with the Nationalist forces for *The Times* left for Spain on 10 June by way of Paris and Hendaye, on the southwest French border.[58] Although authorship of articles in *The Times* was either anonymous, or, in this case, pseudonymous (as from "Our Special Correspondent"), we can be fairly safe in assuming those from Franco's headquarters in Salamanca, and later in Burgos, were written by Kim Philby, as were many of the others reporting on Nationalist operations, political and military. (Reports from the government and military of the Republic were filed by a different correspondent, or correspondents, also designated as "Our Special Correspondent," but usually easily identified by location and tone, referring to "the Government" and the "insurgents," while those from Philby refer to the "Valencia" or, later, "Barcelona" government, and the "Nationalists.")

The Sunday Times team of reporters that produced the excellent first study of Philby (much praised by Philby in the introduction to his own book) were naturally knowledgeable about the ways of journalists. They wrote that during 1937, when Franco's headquarters were in Salamanca, the foreign journalists passed the time in their accustomed manner, in the city's cafés and bars. From time to time, watched over by fascist officers, they were driven to the front. And every morning they were fed the news of the day by Franco's press officer in the gallery of the ancient university's quadrangle.[59] Bilbao was reported "Hard Pressed" in *The Times* on the 15th, encircled on the 16th, its "Defence shattered" on the 17th, a "tighter hold on Bilbao" was announced on the 18th, "Closing on Bilbao" on the 19th, in reports from Vitoria, probably by Philby, based on Nationalist communiqués. Finally, on the 21st, "How Bilbao Fell, From Our Special Correspondent, Bilbao, June 20." On the other hand, a report on "Bilbao's Last Stand," as from "Our Special Correspondent" in Santander on 21 June was clearly written by Philby's colleague embedded with the forces of the Republic ("Heroism Versus High Explosive"). The following day, Philby, writing from "On the Franco-Spanish Frontier," filed a story headlined "Onward from Bilbao," the Nationalists having taken the Basque country, vital for its mines and industry, leaving the Republic the Mediterranean coast and a jigsaw-puzzle-shaped piece around Madrid.

And so it went, with articles in *The Times* from Philby every few days—interspersed with those from his colleagues with the forces of the Republic—printed among the cricket scores, reports on flower shows, and the doings of the King and court, as well as those on the Soviet purges and increasing German aggression. On 16 November *The Times* ran a political analysis from Philby in Salamanca, his first of what would become an occasional series: "While the Nationalist armies are pushing the frontier of Nationalist Spain towards the Atlantic and Mediterranean, General Franco and his advisers are proceeding with the less spectacular task of consolidating the new State," giving the history of the Falange, the relationship of it to the army and the monarchy and so forth. The Nationalist censors could find no fault with such reports by the young gentleman from *The Times*. When not at work on his newspaper stories, Philby visited the German embassy twice a week and made a habit of speaking with the German ambassador before each of his monthly or bimonthly trips to report to Orlov in Narbonne or Perpignan in southeastern France.[60] On one occasion he traveled to Bayonne to meet his mother and sister, who were driving to Cairo.[61]

In the first quarter of 1938 Philby himself twice became the subject of two of his own reports. The issue of *The Times* for 3 January 1938 ran the dramatic story of Philby's wounding by artillery fire and that for 4 March on his subsequent decoration from Franco. In the first, readers were told: "Three journalists—two American and one British—who were visiting the Teruel front lost their lives as the result of their motor-car receiving a direct hit from a long-range shell on Friday.

Mr. Bradish Johnson (American), of the News-Week, was killed outright; Mr. Richard Sheepshanks, Reuter's Special Correspondent, and Mr. Edward Neil (American), of the Associated Press, were seriously wounded. Mr. Sheepshanks died from his wounds in Monreal Hospital on Friday night, and Mr. Neil in the Red Cross

Hospital at Saragossa to-day. Your Correspondent, who was in the same car, escaped with slight wounds and has recovered.

The incident occurred in the main square of Caude, a little village a few miles from Teruel. Press cars were drawn up there awaiting one which bad lagged behind; and the journalists, after a few minutes' wandering round the village, returned to their cars to shelter against the intense cold. Your Correspondent joined Mr. Neil and Mr. Sheepshanks in their car, and Mr. Johnson, who was a photographer attached to News-Week, took his place at the driver's wheel a few minutes later. The party was smoking in an effort to drive up the temperature when a shell landed near the radiator and riddled the car with shrapnel.

Your Correspondent was able to leave the car and cross the square to a wall where a group of soldiers was sheltering. Thence he was taken to a first-aid station, where light head injuries were speedily dressed. Meanwhile Spanish Press officers worked gallantly in an attempt to rescue the other occupants of the car regardless of falling shells. Mr. Johnson, however had received a shrapnel wound in the side and must have died instantly. Mr. Sheepshanks was still breathing when the rescue party arrived with stretchers. He had been wounded in the face and head and from the first it was clear there was little chance of recovery. He died in hospital at Monreal at 7 p.m. without having recovered consciousness.

Mr. Neil was fully conscious when taken to a first-aid station at Caude on a stretcher, and showed concern about the fate of his typewriter. His leg was fractured in two places, and later 35 pieces of shrapnel were removed from it. He was taken to Saragossa and operated on. Gangrene had set in and he died at mid-day to-day."

Philby had been wearing a coat that his father had given him, which he in turn had received from "one of his Arab princes. It was a very amusing piece of tailoring: bright green fabric on the outside and bright red fox fur on the inside . . . nothing better in the world for the cold Spanish winter."[62] In some accounts this was misidentified as a woman's coat.

Three months later, Philby wrote: "Your Correspondent was received yesterday by General Franco, who conferred on him the Red Cross of Military Merit

and also handed to him the diplomas of the same decoration award-
ed to Mr. Neil, Mr. Sheepshanks, and Mr. Johnson, the foreign war
Correspondents who lost their lives when a shell struck their car at
Caude, on the Teruel front, on December 31. The Generalissimo
expressed deep sympathy with the families and Friends of the dead
men."[63]

This did not seem unusual at the time. Why should Franco not
publicize in this way the support he was receiving from *The Times*,
tantamount to an official endorsement by the British government
itself? This event also demonstrated Philby's access to Franco, which
may have something to do with the otherwise rather odd stories
about Comintern plans to use him as an assassin of the fascist leader.

On 24 April 1938 Philby reported from Burgos on "Press Control
in Franco's Spain": "Sweeping powers over the organization of the
Press have been given to the Minister of the Interior at Burgos—
another milestone on General Franco's road to totalitarian rule."
"Totalitarian" was a term of praise, not opprobrium, at that time,
in those circles. For the remainder of the spring, Philby reported the
Nationalist advance in a series of short dispatches. But it was his
colleague on the side of the Republic's forces who reported from
Hendaye that "Mr. David Guest, son of the British Labour M.P.,
Dr. Haden Guest, is reported here to have been killed while serving
with the Republican Army," during the desperate battle of the Ebro
River. "Imagine yourself . . . on a Spanish hillside above the Ebro,"
Anthony Blunt was made to say to his students in a radio play by
Corin Redgrave:

> On the opposite side sits Franco's army . . . And your position is
> absolutely hopeless . . . Your ammunition is almost exhausted, food
> and water running low. All the non-communist brigaders have been
> sent home, only communist volunteers are left. So you are going
> to die. Almost certain to. How do you face that? . . . you're a com-
> munist in Spain, in 1938, and you don't have to ask, you *know* why
> you're here, you've volunteered for it.[64]

Another of the leading, overt, Cambridge communists, John Corn-
ford, had died much earlier, on 28 December 1936, soon after arriving
in Spain. That left James Klugmann from among the Cambridge

group who had not publicly abandoned the Party, and, of course, Burgess, Maclean, and Philby, who had.

By May 1938 Franco's army had reached the Mediterranean south of Catalonia, cutting in half what remained of the Republic beyond the Madrid area. On 10 August 1938 *The Times* ran among its "Special Articles," Philby's "In Franco's Spain: Analysis and Survey: Structure of the New State," concluding lyrically, after a thorough political and economic account over two pages, with: "And so the State under Franco struggles confidently forward through another summer.

> Beset by economic difficulties and by a stubborn foe, it is bravely facing the twin tasks of military victory and national reconstruction. The sun blazes down with dreadful intensity. All who possess the necessary means have migrated to the north, and the Embassies are grouped round the blue bay of San Sebastian. But for the people and the Army there is no respite. Blood still flows in Valencian orange-groves: still girdles the doomed, white city of Madrid; still mingles with the streams that water the sun-smitten vale of La Serena, serene in nothing but name."

Philby's articles had a similar tone that winter: "Snow is falling on the Spanish mountains.

> The nation stands on the threshold of the third consecutive winter of warfare. Bitter winds that sweep over Aragon and Castile—an enemy more relentless perhaps and more feared than most modern instruments of war—are gathering strength. They bring back memories of last year's cruel struggle for Teruel, of agonies that must be repeated. Troops that struggled naked to the waist over the sun-scorched hills around Gandesa are now huddled into rugs and greatcoats."[65]

The Nationalists took Barcelona at the end of January. Philby went into the city with them. "A solemn field mass was celebrated in the Plaza de Cataluña at noon to-day . . . At the end of the ceremony the vast concourse assembled in the square and knelt with right arms upraised, thus saluting both the spiritual and temporal powers to which the New Spain owes allegiance . . ."[66] On 30 January 1939 there was a "Special Article," a feature flagged in the bordered index on the top left of the page, occupying the entire far-right column of that page and the first column of the next. "In Barcelona To-day: Gradual Return to Normal: Horrors of Montjuich Prison." "Barcelona is returning to normal . . . The mood of delirious excitement has given place to one of quiet satisfaction . . .

> Those returning exiles who are not searching for relatives are searching for property. A lieutenant of the Requetes [Carlist militia] entered your Correspondent's bedroom this morning and explained briefly that he was the owner of the flat, put a chair on the bed and extracted from the recesses of a lamp hanging from the ceiling a small piece of screwed up tissue paper. Having examined its contents he pocketed it, apologized for the intrusion and disappeared as quickly as he came with the recovered treasure . . . Long files of Republican prisoners, lightly guarded, are straggling up the rough road leading to the terrible prison fortress of Montjuich which frowns over Barcelona . . . The place is redolent of tragedy. In the western moat are visible the walls where the firing squads did their deadly work . . ."

And then, on 22 February 1939: "Barcelona, Feb. 21. Barcelona En Fete. Franco Reviews His Army." Philby wrote: "General Franco reviewed his army in Barcelona to-day . . . At the head of the parade rode General Gambara, the Italian commander of the Legionary Army Corps . . ." He mentioned prisoners, refugees, a purge of school teachers.

Meanwhile, Philby apparently continued to make occasional visits to Paris: "In late March 1939 a fairly typical letter came to the [Moscow] Centre from the Paris residence: [Donald Maclean] has a friend here—a British journalist, allegedly tied to us in our work, loyal, and very valuable . . . [Maclean] often meets this man . . ."[67]

Then came the last phase of the siege of Madrid. "The thoughts of all Spaniards to-day centre in the great plain which sweeps southwards from the foothills of the Sierra Guadarrama, in the middle of which lies the beleaguered city of Madrid."[68] By this time, when Philby's articles refer to "the Spanish Government," they are referring to the Nationalists. Philby was given another "Special Article" on 28 March 1939, headlined: "The Ring Round Madrid." "The greatest concentration of infantry, artillery, and aircraft yet seen in the Spanish civil war is being assembled gradually on the Madrid front." And then two days later, Philby reported "How Madrid Fell" from Nationalist sources. It was seized, they said, by the "Fifth Column" of the Falange in advance of Franco's army.

Then, "The streets of the capital on the eve of the victory parade are ablaze with red and gold, the colours of the new Spain . . . The parade will be headed by General Saliquet . . . Immediately after him will come the Italian volunteers . . ."[69] and finally: "Madrid Victory Parade. Italians at the Head . . . From Our Special Correspondent. Madrid, May 19. The great Victory Parade, 16 miles in length, began here at 9 o'clock this morning under grey skies."[70]

Kim Philby went back to London in July 1939, after two and a half years in Spain. The Munich Agreement had been signed nine months earlier; the purges of the Red Army had begun more than a year before that; the Anschluss occurred in March of 1938; the occupation of Prague took place as Madrid was falling to Franco; the Molotov-Ribbentrop Pact would be signed within a month. Philby had experienced socialism and counter-revolutionary terror in Vienna; he had pledged himself to the communist underground; he had lived through and reported on a fascist-initiated civil war in Spain that left perhaps half a million people dead. Kim Philby was twenty-seven years old and the world was growing darker. He was five years into his own silent war.

In January 1938, in an event little-marked at the time, as they say, the British Museum of Natural History had found "Evidence of Oil in Arabia [from] Mr. Philby's Collection of Minerals" donated to the Museum.[71] St. John Philby had continued, for a while, to move back and forth between Mecca and London, living in the former in the spring of 1938, in the latter the following winter, moving steadily further out on the fringe of Establishment opinion in London, closer to the ways and attitudes of his royal friends in Arabia. In July 1939 he contested a by-election at Hythe, Kent (necessitated by the death of Philip Sassoon, with whom the Philbys had some sort of family connection, perhaps dating back to Iraq). Whereas St. John Philby had identified with Labour earlier, in this effort he was the candidate of the British People's Party (which "stands for 'peace by agreement with our adversaries'"), receiving fewer than 600 votes out of more than 20,000.[72]

JAMES ANGLETON: POETRY AND YALE

Shortly after the Angleton family arrived in Milan, in 1933, Hugh Angleton, who had barely more than a rural high school education himself (and his wife, Carmen, probably not even that), went to England, looking at schools for his children. James was sent to a prep school, Chartridge Hill House in Buckinghamshire, then after a spring and summer traveling in Europe, to Malvern College in Worcestershire, where from 1933 to 1936 he added some French and German to whatever he may have had of his mother's Mexican Spanish and his father's business Italian.[73] The transformation of the Angletons from Mid-western farmers to members of a cosmopolitan elite in a single generation was dazzling, even by the American standards of the time.

Hugh Angleton ensured that his son's education was broader than that typically afforded his peers at Malvern College, including, "in 1936, when he was 18 . . . working through a summer holiday as an apprentice mechanic in National Cash Register's Paris factory." James Angleton later told a colleague that when they heard about the German reoccupation of the Rhineland "The workers to a man threw down their tools and standing at attention sang the *Marseillaise*. Then they streamed into the street, cursing the government. I stayed up all night, listening to the furious talk of the workers in the bistros. It was my first political experience—an experience in despair."[74] If the story is true, it is more likely than not that the workers were communists, which is interesting. The image of Angleton as an apprentice mechanic is also interesting.

In the autumn of 1937, just after Kim Philby became "Our Special Correspondent" for *The Times* in Salamanca, James Angleton, five years younger, enrolled in Yale University, New Haven, Connecticut.[75] He had returned to a country in the second crisis of the Depression. The New Deal by May 1937 had brought unemployment down from a peak of 25 percent to under 15 percent, at which point Roosevelt had ill-advisedly abandoned deficit spending and balanced the federal budget. Unemployment went back up, as Keynes would have predicted it would, a year later reaching a secondary Depression peak of 19 percent. The stock market, which had been rising steadily since late 1934, crashed, erasing its gains for that entire period. The agricultural Mid-west remained devastated by the "dust bowl" drought and the worldwide agricultural depression. Father Coughlin, the Nazi-supported "Radio Priest," had an audience of millions of listeners, and Julius Kuhn, Führer of the German-American Bund, attracted 20,000 people to a rally in Madison Square Garden in New York City. Across the aisle, as it were, the Communist Party was still growing in influence. After the factory occupations earlier in the year, General Motors had been forced to recognize the then-radical United Auto Workers with its communist shop-floor organizers. There were similarly communist-influenced, when not communist-led, strikes on the docks on the West Coast and in cities across the country. If there was ever to be a communist uprising in the United States, this was the time. All this would have been familiar to a young man fresh from crisis-stricken Europe.

There was another factor, this unique to the United States among industrialized countries: the situation of the descendants of enslaved Africans, then concentrated in the former Confederate states, where they were disenfranchised and living in conditions approaching serfdom: systematically subjugated and isolated in a way admired by Nazi legal theorists. The pariah status of the descendants of enslaved Africans was, and to some extent still is, a fundamental issue of American society. It was, and to some extent still is, particularly fundamental to social, political and economic arrangements in the former slave states, but the racist attitudes dominant among white residents of the southern United States were not confined to them. The Ku Klux Klan was still an important political and social factor in most states, north and south, east and west, electing officials from the village level to Congress. And in the late 1920s and 1930s attitudes such as the following were intellectually, not to mention socially, respectable: "The white South denies the Negro equal participation in society, not only because it does not consider him entitled to equality, but because it is certain that social mingling would lead to biological mingling, which it is determined to prevent, both for any given contemporary generation and for its posterity."[76] This was written by Donald Davidson, a Vanderbilt

University professor of English, whose students included Cleanth Brooks and Robert Penn Warren (always "Brooks and Warren," like "Burgess and Maclean"), who edited the anthology *Understanding Poetry*, which included Davidson's dramatic monologue *Lee in the Mountains*:

> *God too late*
> *Unseals to certain eyes the drift*
> *Of time and the hopes of men and a sacred cause.*

The "sacred cause" of the Confederacy, that is, slavery. Another member of the group, the poet Allen Tate, wrote that "The negro race is an inferior race . . . Our purpose is to keep the negro blood from passing into the white race." Tate wrote on another occasion "lynching will disappear when the white race is satisfied that its supremacy will not be questioned in social crises."[77] And so on, and so forth, while in Harlem jazz clubs white customers heard ironic laments of the "pastoral scene of the gallant south."

The cultural manifestations of this racism among white intellectuals, such as those expressed in careful prose and even more careful verse by Davidson and Tate, were in the first instance expressed defensively, as if efforts to defend African-Americans from the everyday violence in which they lived were an attack on the elegant cultural practices of those, living in shacks, committing, and those, living in pillared mansions, benefitting, from that violence. In the anthology *I'll Take My Stand: The Twelve Southerners* (1930), "All the articles bear in the same sense upon the book's title-subject: all tend to support a Southern way of life against what may be called the American or prevailing way; and all as much as agree that the best terms in which to represent the distinction are contained in the phrase, Agrarian *versus* Industrial." "The Southern way of life," for these twelve (white) southerners, it should, and did, go without saying was the *white* southern way of life, denying "the Negro equal participation in society." The authors committed to supporting it included Donald Davidson, Allen Tate, John Crowe Ransom and Robert Penn Warren. Davidson and his disciples, as most were English professors, thought to valorize the white southern way of life through cultural production, essays, stories, and especially the writing and criticism of poetry.

All this would only have been of provincial interest except for
the circumstance that Cleanth Brooks and Robert Penn Warren,
colleagues in the English Department of Vanderbilt University,
produced *Understanding Poetry* (1938), a textbook still found
in American high school and college classrooms. The influential
introduction to *Understanding Poetry* with odd stylistic emphases,
proclaimed "as error" the prevailing orthodoxy "that all students of
literature should be regarded as historians . . .

> More important still, and much more fruitful than the problems
> of origins and development, are those of content and significance.
> What is the human matter, what the artistic value of the work? . . .
> [T]he student of literature must be instructed, partly at least, in the
> mysteries of the art."[78]

And who would, or had ever, denied that? However, their aim was
not so much to save the study of the human matter and artistic
value of the work as to deny the importance of the study of origins and development, to deny the then Marxist-tainted historical
scholarship.

Brooks and Warren (both from Kentucky, educated and then
teaching in parallel at various southern colleges and universities)
instructed their readers, their students, that literature is best studied
without regard to its historical and biographical setting. More than
that, it is to be taught and read as a nearly religious mystery. This
was not a neutral prescription in 1938, halfway through the Spanish Civil War, with pitched battles between American workers and
police in northern factories, mines, and waterfronts, with lynch-
ings a common occurrence across the southern states so that the
supremacy of the "white race . . . will not be questioned." Despite
this background, in the opinion of Brooks and Warren, the student
should read, say, "Lee in the Mountains" or "Ode to the Confederate
Dead" without thinking about the details of the slavery for which
General Lee and the soldiers serving with him fought, thinking,
instead, of the mysterious glamor of it all.

In addition to its function as an anthology, *Understanding
Poetry* was an introduction to a methodology for reading poetry.
To this end, Brooks and Warren prefaced it with a "Letter to the
Teacher."

The editors of the present book hold that a satisfactory method of teaching poetry should embody the following principles:

1. Emphasis should be kept on the poem as a poem.
2. The treatment should be concrete and inductive.
3. *A poem should always be treated as an organic system of relationships, and the poetic quality should never be understood as inhering in one or more factors taken in isolation.*[79] [Emphasis added.]

For the New Critics, a poem is a poem because it has a *poetic quality,* something that is not to be isolated in one part or another—it is not verse, nor is it imagery—but "inheres" in the poem as a whole. Only when the student has the whole picture can he (always "he" in this tradition) make sense of any particular factor, then, in a version of the hermeneutical circle, once the whole is grasped, the merest fragment makes sense, is meaningful, is *imbued* with the quality of the whole. It was a method that could be, would be, applied to much beyond the study of poetry. Thomas Powers has observed that "At some point about a decade into Angleton's career as a counterintelligence analyst he began to adapt the close reading of the New Criticism to the identification of KGB penetration agents.

> You might think of it like this: the discrete bits of information in a chronology are like the words of a poem, each with its own freight of implication. When you quit thinking about the real world (the life and times of the poet) and concentrated on the meaning of the words (how the bits connected) then you began to see what the Russians had hidden . . ."[80]

The New Critics argued that theirs was a method deeply rooted in a particular set of values; that it was, in the final analysis, a method for promulgating and inculcating those values: agrarianism, Catholicism, and, for some, such as Davidson and Tate, racism. It could be argued that, as it were, a covert purpose of the New Criticism was to "imbue" in the student a unified world view applicable to all manner of things. The student was taught to choose between poetry and Christian civilization or historicism and the pagan barbarianism of Communism. The choice was clear enough to someone like the young James Angleton, who read the daily newspapers through a sensibility formed in Mussolini's Milan, or, on the other hand, would have been as well to someone like Kim Philby, a communist, who read, and who at this date wrote, the daily newspapers through a sensibility formed in the libraries of Trinity College, on the streets of Vienna, on park benches in London, in Spain.

Yale itself was isolated from much of the effects of the Depression by its own extensive building program, funded by the Standard Oil-derived fortune of anglophile Edward Harkness, who had given the University $10 million in 1930 (about $150 million in 2018 dollars) to build a nine-residential-college simulacrum of Oxford. The construction of those neo-gothic structures provided employment to New Haven residents through much of the decade. Just about the time, then, that Kim Philby was beginning to report from Franco's ancient gothic university headquarters in Salamanca, the similarly multilingual, well-traveled, somewhat younger and much less experienced James Angleton moved into his neo-gothic rooms in the New Haven construction site of Yale University and decided that it was the purpose of Yale, and his own purpose while there, to study and to write and to support poetry, as Lincoln Kirstein had done at Harvard with *Hound and Horn* and as James Laughlin was doing with *New Directions*. Almost immediately upon his arrival at Yale, Angleton was in correspondence with the prominent poets of the day concerning a college literary magazine, *Vif,* which Angleton and his friend Reed Whittemore called a "Revue Francaise Inter-Universitaire." Soon, they turned from *Vif* to produce *Furioso*, a journal that would continue under Whittemore's (and, for a time, Carmen Angleton's) editorship into the 1950s. *Furioso* was, according to at least one observer, "one of the major literary periodical voices of its era, as important as the *Sewanee Review* or the *Kenyon Review* or the *Partisan Review*."[81]

After that of Brooks and Warren, it was the English poet and critic William Empson's work that was particularly crucial for James Angleton. Empson's *Seven Types of Ambiguity* begins: "I propose to use the word [ambiguity] in an extended sense, and shall think relevant to my subject any verbal nuance, however slight, which gives room for alternative reactions to the same piece of language." Empson continues: "in a sufficiently extended sense any prose statement could be called ambiguous . . . Thus a word may have several distinct meanings.

> Several meanings connected with one another; several meanings which need one another to complete their meaning; or several meanings which unite together so that the word means one relation or one process. This is a scale which might be followed continuously. "Ambiguity" itself can mean an indecision as to what you mean, an intention to mean several things, a probability that one or other or both of two things has been meant, and the fact that a statement has several meanings."[82]

Angleton would remember of this careful exposition, if nothing else, "the fact that a statement has several meanings."

That first summer of the European war, while visiting his family in Italy and becoming, at least *ex officio,* a junior partner in his father's National Cash Register enterprise, Angleton wrote to the poet E. E. Cummings about his desire to meet Ezra Pound:

> Dear E.E.
> If a bomb or the food doen't [sic] lay me low I am going to see Ezra next week. The old boy has got plenty on his balls and every time I get the least bit worried he lifts me up to the point that I feel like murdering professors, or at least cutting off their dung-dragging beards. However . . . however . . . however.
> Milan has been very pleasant and there is nothing to do which means that I read one novel and dream about the next issue of *Furioso* . . ."[83]

Angleton spent most of a week with Ezra Pound in Rapallo, establishing a relationship—mentor and disciple—that lasted for two or three years, much like that James Laughlin had developed with Pound slightly earlier. Pound's politics were apparently not an impediment for either young publisher, perhaps the opposite, especially for Angleton, raised in Mussolini's Italy, steeped in the intellectual world of agrarian poetics. Unlike Kim Philby, he did not need to wear a mask to display fascist sympathy.

Angleton returned that autumn to a university seemingly oblivious to events in Europe. For the most part he worked at *Furioso*

---

and at his own poems. He lived, as many undergraduates lived, in a nocturnal welter of papers and cigarettes, habits he kept throughout his life. He was also athletic, playing tennis and soccer for Yale (mentioned a few times for the latter in contemporaneous issues of the *New York Times*). Angleton initiated his sister Carmen into his new literary world.[84] Their close lifelong relationship supported a strong connection between James Angleton and a postwar transatlantic café society that eventually intersected with the CIA-supported Congress for Cultural Freedom and included literary figures like Mary McCarthy, Bernard Berenson, Peggy Guggenheim, and Hannah Arendt.[85]

The first three issues of *Furioso* characteristically contained short poems by Pound, Williams, Eberhart, and Empson that they seem to have sent to Yale as an alternative to being discarded. The remaining authors were less distinguished, their poems with vocabularies decades out of date, with inward-looking subject matter and much use of the vocative. The fourth issue, summer 1941, was different. There were poems by Auden, Marianne Moore, Wallace Stevens, Cummings, and Lawrence Durrell, more than fifty pages of reviews (including a reprint of a lecture by I. A. Richards), and "The Spanish Dead," by Archibald MacLeish: "The children of Almería they are still/They do not move they will never move those children . . ." Almería was the site of a Nationalist atrocity in the Spanish Civil War. MacLeish's poem is unique in *Furioso*, a journal, like Laughlin's *New Directions* anthologies, otherwise strongly oriented to the political right. Both Angleton and Laughlin were disciples of Ezra Pound, both accepted his admiration of Mussolini and his anti-Semitism and for a time adapted the latter, if only in their letters to the Master. Angleton's lifelong close friend Cummings remained in touch with Pound, despite the war, and shared some of Pound's political views.[86]

Angleton wrote to Pound in February 1940 about politics and offering money: "There is hell of a lot of Roosveltian shilly-shally here in America.

> Everything is definitely British and the jews [sic] cause a devil of a lot of stink. Here in New York will be the next great pogrom, and they do need about a thousand ghettos in America. Jew, Jew and Jew, even the Irish are losing out . . . I talked to Dad on the

telephone the day before the war and mentioned the little shekel you might need, say a couple of thousand, and he said o.k. So I hope you will oblige by writing him and accept it as a favor."[87]

Pound replied to the offer of money, "thanks but no thanks," more or less. Angleton's letters in 1940 became if anything more frantic, reflecting the tensions of the coming war and his peculiar position: caught between two or three languages, half attached to Italy, half to New Haven, with the complication of Pound on both sides. In a letter to Cummings, Angleton said, "I am looking for some sort of myth, something that will bring things all around to a solution." Those looking for a myth usually find one. It might be said that Angleton was to find one in the Cold War itself.

James Angleton had made a position for himself on the margin of the transatlantic literary world. He was a friend of Pound, one of the many drinking companions of William Empson, a frequent correspondent of Cummings and Williams. All these famous poets took this young man very seriously. One of the few Yale teachers whom Angleton himself took seriously was Norman Holmes Pearson, who was to become one of the more significant American spymasters, and, based first in London, later back in New Haven, a mentor of generations of American intelligence professionals. It was Pearson, as it happened, not Pound, who was to stand godfather to Angleton's career, which made all the difference.

Angleton graduated from Yale in June 1941, in the lowest quarter of his class, a consequence of not often going to classes.[88] Soon after graduation he tried to join the army. But Angleton's health was never good—all his life he had periodic bouts of emphysema and tuberculosis—and the army was not yet ready to overlook that sort of thing. Angleton also applied to Harvard Law School. That application too was rejected. He then asked Norman Pearson for a recommendation, which Pearson supplied:

Angleton is a young man of great, and on occasion, not always practical enthusiasms . . . I have known Angleton for several years in an academic way, despite the fact that he has taken no classes from me. I can say quite flatly that he is one of the few undergraduates who has made their mark on Yale.[89]

Harvard relented and Angleton settled into the life of a Harvard law student. He was soon interviewed by the FBI, which was collecting information about Pound for a treason indictment for his radio broadcasts from Rome.[90] Angleton told the FBI that he admired Pound's poetry and agreed with his political theories, but not with Pound's prejudices against Jews and international bankers. He thought the radio broadcasts that were the grounds for the treason indictment incoherent, and agreed both to testify and to name names. It was a well-balanced performance: as loyal as was prudent to his friend, yet helpful to the authorities.

James Angleton became engaged to Cicely d'Autremont, a Vassar student from Tucson, Arizona, in April 1943. They were married in July. Cicely d'Autremont's parents were leading citizens of Tucson, with a considerable fortune that derived from Duluth mining and lumber interests on both sides of the family. Her maternal grandfather, Chester Congdon, was a lawyer associated with a long list of mining and steel companies, owner of the thirty-nine-room Glensheen Estate in Duluth, Minnesota. Her parents' local Tucson investments included mines and a hotel. Her father, a banker, served in the Arizona state legislature; her mother was active in the community, occupied with charitable work among the African-American and Mexican-American peoples there. The family's way of life included trout and bass fishing in private streams along the Canadian border, visits to New York, vacations on Cape Cod. The aura of independent means noticed by observers of Angleton in later life—the English bespoke suits, the Mercedes, the private streams, and the Tucson "mansion"—was based at least in part on the wealth of his wife's family as well as that of his own.

By March 1943 the army was prepared to overlook Angleton's health problems. He was twenty-five years old, well-educated, multilingual, about to be married into the American business elite, already part of the international section of that group through his own family. He was a few years older than Kim Philby had been when Philby had committed himself to working with the communists; in comparison to Philby at that age, Angleton was still somewhat cosseted and aimless.

WAR AND SECRET INTELLIGENCE

PHILBY

Kim Philby had returned to London from Spain in the fall of 1939—early in the Phony War in the west—a well-known and well-regarded war correspondent beginning to emerge from his father's shadow. *The Times* almost immediately sent him to France, once more as "Our Special Correspondent," now to cover the operations, or lack thereof, of the British Expeditionary Force (BEF), stationed amid the quiet, death-haunted fields on the French/Belgian border. Philby had obtained permission to wear on his war-correspondent uniform Franco's medal, and perhaps with the same false flag endeavor, made sure to be seen from time to time in Paris with Lady Margaret Vane-Tempest-Stewart, a daughter of Lord Londonderry, that stalwart of the Anglo-German Fellowship. Philby had other meetings as well during his visits to Paris. Some had to be carefully arranged in advance as neither he nor his Soviet contact knew one another by sight:

> Terms of the meeting: 12 or 13 October from 12:00 to 12:15 p.m. at the Place de la Madeleine on the street near the entrance to the Thomas Cook tourist office, across from the Cathedral of the same name as the street. Identification signs: [Philby] will carry the English newspaper, the *Daily Mail*. Our person should have the same paper. The password our man has to ask . . . "Where is the Café Henri around here?" in English or French. The answer: "It's near the Place de [sic] Republique." The back-up meeting is on 1 or 2 November. Same time, terms and place."[1]

Others Philby saw in Paris he knew very well. Cookridge has it that when Philby "looked up" Donald Maclean at the British embassy in Paris, Maclean introduced him to his American "girl friend"

Melinda Marling and the bohemian set at the Deux Magots, Flore, and Coupole cafés.[2] This is not otherwise attested—which does not mean that it is not true.

Philby's reports to *The Times* (from "Our Special Correspondent, Somewhere in France") began on 2 October 1939: "It has been my privilege to spend the past 48 hours with the British Army in France," he wrote.

> During that time I have been able to visit the present G.H.Q., to make contact with all arms and all ranks, to see troops at work, at rest, and on the move. Everything that I have seen and heard justifies the conviction that no finer body of men than the "Young Contemptibles"—as they have already christened themselves—has ever left the shores of Great Britain . . . As for their equipment, it must be seen to be appreciated.

That was the equipment that would be left on the beach at Dunkirk. While the British army was preparing to fight the Germans on the familiar ground of Flanders, in Whitehall important officials were already contemplating a reversal of alliances, the fear of which would haunt the Kremlin for the duration of the war. John Colville, then one of the Assistant Private Secretaries to Prime Minister Chamberlain, commented in his diary under 13 October: "It is thus vital that we should play our hand very carefully with Russia, and not destroy the possibility of uniting, if necessary, with a new German Government against the common danger. What is needed is a moderate conservative reaction in Germany: the overthrow of the present regime by the army chiefs."[3] This does put an interesting light on the July 1944 attempt to "overthrow the present regime by the army chiefs," or, at least, some of the army chiefs.

On 14 October *The Times* published a report from "Our Special Correspondent" submitted the previous day: "The British Field Force is moving gradually into line. Its massive equipment, rumbling steadily eastwards, is strung out far and wide along the roads of France . . . Hitherto our troops have taken no part in the land fighting on the Western Front . . ." And on the 15th, "In spite of intense military activity, life appears to proceed with little change.

From misty dawn to the sinking of the pale autumn sun, men, women, and *children* labour in the fields, gathering in the great stores of foodstuffs which lie embedded in the soil of France. Their labour, like that of the khaki-clad figures who rumble past them in their cumbrous lorries, is one of the many factors that guarantee the British and French Empires against defeat." [Emphasis added.]

One thinks of the mud-colored images of those "men, women, and children" laboring in those fields as put down on canvas by van Gogh, say, and considers their role in the great empires benefiting from that labor, the "benefits" they received in return.

Published in *The Times* on 18 October, next to another of these optimistic articles, was an appraisal by Philby's colleague, "Our Military Correspondent," that "a blow against the Maginot Line" by the German army, "or a combination of such a blow with a turning movement through neutral territory . . . would be out of the question from the purely military point of view." Thus assured, Philby reported on 25 October that "The British Army is still preparing for war, not waging it." The following day he wrote that "In spite of the severe weather the health of the troops has suffered but little. All day they are in the open air engaged in strenuous digging; at night they have a change of socks . . ." (There seems to have been a fixation on the socks of the infantry by those at home.) On the 30th, "It is the opinion of the Quartermaster-General that, both as regards mobility and fire power, the British Army is capable, other things being equal, of meeting and beating the Germans under any conditions." All through November and December 1939 the reports are of visits to the front line by various dignitaries—Anthony Eden, Chamberlain, the King—and little else.

Philby missed his first planned meeting in Paris with his Soviet contact, explaining that travel was difficult and that the meetings could only be held once a month. The material he handed over, however, "was detailed and . . . valuable." In a report of 1 April 1940 "the chief of the London Soviet Secret Intelligence residency would write:

Contact with him has been very irregular, especially recently . . . [Philby] is undoubtedly a very cultured and highly erudite individual, endowed with a broad outlook. He reads a lot of serious literature, particularly scholarly works on the history of music. He has repeatedly emphasized that he has no other goal in life than working for the Revolution . . . At the same time . . . he was beginning to experience a certain disillusionment with us . . . A few times, he complained that the casual, irregular and unsystematic contact with us during his time in Spain often left him with one or another unresolved political and party questions. The signing of the Soviet-German Non-Aggression Pact caused [Philby] to ask puzzled questions such as, 'Why was this necessary? What will happen to the single-front struggle against fascism now?' . . . [Philby] greeted the liberation of the peoples of the Western Ukraine and West Byelorussia by the Red Army with a burst of wild enthusiasm . . ."[4]

The answers to his questions about the "Soviet-German Non-Aggression Pact" are not recorded.

On 10 May 1940 the German army finally invaded in the west. Philby reported to *The Times* on 12 May that "After eight months of patient waiting the bomber squadrons of the Advanced Air Striking Force have had their first chance of aiming a real blow at the enemy this week-end, and they have taken the fullest advantage of it.

Raid after raid has been successfully carried out on the German troops moving forward through Luxemburg and Belgium, and many of our pilots have come back with heartening stories showing clearly the havoc they have caused."

On the 13th the report is of "R.A.F. Triumph in 'Total War.'" On the 14th: "The great battle for Belgium is continuing along a front stretching 100 miles from the marshy country north of the Albert Canal to the mining basin of Longwy, where the Germans may try to break through the Maginot Line at the point on which the Allied forces are pivoting in their vast right wheel across the Low Countries." On the 15th, "A Day of Raids: Attacks on R.A.F. in France."

And then, with little, if any, preparation for the readers of *The Times*, on 18 May, "B.E.F. Withdrawn West of Brussels," which was something of an understatement: the Western Front had collapsed not from "a blow against the Maginot Line" by the German army, but from "a turning movement through neutral territory," which, as it happened, was not "out of the question from the purely military point of view." The next day Philby lost all his kit during the chaotic retreat from Amiens. The British war correspondents, so optimistic only days earlier, were evacuated to Boulogne and from there to England, where they saw the preparations for the withdrawal of the BEF from Dunkirk, much of its "massive equipment" to be put to use by the Wehrmacht. Two weeks later Philby was back in France, witnessing the death of yet another republic.[5] *The Times* published a story of his on 14 June, filed from Paris on the 11th: "To-day, with the streets filled with smoke and the sound of anti-aircraft guns in the distance, Paris is slowly emptying. Except for a heterogeneous collection of vehicles piled high with refugees and their household belongings, the streets are almost deserted. The acrid smell of burning permeates the city." Philby wrote a series of stories over the next ten days describing how he and his fellow journalists moved from Paris to Bordeaux with the columns of French refugee civilians and government officials. On the 18th the paper published his report filed from Bordeaux on 17 June. "British and some American journalists left here to-day for a port where a steamer waits to convey them to England." It was the end, for nearly two decades, of his career as a journalist. He resigned from *The Times* on 15 July 1940, to take up quite a different career.

That summer, St. John Philby planned to leave Saudi Arabia for the United States, perhaps to meet with his American oil-company clients, perhaps to speak against British imperial interests, perhaps both. The British representative at Jeddah, Sir Hugh Stonehewer Bird (later ambassador to Iraq), telegraphed London on 12 July 1940: "I received this morning a message from Ibn Saud informing me that Philby was leaving the country and asking me to facilitate his journey.

> Philby was, the King thought, mentally deranged, he never ceased heaping curses and insults and scorn on the British Government. He had told Ibn Saud that he wished to travel to India and the United States of America for the purpose of conducting anti-British propaganda."[6]

When St. John Philby reached Karachi, en route to the USA, he was detained under the Defence of India Rules and packed onto a ship for Liverpool. The India Office informed the Home Office of the background to this matter on 30 August 1940. The Home Office, in turn, decided that Philby's comments about the conduct of the war and the nature of the British government would have come to the attention of "natives" and therefore could be construed as "something approaching an attempt to stir up sedition."

Thereupon followed a complicated exchange of communications between Guy Liddell of MI-5 and Valentine Vivian of SIS. On 19 September Liddell sent the file on to Vivian for his comments. It is worth quoting Vivian's reply at length.

Secret. (Strictly Personal)

My dear Guy,
Your PF.40408/B, dated 19.9.40., about H. St. J. Philby is one of the hardest letters to answer, which you have ever sent me.

I suppose that I have known St. John Philby on and off for about 30 years. As a bullet-headed young Assistant Commissioner in Shahpur in the Punjab, he was singularly devoid of manners and always up against his superiors. He was strongly self-opinionated and expressed himself, often extremely capably and accurately, with such arrogance that no-one had a good word for him. But neither then nor since has he ever been anything of a fool.

Later he gained expert knowledge of Arabic and the Arabs, while High Commissioner in Trans-Jordania. He fell out violently with the Foreign Office and the Colonial Office regarding policy in the Arabian Peninsula and expressed himself with as much force and arrogance as he had done when he was a young Assistant Commissioner in India. He advocated the dropping of the Husseinis and the backing of Ibn Saud, the deadly enemy of the Husseins. He was, of course, dead right in his views, but he expressed them with such lack of restraint and such want of discipline that, where his knowledge and flair should have been invaluable to the Government, it was repudiated.

Later, again, he came to eminence as an Arab-explorer, became a Mohamedan and settled down in Saudi-Arabia more or less as a Finance Advisor to Ibn Saud. During this period he was for the most part out for his own interests, but he was a sore embarrassment to our Government in their Arabian policy. I imagine that his politics are, and have always been, Left Wing, and, if my memory is right, he was intriguing with Dr. Dalton over Egypt and Arabia in the time of the short-lived Labour Government.[7]

You will see that, if he and his views have been unpalatable, that does not prove that he was not both accurate and far seeing. I myself, although I have only seen him a few times both in England, India and Arabia of late years, have found it possible to get on with him and I do not believe that he is disloyal, merely insufferably arrogant.

Now, the curious thing is that his son (the person to whom I believe he refers as "Kim" in one of the letters returned herewith) is one of our D. officers. In that capacity I have met him once or twice and found him both able and charming. He himself told me that his father had cooled down in the strength of his views in the last few years, but that would not appear to be so from the letters. Young Philby was, of course, in D's section long before there was any question of D's section being taken over by Dalton, but, as that has happened fortuitously, the son will be more or less under the direction of a man known to his father, with whom I believe the latter has had quite a number of semi-covert dealings. I mention young Philby simply because I think it will make it more difficult to take any repressive measures against the father.

I am afraid this is a terrible rigmarole, but it is my only way of explaining the difficulty which St. John Philby represents. I do not think he is disloyal and I think it is most urgently necessary not to give him a further grievance. On the other hand, I feel it is a case in which the Foreign Office and the Government would gladly see you using strong-arm tactics. With this uncomfortable problem I must leave you to deal.

Yours sincerely,
/signed/

P.S. Philby's wife, Dora née Johnson, the daughter of an Indian railway official, was a childhood friend of my wife's. She is a perfectly regulation young Anglo-Indian woman, good bridge and tennis player and fine rider. She has no politics and, though she has been out to Arabia once or twice to see her husband, she had rather dropped out of his family life, when I last saw her by accident in my bank. From the letters it would seem that the family is coming together again.[8]

Someone in the Foreign Office read Vivian's letter and took exception to it, stating "that in Mr. Philby's world there is only Mr. Philby. Loyalty and disloyalty are only words to him." Guy Liddell then wrote to Vivian, stating that "I do not know the identity of the person in the Foreign Office who wrote this but in view of what you said I cannot help feeling that it may be a very unintelligent remark and that a gross blunder is being committed. Do you think there is anything to be done, particularly owing to the fact that the son is in your employ?"

Detention of St. John Philby under the Defence of the Realm Act was issued by John Anderson, Home Secretary, on 20 September 1940. St. John Philby arrived in Liverpool on the *City of Venice* from Karachi on 17 October 1940, and was duly arrested. On 26 October Vivian replied to Liddell "I am inclined to agree with you that one of the ugliest blunders is being committed . . . the action could very easily be depicted as political malice, and I have no doubt that, when the circumstances come, as come they must, to Herbert Morrison's notice, there will be quite a nasty sticky row."[9] Vivian also commented that "in view of Kim Philby's employment in the D. Section" he has some justification in interesting himself in the case. Vivian wrote to Liddell on 6 November stating that he had just received a copy of Stonehewer Bird's letter "which I rather think furnishes the substance of the case against Philby. I enclose a copy of the telegram, which certainly gives the impression that he has taken leave of his senses . . . I should be grateful if you could get from the Home Office the actual grounds for his detention and let me know them, as we shall no doubt get some representation from young Kim Philby."

As far as the records show, it was not Kim Philby, but his mother Dora Philby, that "perfectly regulation young Anglo-Indian woman," who intervened, writing to Lord Lloyd, former High Commissioner in Egypt, Secretary of State for the Colonies, on 11 November, asking him to look into the matter as "they have detained my husband in Liverpool prison for nearly a month now. I don't know exactly what it is all about but I can't believe he is as dangerous as all that."[10] Lloyd wrote to a Colonel Harter on the 14th, asking for information, saying "I know Philby well: he is a bit of a brilliant lunatic and has always been a bit 'agin the Government', but he is the last man whom I should have conceived of being anything but a most loyal and patriotic person." Harter replied on the 16th, stating that Philby had said he was going to appeal, but had not yet done so. Liddell and Vivian again exchanged notes on the 19th and 25th, agreeing with one another that a "blunder" had been committed. There was much more correspondence among Home Office, Foreign Office, SIS, MI-5, and Lord Lloyd, and by 12 December, Cadogan at the Foreign Office, intervened, saying more or less that it was all right with him if St. John Philby were released as long as he stayed in England. Herbert Morrison, Home Secretary, revoked the detention order on 15 March 1941. St. John Philby was refused permission to return to Arabia until after the war, when he did so.

The entire affair gives a sense of the closed world of the British ruling class of the time. Everyone had known everyone back in India, their sisters knew their wives, even the often outrageous St. John Philby was—eventually—taken care of, busying himself for the duration of the war with his writing and lectures. And as for Kim, "He looks good. We fixed him up."

Kim Philby's tale of his entry into the British secret intelligence world, as he first told the Soviet secret intelligence service, then told MI-5 in 1951, then, finally, told MI-6 in Beirut, was that on his journey from France to London in June 1940 he met Esther Marsdon-Smedley, a well-connected journalist, who was connected with, among other things, Section D. of MI-6. They chatted, he said; she thought he would be a good addition to Section D., he said; she recommended him to a friend in Section D., who interviewed him in the company of her assistant, who happened to be Guy Burgess. Philby was offered a position organizing a school for training propagandists and saboteurs, which he set about doing, from the ground up, as until then SIS had not had such a training facility. A few years later, the school Philby had organized played the same role for OSS personnel as well. Another story, which does not necessarily contradict Philby's, is that Philby was recruited by Valentine Vivian, second in command of MI-6: "I've got a bright young man for us—Philby, the *Times* war correspondent. Used to know his father in the old days." Vivian, like the original Kim's protector in Kipling's fable, was pleased with his protégé.[11]

He considered the years to come, when Kim would have been entered and made to the Great Game that never ceases day and night . . . He foresaw honour and credit in the mouths of the chosen few, coming to him from his pupil.[12]

After the usual bureaucratic disorders, Section D., in late July 1940, was absorbed into the Special Operations Executive, under the Minister of Economic Warfare, Hugh Dalton, sometime associate of St. John Philby. Kim Philby (as well as, for a time, Guy Burgess) went into the agent training operations of SOE, being trained and training others.

During this period, Philby and the other Comintern agents in Britain had had difficulty remaining in contact with Moscow Center as the purges there hollowed out the Soviet Union's foreign intelligence apparatus. It was not until December 1940 that Philby re-established contact with Moscow.[13] From "December 1940 to March 1941 [Philby] reported, among other things, about the organization of diversionary work by the British, the structure of [the training school], the management staff of the IS [Intelligence Service], and the staff employed at [the training school]. He also reported the names of agents who were deployed by the British to enemy territory, about Czech and Polish intelligence work against the Germans."[14]

Soviet counterespionage may have found this information useful; they may have transmitted it to their then-ally, Germany, or it could have been filed away, disbelieved, taken as a provocation, as happened from time to time, due, as Graham Greene had it, to the human factor.

Six months after Coville's private musings about a reversal of alliances, on 19 April 1941, Stafford Cripps gave Andrei Vyshinsky, the Soviet Foreign Minister, a memorandum warning the Soviet government that "if the war between England and Germany lasted long, Great Britain would be tempted to conclude an agreement to end the war.

> The conditions of which an agreement, the Ambassador wrote, had recently been discussed in influential German circles: Western Europe would return to its pre-war situation, while Germany could thrust all its military forces unimpeded to the East to secure living space there . . . Three weeks later, it seems Cripps's fears received confirmation. A German aeroplane landed in Scotland on 10 May, with no less than Rudolf Hess . . . on board."[15]

The Russian intelligence services released a selection of documents in 2011 for N. M. Dolgopolov's biography of Philby.[16] These contained information from Philby, which had been transmitted to Moscow from the London KGB residency. They included a series of reports concerning the arrival of Rudolf Hess in Scotland. One had it that the deputy chief of the Foreign Office's press department, Tom Dupree, had told Philby that Hess had claimed that he had gone to England to negotiate a compromise peace between the British Empire and Germany followed by an alliance against the Soviet Union.[17]

Philby informed the London NKVD residence that during his talks with British military intelligence officers Hess had claimed that he had arrived in Britain, with Hitler's knowledge, to conclude a compromise peace. It was not clear whether in fact his proposals had Hitler's support. Moscow came to the conclusion that the British might accept Hess's proposals and sign a peace treaty with Germany, which would be followed by a military alliance directed against the USSR, a conclusion reinforced, as we have seen, inadvertently or not, by Cripps.[18] Soon after the German invasion of the Soviet Union, Philby was tasked by the KGB with monitoring Allied negotiations concerning the second front. Everything he was able to discover about this was sent by Lubyanka directly to Stalin, including what the Soviets saw as "the duplicity" of Churchill in continually promising and continually delaying the second front.[19]

A message from the London residency, on 20 June 1941, based on information from Philby, described Foreign Secretary Eden's conversation with Soviet ambassador Ivan Maisky, in which Eden said that "Britain would send a military mission to the USSR, if necessary, and promised to intensify the activities of British aviation against Germany to weaken German pressure of the USSR, in case of the German-Soviet war . . .

> At the same time, the British have recently intensified their preparations for the bombing of Baku. On June 16, under the chairmanship of Churchill, another meeting of the Imperial Defense Committee was held, at which the question of means to stop the receipt of oil by Germany was discussed. In his speech, Churchill insisted on speedy completion of all preparations for the bombing of Baku . . .

Beaverbrook evasively answered that 'the Caucasian scheme seems to him now very remote.'"[20]

Churchill seems always to have been in favor of bombing the Baku oil fields, the reasons changing with the circumstances. This did not sit well with Stalin, whatever the circumstances.

In September 1941, after a year working on the propaganda efforts of Section D. of MI-6, then on those of SOE, writing pamphlets and lecturing, Philby was recruited back into MI-6 as head of the Iberian group in Section V.[21] Section V was not, yet, a large organization. For example, there were only half a dozen officers in the Iberia section, including Kim Philby himself. It was "responsible for the collection of counter-espionage information from foreign countries by illegal means." This is what the British secret intelligence service hoped to accomplish, at that time, in regard to the German secret intelligence service.[22] And the Soviet secret intelligence services then and later hoped to accomplish this in regard also to the German, British, and American secret intelligence services. In part due to Philby's work, both organizations were quite successful.

Timothy Milne remembered a party in Aileen Furse's bedroom, where she was resting a week or two after the birth of their first child. Tommy and Hilda Harris were there, as was, inevitably, Guy Burgess.[23] Kim and Aileen Philby (as they were known, despite being unmarried) were leaving London. They had rented a house in St. Albans, The Spinney in Marshalswick Lane, ten minutes by car or twenty minutes by bicycle from Glenalmond, the Edwardian country house headquarters of Section V. The purpose of Section V of MI-6 was to discover everything possible about enemy intelligence organizations: where they were located, who was on their staffs, the identity of their agents, how they functioned, and how they communicated. This information was conveyed to MI-5 so that the domestic secret intelligence organization could strengthen its defenses against foreign infiltration. MI-6 also endeavored to combat enemy intelligence organizations in foreign countries.[24] There were sections for the Americas, western and eastern Europe, and the Middle East, as well as Philby's Iberia. The way its staff went about studying the structure and activities of the German secret intelligence services would be familiar to any researcher: scanning documents (or, in this case, messages); identifying items of interest, cataloging those;

forming theories, testing them; constructing narratives. Always very interesting, as an intellectual exercise. But, of course, in 1941 this involved the survival of the British empire and the outcome of the war.

The activities of Section V had to, and did, utilize what it learned both from its research and from intercepted German message traffic in order to reduce the effectiveness of the German espionage effort. In this it was successful, using its knowledge of the German intelligence agencies' "order of battle," for example, to convince the Franco government to expel large numbers of German agents from Spain.[25] That notable success was facilitated by Kim Philby's familiarity with Franco and his entourage, especially Philby's familiarity with Franco's touchiness about any German claims of Spanish indebtedness for its help in the Civil War. As Hugh Trevor-Roper put it: "Philby was undeniably competent: the most competent and industrious man in that generally lax organization."[26]

Milne thought that Philby was the person primarily responsible for the quality of the work of Section V. He wrote clearly and concisely, and he was familiar with the relevant files and other paperwork. He had sound judgment. He was admired by his colleagues and superiors.[27]

The high regard in which Philby was held in MI-6 is illustrated by this letter from Stewart Menzies to Peter Loxley of the Foreign Office, 15 March 1943, responding to a transfer request for Philby from Loxley: "Dear Peter, This places me in an uncomfortable position.

> You know as well as I do the valuable work which Philby is doing for me. At the same time, I realize the importance of first-class representation in Spain in the days ahead. I also have some qualms of conscience about interfering with the career of so able a man as Philby is . . . After full consideration of all the circumstances and after consulting those immediately responsible for Philby's work, I have come to the conclusion that the Allied cause will best be served by leaving Philby where he is . . . I hope that when he communicates this decision to Deakin, Roberts will make an opportunity of emphasizing that the essential nature of Philby's contribution to the war effort compels his present employers regretfully to refuse to let him go, and that they hope that this refusal will not prejudice

Philby's own personal interests . . . I have not liked, without your permission, to tell Philby what has happened. May I have your permission to do so?"[28]

It is not clear what position in the Foreign Office Loxley had in mind for Philby, aside from the fact that it was obviously something in the Madrid embassy, perhaps First Secretary. Menzies would remain impressed by, and loyal to, Philby to the end.

On 10 March 1943, while Philby was impressing Menzies and others with the success of his counterintelligence efforts in Spain, his then current NKVD "control" informed Moscow Center that "Meetings with [Philby] take place in London once every ten to twelve days, in the customary way, as with other agents.

> Sometimes, when the opportunity arises, he brings separate files to photograph (only when we ask him). In these instances we meet him in the morning and return the material in the evening. This, of course, is inconvenient and incorrect according to operational procedures, but it's the only way to get the documentary files that [Philby] can't copy, because they're too large. Earlier, as far as we know, he used to have a 'Minox' but his photographs weren't very good, and at your instruction we took the camera from him . . ."[29]

Philby said in a 1981 lecture to junior officials of the Stasi that he had met with an SIS archivist two or three times a week for a drink, which had led to the archivist giving Philby access to documents in which he was interested. He passed these to his Soviet contact in the evenings, who photographed them and returned them to Philby to replace in the archives in the morning.[30] Yuri Modin, one of Philby's KGB contacts, wrote that Aileen Furse worked in the archive section of MI-5, perhaps supplementing this route into the British secret intelligence archives. In any case, it seems that Philby had access to the names of British agents, worldwide, which he duly sent on to Moscow.[31] According to Philby: "The most significant information which I passed on to Moscow while I worked in SIS . . . [was], to begin with, the general overview of SIS, its structure, the areas it was working in, directors, addresses, its most outstanding agents and that sort of thing.

All the information that SIS possessed about the German *Abwehr*, Himmler's secret-service SD [as well] . . . At about this time the SIS began getting serious information about the state of affairs in the O.S.S. as well, the American military-intelligence service . . . I also passed on this information, when possible, to the Centre . . ."[32]

With one hand, Philby helped SIS obtain textbook-quality information about the German secret intelligence organizations, while with his other hand he provided that and similar information about SIS itself and its American counterpart, OSS, to the Soviet secret intelligence organizations.

From early 1943 Kim Philby was in a position to deliver to Moscow not only the entire "order of battle," personnel structure and on-going accumulation of secret information of the British intelligence services, he was able to do so as well in regard to the new American organization, OSS. Cave Brown speculated that because of Norman Holmes "Pearson's relationship with Philby, on whom he was entirely dependent for some time in almost every professional respect, nearly the entire security system of the United States in theory, and also to some extent in practice, was penetrated from the onset, vulnerable to Soviet espionage."[33] In any case, it appears that the professional home that James Angleton found in America's secret intelligence organization was already under Soviet surveillance, penetrated two or three years before he entered it. This would be a lesson, once he learned it, that he would take to heart.

Information and orders passed from the headquarters of World War II combatants by telephone landlines and by radio. The landlines were almost always secure. The radio messages were encoded and transmitted by Morse code. As radio signals can be received by anyone listening in on the proper frequency, the further coding of these messages was crucial to their security. This was the case for commercial purposes as well as diplomatic and military messages. Between the wars an electro-magnetic commercial machine came into use that was believed to produce undecipherable messages. The machine was then elaborated by the Germans and others. However, the British intelligence services, at Bletchley Park and elsewhere, succeeded in developing ways to decipher the various German codes (as the US did with Japanese codes.) The result was known as ULTRA. Using these intercepted and decoded messages, and other means, the British secret intelligence services were able to identify German agents sent to the United Kingdom, imprisoning some and turning others into double agents in a project called "Double Cross." The crowning achievement of years of effort along these lines was the German belief that Overlord, the invasion of Normandy, was a feint, the real invasion, putatively under General Patton, to take place elsewhere along the Channel coast. Double Cross was completely successful, setting an impossible standard for later efforts—and giving rise to the later not unreasonable question that if, incredibly enough, all German agents in Britain during World War II had actually been double agents, controlled by the British, how was any Cold War intelligence service to be sure that the same had not been done to them, that they had not been penetrated?

James McCargar, a particularly colorful American secret intelligence official, commented in this regard that "A successful penetration of the opponent's secret operations organization puts you at the very heart of his actions and intentions towards you.

> You share his mind and thinking to an intimate—and reliable—degree impossible in any other secret operation. This means that so far as intelligence is concerned, you know what he knows. You have therefore annulled, in one stroke, the value of his secret knowing. Even more importantly, through your knowledge of his intelligence interests and of his political operations, as revealed in his policy papers and instructions, you are in the possession of the most reliable possible indications of his intentions. Most importantly, you are in a position to control his actions, since you can, by tailoring intelligence for him to your purposes, by influencing his evaluations, mislead him as to his decision and consequent actions."[34]

That was the aspiration of the intelligence officer; that was the terror of the counterintelligence officer; that was what Philby helped MI-6 accomplish in regard to the Abwehr; that was what he helped the KGB accomplish in regard to MI-6, OSS, and, perhaps, the CIA.

After Double Cross, for counterintelligence officers—British, American, Soviet—that idea lingered for a generation: everything we think we know may be sheer manipulation, betrayal. Much has been written about Moscow Center's suspicions of its British agents. This was not specific to those agents, nor to the Soviet secret intelligence services.[35] As Philby's Russian biographer, journalist Genrikh Borovik, was told by a slightly bored young Russian secret intelligence officer, stating what was for him an obvious point: "[I]n the end, the direct obligation of any secret service [is] to check constantly its agents for 'doubleness'. . .

> There is a special service in the Centre . . . which checks and rechecks all its agents and all its sources of information, not out of maliciousness or capriciousness, but because that is its official duty. In doing so, it is obliged always to assume the worst . . . In receiving any information from a source, the specialists accepting it always ask themselves several questions: Whom does this information profit? Did the source have access to it? How can this information influence the relations between countries? Will it cause harm to our country? Finally, what harm can it cause the intelligence service . . .?"[36]

Borovik tells us that in "a short period at the end of 1943 Philby passed on to his Soviet control:

> Political and war information about the Soviet Union that had been received by SIS, data about its residences, the work of the counter-intelligence section, radio intelligence and counter-intelligence activities, documents related to the Allies' strategic war plans, the correspondence between the British Military Mission in the USSR (Mission No. 30) and the British War Ministry, material on SIS work in the USA, the correspondence between SIS and [its official agent in the Soviet Union], data on SIS counter-intelligence network on the Iberian Peninsula, a diagram of the organization of the American Intelligence service, the telegraphic correspondence between the Foreign Office and the British Embassy in Spain . . ."[37]

In sum, the British secret intelligence services and much of the rest of the British war effort, were, due to Philby, transparent to Soviet intelligence.

ANGLETON

James Hugh Angleton and his wife and daughters arrived in New York City from Milan on 8 December 1941, the day that the United States declared war on Japan, while sons James and Hugh were still at Yale. Hugh and Carmen Angleton and their daughters stayed at the Ambassador Hotel for three months and then moved to the New Weston Hotel on 50th Street, near the Waldorf Astoria. On 16 September 1942, William Donovan, by then Director of the Office of Strategic Services, recommended the appointment of James H. Angleton for duty with the "Strategic Services Command." The duty proposed was "of a secret nature." Under "Applicant's special qualifications," Donovan wrote: "This man's extensive knowledge of foreign affairs, his wide and varied experience in executive positions in foreign areas and his world travels render him extremely qualified to perform the contemplated duties, which could not be performed by him in a civilian capacity." Finally, "Waiver of fourteen (14) days' notice for active duty is attached." Donovan wanted James H. Angleton immediately. It was at first the father, not the son, who was the "Angleton" of OSS.

James H. Angleton was sent to the School of Military Government, University of Virginia, Charlottesville, apparently with the idea of preparing him to be a military governor in Italy. However, his Italian "was of a poor commercial brand and . . . he had practically no conversational ability and did not pick it up readily in the Italian classes." Major Angleton was sent back to OSS, in July 1943, where he was assigned as the X-2 field representative for the North African Theater, stationed in Algiers, reporting to Colonel William Eddy. He was with "S" Force in May 1944, in Rome, which he had reached "just behind the Fifth Army." This unit conducted raids around Rome, arresting various suspects and recovering German records and other materials. Major Angleton worked with military police officials investigating the Ardeatine Caves massacre,* then followed the Fifth Army into northern Italy, providing economic intelligence concerning merchandise dumps, hidden German

---

* Three hundred and twenty Italians, picked at random, were murdered in retribution for the deaths of thirty-two German soldiers.

warehouses, and black-market operations in northern Italy. He used his pre-war personal friendships with Marshal Badoglio, Marshal Messe, the Lieutenant General of the Realm, and past members of Italy's Secret Military Intelligence to provide advice to the Allied Military Government. Major Angleton spent the last few months of the war in Italy in Florence at the headquarters of the Fourth Army. In June 1945 he was given the Bronze Star by General Donovan in a ceremony in Washington, D.C.[38] A year later, he was back in Milan, re-opening the American Chamber of Commerce and resuscitating his company, now called National Cash Register Products.

James Jesus Angleton's CIA personnel form covering the early part of his career recorded that from 1934 to 1938 he had been a "Junior Partner, National Cash Register Company, Rome, Italy. In Paris, Rome, and Milan, spent vacations as sales and mechanical apprentice with view to eventually taking over the National Cash Register Agency for Italy. This is a family business." He listed as "income other than salary: Idaho Ranch, family sources, and securities. Foreign Languages: Italian, fluent; French, fair; German, slight [no Spanish listed]. Qualifications for intelligence position: Extensive travel and residence in Western Europe, education and background, writing and analytical criticism which tend toward the intelligence field." The Harvard Law School advised the FBI that Angleton failed his examinations in June 1942 and was given permission to repeat the year. It would have been difficult to predict the direction his career would take after his service in the army. Would he return to Italy and rejoin the family business? Would he continue to the career James Laughlin followed as a publisher? Or would he finish law school and become a lawyer?

James J. Angleton began his army service specializing in Military Government, as had his father, for which he was stationed at an army school in Michigan. However, on 30 July 1943 William Sherwood of the Office of Strategic Services wired Angleton's commanding officer for approval of the transfer of by then Corporal James Angleton to the OSS. A "Transfer of Enlisted Man" memorandum of 21 August stated that Angleton "has been interviewed by a representative of [OSS], and has been found to possess certain qualifications necessary to the activities of this command." This was the outgrowth of a friendly conspiracy involving his father, James Murphy (head of X-2), and Norman Holmes Pearson.[39] Murphy wrote an expediting memorandum in September 1943: "I would greatly appreciate it if you could get provisional security [clearance] for Corporal James Angleton, in order that he may commence O.S.S. school on Monday. His father is with this branch, and was with O.S.S. previously . . . In addition young Angleton is very well known to Norman Pearson, who recommended him to me before I left London."[40] On 7 September 1943, Angleton received orders to go to the headquarters of the Office of Strategic Services (Room 2047, Building "Q", Washington, D.C.), "without delay." His subsequent performance both at the OSS schools and in the training course further impressed Murphy, who sent him off to London to assist Pearson. Angleton sailed from New York on 28 December 1943.

By the time James Angleton arrived in London, OSS X-2 was established in the Ryder Street building housing MI-6 staff. Pearson's office was 22-A, near that of Kim Philby. Angleton shared office 23-B with Perdita, the daughter of Pearson's poet friend H. D. (Hilda Doolittle).[41] He seemed immediately on arrival in London to have become a different person: the person he would remain. He was no longer an aesthete, no longer a poet manqué, no longer adrift, no longer looking for a myth. He had found one.

Angleton was promoted to second lieutenant on 2 July 1944.

In London, Angleton became a student of Kim Philby in the ways of counterespionage. "Once I met Philby," Angleton said, "the world of intelligence that had once interested me consumed me. He had taken on the Nazis and fascists head-on and penetrated their operations in Spain and Germany. His sophistication and experience appealed to us . . . Kim taught me a great deal."[42] No doubt Philby "seemed enormously intelligent, sophisticated and well-informed" to the neophyte intelligence officer. According to Cave Brown, "It was Philby who taught Angleton the structure of the Secret Service—

There were fifty-three officials whose missions Angleton needed to know about—and how the enemy's wireless and mail messages were intercepted, what to watch out for in the decrypts in regard to enemy sabotage operations; the use of double agents in South Africa and Canada; the nature of British Security Coordination,

the all-in-one British Secret Service in the Americas, and of Security
Intelligence Middle East; a study of the work at Bletchley Park . . .
the personalities and the administrative and security procedures of
the British Secret Service. But above all there was the XX Committee, the agency that handled the double agents, its methods and its
doctrine."[43]

Seale and McConville reported that Section V had a formal intensive six-week course in counterespionage for the X-2 officers.[44]
"Philby 'gave a one- to one-and-a-half-hour talk on the subject of
turning agents—double agents,' one of the Americans recalled. 'I
do remember being very impressed. He really knew what he was
doing.'"[45] Milne recalled that Kim Philby "played a large part" in
supporting MI-5 in the Double Cross operation, with a particular
responsibility for managing double agents.[46]

Beyond formal study, during their apprenticeship with the British Secret Intelligence Service X-2 officers were given a thorough,
hands-on grounding in counterintelligence techniques. According to
the "War Report" of OSS: "Characteristic of the apprentice training
[sic] offered O.S.S. by the British was that given to some X-2 members in the double-agent section of MI-5(B) . . .

> These officers were assigned desks in the offices of that section and
> had free access to the files of double-agent cases, to the traffic of
> current ones, and to the officers who had directed or were directing
> such cases. Normally, in the course of their study, they met both
> double and controlled enemy agents whom the British were operat-
> ing, helped to gather the 'chicken feed' which was to be transmitted
> to the Germans, and learned the relationships between the sections
> to which they were attached, and the other intelligence organiza-
> tions which shared the exploitation of double-agent networks. One
> American officer was given a desk in the room of the director of the
> double-agent section and was made party to all conversations and
> conferences on problems arising in connection with the manage-
> ment of current British cases, some of which were of a long-range
> character and therefore involved the highest security."[47]

It would be interesting to know the name of that officer. Was it
Pearson? Or was it James Angleton? In any case, Angleton would

learn about these things, learn to do them, learn to fear them.

In the opinion of the CIA historian David Robarge, "The impact that working in the Office of Strategic Service's counterintelligence branch, X-2, had on Angleton can hardly be overemphasized . . .

> X-2 from its inception had a culture of intense security and secrecy . . . while in London, Angleton became privy to the Double Cross and FORTITUDE deceptions that were preparing the way for the cross-channel invasion. This knowledge was a major reason for his belief in Soviet "strategic deception."[48]

That is, if the British could operate a project as successful as their deception concerning the target of the D-Day invasion, in theory, the Soviet intelligence services could successfully operate similar projects. Another CIA historian, this one anonymous, recalled that "In later years Angleton often spoke about the success of Double Cross and of the vital need to have a communications intelligence (COMINT) capability as part of any deception operation . . .

> Another likely influence on Angleton was the British practice of limiting to extremely few people knowledge of the ULTRA and Double Cross programs and giving the officers running these programs virtual veto authority over other British intelligence activities. Angleton used this approach as a model to establish similar, unique operational authorities when he later ran CIA's Counter-intelligence Staff (CIS)."[49]

Kim Philby and James Angleton appear to have become friends in London. Philby may have felt he had a mentoring relationship with Angleton. Angleton may have shared that feeling.[50] Or Philby may have believed that Angleton was a good channel into American secret intelligence and therefore to be cultivated. Or they may have liked one another. All those things. By February 1944, OSS X-2 London had a staff of seventy-five. The tide of war had turned with Midway, El Alamein, and Stalingrad, and then there would be Normandy, but the American intelligence officials still had much to learn, and in London James Angleton finally became a good student. He was then in his mid-twenties, a newly minted second lieutenant, chief of the Italian Desk for the European Theater of Operations at X-2, a protégé, an apprentice, of the older, more experienced, more sophisticated Kim Philby.

Angleton had been taught close reading at Yale. OSS, and MI-6, would teach him to read all over again. Interestingly, the kind of student he became was that specifically discouraged by his Yale teachers: he became a student of the history and contemporary context of the texts he studied. Tom Bower observed that "Angleton became fascinated by the refinements of counter-espionage, where the original penetration was turned back on to the enemy.

> The game required not merely traditional skills and patience, but dispassionate intellect to identify unnoticed German successes and constant analysis to protect against deception. [He] explored the Byzantine possibilities open to the counter-intelligence practitioner for exploiting his vulnerable opponents and sowing discord and confusion."[51]

All this was the fruit of his study with Philby and his colleagues in Ryder Street. Angleton, matching the information from ULTRA with reports from Italy, was beginning to establish his reputation. "If 'Philby was the most gifted of the British,' as one intelligence officer said,

> 'Angleton was the most gifted of the Americans.' A fellow X-2 officer said that 'Jim was a very respected American among our British counterparts. He was probably more on a basis of equality with his British counterparts than anybody.'"[52]

Sometime in 1944 he received a unique confidence from the head of British secret intelligence: "'We've been penetrated by the communists,' Menzies told Angleton in 1944, mindful of MI-5 reports, 'and they're on the inside, but we don't know exactly how.'"[53] Perhaps Menzies also shared this confidence with Angleton's colleague, Kim Philby.*

---

* At about this time, Philby's responsibilities were widened to include French North Africa, Italy, and the western and central islands of the Mediterranean, with responsibility for the Special Counter Intelligence Units controlling the feed from Bletchley to the armies in that area.

In October 1944, Philby was made head of a new organization, Section IX of SIS, devoted to counterintelligence operations, especially those against "Soviet espionage and the Communist movement in Europe, and particularly in the Balkans, Italy and France."[54] Moscow must have been astonished. Not only was their agent in charge of the British empire's operations against Soviet espionage activities, but as "chief of Section 9, Philby was also a member of the Joint Intelligence Committee (JIC), consisting of representatives from the SIS, MI-5, the Foreign Office, the army and navy."[55] It is difficult to over-estimate the access this gave him, and therefore Moscow, to Anglo-American secret intelligence information.

Philby's former chief, Cowgill, resigned at the end of December, perhaps as a result of an intrigue by Philby, suggested by Moscow, perhaps partly in a dispute over the handling of ISOS material, perhaps, as Angleton commented in a SSU/X-2 counterintelligence summary of 1 July 1946, because of an intrigue by Richard Brooman-White: "The dismissal of COWGILL brought about a subsequent rise in the star of BROOMAN-WHITE . . .

> BROOMAN-WHITE . . . is personally suffering from a "guilt" complex for having wielded the dagger against COWGILL when the latter took more than a personal interest in his career. This is a cloud on his record which he resents because the episode is so well-known to Norm and others in London."[56]

Timothy Milne, Philby's best friend (barring Guy Burgess), replaced Cowgill as head of Section V.

As the Anglo-American armies were moving from North Africa, across Sicily and up the Italian peninsula, James Angleton was transferred from London to Italy as commander of SCI Unit Z.[57] The Special Counter Intelligence (SCI) units were originally an SIS project. They were developed to solve the problem of getting ULTRA-type material from Bletchley Park into the field, without violating the stringent security protecting it.* Eventually OSS also launched SCI units: "Small groups of X-2 personnel were attached to field armies and army groups . . .

---

* ULTRA was the general designation of decrypted enemy messages.

These Special Counter-Intelligence (SCI) units were directed to (1) Handle distribution of counter-espionage information, advising on its proper use in order to assure maximum security; (2) Provide information regarding secret enemy intelligence organizations, personnel and activities, suggesting, on the basis of this knowledge, counter-espionage objectives and methods of dealing with them; and (3) Help in the examination of captured enemy documents and captured enemy agents of intelligence interest."[58]

The OSS SCI units in Italy reported to the London head of MI-6 counterintelligence for the region, Kim Philby, as well as to his OSS opposite number, Pearson.[59] SCI members "were trained and briefed in the X-2/London office, and, for a group of selected officers, in the double-agent section of MI-5(B).

The training consisted of formal lectures on enemy organizations and their relationship; the study of CE files of invasion areas; classes in codes and communications procedures; work with desk personnel in the preparation of SHAEF cards, target lists and the like; and discussion and study group meetings with experienced British and American officers."[60]

Angleton's access to ULTRA in Italy gave him an enormous advantage as he went about his business, officially described as "the extermination of the German intelligence system so as to make it impossible for that system to continue or be resurrected in any organized form."

Timothy Naftali, in his pioneering and oft-cited article on Angleton's career in Italy, began by stating that "A study of [Angleton's] Italian career . . . serves not only as a primer on what the OSS and the SSU achieved in counterespionage in Italy but also as an introduction to the world view and professional skills of the man who would come to dominate American counterespionage for a generation."[61] He then divided "Angleton's career in two. Until August 1945, most of Angleton's operations were the extension of a program of military security . . . After the war, Angleton's concern became almost entirely 'long-range counterespionage,' in effect the surveillance of all foreign intelligence operations in Italy." It was this second mode, "long-range counterespionage," in which Angleton was primarily interested, not only for the remainder of his time in Italy, but for the rest of his career.

The situation in Italy in late October 1944, when Angleton arrived there, was extraordinarily complicated. The war, and the bungling of American and British generals, had left the peninsula divided between the Allies in the south and the Germans in the north. The Allied zone was politically divided between the British and the Americans. Churchill wanted Italy for his chain of revived Mediterranean monarchies; the Americans were not at all enthusiastic about that project.[62] The German zone was contested by partisans, who were in turn divided in various ways, chiefly between those many who were communists and those who were not, and among the latter, those who were monarchists and those who were not. OSS itself was divided, at the working level, as some members were communists, or "close to the Party," while there was increasing pressure from other factions to purge communists from the organization. In London it was felt, reasonably enough, that the atmosphere among the Anglo-American secret intelligence organizations in Italy was "murky." When "Angleton assumed command of the local X-2 office, [it was]

> a floundering unit that had lost the respect and cooperation of other American and Allied services because of poor management and inability to stay on top of the activities of enemy espionage organizations. Within weeks of his arrival, the energetic young lieutenant had revitalized morale in his new command, renewed contacts with sister services, and reinvigorated counterintelligence operations across the Italian peninsula."[63]

On 27 November 1944 Angleton wrote to "Graham" (perhaps Major Graham Erdwurm, then head of X-2 for Italy), thanking him for "coming up to initiate the new change of command," and to ask for office supplies and to list some activities. "I haven't got my feet on the ground to write you any detailed intelligence reports, but for your interests, we have embarked on or accomplished the following:" a list of six activities, varying from secret intelligence liaison to a Thanksgiving party.[64]

As experts in the personnel and methods of the enemy, Angleton's X-2 officers assisted the US Army's Counterintelligence Corps, a much larger organization, in locating and neutralizing German and Italian fascist agents. X-2 was still virtually an extension of British secret intelligence, with its "superior source" from signals intelligence. Cave Brown speculated that "The working relationship between [Philby and Angleton] undoubtedly owed much to the ISOS decrypts that Philby sent to Angleton, backed by the rich intelligence on the personalities of the German and fascist intelligence services from the SIS and MI-5 central registries . . ."[65] Angleton was in a privileged position to direct aspects of the army's security program because of his relationship with Philby, his access to ULTRA, and the instruction he had received in London in the arts of doubling and controlling enemy agents: skills and access that army counter-intelligence officers did not have.

Part of Philby's work for Section V had been the creation of "Keys." "In the second half of 1944 a joint War Room, staffed by Section V, O.S.S./X2 and MI-5 had been set up to deal with the counter-espionage information coming in from the war theaters of Western Europe, and to give the necessary guidance—and ISOS information—to the SCI units with the various British and American military headquarters."[66] The OSS War Report tells us that in order to do this, "ISCI/Z began the publication of an extensive series of reports, called German Intelligence Service 'Keys.'

These were expert summaries of all available information on the German services in general and on the specific divisions of the SD and Abwehr in the areas ahead, targets giving the locations of all GIS [German Intelligence Service] schools and establishments in northern Italy, and lists of all known SD and Abwehr members and their relationships. These handbooks, periodically revised, gave a nearly perfect record, from all sources, in a form useable by the lowest echelons of the army CI staffs in the field, and provided fully cross-referenced data for the use of CIC and British FSS [Field Security Section] interrogators. In this way it was possible for SCI/Z to utilize the services of over 200 interrogators in the accumulation of still further data from the rapid interrogation of captured enemy personnel . . . X-2 had access to the complete Italian counter-espionage files, which included not only information on German intelligence personnel and operations, but also on those of the services of other countries all over the world."[67]

In the first few months of 1945, Angleton adopted SIS's, Philby's, "Keys," in this case as "an easy-to-revise compendium of information about the various German and fascist Italian intelligence services that could be shown to officers not indoctrinated into ULTRA.

> The trick was to comb POW interrogations for corroboration of facts first learned from ULTRA. Once a detail had been found in a less sensitive place—a SECRET interrogation report instead of a TOP SECRET ULTRA decrypt—it could be disseminated."[68]

When the army picked up an enemy agent in Italy, one of Angleton's X-2 staff would be called in to assess the agent's bona fides and potential as a double agent. If the results of the review were affirmative, X-2 assumed responsibility for the agent.[69] Angleton and his colleagues appeared merely to be carefully collating POW interrogations and the like to assemble materials that could be used as a basis for these assessments; while they were in fact doing that, they were also using these materials as cover for the ULTRA information. Concealing the latter was of the highest importance and not at all a simple matter. This exercise may have been the origin of Angleton's practice, attested to in most accounts of his CIA years, of dropping mysterious comments into a conversation, then, when questioned, dismissing his interlocutors with the statement that they were not cleared to know his sources. In Italy, at least, this had been a simple statement of fact.

The tasks at hand for Angleton in Italy were centered on liaison activities with US and Allied intelligence services, interrogations of line-crossing German agents, meetings with colleagues and officers of other services, the writing of reports. File after file in the US and British National Archives contain the flimsy copies of reports received, reviewed, and sent on by Angleton's unit. There are local situation reports, personality lists, historical studies; reports on the developing situation in Yugoslavia and the efforts by Tito's secret intelligence service to support the Italian communists; reports on the surviving Italian fascist organizations; reports on looted art and caches of gold, relations with the Italian intelligence services, interviews with prostitutes (and lists of them); reports on currency matters, clippings from newspapers; reports on dealings with the Vatican, detailed contracts with newly hired agents for X-2. (These last included a line for the name of the person to receive compensation in the event of the death of the agent.)

The reports show that for counterintelligence specialists, close readers like Angleton suspected enemy agents should be treated as guilty unless proven innocent. Angleton was always surprised by the surprise of others at his systematic suspicions. How else should a counterintelligence officer view the world? This procedure and attitude was taken as a matter of course in OSS. The then head of the organization, James Murphy, "had been recommending to Donovan that no agent be employed by the O.S.S. in any part of the world who had not first been cleared by X-2."[70] Officers in OSS Secret Intelligence in Italy had to have Angleton's approval for their agent initiatives. Arrangements of this kind were—are—standard practice in secret intelligence organizations: not then or later an Angleton-imposed novelty. Angleton's memorandum of 29 November 1944 to Colonel Glavin, C.O., OSS Headquarters, Caserta, concerning the "Use of San Marco Personnel by O.S.S. Marine Detachment," contains a summary of his counterespionage credo and mode of operation: "The question of security, as we view it, is this:

> Every operation involves a known risk which must be accepted. By vetting personnel, X-2 will attempt to discover possible double agents. If our check is negative, it means merely that subject is not included in card files of some 15,000 known agents or suspects. However, the new employee's name will be kept in our Top Secret files in the event further interrogations of captured agents reveal pertinent information."[71]

Three years earlier, Angleton's responsibilities had been limited to soliciting poems for *Furioso*.

In Italy Angleton followed the custom of his Double Cross mentors by calling groups of agents by short, often related names. A circuit of his sources called Rose, Pansy, Briar, and Bloom wandered around Rome, entering houses, stealing documents, recruiting the mistresses of foreign diplomats, and reaching up to Milan while it was still under German occupation to identify sites of interest to the Allied armies. (An activity in which Angleton's father was also engaged.) Others in Angleton's employ recovered caches of fascist documents—and such accumulations as the royal treasury of Ethiopia[72] and some Finnish gold hidden in a specially constructed vault.[73] Other OSS forces in Italy had worked closely with Italian naval saboteurs. One such, Capitano di Fregata Carlo Resio, approached Angleton in November 1944 with two offers: radio operators to assist in penetration work behind German lines in the north of Italy; and the use of the Italian GAMMA school for frogmen at Taranto as a basis for the creation of a US sabotage group.[74] Angleton, deciding that it was worth running the risk of infiltration in order to strengthen X-2 relations with the Italian intelligence services, used these offers as the basis for general cooperation. He gave Resio himself the code name SALTY, and, beginning in January 1945, received from him a series of reports useful for counterespionage operations. The reports concerned both remaining fascist activists and Soviet-supported communist plans. X-2 headquarters found the latter irrelevant, at that moment, to the war effort, writing Angleton in February 1945 that "We would further like to know from you whether you feel that all of this information actually ties in with German activities, either in the present or along the lines of future operations. Without an explanatory tie-in and evaluation, much of this information seems to be rather meaningless."[75] SALTY, and Angleton, were, in Washington's view, premature anti-communists. Angleton dropped the issue, for a time, but he continued to work with Resio and to broaden his relationship with the Italian intelligence services.[76]

This brings us to Plan IVY and Angleton's colorful relationship with Prince Borghese, a minor member of that aristocratic family and a major Italian war hero. Borghese, a fascist loyalist, had developed the use of small—often single-person—underwater units: frogmen, miniature submarines, and so forth, personally conducting a number of such operations against Allied shipping in Gibraltar harbor. Rallying to Mussolini after the latter's disposition by the fascist Grand Council and rescue by the Nazis, Borghese converted his frogmen to a division-size land force collaborating with the Germans in northern Italy. The American goals in relation to Borghese were to detach him from the German forces, using him to prevent "scorched earth" destruction of Italian industrial and other resources and as a counterweight to the communist Italian and Yugoslavian partisans.

By May 1945, Borghese was on the most wanted list of Italian partisans in Milan, where Mussolini had just been executed. Things became rather dramatic. Angleton used the codename SAIL for Borghese in a Top Secret memorandum of 12 May 1945, suitable as the basis for an episode in a drama: "1. While in Milan, the undersigned received information to the effect that SAIL was in hiding from the partisans.

1. In view of the fact that two agents from this unit [SCI Unit Z, Rome] who successfully crossed the lines to conduct counterintelligence missions had become involved with SAIL, it was felt necessary to interrogate him before the partisans overtook him.
2. Through a cut-out, an appointment was made and SAIL was visited in his hideout. He talked quite freely and gave partial information which tends to confirm his intensive knowledge of Allied intelligence activities, including valuable information as to the last few weeks of the Fascist Regime. He promised to submit a complete, detailed report of all Fascist and German activities since the armistice, giving every indication that he had participated with the highest German echelon in Italy.
3. On leaving the apartment the undersigned and his cut-out were confronted by six members of the [Socialist] Matteotti Brigade who were in an automobile; fully armed with machine pistols and other weapons. Two members of the party indicated to the portiere that they were looking for someone in an apartment identical to SAIL's. In view of our interest in obtaining information concerning our operations and the possible whereabouts of valuable documents, a quick decision was made to intervene with these partisans by making SAIL a prisoner of war in the event they should discover his whereabouts. While the two partisans were in the apartment searching for SAIL, the undersigned questioned the occupants of the car concerning their activities. It was evident that they intended to exercise summary judgment and execution of all persons taken by them. After a half hour, the two partisans who had entered the building returned in great haste, jumped into the car and drove away.
4. After waiting several hours, the undersigned went to SAIL and brought him immediately to Rome for detailed interrogation.
5. It is felt that because of SAIL's aid to our agents, we should

prolong his internment in order to enable him to have a fair trial until partisan excitement has calmed down, and in order to extract from him valuable political and counter-intelligence information which he has acquired since the armistice of September 8. Had SAIL been kept in custody at Milan, there is little doubt but that the uncontrollable partisans would have attempted to take him into their custody by force of arms.*

We might contrast this film-noir scene with the usual image of the middle-aged James Angleton, at his desk in a darkened office, moving files from one tall stack of paper to another.

A series of documents in the British National Archives provide another record of Angleton's day-to-day business with SCI/Z. For example, a memorandum of 1 September 1945 from "Commanding Officer, SCI/Z Units, 1st Lt. James Angleton," requests permission to send a group to Venice in order to screen people coming into Italy from the Balkans. Two days later a similar memorandum concerns a group to be sent to Trieste. A memorandum dated 15 April 1946 concerns "Russian control of traffic from Rumania," this signed by "Capt. James Angleton."⁷⁷

In the course of his description of Angleton's "penetration agent," or "mole" in the Italian naval intelligence service, Timothy Naftali noted that the agent "warned the Americans that anti-Communist Albanians had approached the Italian Royal Navy for money and weapons to attempt the overthrow of Enver Hoxha's regime.

> Thus Angleton found himself being asked both by [the agent] and his liaison partners for guidance as to what the Italian response should be. In order to control this relationship between [Italian naval intelligence] and the Albanian dissidents, Angleton risked disclosure of his own penetration by boldly recommending that [the agent] be the liaison between the two groups. [The agent]'s superiors agreed, and for nearly a year, X-2 was able to monitor these discussions through [the agent]."⁷⁸

---

* Borghese, saved in this way by Angleton, was indeed tried after the war, served a few years in prison, became a leading figure in the postwar fascist revival, attempted a coup in 1970, and died in Spanish exile.

This incident has a bearing on two topics we will consider later: efforts to "roll-back" communist control in Albania, and the use of moles by intelligence services.

Naftali sums up Angleton's application of the lessons he had learned from Philby to his work in Italy in this way: "In his use of ULTRA material and the other products of liaison and penetration operations, Angleton demonstrated a firm grasp of the principles of effective counterespionage.

> He knew both how to make use of the intelligence that he had and how to develop new sources. Throughout, his objective was to extend his coverage of foreign activities likely to affect U.S. interests. This implied an exacting definition of counterespionage, which obliged the field officer to monitor all foreign intelligence-gathering in strategic areas and to control every possible channel through which an adversary might acquire American secrets . . . This sureness of touch had its negative side. It nourished a self-confidence that occasionally led Angleton astray . . . Angleton could relax his principles if he became personally involved in a case."[79]

PHILBY

Some time in 1944 Philby learned from "one of the leaders of American intelligence" that the United States and Britain were working together to create an atomic bomb. He sent this information to Moscow. According to Dolgopolov, Philby's news (presumably along with that from other sources, such as Klaus Fuchs and Donald Maclean) spurred Stalin and Beria to commit all available scientific forces and considerable financial resources to develop a Soviet atomic bomb.

On a different front, as it were, there was a notice of domestic urgency in *The Times*, 5 September 1944: "Nannie wanted as soon as possible for girl aged 3, boy aged 1, new baby February; help given; location, Wales temporarily, London soon (Armistice) . . . Philby, 23, Cadogan Gardens, S.W." The location in Wales was that of the senior Philbys' country cottage, that in Cadogan Gardens, Aileen Furse's mother's home. The baby in question arrived a bit early, according to *The Times* of 28 December 1944. "Birth announcement. On Dec. 21, 1944, at the London Clinic, to Kim and Aileen Philby—a son." Kim Philby and Aileen Furse were still not, in fact, married, but this did not seem to bother anyone. The Philbys moved to a large house in a fashionable part of London, Number 18, Carlyle Square, early in 1945, perhaps underwritten by Aileen Philby's mother.[80]

As World War II was winding down Philby was faced with two crises that could have brought his careers to an early end. In August 1945, according to Philby's own account, "A certain Konstantin Volkov, a Vice-Consul attached to the Soviet Consulate-General in Istanbul, had approached a Mr. Page, his opposite number in the British Consulate-General, and asked for asylum in Britain for himself and his wife . . .

> *Inter alia,* he claimed to know the real names of three Soviet agents working in Britain. Two of them were in the Foreign Office; one was head of a counter-espionage organization in London."[81]

Volkov insisted that his information be sent to London by diplomatic "bag," not by telegram, as he said the Soviets had broken some of the British codes. The British agreed. It took ten days for the information to reach London, whereupon the papers landed on Philby's desk. At a meeting with his Soviet contact Boris Kreshin "on 20 September [1945] . . . an agitated Burgess delivered 'an exceptionally urgent message from Philby' who wanted a rendezvous the following day.

> Apparently Philby had called on him at the Foreign Office and had given him an envelope to pass on to Boris Kreshin . . . the following evening; he cautioned Burgess to take exceptional care, which was why, unusually, he had not brought any Foreign Office documents with him. Kreshin, of course, recognized that such an unprecedented breach of tradecraft indicated a crisis: his judgement was correct, for the envelope contained Philby's account of the intended defection in Istanbul of a NKGB officer named Konstantin Volkov."[82]

According to Yuri Modin, Philby quickly composed a report on the affair and gave it to his handler. Moscow advised Philby to slow things down in order to gain time.[83] Three days later, Philby set out for Istanbul to take charge of the case, the plan being to take Volkov to the British base in Cairo for interrogation. Because of weather conditions, it took two or three days for Philby to reach Istanbul. Two or three more days went by in bureaucratic squabbling and protocol activities. By the time Philby and his associates were ready to meet Volkov, nearly three weeks had elapsed and Volkov could not be found.[84] Milne comments that Philby began to drink heavily after the Volkov affair. Perhaps this was because he realized how nearly he had been exposed, how it was only a matter of chance that he could in fact be exposed at some point, at any point, in the future.

There was a virtually simultaneous crisis for Philby, this time in Canada. "The defection in September 1945 of Igor Gouzenko, a cipher clerk at the Soviet embassy in Ottawa . . . became known as the 'Corby' case, the name apparently chosen from the Corby's Canadian whisky favored by the officers working on the case . . ." SIS was notified on 9 September. Philby immediately notified Moscow.

On 12 September Philby produced a draft précis of the case so far . . . which is notable for its cautious and soothing tone, including predictions of developments which he had already engineered himself . . . "in particular that the contact between [Nunn] May and the Soviet agent in the U.K. will fail to materialize."

Philby nominated Roger Hollis of MI-5 to handle the matter for British secret intelligence. Hollis "flew out on 16 September, [becoming] the linchpin of Gouzenko's interrogation. Cables passed between Hollis and MI-5 through Stephenson and Philby."[85]

Oleg Tsarev claimed to have found a report from Philby about the Gouzenko affair in the KGB files. According to Tsarev, in Philby's report to Moscow Center "of 18 November 1945 he described the Nunn May investigation . . .

MI-5 has established four planned meetings of May with his London contact. These meeting [sic] were fixed for 7, 17 and 27 October and 7 November. Neither May nor any of his contacts appeared at these meetings. In London they are of the firm opinion that May, as well as other agents from the Zabotin network, were warned of the impending danger. According to MI-5, May has not put a foot wrong from the time he arrived in England. He did not establish any suspicious contacts. He does not show any signs of being afraid or worried and continues to work quite normally on his academic research. Bearing this in mind, MI-5 came to the conclusion that May was a tough customer who will not break down under questioning until he is confronted with fresh and convincing evidence. The matter was postponed indefinitely for serious political considerations. It is not only a question of friendly relations with the USSR, but also of the future control over atomic secrets."[86]

In an article he wrote in Moscow entitled "Should Agents Confess?" Philby told how he worked with Hollis, on the one hand, to catch Nunn May, and, on the other hand, with his Soviet contacts to help him escape. Despite Philby's efforts, Nunn May confessed and was sent to prison, illustrating Philby's doctrine that agents should never confess.[87]

Following these close calls, Philby's prestige in MI-6 continued, if anything, to increase. When Menzies, early in the spring of 1945, began planning for a reorganization of MI-6, Philby's counterintelligence section was allocated the largest number of officers.[88]

In March 1945, Kim Philby, in his role as head of MI-6 Section 9 "flew to Rome to check out possibilities of organizing work against local [communist] organizations and to find in Rome suitable people among [SIS]'s bureau to do such work," while, in May 1945, in his role as an agent of Soviet intelligence, Philby "reported that the counter-intelligence section of the O.S.S. in Italy has set up a microphone in the building where Togliatti works, thanks to which they can monitor all conversations in the building."[89] It is likely that Philby learned about the Togliatti matter from the head of OSS counterintelligence in Rome, his protégé James Angleton.

Around this time Philby "was made overall controller of MI-6's secret agents in the Soviet Union.

He was also in charge of recruiting spies and mounting sabotage operations against Communist parties in the USSR and elsewhere. Naturally, he kept [the KGB] fully informed of these operations, which were usually carried out by the British, only occasionally by the Americans. [The KGB was] careful not to use his information to conduct a systematic dismantling of the networks concerned . . . because Philby had to show results to his superiors . . . [The KGB] knew in advance about every operation . . . The KGB let some of the agents go free temporarily, to avoid jeopardizing Philby, while others were turned and became [its] own double agents."[90]

In the summer of 1945 Philby flew to Germany "to examine with the [SIS] stations the scope for and strategy of future anti-Soviet and anti-communist intelligence work." He and his colleague Timothy Milne visited Hitler's Chancellery and other sights of the ruined city. During lunch one day Philby accidentally drank a glass of insecticide, having been told it was hock. The incident was nearly fatal. When he recovered, Philby and Milne went on to Austria, where they were when first Hiroshima, then Nagasaki were destroyed and the Soviet Union began eliminating the Japanese army in northern China. The next stop was Trieste, from which they returned north to Frankfurt. After this tour, reminiscent of his student-days European travel with Milne, Philby said he was not convinced that SIS stations in Western Europe were capable of giving much assistance to Section IX's anti-communist efforts.[91] Such as they were.

The efforts of Soviet Intelligence in Germany, on the other hand, were going forward. According to an official history of the Russian foreign intelligence service: "In April 1945 . . . operational groups were set up whose task was to recruit agents capable of identifying members of the Nazi underground, to cover the activities of various political groups, to reveal the secret activities of British and American special services . . .

By the end of 1945 . . . In the field of foreign intelligence, the task was to acquire agents capable of occupying leading positions in the new Germany, and also to cover the activities of the United States and Britain against the USSR and its allies . . . the tasks of obtaining intelligence information about the policies of the United States, Britain and France on the issues of the post-war arrangement in Germany and the creation of a new anti-Soviet bloc with the participation of Germany became priorities in the work of foreign intelligence . . . Employees of "legal" residences in Germany recruited a large number of persons who worked in the administration of the Western powers, from which valuable information on the plans of former allies both in Germany and on their subversive activities against the USSR and countries of Eastern Europe was obtained on a regular basis."[92]

In August 1945, Philby was given the Soviet Order of the Red Banner; later in 1945 he received the Order of the British Empire.[93]

Philby finally divorced Litzy, in absentia, on 17 September 1946 and a week later married Aileen, who was pregnant with their fourth child.[94]

ANGLETON IN POSTWAR ITALY

On 23 March 1944, while James Angleton was assuming responsibility for the Italian desk of OSS, X-2 London and Kim Philby was running MI-6 Section V for the Mediterranean area, "Members of a resistance cell, the Patriotic Action Group (Gruppi d'Azione Patriotica, or GAP), under the leadership of Rosario Bentivegna, detonated a bomb near a column of police marching down the Via Rasella in German occupied Rome.

> Twenty-eight police officials died on the scene; by the next day thirty-three policemen had died. The final death toll would rise to forty-two policemen, with additional casualties among civilian bystanders . . . Field Marshal Albert Kesselring, Commander-in-Chief South . . . authorized the reprisal plan . . . On the following day, March 24, 1944, personnel from the headquarters of the Security Police and SD in Rome, led by SS Captain Erich Priebke and SS Captain Karl Hass, assembled 335 Italian male civilians near a series of man-made caves on the outskirts of Rome on the Via Ardeatina . . . Following the shootings, Priebke and Hass ordered engineers to seal the mouth of the cave through the detonation of explosives, killing any victims who had managed to survive and entombing the dead . . . In 1947, a British court in Venice sentenced Field Marshal Kesselring to death for the shootings at Ardeatine and for incitement to kill civilians."[95]

The "Supreme SS and Police Leader" in Italy, Kurt Wolff appears to have had knowledge of the planned massacre and possibly approved it. Eugen Dollmann, an SS colonel, was one of the lower-level German police officials implicated in the massacre.

Dollmann was an unusual Nazi police official. Born in 1900, he was "intelligent, cultured, highly educated." A historian of sixteenth-century Italian art, he had moved from Germany to Rome in 1927 and gone native, as it were, preferring to be called Eugenio, becoming completely fluent in Italian, dressing in the fashion of the Italian aristocracy, whom he frequented. Nonetheless, he joined the Nazi party in 1934 and the SS in 1937, becoming Himmler's representative in Rome. Dollmann was the translator of choice for high-level meetings between German and Italian officials, including those of Hitler and Mussolini.[96] From October 1943, as a liaison officer with Italian officials for Wolff and Kesselring, Dollmann helped his Italian aristocratic friends, protecting them from the SS, for a price, and claimed credit for Rome's designation as an "Open City."[97] When the German army withdrew to the north, Dollmann went with it.

Which brings us to Operation Sunrise, the highly publicized secret operation that made Allen Dulles's reputation. Dulles often told a story about how his decision to negotiate the surrender of German forces in northern Italy had saved many lives and much property in northern Italy. However, according to Michael Salter, "It appears that, far from being an O.S.S. mission, Operation Sunrise had in fact been planned by [a certain SS Lieutenant Guido] Zimmer and his superiors.

> In a November 1944 . . . Zimmer suggested contacting Allied intelligence in Switzerland through Baron Luigi Parrilli, formerly the representative of the Kelvinator and Nash companies in Italy [perhaps, therefore, known to James Hugh Angleton] . . . Rauff and other regional RSHA officials backed this approach . . . In mid-February 1945 they also got support from Karl Wolff, highest SS and Police Leader for Italy . . . in late February 1945 . . . negotiations with Dulles's assistant Gero von Gaevernitz, Parrilli reported that he was working for Zimmer and that German authorities were interested in sparing northern Italy from a horrible fate . . . On March 3, 1945 Zimmer, Parrilli, and Eugen Dollmann, Himmler's representative in Italy, met with O.S.S. official Paul Blum in Lugano, Switzerland. This meeting set the stage for a visit by Karl Wolff and

his adjutant to Dulles himself on March 8 . . . Dulles and Wolff finally brought about a surrender, but it came late: the fighting in Italy stopped on May 2. What might have been a boon to Allied forces in Italy turned out to be a saving of only five days before the end of the war in Europe . . ."[98]

After reviewing Zimmer's notebooks, OSS and SSU officials concluded that his Operation Wool preceded Operation Sunrise—in other words, the bargain was as much a German initiative as it was an American intelligence coup. It might well be considered part of the—presumably uncoordinated—German and Anglo-American preparations for a reversal of the World War II alliances.

Dulles proclaimed his negotiations as a great success for OSS and, mostly, for himself: the basis for his legend as the Great White [sic] Case Officer. It went further than that: "During the late summer and autumn of 1945 . . . O.S.S. Washington was seeking to capitalize on the organisation's wartime successes as a way of staving off threatened closure. Advancing favourable media publicity concerning the role of OSS officials in Operation Sunrise played a significant role in this propaganda . . ." However, Angleton criticized the descriptions inspired by O.S.S. in the press of the roles Zimmer and Parilli played in Operation Sunrise as an "unfortunate exaggeration". He also objected to the actions of Allen Dulles in the first half of 1946 to reward Guido Zimmer by facilitating and sponsoring his repatriation. In his role as the Commanding Officer of OSS/SSU Rome, Captain James Angleton submitted a memorandum, Angleton stating that:

> In the past, Subject has enjoyed privileged treatment at the hands of non-CI agencies in this theatre because of his role in the Sunrise operation. This fact makes it difficult for this Unit, under present circumstances, to take a position with reference to the above request. It is this Unit's opinion that Subject at the outset was deserving of no better treatment than that afforded persons of much greater importance to the success of Sunrise than he, namely General Wolff and [Eugen] Dollmann. The time that has elapsed and the evident condoning treatment afforded subject, raises some doubt whether at this stage Subject should still be handled in accordance to the directives laid down for the treatment of GIS [German Intelligence

Service] personnel in April 1945. It is in any case certain that once in Rome, this Unit will desire to interrogate Subject in detail.

According to Michael Salter, "Angleton's effort to scupper the continuing 'condoning' and rehabilitation of Zimmer . . . was largely effective."[99]

Angleton remained interested in Zimmer's wartime activities. In late June 1946, he reported to Washington that the so-called Zimmer notebooks had been translated into English. The notebooks, broken into 167 separate memos, covered the period from late 1944 until May 1945, although the months of November and December 1944 were missing. In Angleton's view, Zimmer's notes "provide one of the richest single bodies of information on the activities of Abt. VI Milan and the background of the Armistice negotiations. The notebooks contained detailed descriptions of Italian agents in the employ of the Germans as well as on the activities of the SS in Italy. In reviewing the notes, Angleton observed, 'it is apparent that the pre-armistice negotiations were as much the work of the Intelligence (most particularly Abt. VI) system on the German side as it was from the side of the Allies.'"[100]

Michael Salter found that Angleton "was more sympathetic to Dollmann, possibly because of his potential for use in active or passive (damage limitation) anti-communist missions which became an urgent priority for him even as the war was ending.

> On 13 November 1946, he wrote to G-2 HQ explaining the reasons why he and his colleagues had to date deemed it important to protect Dollmann . . . 'Military honor dictated that we should honor the promises made to these men.' Dollmann and Wenner had acted in a way that had given US military real benefits that had assisted with America's vital national security interests in restricting postwar Soviet territorial gains. Sunrise had nipped various threats in the bud, including 'a redoubt in Austria, which may have resulted in a Tito or Russian occupation of parts of the Venezia Giulia as well as much of the present Allied zones in Austria.'"[101]

Dollmann played a role in, and was played by, many of the groups flourishing in the chaos of immediate postwar Italy.

Although Dollmann was cleared by the British of responsibility for the Ardeatine massacre in July 1945,[102] he went through various POW camps, escaping and taking refuge in Milan under the protection, or as a prisoner of, the Church. Circa December 1945, while he was staying in a Church mental asylum outside Milan, "[A] huge Buick with a US army pennant drew up in front of my private lunatic asylum and I was invited to take a seat in it . . .

> The Negro Chauffeur then drove us off to Rome and on the way we were respectfully greeted by all the Carbinieri we came across. On our arrival in Rome, I was deposited in this flat . . . Two [American officers] then came in . . . They introduced themselves to me as Jim [Angleton] and Joe of the O.S.S. [actually SSU] and shook my hand as though we were long-lost friends. 'We are very glad to have found you, Mr Dollmann' they assured me . . . They inquired solicitously about my 'journey', expressed regret that I had been so bothered and assured me that they were very glad to be able to do something for me."[103]

Angleton told Dollmann that they wished to use his services as part of an anti-communist operation, for which his past complicities and Italian claims concerning his involvement in war crimes were of no relevance: "Well, you see for us of the American Secret Service the struggle against Communism is only just beginning . . . and so we thought of sending you to Germany on a secret mission . . . you would have to take a six weeks' course, and after that you would be able to build up a really good espionage organisation against the Russians.

> I have already informed my superiors in Washington about what I intend to do with you, and the G-2 General in Caserta has already confirmed the plan . . . even before you came here Baron Parrilli discussed the whole matter with General Morgan, our Commander in Chief at Caserta, and they came to a satisfactory agreement about your future . . . You can stay here for a while perhaps . . . but in view of the nature of the struggle we aren't particularly interested in the Mediterranean. Our new frontier lies in Germany."[104]

Dollmann was given "a bundle of currency, and a false identity document in the name of Alfredo Casani, stating that he was an employee of the American government. US intelligence officials in Italy also provided Dollmann with a large and relatively luxurious apartment in Parioli, a residential area of Rome. It was fully equipped with a library, chauffeur and even a maid."[105] Then he was "by chance" arrested by the Italian police and released only when "Angleton . . . personally visited Police President Polito to retrieve" him. After publicity in the Italian press, he was rearrested and held in prison until he was again freed by the American military around Whitsun 1947 and flown to Germany, where he was held in a guest house for high-ranking prisoners.

In an operation supervised by Angleton, according to Michael Salter, between 17 and 19 May 1947, Dollmann and Wenner were finally transferred by Counterintelligence Corps agents from Rome to the custody of the Director of Intelligence EUCOM (G-2/CI). They were transferred together with a "complete brief of [their] past histories." The Heidelberg CIG officials who received them were told by their Italian-based colleagues that these officials were to continue an earlier policy of shielding the two men, even from the British authorities who were responsible for organizing trials of senior German officials for major Nazi war crimes in Italy . . . "Both have information which would place present Italian political regime in bad light if published . . .

Now it becomes clear from this internal CIG memo that one previous unacknowledged factor motivating their protection was that Dollmann and Wenner's involvement in Sunrise meant that they had acquired potentially embarrassing details, possibly relating to the Italian Prime Minister, [Ferruccio] Parri, whose release was one of the terms and conditions of that mission. It is possible that they were aware of Parri's alleged collaboration with the Nazis after his wartime capture, which had ensured his survival rather than immediate torture and execution. If such details had been widely exposed and believed, it would have devastated his popularity as a former socialist partisan leader. American intelligence may have been anxious to support Parri as a popular left of centre, anti-communist during a period in which the Italian Communist Party threatened to come to power through democratic means. If this was the case, then Parri presumably remained indebted to US intelligence officials and generally compliant with their wishes, not least because of their knowledge of this particular skeleton in his cupboard."[106]

It is not surprising, then, that "By the spring of [1946] Angleton had penetrated the office of the Italian prime minister and was securing photographic copies of important documents from the office's files."[107] According to David Alvarez, the Prime Minister, Alcide De Gasperi, was "actually on the O.S.S. payroll, receiving monthly subsidies from . . . American handlers."[108] This no doubt facilitated access to his files.

Dollmann continued to be used by various intelligence agencies into the 1950s.[109] As Angleton later observed: "Once an agent, always an agent, for someone."

From the Soviet point of view, as often articulated by Stalin himself, Operation Wool/Sunrise, and other operations of a similar nature, pointed to the long-rumored and for the Soviets dreaded reversal of alliances, a joint effort by the western Allies and the German forces against the Soviet Union. "In the wake of FDR's death . . . the German Army in the West collapsed . . . German forces began a series of surrenders everywhere except on the Russian front, where the German Army continued to fight.

> Rumors again swept Germany that Britain and the United States were about to join the German armies on the Russian front, fueled doubtless by Churchill's issuance of some veiled directives. Among them was . . . a secret order to Montgomery to stack all the captured German arms 'so that they could easily be re-issued to the German Armies with who we should have to work with if the Soviet advance continued.'"[110]

This order to Montgomery (which was not obeyed) was of a piece with Churchill's "Operation Unthinkable," a planning exercise for exactly that reversal of alliances, also hinted at by the creation of MI-6's anti-Soviet Section IX, a reversal that took effect two or three years later as the Cold War began.[111] The memorandum "Security of the British Empire," prepared by the Chiefs of the Imperial General Staff (of which Kim Philby sent Moscow a copy on 6 November 1945), declared the Soviet Union a major threat to the empire (although not necessarily to Britain itself) and recommended the establishment of a special relationship with the United States that would commit the Americans to the defense of Western Europe, the establishment of military-political blocs, and military bases in Europe and other regions of the world.[112] This was a continuation of Churchill's foreign policy, although it was at odds with that of Attlee in the first years of his government.

After Germany's surrender to the Allies, X-2 in Italy went about finishing its work of identifying and capturing former members of enemy intelligence services. "In the fall of 1945, however, Angleton's unit began to diversify its operations beyond its formal assignment of counterintelligence and security."[113] At that time, "Angleton supervised five field offices, all in north Italy.

> A unit in Genoa was responsible for watching French activity in northern Italy, and to that end it controlled a subunit in San Remo that was particularly charged with monitoring illegal and clandestine activities along the Franco-Italian border. In cooperation with the Italian police the Genoa unit was also responsible for maintaining security in that important port and across the coastal region of Liguria. An office in Milan monitored political and economic developments in the financial capital of the country and directed the work of a subunit in Turin that was chiefly concerned with political activities of leftist groups in Italy's industrial heartland. The unit in Trieste had the most difficult assignment. That city and its hinterland were contested by Italy and Yugoslavia, and both countries considered the region a fertile field for clandestine political, propaganda, and paramilitary operations."[114]

All of this meant that, as "Special Counterintelligence Unit Z suffered from a shortage of personnel . . .

> Angleton realized that, for the foreseeable future, reinforcement from the United States was unlikely. If SCI/Z was to succeed in its expanded mission, it would have to look for help in other places. Angleton decided to look close to home . . . The Americans could compensate for their lack of resources by piggybacking on the operations and agent networks of their Italian friends."[115]

Angleton found that the advantages of the additional resources obtained in this way were counter-balanced by the care needed to interpret reports from Italian intelligence agencies. "By bombarding their American counterparts with alarmist reports of Red conspiracies and revolutionary activities, Italian intelligence, Angleton believed, hoped to scare Washington into adopting an anti-Soviet and anticommunist policy that would include the preservation of the Italian monarchy and support for conservative political organizations."[116] Indeed, "As far as X-2 Italy was concerned

> the specter of fascism did not dissolve with the collapse of Mussolini's rump Republic of Salo and the capture and execution of *Il Duce* by partisans when he sought to escape into Switzerland. Angleton believed that fascism had simply gone to ground and that its adherents, many of whom returned to authority in Badoglio's government of 'experts,' might destabilize the already shaky provisional government in Rome."[117]

From the time of his arrival in Rome, Angleton in practice controlled some—eventually, it was said, all—of the Italian secret intelligence services. The "penetration of the Italian secret services was the highest counterintelligence priority for SCI/Z in the immediate postwar period . . .

> these organizations were providing money and equipment to the various right-wing groups that were emerging among the thousands of émigré Albanians, Croats, Georgians, Hungarians, and Yugoslavs . . . plotting their political return to their homelands. By the fall of 1945 Angleton had recruited his first contacts inside these groups and begun to monitor their activities . . . [a few months later] Angleton would cover Albanian exiles' formation of an anti-Hoxha resistance committee . . . and resistance plans to secure American and British support to overthrow the communists."[118]

Angleton appears to have missed one trick. "Although Angleton's unit kept an eye on the Soviet embassy in Rome . . . the available evidence does not suggest that the Soviets were the main counterintelligence focus in the months immediately following VE Day. Among the foreign intelligence services operating in Italy, the French and Yugoslavs received more attention."[119] But here is the current Russian foreign intelligence service's summary of its predecessor's activities in Italy during this period: "The 'legal' Foreign Intelligence Residency in [Italy] resumed its activities in 1944.

> Communication with a number of [surviving] agents was re-established and a number of new sources were recruited. [The Soviet secret intelligence service r]esident managed to obtain important documentary materials about the country's foreign and domestic policies . . . The residency achieved great success in the field of scientific and technical intelligence, including nuclear physics, because of the close ties of Italian scientific institutions with Western colleagues."[120]

This last may have been a reference to Enrico Fermi's associates both in Rome and Chicago.

David Alvarez found that "By the summer of 1946, James Angleton had largely reestablished the position of American intelligence in the Italian peninsula that had been left in shambles after the closure of [OSS] SI Italy at the end of the war.

> He had creatively expanded the reach of his understaffed and overworked unit by piggybacking on the broad backs of the Italian intelligence and police services, while cleverly avoiding becoming a creature of those services by penetrating their ranks with his own secret informants. Similar penetrations of the government, particularly in the office of the prime minister, the ministries of finance and foreign affairs, and various political parties ensured broad coverage of Italian political affairs, while contacts with the Vatican provided a window on the policies and activities of this important international actor. Finally, liaison relations supplemented by coverage of émigré organizations and the occasional recruitment of foreign agents generated information concerning such targets as Albania, Hungary, and Yugoslavia. Given the small size of his unit and the minimal support of headquarters, Angleton's achievement was probably the equal of any American intelligence station in early postwar Europe."[121]

Alvarez also notes that "By the late summer of 1946 . . . At the

initiative of James Angleton, the American intelligence representative in Rome who had developed productive relationships with
[Polish General Władysław] Anders's intelligence staff, arrangements were put in hand to transfer to American control the most
experienced Polish operatives and their networks in Eastern Europe,
but nothing is known about the fruits, if any, of this plan."[122] That
cautious statement may point to the WiN disaster, of which more
below.

OSS was dissolved on 1 October 1945. Its Research and Analysis
Branch was transferred to the State Department, and the War Department acquired the espionage and counterintelligence branches as
the Strategic Services Unit (SSU). A 15 January 1946 memorandum
by General John Magruder, Director of the SSU, lists the "Assets of
SSU for Peacetime Intelligence Procurement," as if for a bankrupt-
cy sale. One of those "assets" was "Counter-Espionage—the X-2
Branch." The "advertisement" went as follows: "The X-2 Branch
is in the unique position of being the only operating American
counter-espionage organization with coordinated coverage in both
military and non-military areas outside of the Western Hemisphere.
Its tasks are to:

1. Observe, report on and correlate information concerning the
   activities of all foreign intelligence services and related secret
   organizations.
2. Advise and assist the appropriate executive agencies of the
   United States Government in frustrating such activities of these
   interests.
3. To protect clandestine intelligence operations of United States
   Government agencies.

The branch operates by the use of agents and double agents to obtain
information concerning not only foreign intelligence personnel and
their activities but also the structure and policies of their organizations. It works in close liaison with related American agencies
in obtaining relevant information. On matters where the securing
of American interests is not jeopardized, it works in liaison with
foreign counter-intelligence agencies to obtain data on matters and
individuals of mutual interest. The intelligence services of smaller

nations in particular show a marked interest in making available to SSU, which they regard as their American counterpart, counter-intelligence material on subjects which they wish made known to the United States Government and which might otherwise not reach American sources . . .

X-2 has developed a staff of specialists in procuring and corre-lating counter-espionage intelligence with over three years' active operational experience. They work in close liaison with such execu-tive and law-enforcement agencies as State Department, G-2, ONI, FBI and Treasury supplying them with incoming information of special interest. In military areas, such as Germany, Austria, Italy and China, X-2 personnel operate as Special Counter-Intelligence Units which work in close liaison with G-2 Headquarters to conduct clandestine operations against foreign intelligence and sabotage organizations, assist in the interrogation of captured enemy agents and intelligence officials, analyze relevant captured enemy docu-ments . . .

In non-military areas, X-2 personnel generally operate in State Department diplomatic and consular offices particularly in major countries in Europe and the Near East. The X-2 representatives serve American Foreign Service Officers with advice and assistance on security against penetration by foreign intelligence services, and with security checks on native employees, applicants for United States visas or other individuals with whom the officers are in touch. They also maintain appropriate liaison with local counter-intelligence and police officials . . .

Washington X-2 headquarters are the central operational center and collecting point for all information sent in by the field stations and representatives. Here exists a central file of information on over 400,000 individuals who are in one form or another connected with foreign intelligence and otherwise secret organizations whose activ-ities are or may be inimical to American interests. In addition there are maintained comprehensive detailed studies of the structure, politics and operations of foreign intelligence agencies."[123]

"It has been the policy of the Branch," Angleton wrote in a secret memorandum on the status of liaison relations of SSU/X-2 with the counterintelligence branches of foreign special services, "To main-tain friendly relationships with the counter-intelligence branches of indigenous foreign Secret Intelligence and Security Services of those friendly countries in which SSU maintains official stations . . .

Those countries presently defined as 'friendly', with whose Special Services appropriate official liaison has been established on the above terms, are as follows: Norway, Denmark, Sweden, Belgium, Netherlands, France, Switzerland, United Kingdom, Italy, Turkey, Greece . . . The maintenance of such liaisons has distinct benefits. An official relationship is essential in effecting the easy liquidation or neutralization of activities inimical to the United States when sponsored by other nations operating in the area concerned. *The constant frequenting of the headquarters of foreign intelligence services makes it possible to maintain continuous check upon their personnel and activities. By this means, and by social contact, it is possible to make valid deductions about directions and shifts in policy . . . A bi-product of these contacts has been the establishment by personal relations of unofficial channels of information from within the services* . . . The period of hostilities offered a uniquely fortunate situation for the acquisition through liaison of counter-intelligence from the files of Allied Services. At the beginning of the war the United States had substantially nothing. At its end, SSU had the accumulated results for a common effort. From the files of the British services came all their counter-intelligence on France, North Africa, Belgium, the Lowlands, Norway and Denmark; the large majority on Greece and the Balkans; everything on Germany, Austria and Italy; a complete record of their reporting on Spain since 1930; their war-time records on Portugal; and the greater part of their material on Switzerland, Sweden, Turkey and Syria. Complete records were also obtained on all German activities in Eire. Varying amounts were received relating to all other countries outside the Western Hemisphere . . . From the files of the French came all their counter-intelligence on Germany and Austria; enemy-inspired activities in France and North Africa, including collaboration; and all their information on enemy activities in the Iberian Peninsula . . . the Paris station has received from nine French security services reports of checks made on behalf of the Embassy on a monthly average of 1800 names over a period of the past six months . . . From the Swedes come their intelligence on Russian activities . . . The Greek Service gives regularly their

reports on Communist groups and Russian Intelligence activities
. . . The Turkish Service supplies complete reports on Russian
agents or suspected agents . . . This provides a most useful coverage
of the Balkans and eventually within Russian territory itself . . ."[124]
[Emphasis added.]

This was the condition of the American foreign counterintelligence
effort as the United States and the British empire turned from the
defeated Axis enemy to confront the Soviet Union.

During this period Kim Philby's organizational advice was sought
not only by his own chief, Menzies, as we have seen, but also by
his American colleagues. There is, for example, this, from Angleton
to Colonel William W. Quinn of the SSU, dated "London: 30 April
1946 . . . SUBJECT: London Station, Status: 'events of very recent
date have emphasized the necessity for an immediate clarification of
our status unless we are to lose . . . links which it has taken years and
a great deal of effort to establish . . .

> Our difficulties with American agencies in London have all been the
> result of a lack of charter under which we operate . . . About two
> weeks ago Lt. Col. Timothy Milne,* an assistant to the Chief, SIS,
> and H.A.R. Philby, Chief, Counter Intelligence, MI-6, and I had
> dinner and a long conversation. They both would like to have X-2
> as the channel for American liaison for C.I. matters but are aware
> of the possibility that we are not permanent and of our lack of a
> definite sphere in which we are the American agency . . . they both
> expressed a hope that we could soon be established permanently
> and have access to 'certain materials' which are now kept from us
> at the direction of American authorities . . . Both of them expressed
> a hope for immediate clarification of our status; delineation of our
> jurisdiction.'"

It would be interesting to have a full account of this dinner and "long
conversation." However, in the absence of such detail, this brief note
does indicate the intimate relationship between James Angleton and
Kim Philby at this point and that the postwar Washington lunch

---

* This meeting is not mentioned in Milne's memoir of Philby.

conversations of Angleton and Philby were a continuation of a well-established custom.

In regard to Philby's helpful advice concerning the organization of the Anglo-American secret intelligence effort, there is also a 16 August 1946 memorandum from Quinn to Colonel Galloway, relating his opposition to the virtual merger between British and American secret intelligence organizations favored by the former: "Incident to my trip to Europe, I arrived in London on 6 August and immediately made appointments to meet the various members of British Intelligence Services.

> I called on Sir Stuart Menzies, Chief of British Secret Intelligence Service and MI-6; Commander Dunderdale, who maintains liaison with us for MI-6, and Mr. Kim Philby, Chief of Section 5, MI-6 (counter-espionage) . . . I was greatly impressed with the British attitude of cooperation and coordination of our two secret intelligence organizations . . . Sir Stuart repeatedly indicated his desire to join forces, i.e., joint operations in the various areas in the world which were adaptable to that type of operation . . . there is no need for both of our services to effect positive penetrations on the same target . . . it would be more advantageous for one party to procure such information, which the other party could work in another area . . . My answer to this was that we desired, particularly in SSU as long as it lasted, to operate without the aid and guidance of the British intelligence services in order to determine our capabilities for the long pull . . . we preferred to exchange information instead of operating jointly . . . I further feel that we should not permit working liaison here in Washington which entails members of the British SIS in our Special Operations offices, or for that matter in the offices of CIG."

Quinn was eventually overruled in regard to the location of British and American secret intelligence liaison. A few years later, that activity was performed by "Mr. Kim Philby" in Washington, D.C.

British counterintelligence practice was still exemplary for Angleton as World War II ended and the beginnings of the Cold War appeared on the horizon. OSS Counterintelligence summaries for Italy in the summer of 1946, when Angleton was head of X-2 for Italy, include the comment that "JOYCE fully appreciates the mess caused during the war when no agents' files were kept in Italy.

> This old O.S.S. J-1 period contrasts sharply with the British policy of detailed documentation on all the agents and sub-agents, payments made, etc. (The British now find that they have several hundred potential recruits who were recruited and debriefed in an orderly and businesslike manner. There have been few sour British agents and the files of their war-time operations serves as one of their more important war-time intelligence documentations . . .) I desire to emphasize that these [Italian police and intelligence] documentations represent the most important single intelligence item to be gained in Italy . . . It is not too much to state that the complete documentation will no doubt influence all future American activity vis-à-vis the Italians in the fields of commerce, diplomacy, as well as security."[125]

Angleton saw his role in Italy that summer as extending beyond counterintelligence operations. The X-2 operational summaries note that "What is important, is the possible change which will be effected if the Monarchy loses [the 1946 balloting].

> With the advent of the Republic most every I.S. service will be revamped to satisfy the Socialists and there is the danger that the Communists will effect a penetration . . . To meet this eventuality, we are working together with certain CS-Land [Italian] officers, such as JK1/1 to anticipate a Socialist landslide and make sure that apolitical officers are ready to step into the key position. This is the only way that we can possibly preserve our equity."[126]

We also have what is, in effect, a "help wanted" advertisement from James Angleton on behalf of both X-2 and his father: "As GINO should have explained, my father is willing to take on an X-2 trained girl as a permanent secretary to the Chamber of Commerce in Milan.

> She would receive the usual salary from the Chamber in addition to anything paid by SSU. She must be social-minded and have good knowledge of office procedure. She would be used for all official

functions and as the liaison member between the Chamber and Italian industrialists. In this position, we would have a good under-cover contact, who would be <u>au courant</u> with all the chief financial and industrial personalities doing business with the U.S. Qualifications must include dictation, typing and excellent Italian."

The end of the war was marked by the presentation of awards. James Angleton received a Legion of Merit. The citation summarized his career in X-2: "JAMES ANGLETON, 0886353, Captain, Army of the United States, 2677th Regiment, Strategic Services Unit, for exceptionally meritorious conduct in the performance of outstanding services in the Mediterranean Theater from 28 October 1944 to December 1945.

> As Commanding Officer of the Special Counter Intelligence Units in the Mediterranean Theater, Captain Angleton directed the operations of the personnel of those units in the practices which enabled them to apprehend over one thousand enemy intelligence agents. The dissemination of clear, concise and comprehensive descriptive material in a form originated by him [the 'Keys'] was a contributory factor. He personally undertook the compilation of a complete brief on the enemy intelligence services known to be operating in North Italy. By this means the agencies operating with the Fifteenth Army Group were furnished a clear picture of what they could expect in North Italy. Since the surrender of the enemy his review of enemy intelligence material has resulted in the detection of a large number of lesser collaborators. During personnel redeployment, Captain Angleton has been able to obtain a superior quality of results which has gained the commendation of executive intelligence agencies associated with him."

It would seem reasonable of the army to recognize such achievements. Identifying over a thousand enemy intelligence agents in little over a year would as well indicate that the species was not altogether rare, either in Italy or elsewhere.

On 22 January 1946, SSU became, briefly, the Central Intelligence Group (CIG). It would soon be folded into the new Central Intelligence Agency as its Office of Special Operations. According to a

Memorandum for the Assistant Director for Special Operations, 25 October 1946, from then Director of Central Intelligence Hoyt Vandenberg: "The mission of the Office of Special Operations is the conduct, under the direct supervision of the Director, of all organized Federal espionage and counterespionage operations outside the United States and its possessions for the collection of foreign intelligence information required for the national security.

> Such espionage and counterespionage operations may involve semi-overt and semi-covert activities for the full performance of the mission . . . The Office of Special Operations will be responsible for the collection, processing, and distribution of foreign counterespionage intelligence information and will be the repository for such information."[127]

Angleton joined the Office of Special Operations of the new CIA in November 1947.[128]

Captain James Angleton left the army, but, in effect, he never demobilized. Moving from OSS to SSU to the CIA itself, his attitudes and activities were consistent from his Ryder Street days until, if not beyond, his retirement thirty years later. His first postwar field of activities took place in the scene where he had made his wartime reputation: Italy. Kaeten Mistry found that "Italy may have escaped the worst of the devastation wrought by World War II, although the problems it faced were no less real.

> With close to 450,000 lives lost, orphaned and homeless children wandered the streets. In Rome, the Quirinale Gardens became 'notorious as a gathering place for thousands of Italy's mutilated, disfigured and unclaimed children.'"[129]

Between the fall of Mussolini and the Italian election of 1948 the losers were quickly identified: first of all the fascists, of course, hung from lampposts, paunches displayed across the front pages of newspapers. And, a bit later, the king and his party, who had moved too late and too timidly for the British to rescue them. The monarchy was abolished in a referendum on 2 June 1946. At first the struggle between the Church and the Communist Party remained in the balance, tilting now in favor of the one, now in favor of the other. Palmiro Togliatti, the leader of the Italian Communist Party, was successively justice minister and minister without portfolio in the Badoglio government, then vice-premier to Alcide De Gasperi. There were those in the Italian Communist Party, partisans and union leaders, who wished to try for power with the guns they had used against the fascists and Germans. Togliatti, convinced this would bring reprisals from the American army, disarmed his comrades and, supplied with funds from the East, tried to best De Gasperi in the national elections.

The regional elections of spring 1946 gave a majority to the Left alliance of socialists and communists,[130] as did the June Constituent Assembly election. The Christian Democrats continued to lose strength in the November regional voting.[131] Italy's World War II formally ended with the signing of the Italian peace treaty in February 1947. De Gasperi "removed the Marxist left from the coalition government in May, 1947."[132] That autumn, Ambassador James Dunn warned that "it may be 'a question [of] when Communists find it suits their purpose . . . to assume the Government by legal means'"[133] The reason for this was that the communists, the PCI, "were doing a superior job in organizing at the grassroots level. Of course, the CIA also knew that the Popular Front had 'ample funds,' energetic leaders, and dedicated followers, three assets that neither the DC [Christian Democrats] nor the other non-Marxist parties could boast."[134] Ambassador Dunn in Rome said that $10 million would be needed to produce an anti-communist victory in the next election.

On 8 March 1948, the United States National Security Council authorized covert funding of the Italian Socialist Labor Party and the Christian Democrats by the CIA's Office of Special Projects, with James Angleton coordinating the effort from Washington.[135] The principal task of the CIA's operation was to make up for the deficiencies of the Popular Front's opponents.[136] The way in which this was accomplished was that "the CIA used American money to help rig the results in certain constituencies and to provide DC candidates with a pool of money to entice prospective voters with promises of just rewards if they voted the 'right' way . . .

It was decided that the bulk of the earmarked $10 million would come from the Economic Stabilization Fund (ESF) . . . There is reason to believe that much of the money taken from the ESF did not, in fact, come from U.S. coffers, but rather from Nazi assets captured by the Allies during the war. These seized assets included money and gold that the Nazis had taken from the Jews of Eastern Europe."[137]

The money, whatever its origin, was disguised as voluntary funds from various non-governmental organizations in the United States and, perhaps especially, from the American Federation of Labor (AFL) and its Free Trade Union Committee, that is, Jay Lovestone and Irving Brown.[138] Lovestone, one-time head of the American Communist Party, became one of Angleton's personal agents. The funds were transferred through the labor unions themselves and through such groups as Common Cause of New York City, which had connections with the liberationist emigrant communities in the city.[139] The services of Swiss banks were used for more direct transfers. President Truman, in violation of international agreements, also authorized covert shipments of arms to right-wing groups in Italy.[140]

CIA Director Roscoe H. Hillenkoetter "met personally with [Stewart] Alsop 're Italy' in early March 1948.

> The following month, during what [Joseph Alsop] described as 'one of our regular trips of inquiry,' Stewart [Alsop] visited Angleton in Rome, bearing a letter of introduction from his older brother, who had stayed with the erudite spy in the Italian capital the previous summer. Joe had cryptically written to Angleton, "Stew has all sorts of messages from me to you . . . [but] I can tell you one thing: the powers that be here are delighted with what you are accomplishing—they have told me so rather boastfully, and I think I have noticed some of the reasons for their approval in the papers . . ."

The 18 April 1948 election gave De Gasperi's party majorities in the Chamber of Deputies and the Senate. Ambassador Dunn sent his thanks to Lovestone. And "all my friends" in the AFL.[141] Within the CIA, Angleton's Italian operation was hailed as the agency's first real success and both a model and a precedent for dirty tricks to come."[142] James McCargar remembered that "It was embarrassing (I thought) to see American Ambassador Jimmy Dunn going up and down the Italian peninsula making speeches in favor of the Christian Democrats.

> The phrase later used, obviously a vast exaggeration, was that Eddie Page[143] was leaning out the windows of the Embassy passing money to all the Christian Democrats. The money was plentiful. Of course we went all out, and there was, in all fairness, plenty of other money going to the Communists."[144]

Historian Robert Ventresca believes that covert funding of anti-communists in the 1948 Italian elections was a "monumental decision, which was clearly unconstitutional and set a damaging precedent for subsequent Italian elections" and yet "No spirited objections were made to the use of America's technical and economic might to subvert a legitimate democratic process in a country that was both a friend and an ally . . ."[145] The National Security Council "granted the CIA a blanket authorization for covert operations" as a reward for a job well done.[146]

In April 1948, Cicely Angleton had written to Marion Cummings from Tucson that "Jim is home and things are much better . . . At least the Italian elections went off all right which ought to relieve some of the pressure off both Jim and the Pope."[147]

ISTANBUL AND WASHINGTON

Near the beginning of 1947 Kim Philby was sent to Turkey as SIS station chief under fairly thin cover as a Foreign Office's First Secretary.[1] While traveling to Istanbul, Philby flew to Jeddah to visit his father, who took him to Riyadh and, rather oddly, to Al Kharj, the principal claim of fame for which was as an early experimental dairy farm. In Saudi Arabia he was his father's son. In Istanbul he was the representative of what was arguably still the pre-eminent Western foreign intelligence service, and the agent of another yet more powerful.

Istanbul was almost, but not quite, a front-line posting in the Cold War. Across the Aegean, Greece was in a state of civil war between the communist KKE and the government, the former claiming descent from the partisans of World War II, the latter, including former Nazi collaborators, supported by British troops. Nigel Clive, Philby's MI-6 opposite number in Athens, wrote: "Greece was a kind of British protectorate, but the British ambassador was not a colonial governor," which was more or less the definition of membership in the informal empire. In January and February 1947 American diplomatic personnel were of the opinion that the Greek government might collapse at any moment.[2] The CIA agreed, reporting that "Without immediate economic aid . . . there would appear to be imminent danger that the Soviet-dominated Left will seize control of the country, which would result in the loss of Greece as a democracy of the Western type."[3] At the end of February, the British government abruptly informed the United States government that it would withdraw economic and military support from Greece and Turkey by the end of March. This was a consequence of the economic crisis in Britain subsequent to World War II, in turn itself partially a result of the sudden cancellation of Lend-Lease at the end of the war and the terms of the Anglo-American

Loan,* which, taken with the strain of the war itself, had, in effect, bankrupted Britain. On 12 March, US President Truman declared in a speech to a joint session of Congress that the United States would replace Britain in providing military and economic funds to Greece and to Turkey.[4]

The American ambassador in Turkey wrote that: "In an aggressive war by Russia in the foreseeable future, Russia for strategic purposes must overrun Turkey rapidly before aid can arrive. Because of her strategic position Turkey becomes actually the first line of defense for the United States in any aggressive move by Russia."[5] British and American diplomats believed that Turkey was capable of maintaining the then current, and marginally adequate, level of its armed forces, but did not have resources beyond that. US Public Law 75 of the Eightieth Congress therefore provided $100 million in aid to Turkey. The American ambassador, Edwin C. Wilson, recommended that an equal amount be given each year for five years in order to modernize the Turkish armed forces. An American Mission for Aid to Turkey was established and instructed to "maintain loose informal contact with the British authorities in Turkey . . . You may . . . conclude such operating arrangements and agreements with the British authorities as will facilitate the American aid program, for example, in relation to the procurement of supplies or the use of British facilities, installations, and personnel in Turkey."[6] In this context Philby in Istanbul and Clive in Athens were in key positions to facilitate the transition as the dominant power in the region from Britain to the United States, while doing their best to maintain British influence and acting as observers of Soviet and, in the case of Greece, local communist actions in the area.

Kim Philby's MI-6 office was in Istanbul, rather than in Ankara. The Istanbul British offices were in the former embassy building, an imposing Imperial edifice in Pera, the old European quarter of the city, on the trolley car line between Taksim Square and the Golden Horn. It had been about two years since Philby had visited that building while dealing with the Volkov affair. Philby at first rented a villa in Beylerbey, on the Asian side of the Bosporus, next to a landing-stage, from which he commuted to Pera. The villa "commanded a fine view: from the minarets of Hagia Sophia

---

* Especially the convertibility of sterling to come into effect in July 1947.

in the distance to an ancient fortress on a bend of the Bosporus.

> The house itself was huge and the garden and orchard ran nearly
> down to the water . . . The rent even included a private lobster har-
> bour . . . Aileen and the four children soon joined him . . . There
> was the round of diplomatic parties, dinners, picnics and cruises."[7]

John, the eldest child, remembered "the idyllic time the family spent
in Istanbul . . . [he] recalled carefree days playing with local Turkish
children on the beach."[8] The Philbys (including Aileen's mother and
the nanny for their four children) soon moved further up the Asiatic
coast of the Bosporus to another suburb, Vaniköy.

Across the Aegean, Greece was descending into its third civil war
in as many years. In June 1947 the communist rebels against the
British- and American-supported government attempted to set up
a provisional capital near the Albanian border. On Christmas Eve
1947, the Communist Party declared a free government in northern
Greece, which led to the Athens government outlawing the Communist Party. By late 1949 the communist army had been defeated by
that of the Athens government and the RAF and its leaders driven
into exile. Things were quieter in Turkey. While working as MI-6
station chief in Istanbul, Philby accomplished such tasks as would
be expected of secret intelligence station chiefs. He met with Turkish
political figures. He established liaison relations with the police and
various Turkish intelligence agencies and with the representatives
of the intelligence agencies of other countries who were stationed
in Istanbul, especially, no doubt, the CIA station chief, obtaining
and exchanging price lists for information, cooperation, operating
expenses, and so forth. Less routinely, Philby spent the summers of
1947 and 1948 surveying eastern Anatolia on the Soviet border for
both of his services. This was an area close to Iranian Azerbaijan,
from which the Soviet Union had only recently withdrawn.

In the summer of 1948, while photographing the border for MI-6,
Philby sent across two young Georgians, with the aid of the Turkish
service. They did not survive.[9] It was theorized by the Knightley
group of journalists that at this time Philby was assigned by SIS to
pretend to the Russians that he was an MI-6 agent willing to become
on their behalf a double agent. Knightley and his colleagues believed
that this was the only explanation for the way in which, years later,

SIS insisted that he was innocent of the suspicions of MI-5.[10] Philby
was to pretend, to the Soviets, on behalf of SIS that he was working
with them against SIS, while, in fact, he was. Angleton's wilderness
of mirrors is barely adequate as a descriptive metaphor.

Shortly after Philby returned to Vaniköy from his expedition
to eastern Anatolia and the Soviet border, Guy Burgess arrived in
Istanbul, on leave from his work as assistant to the Foreign Office
Minister, Hector McNeil. International tension was reaching a level
not seen since Munich. Important elements in the American government and military were advocating and to some extent preparing for
a nuclear first strike on the Soviet Union; in February the Communist Party took control of the Czechoslovakian government; in May
1948 the state of Israel was proclaimed and the Middle East began
decades of war; in June 1948 the Soviets blockaded Berlin. Against
this background it is unlikely that Burgess was also on leave from his
duties as a Soviet "linking agent": collecting information from other
agents and forwarding it to Moscow. There is, for example, a group
of documents in Dolgopolov's biography of Philby that come from
Philby's posting to Turkey. These are two dozen copies of telegrams
to the Foreign Office in 1948, labeled "political reviews" from the
British ambassador in Ankara during this crisis period.[11] Burgess's
role in collecting and transmitting these, making the necessary contacts with Soviet officials, would have been easier in Istanbul than
in London.

While Burgess and Kim Philby worked, talked and drank, Aileen
Philby had what appears to have been a psychotic episode, involving
self-mutilation and several months in hospital. She "resented Burgess
and his close relationship with her husband, and [had begun] staging
accidents to claim attention; she once reported being mugged in her
car, and on another occasion set fire to the living room, suffering
serious burns. She was later sent to a Swiss clinic for treatment."[12]
That is the sequence laid out in the *Daily Telegraph*'s obituary of
Kim and Aileen's son John Philby. On the other hand, Philip Knightley has Aileen's breakdown *preceding* Burgess's arrival: "While
she was in hospital, Guy Burgess turned up in Istanbul to spend a
holiday with the Philbys . . . Philby welcomed him. They went for
long walks; they drove off for days on end in Philby's office jeep;
they dined at the fashionable Moda Yacht Club . . ."[13] According
to this account, it was *after* Burgess left Istanbul that Aileen Philby

injured herself, was sent to the clinic in Berne for some months, Kim Philby staying with her for the first three weeks. And, according to Seale and McConville, it was in the winter of 1948, while Kim Philby was in London for briefings and, it is said, training in hand-to-hand combat, that Aileen Philby apparently set herself on fire while staying with their expatriate friends Zeki and Hazel Sporel and was taken back to Berne, not returning to live in Istanbul.[14] Whichever of these accounts we believe, it is evident that Aileen Philby, who, apparently unknown to her husband, had had a history of mental illness characterized by episodes of self-mutilation before they began to live together, was increasingly unhappy, increasingly unstable.

According to Cookridge, Kim Philby visited the Macleans in Cairo in the spring of 1949.[15] But that is another story.

Unlike Kim and Aileen Philby, who lived together until near the end of their marriage, James Angleton had left the United States in 1943, shortly after marrying Cicely d'Autremont, and did not see her again until November 1945, when he stopped in New York City for two days on the way to OSS headquarters in Washington for a consultation. Their reunion was not a success. As Cicely Angleton saw it, "We just didn't know each other anymore . . . Jim no longer cared about our relationship, he just wanted to get back to Italy—back to the life he knew and loved. He didn't want a family. The marriage seemed to be annihilated then and there.[16] James Angleton returned to Rome and Cicely Angleton went west to her family's compound in Tucson.[17] James Angleton did not again return to the United States until almost two years later, when the successor organizations of the OSS had become the Central Intelligence Agency.

A description of James and Cicely's extended family housing arrangements will throw some light on what might pass for the class status of the Angletons in mid-century America. Like millions of other white Americans in those years, the Angletons bought a house, this in suburban Alexandria, Virginia, which was to be their home, in their case, until the end of their lives. The small, more or less typical civil servant's house across the Potomac River from Washington, D.C., was deceptive. They also owned a ranch in Idaho, and James Angleton's parents lived in a palazzo in Milan, later in a villa in the Parioli, the diplomatic district, of Rome. His sister,

Carmen, lived there and in a succession of apartments in Rome's historic center. Cicely Angleton's family owned various properties in Tucson, including a house in something like a private park, suitable for one of that semi-colonial city's leading families. James and Cicely Angleton also had vacation homes along rivers near the Great Lakes and rented summer homes on Cape Cod. This was a way of life well into that of the top 1 percent of postwar America, in contrast, say, to Philby's semi-bohemian existence.

As World War II gave way to the early Cold War, the initials on James Angleton's paychecks changed from OSS to SSU to CIA. Once established in the last of these, Angleton worked in the early Central Intelligence Agency's Office of Special Operations (OSO). Foreign Division M of OSO was headed by Angleton's friend Richard Helms, who had responsibility for both intelligence and counter-intelligence activities in Central Europe.[18] Counterespionage, or Staff C (all that remained of X-2), was in the hands of ex-FBI agent William Harvey.[19] James Angleton's Special Procedures Group of OSO was described in a 22 March 1948 memorandum as responsible for covert operations. "The primary objectives of such operations will be:

(1) to undermine the strength of foreign instrumentalities, whether governments, organizations or individuals, which are engaged in activities inimical to the United States; and,
(2) to support U.S. foreign policy by influencing foreign public opinion in a direction favorable to the attainment of U.S. objectives."[20]

It was through the Special Procedures Group that Angleton had worked to influence the Italian elections in 1948.

In 1949 Angleton became chief of OSO's Staff A: foreign intelligence gathering, agent operations, double agent operations, provocation, defectors, operational interrogation, and liaison with the CIA's counterpart organizations abroad. This was a wide range of responsibilities for what was still quite a small organization. He was responsible as well for the all-important files inherited from OSS X-2—those thousands and hundreds of thousands of names.[21] Angleton continued to take care of liaison with foreign intelligence services,[22] which remained vital as "the CIA still relied heavily on the British, French, Germans, and other 'partners' to do much of the recruitments and covert actions in postwar Europe, these so-called liaisons were the very mechanism through which the CIA organized the secret war against the Soviet Union."[23] The CIA was dependent for most of its foreign intelligence on such liaison relationships until the 1960s. Angleton's expertise in the area, and his continuing contacts, were central to his influence in the Agency.[24]

James Angleton's liaison activities for the early CIA included three that were to be career-long special interests: those with the intelligence services of Italy, Israel, and Germany. Continuing Angleton's OSS efforts, "OSO operatives were able to infiltrate and ultimately pretty much co-opt the Italian security services.

> 'This was an Angleton-Rocca thing,' a participant observes. 'We had officers working right in with every branch of Italian intelligence . . . and the relationships were extremely close . . . You were able to get very senior officers in the service to focus on what we wanted done unbeknownst to their bosses.'"

Of course, "'You have to see that they're happy.

> Their motivation is high, they want to work with you, deep down, but at the same time you want to have an element of control . . . You're not only offering gifts but you're saying, Geez, you're trying to put that son of yours through college, and it's a little rough, and we'd be delighted to assist you . . . I don't think that's venality. I think that's good common intelligence sense.'"[25]

Italian consulates in the Soviet bloc furnished information about rail junctions and military bases; Italian businessmen provided information through the CIA's Legal Traveler program.[26] There was also the Vatican. Pope Paul VI, especially, was said to be close to Angleton.

The relationship between Kim Philby and James Angleton evolved from that of teacher and student in London through a quasi-supervisory one when Angleton first went to Italy to one of informal mentorship as the American secret intelligence organizations nearly vanished, then expanded once more. When Angleton went to

London in September 1949, for "a week of meetings with senior British and American colleagues at SIS headquarters . . .

> The meeting of the minds in London in September 1949 settled on the requisite Anglo-American division of labor. The CIA needed expertise in running covert operations, an improved central file registry, and a more robust communications system—all of which the British had in place. SIS needed money and manpower—of which the Americans had a surplus. Kim Philby, all agreed, was just the man to make the new arrangements work in Washington . . ."[27]

Cave Brown claimed that "C had written to the chief of the new CIA, proposing Kim Philby as the liaison officer between SIS and the CIA.

> But Philby's was not the only name proposed. Two other SIS names were offered in the same letter. It was the CIA that selected Philby's name. In the view of Dr. Ray Cline, an assistant director of the CIA during the Philby case and a noted historian of the CIA, it was James Jesus Angleton who selected Philby's name."[28]

Cline may have had his own reasons for offering Cave Brown this story. Perhaps there was an informal notification process, as with diplomatic appointments, in which Angleton participated. Perhaps not, and perhaps Cave Brown misunderstood Cline. In any case, in August 1949, Philby, while still in Istanbul, was offered the position of chief officer of the SIS bureau in Washington in charge of liaison between the SIS and United States intelligence agencies.[29]

Philby was very pleased with the assignment because, as he wrote, "The intention was to upgrade the job for a significant reason. The collaboration between CIA and SIS at headquarters level (though not in the field) had become so close that any officer earmarked for high position in SIS would need an intimate knowledge of the American scene."[30] The KGB, in a completely disinterested fashion, also approved of the choice. Philby's predecessor as SIS liaison in Washington, Peter Dwyer,[31] was believed to have favored the FBI at the expense of the CIA. Therefore, in addition to helping out the CIA with its bureaucratic problems, and in that process gaining the familiarity with the CIA thought necessary for a possible future director of the SIS (and useful to Moscow Center), Philby was charged by SIS with rebuilding good relations between MI-6 and the CIA without offending J. Edgar Hoover.[32] Philby had his work cut out for him. Not offending Hoover would have been a full-time job in itself, as became evident a bit later.

While being briefed in London for this posting, Philby was told about the search for "Homer," the Soviet cover name for a spy in the Washington British embassy.* "The leak from the British Embassy, he was told, involved high-grade diplomatic communications and had taken place in 1944–5, details which were enough for him to be pretty sure in his own mind about who the spy was."[33] Peter Wright claimed that "Meredith Gardner . . . used to tell me how he worked on the matches in his office, and of how a young pipe-smoking Englishman named Philby used to regularly visit him and peer over his shoulder and admire the progress he was making"[34] The minute-by-minute progress of the American and British cryptographers has been obsessively recounted in the literature, usually emphasizing the cryptographic handicraft of Meredith Gardner. However, that was not all there was to it. According to a 17 April 1950 report from Burgess to his Soviet contact, Philby "asked to communicate that the Americans and the British had constructed a deciphering machine which in one day does 'the work of a thousand people in a thousand years'.

> Work on deciphering is facilitated by three factors: (1) A one-time pad was used twice; (2) Our cipher resembles the cipher of our trade organization in the USA; (3) A half-burnt codebook has been found in Finland and passed to the British and used to decrypt our communication. They will succeed within six to twelve months."

A meeting on 4 June "with Korovin, was held in a quiet suburban park and lasted six and a half hours.

The marathon length was accounted for by the Cambridge ring's anxieties about the threat posed to them by the new decryption

---

* Dolgopolov (page 63) says that Philby was told about this effort by Maurice Oldfield, then deputy head of MI-6 counterintelligence.

machine. This, of course, was the latest generation of GCHQ's computers, then completely unknown to the wider public."[35]

The British machines seem to have been both single-purpose mechanisms, like the World War II "bombes" that had helped decipher the Enigma transmissions, and advanced versions of "Colossus," an early programmable machine. The American group seems also to have had some machine assistance, perhaps involving punch cards and similar electro-mechanical devices.

Kim Philby arrived in Washington on 10 October 1949.[36] He "had been in America a bare couple of weeks when [news of] the explosion of Russia's first atomic device in September 1949 threw the whole intelligence apparatus of the Western world into a fever."[37]

> On 3 September 1949 a diverted American WB-29 (weather B-29) flying between Japan and Alaska collected routine atmospheric samples at 18,000 feet.
>
> These revealed an unmistakably higher-than-normal radioactive content . . . Analysis at 3.30 in the morning of 7 September proved that the samples were artificial—that they had been injected into the atmosphere by a non-natural occurrence . . . The first British confirmation came from a UK-based flight leaving on the evening of 10 September."

Michael Goodman writes: "According to Dr Wilfrid Mann, although he occupied the exalted position of atomic intelligence liaison with the Americans, his 'sole job' was to notify Eric Welsh and SIS if and when the US detected a Soviet atomic bomb test.

> Wilfrid Mann learned about the news at 11.30 on the evening of 14 September. 'I had one foot in the bathtub', he recalls, 'when the telephone rang with a request that I go down to the War Room near the White House.' . . . Returning to his office in the British Embassy, Mann sent a series of telegrams through the secure SIS link. With the help of the SIS liaison officer at the Embassy, Kim Philby, Mann spent three to four days in extended communication with London, sending Top Secret messages to Welsh and even more sensitive messages to 'C'. One of the messages to 'C' advised him

that he should inform the Prime Minister of the news. Accordingly, on 17 September [Michael] Perrin accompanied 'C' to Chequers to tell Prime Minister Clement Attlee 'that there was evidence that 'Joe 1' had taken place.'"[38]

Which, among other things, shows that Philby controlled the most secret British communications between Washington and London.

The first test of the American atomic bomb had taken place at the Trinity site on 16 July 1945. Hiroshima was destroyed three weeks later, on 6 August. The Soviet atomic bomb test was on 29 August 1949. It could therefore be inferred that by the time that Attlee was informed of the Soviet test the Soviet armed forces would have had at least one, probably more, atomic bombs of the size used on the Japanese cities. Although Washington would remain out of range of Soviet bombers for a few more years, that was not the case for London. Anglo-American war planners now had to take into account not only the possibility of Soviet retaliation for an atomic attack by a ground invasion of Western Europe, but also by means of a simultaneous nuclear attack on London.

The Philbys found a house in Washington similar to, but slightly larger than, that of the Angletons and in a more fashionable area, at 400 Nebraska Avenue, near the embassy district. Kim Philby's days in Washington "were crowded with meetings, briefings, dictating reports, sifting the mass of material thrown up by one international crisis after another, channeling a flood of top secret traffic to his overworked cipher clerks for transmission to London.

> There were conferences with OPC to plot the Albanian opera-
> tion, sessions with James Angleton and his colleagues at OSO to
> co-ordinate Anglo-American penetration of European Communist
> movements, long painstaking hours with the FBI."[39]

Not to mention the perhaps duplicate traffic that passed, by different routes, between Washington and Moscow. In addition to periodic trips to London, such as one early in 1950 to discuss the Klaus Fuchs affair, Philby also made several to Italy and Greece, "accompanied by high-ranking C.I.A. officials."[40] Perhaps it is *a propos* of these latter visits that Cicely Angleton commented about the pleasure trips of secret intelligence officials taken in the guise of official business.

Klaus Fuchs was a nuclear physicist, a refugee from Nazi Germany, who had become one of the two or three most important British experts working on the development of the atomic bomb, first in the British Tube Alloys project, then at Los Alamos. He had been a communist activist while at university in Germany and early in World War II had become an informant on atomic energy matters to the Soviet Union. In early 1950 he was arrested in England for the latter activities. The Fuchs affair was devastating for the British government, which had been desperately trying to resurrect the "modus vivendi" allowing cooperation in nuclear matters with the United States. Wilfred Mann was kept informed of the progress of the affair by Michael Perrin, as was the Nuclear Energy Group in the CIA. A secret telegram from Washington to the Cabinet Office in London on 7 February noted that, despite Hoover's personal denials which he gave over the telephone to the MI-5 representative, reports were circulating in Washington that he had criticized British security and judicial procedures to a Congressional Committee and that "such reports . . . are bound to confirm the impression in the American mind that the British were negligent about Fuchs' security clearance during the war and are now being uncooperative in helping the American authorities to deal with a most serious breach of American security.

> This impression if allowed to grow will strike at the root of the mutual confidence between America and Britain which is the basis of their cooperation and partnership in the intelligence research and strategic fields and in many others besides."[41]

The next day the Cabinet Office was informed that US Secretary of State Dean Acheson "has now said that he thinks we must break off the Tripartite Anglo-American-Canadian talks on Atomic energy for the time being." Fuchs pleaded guilty on 1 March.

The "Cold War sub-committee" of the British Foreign Office's "Russia Committee," chaired by the ubiquitous Gladwyn Jebb, had decided in November 1948, while Kim Philby was in Istanbul, "to liberate the countries within the Soviet orbit by any means short of war."[42] Albania, between British-controlled Greece and Tito's Yugoslavia, seemed to them a good place to start. Jebb and Lord Jellicoe went to Washington in March 1949 for a three-day meeting on Albania with Robert Joyce of the State Department and Frank Wisner of the Office of Special Operations (OPC).* They agreed on an attempt to "detach Albania from the orbit."[43] Angleton, in the rival OSO, was not included in the meeting. He was known to be opposed to most covert operations, thinking they attracted too much attention and interfered in the collection of intelligence. He also had connections in the exiled Albanian groups from his Italian days, which might have given him the information that conditions in the country were unfavorable to the planned activities. Nonetheless, Wisner and Joyce went to London in August 1950, accompanied on this occasion by Kim Philby, to confirm the operation[44] in a meeting with the Russia Committee of the Foreign Office. "There were to be two main items of business . . .

> To coordinate with the British operations to overthrow the pro-Soviet or Soviet governments of Albania, Latvia, and the Ukraine . . . [and to] reach a consensus with the London intelligence community on the probable date that the Russians would start World War III . . . At these meetings, Philby kept the British minutes while Joyce kept those of the United States. Wisner announced that the CIA would take an active part in the Albanian operations, its first landings to take place in November."[45]

James McCargar recalled "That [the Albanian] operation was originally a British idea, pushed forcefully by Julian Amery, who had been in Albania during the war with the SOE, and he and his colleagues had been treated very badly by Hoxha and his nascent Communist Party . . .

> The British were very strong for this operation. It was, of course, ultimately discussed by Bevin and Acheson, and agreement reached at that level. On the lower, operative level, we were engaged in joint

---

* OPC, which Bedell Smith absorbed into the CIA, was committed to "rolling-back" Soviet power as opposed to simply observing its activities. It was more like the wartime British Special Operations Executive than like MI-6.

planning with the British. Their enthusiasm was evident when I went on a mission to London to discuss it with them . . . The American understanding of the operation was that it was a probe. That is to say, the idea was to send people in who would come back out, or report by radio, as to whether there was any real possibility of a sufficient resistance movement in the country to combat the Hoxha Government . . . the British then sent over H. A. R. Philby, Kim, as he was called, to the British Embassy in Washington, representing the heads of both MI-5 and MI-6. When Philby and I were together, we constituted the command of the operation. We had a room assigned to us in the secure part of the Pentagon, the Joint Chiefs of Staff area.

There we would meet and issue our instructions as they became necessary . . ."

McCargar and Philby, marshals' batons in their knapsacks, set about with this first effort to reverse Soviet World War II gains. McCargar recalled that "We did have three expeditions from Malta by ship.

When the first one went, I got a call from Jim Angleton . . . He called me to his office, and with great glee he read me—Angleton, I should add . . . had totally penetrated the Italian secret service; he ran it—he read me a report which obviously he'd gotten from the Italians about our first physical operation in Albania: the name of the ship was "Stormy Seas" (correct), it passed the Strait of Otranto at such-and-such a time, on board were so-and-so, the whole thing . . . What he didn't tell me, of course, was that the OSO itself was running operations into all these areas, Albania included, which they never told us about. We didn't consult them about our operations, either. But it would have helped a bit if we'd known that the OSO had agents in Albania . . . Notwithstanding what Philby subsequently wrote from Moscow in his memoirs . . . I have always insisted that it was not Philby who gave away the Albanian operation to the Russians and thus to the Albanians. The Albanian community in Italy was so thoroughly penetrated, not only by the Italians but by the Communists, that to me that was where the Russians were getting their information, as were the Albanian Communist authorities . . ."[46]

On the other hand, Yuri Modin claimed that Philby was part of the group planning the operation, details of which he sent to Burgess to pass on to Moscow. His letter to Burgess included the date and hour of the proposed landing, the number of men in the group, their weapons, and their operational programme.[47] Modin's account is confirmed, or perhaps simply repeated, by Dolgopolov.[48]

Philby sent seventy-five documents, comprising 185 pages, to Moscow in 1949. It was noted that most were sent on to higher authority and action followed from about a third. There are telegrams from London, among the Dolgopolov materials, concerning the Albanian operation. For example: "TOP SECRET TO Comrade Stalin [and] Comrade Molotov [from] Resident in London on the night of September 23 [1949] . . .

> reported that he received from an agent that the intelligence agencies of the United States and England jointly have developed a plan for subversive activities against Albania, called Operation 'Valuable.' This plan provides for the sending to Albania of diversionary-insurgent groups, manned from Albanian emigrant Fascists, with the task of raising the 'guerrilla movement' in Albania in the spring of 1950 against the government of Enver Hodja [sic]. The implementation of the plan [includes] establishing the bases on the islands of Malta and Corfu for the first two groups of five people each, who were to be thrown into the territory of Albania . . . There is a half-year training for such groups . . . Information about the sabotage of subversive and insurgent groups on the night of September 24 was transferred to us through our secret secretary at the Ministry of Internal Affairs of Albania."[49]

Kim Philby wrote a colorful, if customarily untrustworthy, account of Angleton's position in the CIA in 1949, when Angleton was still in the CIA's intelligence gathering division, the Office of Strategic Operations, reporting to Colonel Robert A. Schow.[50] According to Philby, "The driving force of OSO at the time was Jim Angleton, who had formerly served in London and had earned my respect by openly rejecting the Anglo-mania that disfigured the young face of OSO.

We formed the habit of lunching once a week at Harvey's . . . Our
. . . close association was, I am sure, inspired by genuine friendliness
on both sides. But we both had ulterior motives. Angleton wanted
to place the burden of exchanges between CIA and SIS on the CIA
office in London—which was about ten times as big as mine. By
doing so, he could exert the maximum pressure on SIS's headquarters while minimising SIS intrusions into his own. As an exercise
in nationalism, that was fair enough. By cultivating me to the full,
he could better keep me under wraps . . . Although our discussions
ranged over the whole world, they usually ended, if they did not
begin, with France and Germany. The Americans had an obsessive
fear of communism in France, and I was astonished by the way
in which Angleton devoured reams of French newspaper material
daily . . . Angleton had fewer fears about Germany. That country
concerned him chiefly as a base of operations against the Soviet
Union and the socialist states of Eastern Europe."[51]

It does not seem from this that Philby knew about Angleton's use of
Lovestone and the American trades unions to intervene in France at
this time, when French politics and society were in turmoil, which
would have explained Angleton's interest in the French press. Even
perfect spies are not omniscient.

The JFK Assassination Files, which contain much detail about
everyday operations of the Central Intelligence Agency, including
personnel action documents, agent employment forms, and the like,
provide information about Angleton's routine in the early days of the
Agency. For example, he met with DCI Hillenkoetter on 13 January
1950, accompanying Schow and ex-King Peter of Yugoslavia as part
of his liaison responsibilities. After this we have some indications of
Angleton's work with Italian intelligence. On 12 April he had a telephone discussion with Captain Baslini of Italian naval intelligence,
regarding the guest list for a dinner hosted by the Italian ambassador in honor of Vice-Admiral Emilio Ferreri, Chief of Staff, Italian
Navy. The dinner took place at the end of the month, on Saturday,
29 April, including DCI Hillenkoetter and his wife; Vice-Admiral
Ferreri; his Aide; Rear Admiral Carlo F. Tallarigo, Director of Italian Naval Intelligence; the Chief of Naval Operations and his wife;
Schow and his wife; the Angletons; and a few others.[52] The next
month's activities began with a 1 May conference, then luncheon

with Tallarigo, Schow, Angleton, and the DCI. In the following weeks there were many meetings and telephone calls among Angleton, Hillenkoetter, Schow, and Winston Scott,* including one about "machine records," a longtime interest of Angleton's.

A letter from William Harvey on 10 August 1950, asserted that Frank Wisner's fixer: "Mr. [Carmel] Offie is not carried on the government payroll; that presently he is working with the American Federation of Labor, dealing with foreign labor leaders; working directly with Mr. Jay Lovestone in New York."[53] That is, he was working for James Angleton.[54] A "Memorandum of Conversation" ("no.3"), of 20 January 1951, from James Reber, Acting Assistant Director for Intelligence Coordination, CIA, had as its subject "Intelligence Support for OSO." It involved Allen (sic) Evans and Charles Stelle of the Department of State and James Angleton and Reber, of the Central Intelligence Agency. They had discussed two subjects: background research needed to prepare questions for OSO operatives and the relationship of what is known generally as International Communism and the Communist Party. Angleton had argued that international Communism was inseparable from the Communist Party. On 16 January, Reber and a colleague had lunch with Angleton, at which they agreed that OSO required studies on Communist Party activities, which in turn required "a group of high intellectual caliber to produce integrated and organized studies on Communist Party activities" based on "research and on highly classified information in the possession of OSO." "Action" items included "The appropriate study of International Communism . . . [as decided] in the conversation between Mr. Evans and Mr. Angleton."[55] The point here is that Angleton's interest was international Communism, not the more or less American version that interested a figure such as Senator McCarthy.

In a February 1951 a high-level meeting to discuss the integration of OPC and OSO, "O/PC raised the question of the responsibility for dealing directly with resistance groups.

It was pointed out that it was the O/PC function to run resistance groups although it is recognized that it is the O/SO function to get intelligence from these groups. A task force composed of Mr.

---

* Later prominent in the 'Lee Harvey Oswald' investigations.

Angleton, Mr. [name not declassified], and Mr. Rositzke was named to reach an agreement on this subject and to present any points of controversy to the Assistant Directors for referral, if necessary, to the Deputy Director."[56]

At this point, then, James Angleton was responsible for "the O/SO function to get intelligence from" so-called resistance groups.

It is perhaps relevant to these discussions that the next month Kim Philby reported to the KGB on Anglo-American plans to send agents into the Baltic states and the Ukraine: "In March 1951, Philby gave Burgess, who was heading home to London,* the names and arrival points of three groups of six men who were to be parachuted into the Ukraine . . . the KGB made good use of it."[57] This is another illustration of Burgess's role as "linking agent" as well as demonstrating that even as Burgess and Philby were beginning to realize that it was only a matter of weeks before Donald Maclean was identified as a Soviet agent, they continued to send operational intelligence, obtained from the CIA and British sources, to the KGB.

The Washington in which the Philbys and Angletons lived, circa 1950, unlike London, was, even more then than today, a "company town," the company being the government of the United States. Social life, as in most company towns, consisted of hierarchical groupings of employees within and between departments, including those who worked with, rather than literally for, the government. At the top, there were the cabinet officers, senators, ambassadors, and the grand commentators, the Alsops, for example. At the point three levels below, where much of the work was done, the Angletons socialized with other CIA, State Department, and FBI couples, and with the occasional reporter, such as Ben Bradlee of the *Washington Post*. James Angleton brought some of his colleagues home to their small Alexandria, Virginia, house, sometimes for dinner, more often for drinks. Those guests included such as Cord Meyer, William Harvey, and Jay Lovestone. The Angleton gatherings were slightly unusual in that milieu, as noted earlier: he maintained connections with poets he had known at Yale and she, increasingly, extended her circle to include artists: women of her own generation and class.

---

* About which more later.

There may also have been contacts with Carmen Angleton's circle of European and American intellectuals. These were different social groups than those in which the semi-bohemian Philbys moved.

The Philbys' house at 4100 Nebraska Avenue, near American University, contained Kim and Aileen Philby, their four children (one a baby), a Scottish nanny, Philby's secretary, who lived in an attic room, and Guy Burgess in a room in the basement.[58] There is nothing in the usual sources about Aileen Philby's mental condition during her Washington years. Perhaps she was in remission, or perhaps her condition was camouflaged by the mist of invisibility covering women in those years.

Burgess seems to have been sent to Washington, as had Philby, in order to prepare him for the next stage in his career, in his case promotion in the Foreign Office. Or, perhaps, he was sent as a last opportunity to demonstrate that he was to have a career in the Foreign Office. He could not have been expected to adjust well to McCarthy-ite, homophobic Washington, or, indeed, to America itself, and did not. Philby told his London and Moscow colleagues that it would be best to have Burgess in his house, rather than let him rent a room somewhere in that still quite provincial city. He may have been right in principle. It did not work out well in practice. Alcoholic, devoutly homosexual, anti-American, quasi-aristocratic British intellectuals were not as familiar in Washington as in London, nor, naturally enough, as well understood. On the other hand, Burgess managed to make something of a life similar to that he had led in London. He soon had aristocratic friends in the Virginia horse country and on Long Island; he became an occasional "roommate" of Alan Maclean, Donald Maclean's younger brother, who was an assistant to Gladwyn Jebb, then British representative to the United Nations in New York. Burgess made new acquaintances in bohemian circles and enjoyed the bathhouses of New York. It was not Mayfair and Soho, but it worked, for a while. And then there were Burgess's visits to New York, which he used to carry messages and documents from the high-security, claustrophobic, Washington environment to New York City, with its many official Soviet personnel and undercover agents.[59]

The United States entered the Korean War shortly after it began on 25 June 1950, pushing the North Korean army back nearly to the

Chinese border. In October 1950, China sent vast numbers of "volunteers" into the conflict, threatening to turn the tables and force the United Nations armies south into the sea. Philby, Maclean, and Burgess were able to communicate information about the actions and plans of the United Nations forces to Moscow, to be relayed, if Stalin chose, to the North Koreans and Chinese. Yuri Modin recalled that when the North invaded the South on 25 June, Burgess and Maclean swung into action. Burgess gave Modin as many documents as he could, annotating them as necessary. Maclean did so as well. The American commander of the United Nations forces, General Douglas MacArthur, asserted that "Philby, as well as Burgess and Maclean had betrayed the plans and the order of battle of the U.S. 8th Army in Korea to the communist intelligence services, and that thirty thousand men had been killed, wounded or captured through that betrayal." Robert Cecil, Maclean's deputy at the time, commented, "He (Maclean) enabled Stalin and Mao to know not only which cards Truman and Attlee held, but how many chips Peking and Moscow would have to push into the center of the table to get London to insist that the West should fold its hands."[60] According to Dean Rusk, later Kennedy's Secretary of State: "It can be assumed that (1) anything we in our government knew about Korea would have been known at the British Embassy and (2) that officers in the Embassy of the rank of [Philby and Burgess] would have known what the British Embassy knew."[61]

More generally, Cave Brown wrote that James McCargar told him that there were two views about Philby's work with US intelligence when the Korean War began: "That Philby's collaboration was confined to preparing for the clandestine war that would develop in the event of general war with Russia—

the establishment of cadres and infrastructure throughout western and central Europe for espionage, sabotage, political warfare, rebellion, similar to that developed by the Churchill government in World War II. But that he was not involved in that other aspect of general war with Russia, military and especially air operations against the Soviet Union, except in the handling of certain grades of the secret signals traffic between the embassy and the London government . . . The second view is that he was not only involved in the planning of the clandestine war but also air operations involving the movement of bombers and atomic munitions to British bases in Britain and the Empire, and particularly to the complex of British air bases in the Cairo-Suez area."[62]

If there is any truth in that second view, Moscow would have had the benefit of Philby's reports from Washington concerning these matters as well as the highly detailed reports from Maclean in Cairo, who was deeply involved in the planning of preparations for atomic warfare against the Soviet Union.

McCargar stated in his oral history of service in the US government that he "considered that Philby and I were friends.

> Philby was a man of great charm. He had a pronounced stammer, which somehow didn't affect one's relations with him. When he started to stammer, you just waited and he eventually found the word and went on. As I said to somebody later, we all came out of the Second World War floating on a sea of alcohol. Drinking was not a sin during the Second World War and these habits stayed on. But Philby was the most extraordinary drinker I've ever come across . . . Many and many a night I saw him very, very drunk. His idea of heaven was a pitcher of martinis that you drank all night."[63]

The Philbys, like the others in their set, frequently hosted parties. One of those, on 19 January 1951, was a dinner party that was to become legendary. Among the more than two dozen guests that unseasonably warm night were James and Cicely Angleton; William Harvey, then responsible for counterintelligence at the CIA, and his wife; Robert Lamphere (the FBI liaison to the CIA and MI-5 and, although he later denied it, a close friend of Kim Philby) and his wife; Robert Mackenzie, the British embassy's regional security officer, with Geraldine Dack, one of Philby's secretaries; and Dr. Wilfrid Mann, MI-6 representative in Washington for atomic energy matters,[64] and Miriam Mann. Gathered in this way at the Philbys' were those responsible for US foreign intelligence collection, for liaison between CIA and the FBI, for liaison between the British and the US intelligence services for, inter alia, the VENONA code-breaking project, and for liaison between the British and the American atomic programs. Accounts of this party tend to focus on an incident involving Burgess and the Harveys. It may have been more significant for the conversations among the various CIA, FBI, British embassy, and MI-6 figures, some of which may have related to atomic energy matters and the Fuchs case, then just coming to a climax. As S. J. Hamrick observed: "In 1948–1949 there were far more serious issues at stake for Britain and more devastating implications in the search for HOMER than were apparent to the FBI. Among those issues was the Attlee government's determination to create an independent nuclear deterrent."[65]

From late 1950 Philby became increasingly preoccupied with what is usually called "the Hunt for Homer": the decoding of secret messages that eventually revealed that Donald Maclean and Klaus Fuchs were Soviet spies. American agencies, as a matter of routine, had recorded coded Soviet radio messages during World War II. The Soviets (as well as other countries) first changed the letters in their messages into sets of numbers, then changed those numbers to other numbers selected from one-time pads of randomized numbers, adding various elaborations to this process. As the Germans had closed in on Moscow early in the war the Russians were unable to print sufficient numbers of one-time pads and some of these were therefore reused. The result was that after the war, experts in Washington and London began to be able to decode parts of some of the messages that had been sent by Soviet agencies in the United States to Moscow during that period. The received narrative is that US Army personnel at Arlington Hall, near Washington, eventually succeeded in decoding parts of messages from someone in the British embassy in Washington. The leaks at first were thought to come from the embassy's code-room staff, then from one or another high-ranking British diplomats, and finally, in part because of a reference to the travels of the source, to Donald Maclean.

As often is the case with such popularized historical accounts, matters were more complicated than that. Among other things, in the larger world of international relations, the British government, at its highest levels, was occupied with atomic bomb development, the Korean War, relations with the United States in general, crucial economic and financial problems, and negotiations about the Schuman Plan, the suggestion of the eponymous French foreign minister to merge French and German coal and steel production. The plan was proposed in May 1950, and in April 1951 culminated in the creation of the European Coal and Steel Community, the forerunner of the European Union. The British ambassador in Washington, Oliver Franks, was fully engaged during these negotiations, relaying British positions to the American State department and vice versa. And there were the usual issues around Berlin. In addition, Prime Minister Attlee had been sufficiently concerned about MacArthur and the situation in Korea to travel to Washington in December 1950 to meet with President Truman for discussions. In a highly controversial event, MacArthur was relieved of his command in April 1951 for planning to expand the war into China, against US governmental policy.

It was in this context that we must place the hunt for Homer. The first information about leakages of British cables from Washington to London had come to light in January 1949. The original cables were sent from Arlington Hall to London that same month.[66] According to S. J. Hamrick, the agent was then identified by a British analyst as the person referred to in the cables under the codename "HOMER". When Kim Philby was in London for his pre-Washington briefings, in September 1949, Maurice Oldfield used the HOMER codename in mentioning the reports he received in Washington. Then, in "August 1950, [a] Mrs. Gray of the Army Security Agency (ASA) recovered two stretches [of text] which read 'work including the personal telegraphic correspondence of Boar [? Churchill] with Captain [Roosevelt]' and 'weeks ago G. was entrusted with deciphering a confidential telegram of Boar's [?] to Captain'.

These recoveries were communicated to the British 11 August 1950, who thereupon set up work-sheets* for further recovery work. The suspicion that 'G.' was the source of material 'G' occurred to people at AFSA immediately upon seeing Mrs. Gray's work, and this suspicion was suggested to the British at the same time."[67] ["G" equals "H" in the Cyrillic alphabet.]

It seems from this that in addition to the Arlington Hall efforts, there were similar efforts by GCHQ in the west of Greater London,

---

* "Work-sheets" may refer to the means for setting up electro-magnetic computing machines.

at a place called Eastcote,[68] which led the American effort by several weeks.

The "TOP SECRET" British message traffic concerning the wartime spy in the Washington embassy intensified during spring 1951. "On 30 March 1951, [redacted ?Meredith Gardner] transmitted to England the suggestion that G. was 'Homer, and GOMER in Russian'. This identification, if true, allowed the placing of G. in New York in June 1944."[69] Philby became an integral member of the hunting party. On 31 March 1951, Geoffrey Patterson, MI-5 representative in Washington, wrote to the Director General of MI-5: "Kim Philby and I have discussed these latest developments with Bob Lamphere [FBI liaison to MI-5 and the CIA] . . . On reading these documents one gets the impression that the source is a diplomat, probably British, who has access to high-level papers and who may attend important policy meetings."[70] Patterson, Robert Mackenzie, and Philby told the Foreign Office and MI-5 that they suspected that Homer was Paul Gore-Booth, while not mentioning this to the FBI. But in mid-April, British suspicion began to shift to Donald Maclean. MI-5's Arthur Martin wrote to Patterson on 18 April 1951: "we are about to investigate MACLEAN's current activities with all the means at our disposal." However, on 5 May we find from London: "Since investigation of MACLEAN's current activities began on 23rd April, 1951, nothing of security significance has come to light."

In late April and early May, GCHQ recovered new information from the Soviet encoded messages. A Foreign Office document of 18 May entitled "Considerations Affecting the Action to be Taken in the Case of D. D. Maclean," stated that "His actions have been under investigation by the Security Service since 20th April, 1951."

> G.C.H.Q. is responsible for the Signals Intelligence source from which the evidence of espionage is derived . . . The Americans have supplied G.C.H.Q. with most of the firm evidence which is so far available from the signals intelligence source. G.C.H.Q. have themselves produced additional evidence, of great significance to the identification, which as yet can only be graded as 'possible' . . . *G.C.H.Q. have withheld their evidence from the Americans.* [Emphasis added.]

GCHQ, using machines descended from those at Bletchley, had made their discovery "some fortnight ago" by the date of this message. The Foreign Office became concerned that the FBI and Arlington Hall might begin to concentrate on Maclean before the Foreign Office was ready to inform the FBI of the Eastcote recovery of information pointing to Maclean (that is, his visits to his wife, Melinda, who at the time of the leaked messages had been staying with her mother in New York City). Patterson wrote to the MI-5 Director General on 8 May that "It is clear that a decision will soon have to be made as to when, and how much, we should tell the Americans of the progress we have made on the case . . . Mackenzie and I hope to meet Sir Roger Makins tomorrow to discuss the matter thoroughly: Philby may also be present." In mid-May MI-5 and the Foreign Office began considering the interrogation of Maclean.

It had taken nearly two years to progress from the break into the VENONA traffic with its references to "Homer" to the identification of "Homer" with Maclean. British cryptanalysts finally decided in May 1951 that "Homer" was indeed Donald Maclean, noting that Maclean's qualifications filled out MI-5's Homer checklist.[71] Philby would have learned of the decision very soon after it was made. On the morning of 9 May 1951, Philby, Sir Roger Makins, Geoffrey Patterson, and Sir Robert Mackenzie met to discuss the Maclean matter. Mackenzie drafted a letter to George Carey-Foster (Head of the Security Department, Foreign Office) about a proposed interrogation of Maclean and, in Philby's absence, sent it off. When Philby returned he was shown a copy. Mackenzie commented, later, in a letter of October 1951, that Philby "was annoyed at my having sent it without consulting him and said that he thought that we should put the arguments both in favour of and against an early interrogation of Mr. Maclean more fully, as he was not entirely convinced that this was the best course . . .

[T]he impression left on my mind at the time was that Mr. Philby was not in favour of early action . . . he still felt that Mr. Gore-Booth was an equally good, if not a better candidate than Mr. Maclean . . . I think [in retrospect] that it is highly significant that Mr. Philby . . . never told us that he knew, as he must almost certainly have done, that Mr. Maclean was at one time a Communist."[72]

And then, probably because he had been ordered back to London by the KGB to warn Maclean of his danger, Guy Burgess got himself into serious trouble during a journey to South Carolina to lecture at the Citadel: collecting traffic tickets, falling asleep on the rostrum, insulting his hosts. The local authorities were satisfied that, through clever interrogation of one of his pick-ups and similar strategies, they had forced Burgess out of the country. Burgess's story seems to have been that he had set up a charade to get himself ordered out of the country so that he could warn Maclean. The stories are not incompatible. In any case, the result was the same: the State Department complained to the British ambassador and Burgess was sent back to London to universal satisfaction, not least his own.

On his arrival in London on 7 May 1951, Burgess contacted Maclean, then head of the American Department in the Foreign Office. Maclean told Burgess that he felt it necessary to defect to the Soviet Union as he did not believe he could withstand interrogation. Burgess worked with his Soviet contacts to arrange Maclean's exfiltration. Not knowing anything about this, of course, on 10 May Patterson wrote to the Director General of MI-5: "Mackenzie, Philby and I have had some difficulty in agreeing on the timing of an announcement to the F.B.I.

> We, of course, realize that it is a decision for London and not for us, but we felt that it was up to us to make a recommendation. Whether it is decided to tell the Bureau before, during or after the interrogation is clearly dependent on a number of important factors and our natural desire to be frank with the Bureau may be overruled . . . While talking over the matter we agreed that a plausible excuse for sudden action by you, without an opportunity of warning the U.S. authorities, would be that you discovered during your investigations that the suspect was planning to leave on a motoring holiday on the Continent and urgent action [without notifying FBI] was necessary in case he attempted to join Pontecorvo."*

On 15 May, in a "Proposed Programme for Exchange of Information with the U.S. on the Case of Donald Maclean," Arthur Martin of

---

* Bruno Pontecorvo, a physicist, had defected to the Soviet Union on 1 September 1950.

MI-5 suggested that Maclean should be interrogated on approximately 8 June 1951.

On 22 May Patterson wrote to Arthur Martin that "The Mac-Arthur affair has been quite extraordinary and tempers have risen very high.

> The F.B.I. are of course almost all Republicans and they have been taking MacArthur's point of view. This means that Kim Philby and myself have come in for a lot of criticism and we have had many battles as MacArthur's discharge was an unpopular move and it was natural to blame the unfortunate British."

And on 25 May Patterson wrote similarly to Carey-Foster that "Washington is, as you know, a complete madhouse

> and now with this MacArthur controversy (in spite of his promises the gallant General shows no indication of 'fading away'), tremendous anti-Truman pressure and a hysterical 'ouster-Acheson' campaign the place is, politically, more astonishing than ever . . . The F.B.I. told me this morning that they were unwilling to approach any of the 'left-wing' or pro-Acheson State Department officials: they were thinking of Hiss no doubt."

Carey-Foster wrote the same day to the head of MI-6, Stewart Menzies: "In order to keep you up-to-date with the proposed action in the MACLEAN case, I am sending you copies of instructions I have today approved for dispatch to Patterson. These will of course be available to Philby."[73]

It was decided in London about 24 May that Hoover was to be informed of the "principal suspect's name by Sir P. Sillitoe on June 12/13 and that the interrogation of Maclean was to take place June 18th or 25th:

> The foregoing programme has been influenced by the fact that Mr. Maclean's wife is due to have a baby on or about the 17th June. Until Mrs. Maclean has gone to a nursing home it would not be possible to interrogate Mr. Maclean since it might be necessary to make a search of his house."

The key information recovered by the British cryptographers at
Eastcote, that of the visits of Maclean to see Melinda in New York,
was finally sent to their American colleagues at Arlington Hall on
28 May 1951.

Burgess and Maclean had left for Moscow on 25 May. A telegram
of 30 May 1951 from Arthur S. Martin (B.2.b.) to S.L.O. Washington (Patterson) read: "1. Donald Duart MACLEAN, present head of
American Department Foreign Office, has failed to return U.K. from
weekend visit to St. MALO . . . Please inform F.B.I." In a second
telegram on 30 May, Martin told Patterson that "(i) M.I.5 should
inform the F.B.I. at once of the disappearance of Mr. Maclean and
Mr. Burgess,

> pointing out that the former had been in Washington at the time
> of the known leakages and adding that they were therefore concen-
> trating their enquires on him. (ii) On the 1st of June they should
> take the action previously planned for the 9th June, viz. inform the
> F.B.I. that Mr. Maclean fitted the known facts about the leakage . . .
> F.B.I. must be told as matter of routine of disappearances . . . You
> may add that their help not required at present into MACLEAN
> investigation but we will keep them fully informed."[74]

And again: "Draft Telegram to S.L.O. Washington to be dispatched
on 2.6.51 . . . Please convey following message Personal from Director General to Mr. HOOVER:

> 'It is my personal view that the disappearance of MACLEAN may
> be no more than coincidence and I would not wish you to think that
> I am yet convinced he is spy we are both looking for. If I receive any
> new information vital to us both I would appreciate opportunity of
> personal meeting with you in WASHINGTON.'"

On 29 May Patterson had stated in a telegram to Dick White. "There
is one point on which I would like your advice.

> I have an appointment to see General Smith, Chief of C.I.A., at 1100
> a.m. on June 12th. This is a courtesy visit . . . He will think it very
> odd if I say nothing about the D.G.'s impending arrival (perhaps
> on the following day [to discuss Maclean's disappearance]). The

C.I.A. representative in London will no doubt learn of the D.G's departure, so I may as well tell the General the same story as you give C.I.A. London. Any suggestions you may have for my meeting with the General will be welcomed by me . . . P.S. Since dictating the above I happened to meet Lamphere of the F.B.I. He had just received the latest addition and he said it confirmed his views on Robert Fisher* [as the spy] . . . *I agreed with Lamphere that Fisher's case certainly looked blacker. So far so good."* [Emphasis added.]

As soon as Burgess and Maclean disappeared from the view of the British government's "watchers," attention turned to Philby.

On 1 June, Arthur Martin "telephoned 'C', reminded him that BURGESS had been staying with Philby in Washington, and suggested that he should make enquiries." The same day Patterson telegraphed London: "(1). I have informed F.B.I. of both persons absence. (2). F.B.I. initial reaction is that both men are taking French leave and will shortly return with chronic hangovers. Lamphere still pursuing Fisher angle . . . We can probably maintain this only casual interest for a few days . . ."[75] Kim Philby himself wrote to "C" on 4 June: "During the last few days, careful reflection on this distressing affair has led me to modify sensibly my reactions to the disappearance of Burgess . . .

> In my telegram, I stated that Burgess was undisciplined and irresponsible to a degree that makes it scarcely conceivable that he could have been involved in any clandestine activity. While it is still most difficult for me to believe that a man of his character could have been employed as a Soviet agent, a few isolated facts about his behaviour in Washington, which I have been piecing together in my memory, suggest that the possibility cannot be excluded. Each fact is perfectly explicable in itself, but Burgess's disappearance with MacLean [sic], and his continued failure to reappear, give then a possibly sinister significance . . . The facts are as follows . . . Burgess had a sun-lamp [for photography?] . . . he possessed a camera . . . Very occasionally, Burgess was in the habit of working at home after office hours . . . Burgess travelled fairly frequently to New York . . . During these visits, he saw Jebb and his staff, and doubtless sought

---

* Robert Fisher was finance specialist in the British embassy.

an outlet for energies normally repressed in the polite atmosphere of Washington . . . Finally, Burgess left behind . . . Stalin's 'Marxism and the National Colonial Question' . . . There is, I am afraid, very little doubt that Burgess had available the essential requirements of an espionage agent . . ."

Patterson wrote to London on 5 June: "F.B.I. continue to be surprisingly calm and full significance of disappearance has not yet sunk in. This may be because they still regard FISHER as most likely candidate."[76] And then on 7 June: "U.S. wireless and news agencies this morning splashed story. They gave both names . . . Alleged gone to Russia." Arthur Martin wrote to Patterson the same day: "Suspicion now thrown on whole circle Burgess's acquaintances who include Philby. 'C' has been informed of this . . . From receipt this telegram you are to show NO (R[epeat]) No telegrams or other papers to Philby or his secretary." The next day, the British embassy in Washington informed the Foreign Office that the "Following item was put out by United Press in Washington this afternoon:

United States officials said today the Central Intelligence Agency and the State Department are highly disturbed over the disappearance of Donald Maclean and Guy Burgess British Foreign Office officials. They said there is not the slightest doubt that both the agencies will make strong representations that the Foreign Office should clean house regardless of whom may be hurt. They said that in view of their records, the two men should not have continued to occupy posts in the British Foreign Office. They pointed out that in the State Department repeated drunkenness, recurrent nervous breakdowns, sexual deviations and other human frailties are considered security hazards, and persons showing any one or more of them are dismissed summarily. The incident, these officials said, has severely shaken the State Department's confidence in the integrity of officials of the Foreign Office. The reaction here was all the more severe because Maclean was in charge of the Foreign Office's United States Section and Burgess had access to Far Eastern information.[77]

At MI-5 Dick White telegraphed to Patterson: "Jones (Eastcote) points out possibility his opposite numbers might enquire when recoveries sent to them on 28th May were first made . . . In circumstances recommend you avoid making definite statement on date we receive recoveries . . . Eastcote's reply to opposite numbers would have to be honest one because of presence of American officer in section concerned."

Arthur Martin went to FBI headquarters in Washington, as if into the lion's den, for interviews with Belmont and Lamphere, writing on 16 June to Robertson: "I was questioned very severely, but not, I suppose, unfairly.

I stuck to May 25th as the date on which we had received the new recovery, but threw in that I had heard about the possibility of such a recovery being made a week or two earlier when I had been paying a routine call at G.C.H.Q. I do not think they have the slightest suspicion that Eastcote had withheld it from them, but I have covered the point would they find out later . . . The danger spots which I had expected were negotiated without much difficulty."

On 25 June, Patterson wrote to Martin from Washington that "we must maintain a steady flow of reports [to the FBI], however unimportant they may be,

in order to satisfy the F.B.I. that we are honouring the D.G.'s promise of full and frank collaboration. Therefore, politically, volume rather than substance . . . really matters . . . As long as we can flood them with other, even inconsequential, material we should be able to get away with interim replies on the more delicate matters—such as the Philby business."[78]

Why did the British government delay for a month telling the Americans that they had identified Maclean as the Soviet agent code-named "Homer"? The answer to this goes beyond relations between Anglo-American secret intelligence agencies and encompasses two other issues: Anglo-American economic relations and atomic energy. Britain was in dire straits economically at this point, and the government was particularly apprehensive about the cessation of Marshall Plan funding scheduled for July 1952, which was connected as well with delicate negotiations with Egypt and other former sections of the empire holding large amounts of sterling debt. It was feared that a major scandal would weaken Britain's hand in these negotiations. More specifically, "the negotiations for a comprehensive agreement on cooperation in [atomic energy matters] were well advanced at the time when the Fuchs case broke and [had] led to a suspension of the talks on the American side."[79] These talks were scheduled to resume in the first half of 1951. The UK was very concerned to return to cooperation, as it was believed that possession of an atomic weapon was essential and without American cooperation it would be excessively costly.[80] Donald Maclean had been a central actor in atomic energy matters. It was feared that Maclean's espionage and defection, following that of Fuchs, would convince many in Washington that Britain was not a good partner for the development of atomic weaponry. Which, as a matter of fact, is what happened.[81]

CIA Director General Bedell Smith ordered everyone on his staff who had met Burgess to write a report about him. An article in the CIA's house organ in 2011 stated that "Reflecting on the defection of Burgess in 1951, Angleton wrote a detailed memo to the DD/P [Deputy Director for Plans] on 7 June in which he described the relationship of Burgess to Philby and to himself.

> Angleton said he knew Burgess well, having encountered him regularly in many social engagements with Philby. He described Burgess as a 'close and old friend' of Philby. He noted that Burgess was present 'at almost every social function which the Philby's [sic] gave for CIA personnel.' He wrote that throughout, Burgess had 'always evidenced considerable knowledge regarding the SIS and Philby's intelligence activity.' Angleton ended the memo by writing, 'If Subject [Burgess] has defected to the Soviets he will be capable of supplying them with a great number of secrets which involve CIA/SIS accords.'"[82]

This indicates, inter alia, that the well-known January 1951 dinner party at the Philby residence was just one of many involving the same or similar groups. The exclusive focus on it in the stories about Burgess and Maclean emanating from Anglo-American secret intelligence sources is a customary way of minimizing embarrassing facts such as this.

William Harvey wrote a five-page memorandum "which traced

Philby's recent career and contacts, and asserted that Philby had to be a Soviet agent. Smith sent the Harvey material to 'C,' Stewart Menzies, in London, accompanied by a typically uncluttered cover letter: 'Fire Philby or we break off the intelligence relationship.'"[83] The Harvey memorandum has been featured, but never published, in the literature.*

Philby was "'withdrawn' from the British Embassy on June 3 [1951],"[84] but he stayed in Washington on leave for some weeks until MI-6 recalled him "for consultations." The consultations turned out to be with MI-5, which decided that Dick White [D.B.] would interview Philby "probably on Tuesday, 12.6.51. A brief for this purpose is being prepared by B.2.b [Arthur Martin]. D.B. is also endeavoring to obtain from SIS information regarding Philby's prospective address and telephone number on arrival in the U.K., in order that a telephone check may be imposed."[85] Philby wrote in his memoir that the day he left Washington: "Angleton rang me and arranged for us to meet in a bar before I went to the airport.

> He began by asking me how long I was going to be away and I said about a week. We chatted on for a bit and then he said: 'Can you do me a favour in London?' I said I would and he handed me an envelope addressed to the head of counter-intelligence in London [Oldfield? White?]. He said he had missed the bag and wanted London to get the message as soon as possible . . . Now that's an unlikely act for a man who was already supposed to be suspicious of me . . . Unless, of course, the envelope contained a blank sheet of paper and Angleton wanted to see what I would do with it."[86]

A 25 June letter from Air Chief Marshal Sir William Elliot to Sillitoe includes this comment about "The other matter about which I was to enquire [of Bedell Smith] concerned the message which Angleton was to give Philby from Bedell Smith

on the evening of the day on which the news about MacLean [sic] and Burgess broke. When I saw Bedell Smith last week he had not

---

* It would be interesting to learn how Harvey established the difference between the "contacts and activities" of a British—or American—foreign intelligence officer and a Soviet agent.

seen Angleton since he had given him his instructions. He accordingly sent for Angleton whilst I was talking to him in his office, but the man was on leave."[87]

This somewhat clarifies the mysterious letter. It was from Bedell Smith, not Angleton. Perhaps it was one of those *Arabian Nights* letters, requesting that the recipient behead the bearer.

Rather late in the day, it would seem, on 26 June 1951 the Federal Bureau of Investigation reported to AFSA that Homer (GOMER), GOMMER, and 'G' were believed to be identical with Donald Duart MacLean [sic]."[88] In a letter of 11 August 1951 from Strang in the Foreign Office to Steel in Washington, the former stated that Hoover had not wanted Bedell Smith told about the Eastcote material. The CIA ranked high on Hoover's enemies list. There is this 14 September 1951 message in the files, apparently from "C" to Brigadier John Tiltman, Chief Cryptographer for the Government Code and Cypher School: "When the matter of Burgess's disappearance became public news, there was, as you are doubtless aware, a great feeling of uneasiness regarding British security in U.S. official circles.

> Because of the close association of Philby with Burgess, C.I.A. was particularly unhappy, and I had no alternative but to withdraw him, and he subsequently resigned. Even so, C.I.A. continued making wild suggestions as to the success of the Russian Intelligence in its penetration efforts, and clearly General Bedell Smith was himself affected . . . The situation could have been greatly improved had the General been aware of the revelations in the 'Sock' material [?] and the role which Kim Philby himself played during the very delicate investigations in U.S.A. F.B.I. had, of course, complete access to the information, but Hoover refused to pass on the evidence to Bedell Smith, which was the more embarrassing in that the latter is Chairman of U.S.C.I.B."*

Bedell Smith was finally told about "the true nature of the original evidence against Maclean" by Menzies himself during a visit to London shortly before 2 October 1951. On 17 October, C. "Kit" Steel in the British embassy in Washington wrote to Patrick Reilly at

---

* United States Communications Intelligence Board.

the Foreign Office that "Bedell's principal worry is concerned with how much Burgess may have learned casually from Philby and in his house about his, Bedell's, organization.

> He was very anxious to be reassured that we had not had any previous cause for suspicion of Burgess as we had of Donald Maclean and that we had let him know about Burgess as soon as our suspicions were aroused. He is naturally not very happy about what B. may have picked up but appeared much more interested in a vindication of our own bona fides toward himself. I think this shows how right we were to come clean with him and that we should go on doing so."[89]

When Philby reached London, "The first session of questioning was done by Dick White [of MI-5, as laid out in Arthur Martin's program], . . . [who] behaved in a friendly way, trying not to make Philby anxious, and asked for his help in working out 'this horrible business with Maclean and Burgess', since everyone knew of his long-standing friendship with the latter."[90] Two more interrogations by White followed. Philby was asked to write an account of his responses. At which point, Philby, knowing that he had no choice, resigned from SIS. A pension was refused, as Philby had not served the statutory number of years.* As a substitute for the pension a one-time payment of £2000 spread over three years was provided. All this was to make it clear to MI-5 that MI-6 was taking its responsibilities seriously, in spite of its doubts about Philby's guilt. We read in a letter of 7 November 1951 to Dick White: "I saw Nicholas Elliott [of MI-6] on Saturday. He told me that the Philbys had taken a house near Rickmansworth and that Malcolm Muggeridge is trying to get the 'Daily Telegraph' to give Philby a temporary job as a correspondent abroad, probably in India . . ."[91] Muggeridge had been one of the leaders of the press pack baying after Burgess and Maclean.

On 27 November Carey-Foster wrote to White urging that action against Philby should be taken very soon as he might hear of the investigation and defect, which should be prevented "since by implication [Philby] is responsible in large measure for the penetration of

---

* As later with Peter Wright, the "spycatcher."

the Foreign Office."[92] On 30 November 1951 Carey-Foster sent the
Foreign Office Permanent Under Secretary White's summary of the
evidence that Philby had tipped off Maclean (including some interesting alignment of dates and stories from Soviet defector Walter
Krivitsky and Volkov).[93] On 6 December D. P. Reilly wrote that
Philby "is expecting to go to India soon after Christmas as a correspondent for the 'Daily Telegraph'."[94] On 7 December Carey-Foster
informed White that a decision had been made to interrogate Philby
as soon as possible and to cancel his passport if necessary to prevent
defection.[95]

Sir Helenus Milmo, QC, was brought in to begin the interrogation.
It was very much a family affair. Milmo had attended Trinity College, Cambridge, as had Philby, Burgess, and Maclean, and during
the war had served in MI-5, working with Philby on Iberian matters
and later as an interrogator of prisoners of war (sometimes with
Anthony Blunt), another role in which, it seems, Philby had known
him.* Philby was interviewed by Milmo at Leconfield House, MI-5
headquarters, on 12 December 1951.[96] When Philby took out his pipe
as Milmo began his interrogation, Milmo attempted to establish
dominance: "This is a legally official investigation. Please do not
smoke." (Sometimes recorded as "You will not smoke.") Of course,
for an experienced secret intelligence officer like Philby, that established *his* dominance. For four hours Milmo shouted and banged
the table with his fist while Philby responded politely, stuttering
when necessary.

> At the outset he was told that certain statements he had made ear-
> lier were unacceptable and he was invited to correct any conscious
> falsehoods he had then told. Philby denied that any of his earlier
> statements were consciously false and, showing complete self pos-
> session, maintained this attitude throughout four hours of hostile
> questioning.[97]

Philby did not confess. The security professionals listening in were
not impressed with Milmo. By the 12th, sentiment had reversed
and it was thought the decision would "almost certainly be not to

---

* Philby's last interrogation, in Beirut, was also by a longtime acquaintance,
Nicholas Elliott, also Trinity.

prosecute."[98] Philby was strongly supported by MI-6 in the person of its director, "C": "In the meeting on 14 December, 'C' said that he thought Philby was innocent of anything other than concealing his Communist past and had not compromised any secrets."[99] "C" said Bedell Smith agreed.[100] "C" wrote to Strang, a month later, on 17 January 1952, objecting that the "case for the prosecution" against Philby had been made by Milmo but no case for the defense had been presented.[101] Nonetheless, Philby was asked to surrender his passport.

Then came William Skardon, who interrogated Philby at Philby's house five or six times until January 1952. (Philby was also interrogated once by "senior officers" of MI-6.)[102] Skardon was polite, did not shout, did not bang his fist on the table, but also did not succeed in obtaining a confession. Perhaps the fame within the secret intelligence community of his "friendly" method that was said to have led Klaus Fuchs to confess had preceded him. Philby's passport was returned. In his 1977 lecture to members of the KGB, Philby said: "in the summer of 1951, Maclean and Burgess arrived in the [Soviet Union], leaving me in serious trouble . . .

> What to do? . . . I enjoyed three great advantages . . . Many senior officers of SIS—from the Chief downwards—would be greatly embarrassed if it were proved that I was working for the Soviet Union. They would certainly want to give me the benefit of any doubt . . . Second, I knew the SIS and MI-5 archives in great detail. I knew the sort of evidence they could bring against me . . . Third, I knew British security procedures inside out . . . I knew that much of the information in the possession of the security authorities cannot be made the basis of a charge in the courts, as it either cannot be corroborated or comes from sources too delicate to be revealed . . . It was a long battle of nerve and wits, lasting—on and off—for five years . . . Then . . . I was informed by SIS that they had finally decided in my favour—they actually offered me a job as SIS agent in the Middle East operating under journalistic cover."[103]

But that was not until 1956. In early 1952 Philby sought "an appointment" in Egypt, but was unsuccessful.[104] This was one of many attempts he made to find employment as a journalist in this period.

In a 4 March 1952 letter from Dick White MI-5 to Carey-Foster, at the Foreign Office,[105] White wrote: "As you know, I visited Washington in January and February with the primary purpose of informing the two U.S. intelligence authorities, the F.B.I. and C.I.A., of the results of our enquiries to date in the [Philby] case.

    F.B.I. Before my arrival in Washington, the Director General had sent Mr. Hoover a full case history and the F.B.I. case officers had already studied this and briefed Mr. Hoover before my first interview with him. Mr. Hoover was therefore able to deliver the official F.B.I. verdict on the case. His actual words were: 'For my part, I conclude that [Philby] is as guilty as hell, but I don't see how you are ever going to prove it.' In a subsequent discussion of the matter he did not ask what restrictions could now be put upon [Philby], nor did he express alarm at the damage which might have been caused by [Philby] to F.B.I. security. Indeed, on this point, Mr. Ladd—Mr. Hoover's Head of Intelligence—had already hinted to me that it was not thought likely that [Philby] had spied for the Russians while in the U.S.A. In this hint of Ladd's, and in Mr. Hoover's obvious lack of curiosity to hear more about the [Philby] case, I discerned a fear that it would do the F.B.I. no good to have to admit that they had had a Russian spy going in and out of the Bureau and enjoying excellent relations with many of its senior men [such as Ladd].

    C.I.A. For the purpose of reporting to General Bedell-Smith I represented both my own D.G. and 'C' and I was accompanied to my first interview with the General by Bruce Lockhart, 'C's' representative in Washington . . . Much more plainly than Mr. Hoover, General Bedell-Smith took the line that this was essentially a British matter, that he did not wish to pry into the detail of it and that, despite the possible damage his organisation might have suffered therefrom, he was anxious that it should not affect the close working relations between his organisation and 'C's'. He showed himself very appreciative of our frankness in informing him of the interim verdict we had reached and argued that such frankness gave him increased rather than less confidence in the British alliance. He also admitted ruefully that what had happened to us today might, after all, happen to him tomorrow. Unlike Mr. Hoover, he has a mind which remembers and connects related facts on the U.S. side—for example, the Alger HISS case and the wide penetration of

U. S. Government Department by the Silvermaster Group. He can therefore see our disasters in due proportion to the American ones.

To sum up U.S. reactions: I think we were certainly wise to be frank with both the F.B.I. and C.I.A. I do not think that either Mr. Hoover or General Bedell Smith harbours bitter reflections against us and I think that the former has probably a personal interest in regarding the case as a purely British one and in not advertising it to a wider public in America. In any case, both realise that [Philby's] guilt is not proven though I think that, on the facts available, both consider him guilty."

It is improbable that General Bedell Smith did not brief his senior staff, including William Harvey and James Angleton, on his conversation with Dick White. What lessons were available to them from the hunt for "Homer" and the identification, however provisional, of Philby as a Soviet agent? One, moral, as it were, in the language of the times, is that anyone can be an enemy agent. From this John le Carré would spin his plots. The other lessons were more mundane, simply methodological: casting the net as wide as possible (including both clerks and first secretaries), going as far back into the past as possible (back beyond the beginnings of careers to school days), exploring each link, each question to the end. "There must be a wide range of data because there are so many pertinent questions always being asked about people.

> What sort of man is he? What are his political and economic views? What are all his names and when was he born? Can he speak English? Who are his intimates? What are his weaknesses? How long is he likely to hold his present standing? Where was he in 1937? etc."[106]

That, again, is from Sherman Kent, but it could just have well come from James Angleton, or from Kim Philby's Ryder Street tutorials.

In his end-of-career oral history, James McCargar recalled about Philby: "As I say, he was my colleague and I thought he was a friend.

> In fact, when I was in the Paris Embassy, after I left OPC, I didn't know what had gone on here in Washington, but I suspected that the Americans had forced Philby out of the British service, MI-6. That this was American pressure. I bumped into Angleton one day

in the lobby of the Crillon Hotel in Paris. I said, 'Jim, my wife and I have access to a flat in Lowndes Square in London. We frequently go there on weekends, when it's possible. I plan the next time I'm in London to invite Philby for a drink, unless you tell me that this would not be a prudent nor a wise thing to do.' 'On the contrary,' said Angleton, 'I think it would definitely be the thing to do, because I still believe that someday Philby is going to be head of the British Service.' So the next time I was in London I got in touch with Philby. I can't remember how, but I did. He was living down in the country. He came, looking somewhat seedy but generally well. In conversation over drinks, I said that if there was anything I could do to help him, I'd be delighted. He said, 'No. Everything is all right.' He was going to Spain, sponsored by The Times, to write a history of the Spanish Civil War, which he had covered for The Times from the Franco side. I said, 'Good. Let me know.'"[107]

McCargar's meeting with Angleton in Paris seems to have been very late in 1951 or early in 1952. McCargar's subsequent meeting with Philby seems to have taken place in 1952 or 1953. It would be surprising if Angleton had not asked McCargar for a report on his meeting with Philby.

After Philby had departed for London and his various unsuccessful interrogations, the CIA's other business went along as usual, as described in the DCI Bedell Smith's "log" of activities in September 1951:

- In order to strengthen its *control* of the Indonesian Intelligence Service, O.S.S. [sic] proposes to invite for conversations and orientation in Washington [the Governor of the Indonesian Ministry of Interior][108]
- The balloon launchings recently conducted from a site near Munich by the CIA-controlled Crusade for Freedom in conjunction with seven other organizations carried 10,000,000 [sic] leaflets into Czechoslovakia and 700,000 into Poland. *The CIA-controlled Radio Free Europe* gave close support to the operation in its broadcasts.[109] [Emphasis added.]

The Director's log is quite explicit about the then highly secret

CIA role in these front organizations. In addition to Radio Free Europe, there are similar references to: The German "League of Freedom Loving Lawyers, *a CIA-sponsored organization* . . . the *CIA-controlled* Committee for a Free Asia . . . the *CIA-controlled* International Federation of World Veterans' Organizations . . ."[110] and "the *CIA-controlled* Far East Broadcasting Company." [Emphases added.]

In October 1951 the Director was informed that "Twenty-one Albanian agents . . . are being flown from CIA's covert training school in Germany to Athens. It is expected they will be infiltrated into Albania immediately following their arrival in Greece. Twenty-six additional Albanian recruits will be sent to Germany for training on the return flight."[111] This last did not go well. On 11 October Radio Tirana announced the trial of fourteen captured spies.[112] An Associated Press dispatch of 23 October reported their conviction,[113] and Radio Tirana on 24 October announced "the liquidation of 13 U.S. espionage agents." The CIA concluded that "This announcement, coupled with testimony at the Tirana spy trials, indicates that the Communists may know of the covert training school for Albanian and Bulgarian agents at the Hambuchen Estate near Munich.

> It also raises the possibility that Communist agents have penetrated the National Committee for a Free Albania as well as the possibility that a 2-man team which parachuted into Albania last May is under Albanian control."[114]

Similar "covert operations designed to compromise Soviet-backed governments also took place throughout Eastern Europe and Asia during Truman's second term in office . . .

> The campaigns most frequently discussed in the literature are those that took place in Poland, the Ukraine and the three Baltic states: Latvia, Lithuania and Estonia. During these years, however, OPC was also active in the Philippines, Hungary, Romania, Czechoslovakia, East Germany, Korea, Tibet and China. Yet, none of these operations were successful and countless men and women, loyal to the western cause, lost their lives."[115]

Some think that Kim Philby was still in the game in 1954. According to Morris Riley, during one of the "Roll-Back" operations, "The NTS* men, and men belonging to Bandera, formed a large team of infiltrators in 1954 who landed in an isolated region in the Carpathian mountains (en route to Ukraine) . . .

> they were ambushed by border police, and the entire unit wiped out . . . information about the operation had been passed from Philby, then (officially) out of SIS, to the Soviets. Philby had gained his information from George Blake (then an RIS agent) who was then working at the Foreign Office in London."[116]

And again, "In November 1950 the young Office of Policy Coordination (OPC) . . . took over from the British as WiN's principal supporter . . . within two years, they had invested several million dollars . . . on 27 December 1952, WiN came to an explosive end . . . 'Foreign spy centers discovered!' screamed Soviet bloc headlines."[117] CIA propaganda activities were more successful than these "Roll-Back" projects, at least operationally. The mid-September "editions of LIFE and TIME publicized a map of slave labor camps in the USSR prepared by the CIA-supported Free Trade Union Committee of the American Federation of Labor."[118] While "Between 28 and 31 October 105,000 copies of 'Animal Farm' were distributed through Austria as an insertion in a CIA-subsidized newspaper. A sellout at the news-stands necessitated an extra run of 15,000 copies."[119]

In May 1952 things began to look up for Philby. He was in Madrid (once more) when he received "a letter from a friend in London who had worked with him during the war [which probably meant he was, or had been, in MI-6]. He was offering Philby a job in London in an export-import company. This meant a solid salary, and Kim readily accepted."[120] However, after he had been there for eighteen months the firm went bankrupt. In any case, Philby had not liked the work, but it had meant a good income for the time. Then other friends came to his aid. There are two stories about this. One, from Borovik, that is, from Philby, is that in 1954 Blunt (who had stayed in touch with him), gave him £5,000 that had been passed to him from the KGB.[121] The other is an odd story in Knightley's second book

---

* Narodno-Trudovoi Soyu, anti-communist Russian exile group.

about Philby involving an abortive writing project for the publisher Andre Deutsch in the summer of 1955, which Knightley appears to believe meant that Deutsch was in effect laundering money from Tomás Harris for Philby. Harris and Philby were old secret intelligence friends and Harris, a retired art dealer living in Majorca, had recently been visited by Philby. He may have decided to give Philby the £600 (about $20,000 in 2018) in question, but why do it in this way? Why not just give him a check? It was about this time that Philby "had heard from the Russian intelligence service.

'I received, through the most ingenious of routes, a message from my Soviet friends, conjuring me to be of good cheer and presaging an early resumption of relations. It changed drastically the whole complexion of the case. I was no longer alone.'"[122]

It may be that the source of the funds was not Harris at all, but, again, Moscow Center.

FOREIGN LIAISONS

JAMES ANGLETON

James Angleton's career from 1948 to 1954 was that of a foreign intelligence (as opposed to counterintelligence) officer. In addition to his more general foreign intelligence collection responsibilities he controlled the Israeli "account"; he had a special relationship with the Italian intelligence services and the developing West German foreign intelligence service; and had what was in effect his own foreign intelligence organization, based in large part on his relationship with Jay Lovestone.[1] Lovestone, a one-time head of the American Communist Party, had built anti-communist networks for the American Federation of Labor, with well-established contacts and funding conduits to anti-communist political parties and trade unions in Europe and elsewhere. Lovestone's operations were aligned with the CIA's general strategy of providing resources to both center-left and center-right parties throughout Europe, funding both Socialists and Christian Democrats. Lovestone collected intelligence for Angleton from agents in Europe, Asia, and Africa.[2]

In mid-1949, Angleton, as chief of Foreign Intelligence Operations, recruited Louise Page Morris, sister of "Eddy" Page of the US Department of State, as another of his personal intelligence agents.[3] According to Matthew James Connelly, Morris had a "long-running affair with . . . Henry Cabot Lodge" and when Lodge was US representative to the United Nations worked with the Algerian representatives there during their struggle for independence from France.[4] She was also the companion of Lovestone. In 1954 Angleton sent Morris to Cairo, Karachi, Bombay, Rangoon, Bangkok, Djakarta, and Taipei, and, no doubt, to many other places through the years. She went to Iraq for Angleton in 1959, where it would have been difficult for her to avoid meeting Kim Philby.[5]

Angleton's connections with the Israeli intelligence establishment began in Italy during World War II, when he had established strong personal relations with some of the leaders of the fledgling Israeli secret intelligence services. Mossad, "the Institute for Intelligence and Special Tasks," created in 1951, was modeled after the CIA and was particularly concerned to maintain close liaison relations with that agency. David Ben-Gurion and his intelligence adviser, Reuven Shiloah, traveled to Washington in May 1951, and in June Shiloah returned to Washington to formalize liaison arrangements in meetings with Bedell Smith, Allen Dulles, and James Angleton.[6] The secret intelligence agencies of the two countries agreed not to spy on one another and to exchange information, an alliance analogous to that between the United States and the United Kingdom. A reason Angleton and his supervisors decided that it was in the American interest to build up the Israeli intelligence services was their possible utility in the Cold War. The Israelis convinced Angleton that the Jewish refugees from the East were a unique resource for gathering intelligence in the Soviet Union. Angleton came to see Tel Aviv as the eyepiece, as it were, of a telescope, the business end of which was focused on Moscow. As he controlled the relationship with the Israeli intelligence services, he controlled their intelligence product and that gave him enormous power in the Agency—not because of Tel Aviv, but because of Moscow.[7]

One product of this arrangement was the spectacular *coup de théâtre* concerning Nikita Khrushchev's "secret speech." Khrushchev denounced Stalin's crimes to the Twentieth Congress of the Communist Party at the end of February 1956. There are many stories about how a copy of the speech was obtained by the CIA. The most circumstantial account turns on Angleton's special relationship with Israeli secret intelligence. According to this story, the Polish Communist Party First Secretary, Eduard Ochab, had his copy of the speech translated into Polish and sent to the leaders of the local Polish Communist Party units. In early April, someone at this level gave a copy of the speech to an Israeli intelligence officer in Warsaw, who took it to Tel Aviv. The then Prime Minister of Israel, David Ben-Gurion, sent it on to Angleton.[8]

A 2 June 1956 "circular telegram from the Department of State to certain diplomatic missions,"[9] gave the official view of the US government at that time: "Department recently obtained from

confidential source copy of document which purports to be version
of Khrushchev's secret Feb 25 speech as prepared for confidential
info and guidance of leadership of a communist party outside
USSR. Study furnishes grounds for confidence in its authenticity but
Department does not propose to vouch for it." Frank Wisner had
made the following comments in transmitting a revised translation
to the State Department: "The speech as here presented adds a
great deal to our knowledge of the implications of the degradation
of STALIN. It makes clear that the present Soviet leaders lived in
mortal terror for their own lives in the last days of STALIN's rule."[10]
Angleton's role in obtaining the speech added to his standing in the
Agency, and particularly with Allen Dulles. Israel's role in providing
the speech through Angleton to the CIA probably strengthened
the links between Israeli secret intelligence and the CIA, just a few
months before the Suez Crisis.

Angleton, of all senior Central Intelligence Agency officials, was
the closest to America's domestic intelligence organization, the
Federal Bureau of Investigation. He was, from the point of view
of the FBI, their agent within the CIA. A 10 June 1953 memorandum from a certain F. P. Keay of the FBI to A. W. Belmont, one
of Hoover's senior deputies, informed the latter that "James Angleton, Central Intelligence Agency (CIA) official, is in charge of the
Special Projects unit located in the Foreign Intelligence division of
CIA . . .

> [H]e more or less falls in category of Confidential Informant . . . In
> general, he is responsible only to the Director of CIA . . . In addition
> to information regarding security matters . . . he frequently clarifies
> matters which the CIA sometimes camouflages with some of its
> cloak and dagger techniques."

The following year, Keay cautioned Belmont in a 17 May 1954
memorandum stating that Angleton "does not want his liaison
arrangement with the Bureau to become a subject of common
knowledge within CIA."

Such was James Angleton's position within the CIA (and the FBI)
just before September 1954, when Allen Dulles decided to make

Angleton chief of an enlarged counterintelligence staff* "to prevent or detect and eliminate penetration of CIA," or, rather, *another* penetration of CIA, as what else was Philby's time in Washington to be called? According to the official history of Counterintelligence by the Office of National Intelligence, Angleton had "previously served as the DCI's personal advisor on CI problems, sometimes to the exclusion of the more official Staff C, and played a leading part in negotiating this restructuring [of the counterintelligence staff].

> Angleton's aim was to prevent the CI mission of the Clandestine services from becoming subordinate to other divisions . . . [in addition] Dulles decided that the Israeli account was too important to be entrusted to the pro-Arab specialists in the Near East Division. His solution was to give it to the Counterintelligence Staff. One rationale for this move was that Angleton had a wide range of contacts with Israeli leaders, many of whom he had met in Italy after the war."

This may have been the argument Angleton himself had used to persuade Dulles to make this unusual decision. Angleton gave Joseph Trento another explanation: "You know how I got to be in charge of counterintelligence? I agreed not to polygraph or require detailed checks on Allen Dulles and 60 of his closest friends . . . They were afraid that their own business dealings with Hitler's pals would come out. They were too arrogant to believe that the Russians would discover it all."[11] The Office of National Intelligence's account continues that "Another responsibility Dulles gave Angleton was handling all liaison with allied intelligence services . . .

> He became the central figure through whom the director would learn of important secrets volunteered by allied intelligence services and also allowed him to control what information CIA passed to these services."[12]

In other words, about the time he became Director of Central Intelligence, Dulles created a unique position of power within the Agency for James Angleton. Angleton's responsibilities, and his actions,

---

* Made official 20 December 1954.

were those "as assigned" by Allen Dulles, as they would be by his successors, especially Richard Helms, until William Colby became Director of Central Intelligence nearly twenty years later.

Matthew M. Aid, a somewhat controversial national security historian, wrote that the CIA's Soviet Russia (SR) division and MI-6 attempted to infiltrate agents into the Soviet Union during the late 1940s and early 1950s in an operation called Redsox, or Red Sox. The parallel effort to recruit Soviet officials who were outside the Soviet Union was called Red Cap (or Redcap). A joint CIA/MI-6 anti-Soviet operation in the late 1940s would likely have involved Frank Wisner of OPC and Kim Philby of MI-6's Section IX. According to Aid there were operations in Latvia, Lithuania, Estonia, Belorussia, the Ukraine, and Russia itself. As with the Albanian operation, the "Redsox" operations were failures. Again, according to Aid, beginning in September 1949: "more than 85 agents, all of them Russian nationals . . . were infiltrated into the Soviet Union by the CIA . . . The number of agents infiltrated into the USSR by Britain's MI-6 is not known . . . but it is believed to be roughly comparable to the CIA's numbers, if not slightly higher." All, or nearly all, of these agents "disappeared." "It was not until 1952 . . . that CIA and MI-6 counterintelligence officers began to suspect that their agents reporting from behind the Iron Curtain had been 'doubled.'"[13] The effort of Soviet intelligence in this endeavor was no doubt facilitated in the early days of the operations, and perhaps later, by Kim Philby.

The counter-attack in this war of spy vs. spy came in Germany. Paul Maddrell found that early in 1955 the German Democratic Republic's secret intelligence organization, the Stasi, arrested people connected with Radio in the American Sector (of Berlin). With the assistance of Philby and Blake, five of MI-6's networks were rolled up. "On 31 March 1955 the Security Commission of the SED Politburo approved the programme of arrests of British agents, which was thereupon carried out very swiftly . . . In a public statement on 12 April the Council of Ministers announced the arrest of '521 agents of secret services . . .'"[14] It was said by Robin Winks that by this point, at the latest, clandestine services chief Frank Wisner and James Angleton had dual responsibility for Red Sox/Red Cap.[15] Again according to William Corson: "In the several months between Poznan [28–30 June 1956] and Gomulka's election [20 October], the

CIA pushed ahead with plans for uprisings in Hungary, Czechoslovakia, and Rumania, in that order.

> Red Sox/Red Cap groups, like latter-day Trojan Horse forces, were inserted into those nations' capitals and plans were made final for the 'freedom fighters' to throw off the evil yoke of communism . . . On October 23, just two days after Khrushchev's order to the Red Army to stand down [in Poland], the Hungarian revolt against the Soviet-dominated regime began. Unlike Gomulka's threat to pit Polish communists against Soviet communists, the Hungarian revolutionaries, aided and abetted by the Red Sox/Red Cap forces, declared their enemy to be not simply the Russians occupying their country but communism itself."[16]

Angleton, implicitly confirming the accounts of Winks and Corson, told Loch Johnson that "he had helped the Operations Directorate with its propaganda operations . . .

> most significantly, its secret supply of weaponry to pro-democracy rebels in Budapest to encourage their uprising against Communist rule in Hungary. This support helped fuel the 1956 revolt in Budapest, which led to the massacre of mainly young Hungarians—as many as 15,000—in the streets of Budapest, mowed down by Soviet tank fire."[17]

Stephen Ambrose wrote that "The CIA sent RED SOX/RED CAP groups in Budapest into action to join the Freedom Fighters and to help organize them . . . Radio Free Europe, and the RED SOX/RED CAP groups, encouraged the rebels." On 10 November 1956 the FBI tapped a conversation between Louise Morris and Jay Lovestone. Morris said, "I know the whole thing . . .

> Do you remember when I said to you that it was criminal to incite a revolution and a rebellion, and not to follow it through? Well, the Wisner crowd incited it . . . And the Horthy crowd has been in it . . . That Radio Free Europe is the crowd that's behind it."[18]

The "Horthy crowd" being the party of pre-war Hungarian fascism. The bloody fiasco in Budapest brought to an end the Anglo-American efforts to "roll-back" Soviet power from eastern Europe by means of clandestine warfare. Frank Wisner had a breakdown from which he never fully recovered. James Angleton turned his attention increasingly to the discipline into which he had been initiated by Kim Philby: counterintelligence.

PHILBY IN BEIRUT

Philby's career in MI-6 had been ruined by the KGB's operation to save Donald Maclean. And yet, officially, Philby was merely *suspected* of having been a Soviet agent. There was no proof, not even an ambiguous World War II decrypt. After the "trial," in which Milmo's loud argument for the prosecution and Skardon's "exquisite" interrogations, had both failed, there appears to have been, in general, an agreement among those in MI-5, Special Branch, and the Foreign Office that Philby had been a Soviet agent. Philby's former colleagues in his own agency, SIS, remained unconvinced. An "SIS officer would argue that an operation could take a working lifetime to bring to fruition, years and years spent building up the opposition's confidence to make possible the final 'sting'.

> If an officer conducting such an operation were, at some stage before the denouement, to have his actions examined by an outsider, then however meticulous the examination, it would be difficult not to conclude that he was a traitor. His only protection at this time is the loyalty and trust of his colleagues."[19]

Timothy Milne recalled, referring to the period after the interrogations had come to an end and Philby was taking odd jobs here and there, that many people in MI-6 believed in Philby's innocence.[20]

Given that, Milne, who was in a way Philby's successor in MI-6, continued to socialize with him in the winter of 1952/1953, sharing lobster paella dinners and introducing him to an (unnamed) friend of theirs, with whom he conducted an affair for the next few years.[21] It is likely that Milne would have been emphatically discouraged from these social intimacies if Philby were under suspicion by MI-6 higher management during this period. Indeed, "C" himself wrote to Patrick Dean of the Foreign Office on 23 September 1955: "There are . . . certain facts not open to doubt, which in my opinion reduce very considerably the suspicion that [Philby] was a Soviet agent. We are examining these points among many others with the Security Service [MI-5] . . . A careful recent review of his record with this Service has failed to reveal any indication of his having been other than loyal in his conduct of the many cases which he handled."[22]

The Foreign Office published a White Paper about Burgess and Maclean two days later, on 25 September 1955. It said as little as possible about Maclean and Burgess and did not mention Philby. Events then took a dramatic turn. "In New York, the Sunday News of 23 October named Philby as the Third Man, and on the following Tuesday [the MP Marcus] Lipton rose at question time in the Commons to ask:

'Has the Prime Minister made up his mind to cover up at all costs the dubious third man activities of Mr Harold Philby who was First Secretary at the Washington embassy a little time ago, and is he determined to stifle all discussion on the very great matters which were evaded in the wretched White Paper, which is an insult to the intelligence of the country?'"[23]

Harold Macmillan, the Foreign Secretary, advised by MI-6,[24] made a statement to Commons on 7 November: "No evidence has been found that Philby was responsible for warning Burgess or Maclean. While in government he carried out his duties ably and conscientiously. I have no reason to conclude that Mr. Philby has at any time betrayed the interests of this country, or to identify him with the so-called 'third man,' if, indeed, there was one."[25] Philby was, for the moment, saved by SIS group loyalty, personal friendships, and Harold Macmillan's dislike of secret intelligence organizations and what he viewed as their squabbles.

Philby held a triumphant press conference in his mother's apartment on 9 November. *The Times* reported that "Mr. H. A. R. Philby . . . denied the charge [that he was the "third man"] and suggested that Colonel Lipton should either repeat it outside Parliament and publish his evidence, or forward the evidence to a judicial member of the Privy Council, withdrawing his charge until the member had had the chance of pronouncing on it." Two days later, the newspaper reported: "In a personal statement in the House of Commons yesterday Lieutenant-Colonel Lipton unreservedly withdrew the allegation against Mr. Harold Philby . . . Mr. Harold Philby said last night: 'I think that Colonel Lipton has done the right thing. So far as I am concerned the incident is now closed.'" The extensive "Top Secret" file sent to the FBI and CIA (therefore, to James Angleton) on 22 February 1956 explained: "Thus, when the SIS 'reassessment' was presented to the Security Service on 20th July 1955,

> its conclusions were that the charge hitherto held against Philby, viz. that he was a Soviet spy while in SIS service, would not stand scrutiny. It was upon their discussion of the SIS case that the Directors of the Security Service and SIS based their submission for the Secretary of State's speech.'"[26]

Philby's life, if not his career in British secret intelligence, began to look up. "Very shortly after his public clearance he had a[nother] stroke of good fortune.

> His four years in the cold had left him broke . . . A friend from his Turkish days, W. E. D. Allen, who had served as Press Counsellor in the Ankara Embassy, . . . invited him to come to Ireland to give him a hand in writing the history of his family firm, David Allen's, whose centenary was to be celebrated in 1957. [Philby] arrived in Cappagh, County Waterford, in January 1956, and stayed for six months, working hard, climbing in the hills and sending postcards to his children almost every day. He returned to London in July 1956 . . ."[27]

At which point, eight months after his press conference, senior officers in the British Secret Intelligence Service had decided to provide employment for Philby. As Philip Knightley put it, perhaps passing on Philby's own interpretation: "SIS was taking an increasing interest in the Middle East,

> and to have an experienced agent in what was then the centre of intrigue for the area seemed a good idea. Even Philby's enemies were not entirely against the scheme, arguing that making Philby active again might lead him to provide the evidence necessary to prove his guilt and close the case."[28]

The "increasing interest in the Middle East" had to do with the Suez Crisis, the British effort to regain lost ground for what was sometimes referred to as "the British Caliphate."

The British government, dominated by second-string World War II Tory grandees led by Anthony Eden, Churchill's longtime successor-in-waiting, looked at Nasser and saw Mussolini. This time things would be different. There would be no Munich. The dictator would be stopped in his tracks and sent packing. Egypt would return to the informal British empire, joining the Hashemite kingdoms of Iraq and Jordan; the supply of oil would be secured and Britain's place at the top table of international affairs would be secure. The United States would pick up the tab, as was fitting and proper. The maneuvering against Nasser had been going on for months when Nasser's intervention in a domestic crisis in Jordan resulted in rioting there and in March 1956 the firing of Sir John Bagot Glubb, leader of the country's Arab Legion, and that force's other British officers. This traditional British colonial army (created, incidentally, by St. John Philby) had been the centerpiece of British military planning for the region. In the last days of July 1956, Nasser ordered the seizure of the canal, and a blockade of Israeli shipping. Nasser's nationalization of the Suez Canal gave the signal for secret war planning among Britain, France, and Israel, crystallizing as an invasion of the Sinai by the latter and a (re)occupation of the Canal Zone by the former. Among the promised rewards to Israel was assistance from France for its nuclear reactor project.

MI-6's plan was for Philby to be an agent, not an SIS officer. Nicholas Elliott, his old SIS friend, arranged for Philby to become the *Observer's* Middle East correspondent and for the *Economist* to take him on as well. SIS vouched with those newspapers for his bona fides. He was to be paid £500 a year as a retainer, expenses, and thirty shillings per hundred published words.[29] This is about what he had received the previous year from Andre Deutsch (or had it been from Tomás Harris?). He was also to publish articles in the American magazine, the *New Republic,* until recently owned by an old Cambridge friend, Michael Straight.[30] Building on his father's networks, Philby would be able to collect information from government officials across the Middle East and by his own efforts to establish relationships with British governmental representatives, commercial interests, and others. Philby, of course, also reported to SIS and the

KGB and kept in touch with the CIA and other intelligence services in the vicinity.* As a CIA historian later pointed out, it "is very easy for an informed person, in an informal atmosphere of friendliness, to succumb to the skilled techniques of a newsman,"[31] or those of a trained intelligence agent.

Shortly before Kim Philby arrived in Beirut, the *Observer* published a travel article about the city by the newspaper's colorful ballet critic, Richard Buckle: "The first impression a stranger receives of Beirut is one of noise.

> Its narrow streets cling to the slopes of a promontory, and as everyone favours wide-shouldered, swashbuckling American cars, the traffic problem is acute . . . All this is rather putting-off at first, but the Mediterranean charm of Beirut gradually manifests itself. Walk or drive in the morning along the avenue on the south side of the promontory and watch the fishermen on the rocks; loiter in the markets at noon; find your way down to the port at dusk, where, looking uphill, you will see, lit-up, rising one above the other, some of those pretty old Lebanese houses, the central pointed windows of their first floors grouped together in threes, which are so rapidly being replaced by modern blocks; wander through the interesting brothel quarter off the Place des Canon at night, where, from the full-blown tarts who lounge in dressing-gowns at the doors of their houses or from the darting pimps who will promise anything, you are sure of a warm welcome: and after a while you will come to appreciate the atmosphere and amenities of the city . . ."

In the course of this—somewhat—routine, orientalist, description of the exotic east, we find: "One evening we drove up into the hills to visit Hadji St. John Philby, the eminent Arabic scholar, a convert to Islam, who had been chief adviser to the late King of Saudi-Arabia, and was recently turned out by his anglophobe successor.

> We watched the sun set, and . . . we drank a very fierce arak, and on the way home my companions turned on me and accused me of encouraging our host's small sons to make so much noise that the

---

* Summaries of all of Philby's articles from this period are to be found as an appendix to this volume.

Hadji's words of wisdom could hardly be heard above our bilingual caterwauling . . . From above, the promontory of Beirut, with its red, blue and yellow lights, was like a jeweled sceptre defying the dark sea."[32]

Seal and McConville confirm that Kim Philby stayed at his father's house when he first arrived in Beirut, going into the city a couple of days each week.[33] More detail, from slightly later, is added by Borovik: "His father came to Beirut two or three times a week, and sometimes every day, and he always dropped in to see his son at the Normandy [Hotel].

> Kim went into the mountains to spend the night with his father and cool off from the Beirut heat. Their relationship improved. St. John Philby was happy that his son was back in shape and readily introduced him to all his Arab friends . . . He knew personally almost all the Arab nationalist leaders. Kim started meeting them soon, too. The leaders were well-disposed to him because of Philby senior's profoundly pro-Arab position, which they expected Kim to share. Kim tried not to disillusion them in his articles. As a result, the first information that Kim passed on to Paulson based on his conversations with the Arabs got high marks at SIS."[34]

Godfrey (Paul) Paulson was then the SIS station chief in Beirut. He "was authorized to give [Philby] small handouts to boost his meager earnings [sic], and asked him to carry out minor intelligence activities during his journalistic assignments in the Middle East."[35] According to Chapman Pincher, "These involved submitting reports and helping to recruit and run agents* . . . The job kept him in close touch with the MI-6 station in Beirut, and being friendly with those who ran it, he resumed his espionage on behalf of the KGB."[36]

Philby told Genrikh Borovik that he "started every day in Beirut by reading the newspapers and his mail at the Normandy.

> That took approximately an hour. Then he went to the British Embassy, to chat with the press officer and hear the latest embassy

---

* Interesting, if true. There are no other references to Philby recruiting and running agents in Beirut for MI-6.

news. After that, Kim went to the US Embassy, to see the press officer and other diplomats dealing with politics. He was met in a friendly way at both Embassies."

Philby's access to Arab leaders was useful to SIS (as well as to the KGB). According to Borovik, which means, as usual, according to Philby: "At least twice a month [Kim Philby] left Beirut either for Amman or Damascus. Four or five times a year he went to Saudi Arabia . . . The British did not have diplomatic ties with Saudi Arabia then, and any information from there, especially such authoritative information from Philby, who met high-ranking officials, was awaited with impatience at SIS."[37] Philby, as well "continued to do occasional work for the KGB . . . and the information he supplied on British policies in the region proved invaluable to [the Soviet] government in its relations with Arab countries. Philby's contribution came more in the form of political analysis than straightforward intelligence."[38] It is not surprising that one of those watching these various watchers watch Philby was the historian of the bar of the St. George Hotel in Beirut, Said K. Aburish: "American interest in Philby manifested itself in many ways: [CIA official James Russell] Barracks openly wanted him watched, [CIA official John] Fistere extended the rules of the game to the point of hiring Philby's daughter [Josephine] and Miles Copeland, by his own admission a major CIA operative during the Philby years in Beirut, maintained a curious friendship [with Philby] . . .

> Molly Izzard . . . gives innumerable examples of late-night telephone calls to their place every time Kim stayed with them. The callers were always 'drunken American ladies' who were checking on Kim's whereabouts. This degree of American attention to Philby amounted to merciless hounding . . . a great many people, British as well as American, were involved . . . Eventually, the belief in Kim's guilt or innocence practically divided along national lines, with the Americans believing he was guilty and the British defending him."[39]

Cave Brown wrote that Copeland was "one of Angleton's men in Beirut . . . financed in part, at least, by Angleton to watch Philby.

Copeland claimed to have the credentials for the task. Having been trained by Philby in counterespionage in London before D-Day in 1944, he had 'known and liked' him when he as in Washington between 1949 and 1951."

In other words, Copeland told Cave Brown that he and Angleton had, as it were, grown up together under Philby's tutelage. "Copeland further claimed to have served on an *Anglo-American committee* which had cleared Philby of the allegations that he had been a Soviet agent; he claimed also that he knew Philby 'better than anyone else, excepting two or three British intelligence officers.'

Angleton had told Copeland that 'if I would keep an eye on Philby' in Beirut, 'he'd pay all the costs—costs being in the form of entertainment expenses, since it was under the cover of social contact that I was to do my counter-espionage work.' Also, the FBI in Washington and MI-5 in London asked him 'to report signs that [Philby] might be spying for the Soviets' . . . Copeland, for the next five years, until January 1963 . . . would 'throw a buffet dinner for forty people on a night when we were sure Philby was free to be one of them, and send the bill to Jim Angleton.' Philby and Copeland became good friends [like Philby and Applewhite] and Copeland claimed to have employed the Lebanese Sûreté to use its 'street eyes'—teams of streetwise Arabs—to watch Philby . . . However this may have been, Copeland, like [Edgar] Applewhite, obtained not the slightest evidence that Philby was anything more than what he appeared to be: an aging and amiable but able reporter who, through a famous father, was exceptionally well connected with . . . Arab politics."[40] [Emphasis added.]

"I know Philby is a Soviet agent," Angleton had said.* Copeland didn't believe it.[41]

According to Phillip Knightley, "the CIA believed that Philby had a top-level source within the Agency who revealed to him in Beirut some of its covert actions . . .

---

* According to Joseph Trento, Angleton met Philby "several times during this period and [Philby] used those opportunities to reassure his American friend of his innocence." Trento, Joseph J. *The Secret History of the CIA*, p. 274.

the CIA was convinced that one of its own officers, Wilbur Crane Eveland, told Philby about the agency's operations in the Middle East and Africa, including plans to bring down the Syrian government late in 1956 and its efforts to rig the 1957 Lebanese election in favour of the pro-Western Chamoun regime."[42]

The game was played both ways.

The *Economist* published seven of Philby's articles between the beginning of August 1956 and the end of the year.* The first of these concerned the sociological and political situation in Aden.† It was followed by one on the tribal Aden protectorates to the east of the city, colorful and knowing, on 18 August. The next article by Philby in the *Economist* appeared on 19 September, when the paper published "Shall Lebanon Copy Nasser?" about oil pipeline negotiations. The *Observer*, also a weekly, which was associated with the (then *Manchester*) *Guardian* daily, published nine of Philby's articles between 30 September 1956 and the end of the year, one every week or two. His first story in the *Observer* was on the front page of the newspaper's edition of 30 September 1956: "Western Oil Threat by Lebanon;" "Talks between the [European-owned] Iraq Petroleum Company and the Lebanese Government have reached a critical state," on the same topic as the *Economist* article. Philby's "Pre-Election Anxieties in Jordan" (the *Observer* datelined Jerusalem, Jordan, 6 October 1956), described rising tension in the region, with the government of Jordan at odds both with that of Iraq over matters of a military alliance and that of Israel, after the dismissal of the British General, Glubb, and his British officers, had weakened the Jordanian army. Philby noted that an Israeli/Jordanian conflict would activate the Anglo-Jordanian treaty, bringing the UK into war on the side of its Jordanian client state against Israel (which would

---

* Articles in the *Economist* are not signed. Philby's are identified by the designation "from our special correspondent" and dateline and overlap with those he contributed to the *Observer*.

† "Aden . . . served a triple military purpose [for Britain]. Army, navy and air force units and the high command stationed there provided the military force, in support of the smaller advance base in Bahrein, to keep control of Kuwait, Abu Dhabi and the other sheikdoms of the Persian Gulf."

have considerably complicated the Anglo-Israeli arrangements in regard to the Suez Canal). The front-page headline was: "U.S. No Closer on Suez," that is, no closer to the Anglo-French position of strong (in public, non-military) measures to reverse Egyptian control of the canal.

Israel invaded Egyptian Sinai on 19 October. On 5 November, "in order to separate the belligerents," so they said, Britain and France used paratroop forces to occupy the Suez Canal Zone. Both the United States and the Soviet Union were opposed to the British-French-Israeli action. The Soviet Union threatened missile attacks on France and Britain. The United States, more realistically, and therefore more effectively, threatened to cut off oil and financial support. Britain and France folded. Subsequently, "the break-up of the [British] Middle Eastern empire proceeded at a particularly fast pace,

> with a loss of British influence on a scale without parallel anywhere else in the third world. The catastrophic failure of the attack on Egypt in 1956 marked the opening of a new phase in British policy in the area . . . British diplomacy proved to be singularly unsuccessful in adapting itself to changing circumstances in the Arab countries."[43]

This, according to Donald Maclean, writing a few years later from Moscow, was the context for Philby's Middle East journalism. Maclean called it the "Collapse of the British Caliphate."

The articles Kim Philby published in the second half of 1956 are what contemporary readers of the *Observer* and the *Economist* would have expected from those newspapers' Middle East correspondent: factual, informed, well-written. They were all datelined from Beirut or from nearby Amman. None gave a prominent place to either Saudi Arabia or Israel. They were, no doubt, read with care in London and Washington, and in Moscow as well.* Remarkably, for those British readers who did not restrict themselves to *The Times*, understanding of Middle Eastern events after Suez was generally based on reports in the *Observer* and the *Economist* by Kim Philby. This would continue to be the case for the remainder of the decade.

---

* Philby's Moscow readers no doubt included Donald Maclean and Guy Burgess.

In 1957 Philby contributed two or three articles a month to the *Observer* (except in August, when there were five and February, March and November, when there were none), three or four a month to the *Economist* (except in December, when there were none). Many of those concerned a war in Oman, about which, in the *Observer* of 28 July 1957, Philby judged that "The situation in Oman is, in fact, exceedingly obscure." It was, he explained, the manifestation of a long-standing conflict between the Imam of Oman and the Sultan of Muscat, involving the Saudis and the British to some extent, the latter having troops in the area. All this complicated by increasingly rich oil discoveries. On 4 August the *Observer's* gossip columnist "Pendennis," under the headline "Oman Bank Holiday," wrote: "We asked our far-flung correspondent, H. A. R. Philby, how he was getting on this Bank Holiday week-end, trying to report the war in Oman. He cables a most dejected reply. 'Fort Sharjah, [in what is now the United Arab Emirates] where all the great newsmen gathered at the start of the campaign, was bad enough.

> The fort is, in fact, a resthouse, attached to the R.A.F. base, and the air-conditioning broke down, prices were high, and the beer was as hot as the Indian Ocean. There was nothing to do except listen to an R.A.F. spokesman contributing neither to the volume nor to the accuracy of the news put out, and to worry about whether it wouldn't be better to move to Bahrein. Outside, wandering among the sand and scrub, a poor lunatic cried out endlessly that it was he who commanded the R.A.F. station . . . Bahrein is equally depressing and even further away from the scene of action. Reporting the Muscat war from there is like covering Rome from Leeds. The hotel has the feel of an elderly P. and O. liner. Fans whirr in all the rooms, moving the semi-conditioned air. Haddock with bubble and squeak is offered for breakfast."

On the 10th, "Our Special Correspondent" reported for the *Economist* on the situation in Yemen and the Aden Protectorates: "The idea of Mr Khrushchev, in his role of defender of the free, extending his podgy paw of friendship on that personification of ancient regimes, the Imam of Yemen, is a cynical absurdity . . .

By turning the tribal protectorate territories into a tribal free-for-all with modern weapons, Russia hopes to unseat the security of the colony and has dreams of installing a satellite Yemen on the straits . . . In the long run, however, the willing co-operation of paramount chiefs in the protectorates and of political leaders in Aden will be as important as guns in resisting the aggressors."

Plus ça change, plus c'est la même chose.

St. John Philby's book, *The Land of Midian,* was advertised by the publisher, Bodley Head, in the *Observer* on 6 and 27 October, and on 24 and 2 November. Along with an autobiographical account, *Forty Years in the Wilderness,* it was favorably, if briefly, reviewed in the *Observer* on 22 December. A major review of the two books appeared in the *Guardian* of 21 February 1958. The reviewer was James [Jan] Morris. He (as Morris then was) was lavish in his praise of *Forty Years in the Wilderness,* less so of *The Land of Midian.*

About this time, "St. John made his peace with the Saudi royal family and returned to Riyadh."[44]

The rhythm of appearances by "the Middle East Correspondent" of the *Observer* and the *Economist* was interrupted in late 1957 and early 1958. Aileen Philby had died in December 1957. Kim Philby went back to England for the funeral, and he remained there for a few weeks, dealing with the situation left by her long final illness and death.[45] He was back in the Middle East by February. Following a pattern of fewer, but longer, articles, Philby reported in the *Observer* on 30 March (from Beirut), that "Prince Faisal has assumed power in Saudi Arabia to a chorus of approval from the Egyptian Press." Philby again displayed his, or his father's entrée to the Saudi government: "The great 'Red Palace' in the centre of Riyadh, where the Cabinet has its offices, is stirring to new life . . .

Prince Faisal is one of the ablest and most engaging personalities in Saudi Arabia: poised and articulate, with a thin mouth twitching sardonically and somber, sunken eyes . . . It is commonly said there is no public opinion in Saudi Arabia. I can say from recent personal experience that that is quite untrue. Throughout the crisis the King was subject to outspoken discussion over the coffee cups. Opinion is there and plenty of it. All that is lacking are the means of public expression."

The *Observer* carried a letter to the editor on 6 April 1958, from Alan Thompson, Edinburgh (perhaps the professor of Economics and Labour MP): "It is to be hoped that somebody in the Middle Eastern Department of our Foreign Office has read Mr. H. A. R. Philby's article on Saudi Arabia . . ."

Between 1 April 1957 and 19 May 1958, Philby published eight articles in the American magazine the *New Republic*. Two were about Saudi Arabia, three about the Middle East, generally, the others about Egypt and Syria, Iraq,* and Jordan.[46] One was "a letter" (9 September 1957) in response to reader and editorial queries, concentrating on Saudi attitudes toward Israel and the recent coup by the King in Jordan. The *Observer* gave Philby five columns and another half page on 22 June for "Crisis-Country Background: The Lebanon," in which he described for his readers the complexities of the country's politics, the state of play between the government and opposition at the moment, which was increasingly violent, and concluding that "A Western Power has nothing to offer this country. The Lebanese must help themselves." Then, "Our Special Correspondent" wrote in the *Economist* on 26 July: "Muddling Through in Beirut and Amman." "Ten thousand American troops have landed in Lebanon; two thousand British parachute troops are sitting on and around the Amman military airfield" whether or not they had anything to offer Lebanon, aside from Camille Chamoun.

Late in the summer of 1958 the KGB re-established regular contact with Philby, its local resident "Petukhov" meeting him every ten days.[47] And somewhat later in the year, "a new [CIA] station chief arrived in Beirut . . . Edgar J. Applewhite". He "had once squired a sister of Melinda Maclean [presumably Harriet] . . . She was a WAVE and had what Applewhite described as 'the best legs on Fifth Avenue' . . .

In due course, Applewhite and Philby met and became friends . . .
Applewhite and Philby visited each other's apartments, stopped

---

* He apparently spent two weeks in Iraq that year accompanying the Middle East expert, his father's biographer, Elizabeth Monroe.

for conversation when they met in the street, greeted each other at parties . . . Applewhite never lost sight of the fact that Philby might be a KGB agent . . . What was expected of Applewhite in his association with Philby was that he should not be taken by surprise by any move that Kim made. After each session with him, Applewhite made a memo for the record, and this went to the [counterintelligence staff's?] Philby file in Washington."[48]

There was, then, Paulson of SIS, Petukhov of KGB and Applewhite and—many—others of CIA. This is not to overlook Philby's contacts with Syrian, Lebanese, Jordanian, Saudi, perhaps Iraqi, and presumably Israeli secret intelligence representatives. All of these, and beyond them, James Angleton, were watching Kim Philby go about the life of a foreign correspondent: interviews with officials of half a dozen governments, long afternoon hotel bar conversations with other journalists, parties and receptions. Angleton was well known as a fly-fisherman, patiently casting his lures again and again.

Some months of 1958 had been occupied, we are told, with a passionate and highly alcoholic affair between Kim Philby and Eleanor Brewer, the American wife, then ex-wife, of *New York Times* reporter Sam Pope Brewer. In January 1959, Kim Philby and Eleanor Brewer were married in London.

In his third article in the *Observer* for 1959, in February, "Arab Fears of Jewish Influx," Philby reported rumors of "a new massive wave of Jewish immigrants into Israel, largely from Communist countries," which was "arousing alarm in the Arab States . . . The Arab alarm is reflected in highly coloured estimates of the extent of the immigration now contemplated. Semi-official sources speak of a first installment of a quarter of a million, rising in due course to three million." The Arab governments were blaming the Soviets for allowing the immigration and the British and Americans for supporting it with public and private funds. Philby summarized the situation by stating that "The immediate outcome of the dispute is likely to be a heightening of Nationalist-Communist tension in the Arab world . . . The long-term result of the immigration—if it takes place—will be to confirm Arab fears of a world-wide conspiracy against them, with the usual concomitant of alarms, and excursions throughout the region." It would be reasonable to suppose that these articles, in particular, were of considerable interest in official circles in London, Moscow, Tel Aviv, and, of course, Washington. A story in the *Economist* on 10 October, "Cairo versus Peking," argued that "the communists are playing the Middle Eastern game both ways. They do not want to lose the Arab nationalists as levers to be thrown against the West whenever necessary. At the same time they still hope to bring about a communist takeover of Arab lands . . . It calls to mind the situation between the world wars when the Soviet government secretly approved and publicly disavowed the actions of the Comintern." This last being a subject on which Philly could, but would not, claim some authority.

In 1960, Nicholas Elliott,* Philby's sponsor for his employment with the *Observer* and the *Economist,* who, coincidentally, had been sent out to be SIS chief in Beirut, encouraged Philby to become more active: "The idea was to force Philby out into the field, to give him the profile of an active and industrious intelligence officer and thus force the Russians to use him again.

> Philby would be taken into Elliott's confidence; he would be made a part of SIS operations; he would learn information so important that he would have to pass it to his Soviet control. But although some of that information would be genuine, some of it would be a plant and Western counter-intelligence would be waiting to see where it surfaced. If it could be traced back to Philby, and only to Philby, then the British authorities would at last have proof of his treachery."[49]

Nicholas Elliott "began to push Philby to produce a steady flow of high-grade information.

> Suddenly Philby became one of the most active journalists in the area. He was here, there and everywhere, filing copy from Amman, Riyadh, Damascus, Sharjah, Bahrein, Baghdad, Cairo, Kuwait and Yemen. Later, when Philby had defected, the CIA compiled a break-down of these trips and the copy they produced and decided that there was an unjustifiable discrepancy—he had visited too many

---

* The presentation of himself in Elliott's two volumes of memoirs is that of a Tory prig, hardly a match for Philby. Milne writes that when it came down to it, "Philby ran rings around Elliott," Milne, p. 254.

places for too few journalistic results. The CIA attributed this to his work for the Russians, but it was SIS that kept him busy."[50]

So thought, or wrote, Philip Knightley.

St. John Philby died in Beirut on 30 September 1960. His obituary in the *Observer*, by his son, ran the next day: "St. John Philby, greatest of Arabian explorers, died suddenly, aged 75, in Beirut yesterday.

> He was on the way to his home in Riyadh from the Orientalists' Congress in Moscow . . . His greatest contribution to Arabia was . . . the negotiation of the East Arabian concession on behalf of the Standard Oil Company of California, a transaction which brought in its wake changes of which Philby himself heartily disapproved."

A notice by Freya Stark was published in the *Observer* on 9 October: "In these latter years he would pass to and fro between Mecca and the Athenaeum [in London] studying his pre-Islamic histories and sometimes stop off in Venice to sit in my garden and tell me the Arabian news. And every year he seemed mellower, serene in values tested by life as on an anvil, amusement and tolerance growing out of that fine uncompromising climate of his youth." There was also an obituary, in the *Geographical Journal,* by Wilfred Thesiger, one of the trio of pioneering British explorers of Arabia.

Philby wrote just nine articles for the *Observer* in 1961. In a feature article on 12 March, "Oil Village in the Desert," Philby described mechanized Aramco exploration in the Empty Quarter of Arabia that his father had explored on camel-back, and he had recently visited. Philby reported on Saudi government cabinet changes on 18 March in the *Economist* and under the title "Among Africans" on 15 April, concerning the "All-African People's Conference" in Cairo, 25 March to 7 April 1961. On 29 April 1961 the *Economist* published an article "Cairene Anxieties," about the "Resentment, concern and shock" expressed by Tito and Nasser about the Bay of Pigs invasion of Cuba by the United States.

Michael Goleniewski, code-named "Sniper," a Polish intelligence official who had become a CIA asset in early 1959, defected to the

US in January 1961. Another American agent, Oleg Penkovsky, had been brought to London on 20 April 1961. In April 1961 George Blake, an MI-6 official studying at the Middle East Centre for Arab Studies near Beirut, was recalled to London, where he was arrested. He had been identified as a Soviet agent by Goleniewski.[51] There was a notice about Blake in the *Guardian,* on 19 April: "Secrets Charge in Camera: Official accused." On 4 May *The Times* reported "42-Year Sentence on Official Who Spied for the Russians." This was followed by discussions in Parliament and assurances by Prime Minister Macmillan that security procedures would be made more strict. Articles and analyses continued to run in the papers for months, one mentioning in passing that during his last ten days in Lebanon Blake was seen in Beirut (*Guardian,* 9 May 1961). The extraordinary length of the sentence was much commented on. It goes without saying that his case would have been closely followed by both James Angleton and Kim Philby.

During this period, the first six months of 1961, Kim Philby continued to publish in the *Observer* and as "Our Special Correspondent" in the *Economist:* ten articles between them. In the second half of 1961 the two papers published thirteen articles by Philby. On 27 May 1961, a major article, "New Approach by Persia to Soviet?" was published in the *Observer,* datelined Teheran. It began with evidence of privileged access: "Dr. Amini, Prime Minister of Persia, told me to-day that he would dearly like to see better relations established with the Soviet Union." Philby reported that, aside from that, Amini's main concern was to limit corruption as a way to avert revolution. Then on 3 June 1961 the *Economist* ran "Dr. Amini's Fifty-Fifty Chance, " as a leader "From Our Middle East Correspondent," datelined Teheran: "Anyone who knows what is really going on in Persia must be grossly misinformed . . . if every case of corruption were tracked down and the offender punished there would be precious few experienced people left to run the country." Still in Teheran, Philby reported on 10 June 1961, under the *Observer*'s heading "Inside Persia" the next day: "Dr. Amini Starts the Long Haul." Philby lists foreign debt, land reform, the cost of living, and corruption as major issues. There was also the balancing act between Britain and the United States, on the one hand, and the Soviet Union on the other. Philby commented that "Persians must try to live with the Soviet Union . . . This means in effect that the

Russians should ease their propaganda from Moscow Radio and from the 'National Voice of Iran'—a transmitter which purports to be operating clandestinely in Persia but which is located in fact on Russian soil."

In July, Kim Philby became, once more, a war correspondent. The *Economist* carried a 1 July 1961 report "Baghdad Brainstorm," concerning General Qasim's declaration "last Sunday, that Kuwait was a district of Basra province." The lead article on page one of the *Observer* on 2 July 1961, by Philby, datelined Kuwait, 1 July: "Bombers Join British Forces in Kuwait, Troops awaiting any move by Iraq, Sheikhdom is not expecting war." "British troops landing in force in Kuwait to-day ready to defend the newly independent oil sheikhdom threatened by Iraq." Philby reported that the Iraqi General Qasim and his communist allies had been threatening "to enforce his claim to Kuwait by military action." On 8 July the *Economist* published an illustrated article that "Secure Behind the Shield" of British forces, "War clouds over Kuwait are disappearing almost as fast as they blew up." At the end of the month, an article datelined Beirut, 29 July ("Hussein wants cash for Kuwait troops, Discussion with King Saud"), stated that King Hussein of Jordan had gone to Taif, King Saud's summer capital, to meet with the Saudi king. "The strangest and, from the British viewpoint, the most gratifying feature of the Kuwait incident is the reluctance of Arab States to speed the British departure by providing forces of their own to fill the gap." But two weeks later, with "Arab force will take over in Kuwait," the report from Beirut on 12 August stated that "The early withdrawal of all British forces from Kuwait is forecast here as a result of an agreement reached between the ruler and the Arab League mission for their replacement by an Arab Defence force."

In November 1961, Kim and Eleanor were in London on a short visit.[52] The usual accounts of this period of Philby's life emphasize his increased drinking, abetted by Eleanor.

There were only seven of his articles published in the first half of 1962, most in the *Observer*, nearly all about Syrian politics; however, he had twice that number published in the second half of the year, most about the "revolution" in Yemen, filed from nearby Aden; some were feature articles accompanied by photographs. The *Economist* carried an article in its 6 January 1962 paper, "Greater Syria, Pocket Edition," mentioning an abortive *coup d'état* on 31 December 1961.

There were few other articles from "Our Middle East Correspondent" in the *Economist* in 1962, which was the cause for increasing complaints addressed to Philby by its editors. On the other hand, the number of his articles in the *Observer* increased in 1962. On 22 July the *Observer* published a major article across four columns on one page, three on another, "By H.A.R. Philby," about: "Nasser's Pride and Glory." On the occasion of the tenth anniversary of the Egyptian Revolution, Philby reviewed the condition of the country. "If Socialism means nothing more than Government control, then Egypt is one of the most Socialist countries in the world.

> With the very important exception of land, the Government now runs all the basic enterprises of the country . . . There is a minimum wage . . . There is no right to strike in Egypt . . . Nobody in Egypt seriously pretends that the country is already a democracy . . . The Muslim Brotherhood and Communists were crushed and all party activity was banned . . . the Soviet Union remains the chief outside beneficiary of the squalls which beset the Egyptian revolution."

"It is now as difficult to conceive an Egypt without Nasser as a Yugoslavia without Tito or an India without Nehru—and Nasser is still a young man."

On 14 September 1962, *The Times* ran another espionage story: "Admiralty Man On Secrets Charge: Said to have recorded information." "An Admiralty civil servant, William John Christopher Vassall, aged 38, of Hood House, Dolphin Square, Pimlico, S.W., appeared at Bow Street Magistrates' Court yesterday charged under the Official Secrets Act with recording secret information at the Admiralty and elsewhere." Vassall had apparently been identified by a defecting KGB officer called Anatoliy Golitsyn. That same month, Penkovsky, who had returned to Moscow, was arrested there.

For much of the rest of the year Philby was covering (yet another) civil war in Yemen. A feature article under the heading "Inside the Yemen by H.A.R. Philby" was published by the *Observer* at the end of October 1962: "Backward nation that looks for miracles," datelined Aden. He presents the situation of the day, the rebellion against the traditional rulers by an Egyptian backed "republic," the former supported by the Saudis, Jordanians, and traditional rulers in the Aden protectorate. "Meanwhile, British officialdom in Aden maintains an enigmatic silence on all matters affecting the Yemen.

> It seems that, for fear of provoking renewed outcries against colonialism, it is suffering from self-inflicted lingual paralysis, ignoring the fact that many neuroses tend to disappear if freely discussed."

He criticizes the US and Britain for not recognizing the revolutionary government, portrays the Imam in dark colors and concludes: "Given reasonably stable and enlightened government and two or three decades of constructive work, the Yemen could again become Arabia Felix. But those tribesmen will have to be tamed first." Also on 20 October 1962, the *Economist* ran an anonymous piece in the Opinion section, "Arabia Felix: With the Yemeni revolution, all Arabia may have come to the end of a long sleep." It began: "Until something is done about the lacework of British protected states that festoon the eastern and southern coasts of the Arabian peninsula, the Arab portrait of Britain is indelibly adorned with the horn and tails of an old-fashioned proconsul," which sounds like Philby. The article posits that change in Yemen will result in progress elsewhere in the peninsula.

The following week there was another major feature from Philby in the *Observer*, with photographs: "Unshackling the Yemen," datelined Beirut, 27 October. He criticizes official British policy in Aden and the protectorates, in the spirit of his father, but also writes that "the ability of the revolutionaries to fashion a modern State on the ruins of the old must remain in serious doubt . . . The rudiments of administration scarcely exist. Without trying, I saw 20 tanks in Sanaa alone, but despite hours spent in Republican headquarters not one typewriter." Philby's tone seems more anti-establishment, more critical—in both senses of the word—than before. On 23 December the *Observer* ran an article by Philby under the headline: "The odds against the Imam," after the US did in fact recognize the Republican Government of the Yemen. The Jordanian Prime Minister, according to Philby, had stated that "the Imam's forces are 'at the gates of Sanaa,' . . . When that tired claim was first made, I was in Sanaa myself, and could certainly have driven at least 50 miles in any direction without any risk beyond that of a jarred spine

. . . The oddest feature of the situation is Australian recognition of the revolutionary Government. There is speculation whether this foreshadows Australians chewing *qat* or Yemenis playing cricket."

Philby's contributions to the *Observer* continued in 1963 with articles on 13 and 20 January 1963. That of 20 January 1963 was datelined Beirut on the 19th: "League abandons Kuwait." "The Arab League is evidently dying on its feet." It was withdrawing even token forces protecting Kuwait from Iraq. "No official reason for the decision [to withdraw Saudi and Jordanian forces from Kuwait] has been given, but the deplorable increase in tension between the Arab monarchies and republics after the revolution in the Yemen doubtless swayed both King Hussein and Prince Faisal to bring back units which they can ill spare." That was the last article by Philby published in either the *Observer* or the *Economist*.

Anatoliy Mikhailovich Golitsyn, a KGB officer operating under diplomatic cover in Helsinki, defected to the CIA on 15 December 1961, and was taken with his family to the United States. Christopher Andrew states that as a consequence, in January 1962 the KGB suspended agent meetings worldwide, limiting contacts to dead-letter boxes and similar secure means.[53] Rather quickly, in March 1962, the CIA sent MI-5 a list of ten of Golitsyn's "serials:" identifications of KGB agents. One concerned a "ring of five," including Burgess, Maclean, and a third, code-named "Stanley," who had something to do with the Middle East.[54] This seemed to point to Philby.[55] In what may have been a related development, in the autumn of 1962, Tomás Harris, a member of Philby's set from the Comintern period, was killed, it is said, in an automobile accident in Spain.

MI-6 decided that time was running out. When Angleton's trusted source, Golitsyn, told his stories about the five Cambridge undergraduates who had been recruited by the Comintern in the early 1930s, they concluded it was time to confront Philby.[56] In January 1963, MI-5 and SIS sent Nicholas Elliott back to Beirut to confront Philby. Robin Winks, who may be taken as relaying Angleton's account of the matter, wrote that Angleton had two agents in place in Lebanon, planning to have Philby detained by the CIA's station chief in Beirut and interrogated "by someone Philby did not know," presumably an American, but was frustrated in this by the arrival in Beirut of Elliott.[57] Given the by-play between American and British secret intelligence services in the search for "Homer," it is not out of the question that Elliott was sent to Beirut precisely to frustrate Angleton's plans. Be that as it may, Elliott extracted, or, rather, received, a two-page letter from Philby that Elliott called a confession and returned with it to London.[58] Years later, in Moscow, Philby told Phillip Knightley that the encounter with Elliott was a charade: SIS knew he would not accept the offer. They wanted him to go to Moscow to minimize the scandal and subsequent damage to relations with the CIA.[59]

The 3 March 1963 issue of the *Observer* carried a front-page story: "Journalist missing in Middle East." "The Egyptian authorities in Cairo are being asked if they can help to trace the present where-abouts of Mr. H. A. R. Philby, Middle East Correspondent of the *Observer* and the *Economist*, who has been missing from his home in Beirut in the Lebanon for the past five weeks." The journalist Clare Hollingworth published a series of slightly ironic articles specu-lating about his whereabouts, then, on 2 July 1963, the *Guardian* published on its front page her article: "Mr Philby believed behind Iron Curtain, 'Third man' who warned Guy Burgess." She wrote that "Mr H. A. R. 'Kim' Philby . . . is now believed to be behind the Iron Curtain . . .

> Further, he was after all the 'third man' who on May 23, 1951—the very day Donald Maclean and Guy Burgess disappeared—warned Burgess that the then Foreign Secretary, Mr Herbert Morrison, had agreed that Maclean should be questioned by the security authori-ties . . . Mr Philby, who was 51, was charming, witty, and amusing . . . 'Kim' never overworked and appeared to enjoy the social life of Beirut . . . [He and Eleanor] formed a link between Arab and the European social quarters and were greatly in demand at parties of the British and other embassies in Beirut . . . 'Kim' too was friendly with the men from the Services and Foreign Office who went to Shemlam, the Middle East centre for Arab Studies near Beirut . . ."

By whom she may have meant George Blake.

On 6 July 1963 the *Economist* ran an editorial: "A Lost Corre-spondent." "Philby got in touch with us in April, 1956, some five months after his public clearance by Mr Macmillan, saying that he

wanted to return to journalism and was prepared to go to Beirut; he
knew the Middle East and had his family connection there.

> We came to an arrangement with him in June, together with the
> sharing of pay and work that was suggested then by *The Observer,*
> which gave him the position not of a salaried staff member but of
> a correspondent with a regular retainer plus payments for articles
> used . . . He was an excellent Middle East correspondent in 1956,
> 1957, and 1958 . . . As the pressure of explosive crises there began to
> ease off in 1959 and 1960, we began to notice that he failed to find
> non-crisis topics to write about. We had difficulty in getting him
> to respond to our general, as distinct from political, interest in the
> affairs of his part of the world, and we had a growing feeling of a
> lack of real communication with him. By the time he failed to turn
> up for a dinner in Beirut on January 23rd [1963] our contact with
> him had for some time been inadequate . . ."

That explanation may have satisfied some readers of the *Economist*.

The *Observer* tried harder. Roy Perrott wrote in that paper on 7
July 1963 "Philby; All we know." "No inquirer could honestly and
certainly conclude that this man, this modest, somewhat retiring
man, this very capable and straightforward journalist could be
another defector.

> No one then claimed they had heard him utter any Communist
> sentiment under any conditions of stress or liquor . . . The papers
> shared payment of a retainer of £500 a year (which later went up
> to £1,000) plus expenses and payment for news and articles sent.
> In *The Observer's* case alone, this amounted to an extra £1,000 a
> year . . . Mr. Miles Copeland,* the former American diplomat, who
> had frequent political discussions with Philby, told me in March:
> 'If Philby was a Communist he was the best actor in the world
> and this was quite unbelievable. He would have had to construct a

---

* Elsewhere in the article Copeland was identified as "an ex-diplomat who, by
coincidence, had been on the United States Government Committee which had
cleared Philby of complicity in the Burgess and Maclean case." This seems to be
the only public reference to the existence of such a committee reaching such a
conclusion.

fantastic intellectual framework and stick to it moment by moment, all tending to a liberal viewpoint.' . . . Miss Elizabeth Monroe, the distinguished Middle East expert, who was in Philby's company for a week in 1957 on a tour of then-monarchist Iraq, says: 'There was no sign of a scrap of prejudice in him at all. What impressed one was his intense and impartial curiosity about everything and his calm judgment based on a tremendous background knowledge.'"

Philby had thought about Elliott's offer of immunity, concluded that it was not genuine, took his decision—and his opportunity—evaded various watchers, and five days later boarded a Russian freighter and sailed from Beirut through the Straits to Russia. (Leaving his apartment in Beirut for the harbor, he had been trailed by a Soviet agent to make sure he was unharmed until he reached a KGB safe house—which demonstrates the pervasiveness of his Soviet contacts in Beirut.)[60] Three weeks later, on 30 July, a seven-line report in *Izvestia* said: "The British subject Philby, who occupies a leading position in British Intelligence, has applied to the Soviet authorities for political asylum and Soviet citizenship. It is learned that the USSR Supreme Soviet has complied with Philby's request."

The way the Beirut interview of Philby was handled, and Philby's escape, convinced Angleton, Peter Wright, and Arthur Martin that there was a mole inside MI-5.[61] Whether or not that was true, Angleton's belief that there was a mole in MI-5 was significant for later events. According to other recent Russian sources, when Philby defected, Angleton told Helms, "Now you realize that I am capable of more than poetic hyperbole."[62]

Philby's Spanish Civil War contact, Alexander Orlov's 1963 *Handbook of Intelligence and Guerrilla Warfare,* claimed that: "Soviet intelligence officers agree that next to the resident director . . . the most important figure is the 'source,' or the informant, as he is usually called.

If the informant is situated in a strategic position with access to important diplomatic or military state secrets, he is worth his weight in gold every time he produces something of significance . . . The principal task of the resident and his assistants will then consist in guiding the informants intelligently and in seeing that they are not caught . . . Soviet intelligence treats its informants with genuine solicitude. It never violates its promise not to divulge their identity or services on behalf of the Soviet Union, and it rushes to their aid whenever they are in trouble . . . The Soviet intelligence hires the best lawyers when informants are caught and helps their families with generous sums of money, even when the further usefulness of the informants has been completely destroyed. There have been cases when Soviet intelligence saved informants hours before their impending arrest by getting them out of the country, helped their families with ten-thousand-dollar bank drafts, and later did their best to reunite them with their families by bringing the families to them in the Soviet Union."[63]

"THIS IS KIM'S WORK"

On 18 August 1954, approximately at the halfway point of Kim Philby's time "in the cold," between his interrogations and his assignment to Beirut, James Angleton briefed the group working under General James Doolittle that was examining the Central Intelligence Agency. Angleton "was highly critical of Gen. Walter Bedell Smith's administration at CIA . . .

> Angleton . . . claimed that Smith had been hoodwinked by the psychological warfare experts like Frank Wisner. Smith forgot espionage and counterespionage operations and devoted his time and attention to psychological warfare projects, many of which failed miserably."[1]

"Psychological warfare projects," in this context, refers to matters like the Albanian and Ukrainian efforts, which did indeed "fail miserably," at least in part, as Angleton would have suspected by this point, because of what he would later call "Kim's work." The Doolittle report, presented in September 1954, repeated Angleton's and earlier recommendations to strengthen CIA's counterintelligence activities: "Most signally, the report urged CIA to assume the country's leading counterintelligence role . . .

> The United States needed to abandon the law-enforcement route for a 'more ruthless' approach, the Doolittle Report stressed, and that new ruthlessness must be applied to 'intensification of CIA's counterintelligence efforts to prevent or detect and eliminate penetrations. The situation required a new strategy, a new concept for American life, one which would spill across normally restricted areas, legal channels, and departmental lines.'"[2]

"Spill across normally restricted areas, *legal channels,* and depart-mental lines."

Allen Dulles, after maneuvering for the position since Operation Sunrise, had finally become Director of Central Intelligence in February 1953.[3] The Agency at that point had three Deputy Direc-tors: Plans (Operations), Intelligence (Research and Analysis), and Administration. "Plans" was a euphemism for what was usually called the clandestine services. The latter at that time included a Foreign Intelligence Staff, within which Angleton was still chief of the Special Projects unit, "special," having its usual Agency meaning of "secret." In December of 1954, Dulles acted on the recommenda-tions of the Doolittle Committee by creating a counterintelligence staff within the clandestine services and making James Angleton its chief, their conflict over Operation Sunrise now forgotten. Angle-ton, who had helped establish the Soviet branch of the CIA, when his career path had seemed to be following that of Richard Helms in Foreign Intelligence collection, now found his proper niche in counterintelligence: to one side of the main currents within the Agency—the conflict between intelligence procurement and covert action—in some sense isolated, in most others, independent and perhaps central.

Human, as opposed to open source or technical intelligence, is information derived from interactions among people. These can vary from something close to, or identical with, open sources, through the use of agents (paid or ideological, double, or otherwise) to defectors. Dulles "was keenly interested in defections from the Communists . . . realizing that defectors could be a most valuable source of intelligence. Those who had frequent contact with him were aware of the amount of time he spent on CIA efforts to deter-mine the *bona fides* of defectors."[4] Therefore, when James Angleton became chief of the counterintelligence staff, "The main job of Angleton and his staff was giving the bona fides to a source.

> The divisions would recruit a source, whether it was in Europe or Vietnam, wherever, they would do whatever, they would use their own methods, polygraph or whatever, but then Angleton's staff would look at it in the larger picture and say, 'We will not give this person bona fides.' If they didn't, it meant the information that came from him was labeled: 'from a source whose bona fides have

not yet been established,' which, of course, would lead some people [in the Agency] . . . to believe that their intelligence is being paralyzed, because, with this label, they weren't able to count on the people . . . that they believed in."[5]

However, as Angleton saw it, he was simply following best practice, as he had learned in Ryder Street, as he had learned it from Kim Philby, as he had learned it about Kim Philby. For Angleton and Dulles and Helms, for other ex-OSS officers in the CIA, "the lesson of X-2 was that it's preferable to have unfounded suspicions than to be duped by a bogus source."[6] It is true, however, that others, especially later, differed.

From the time that he became chief of the counterintelligence staff, James Angleton was responsible for ensuring that the Agency's secrets would not be known to others. In his view, "whereas the Soviet Division might see a Soviet diplomat as a possible CIA mole, the Counterintelligence Staff would view him as a possible disinformation agent.

> What division case officers would tend to look at as valid information, furnished by Soviet sources who risked their lives to cooperate with them, counterintelligence officers tended to question as disinformation, provided by KGB-controlled sources."[7]

Angleton's proposal was that the counterintelligence staff would be equal in authority to its intelligence collection interlocutors. Although on paper Dulles placed Angleton under the Deputy Director for Plans, on a level with the area division chiefs, Angleton's view of the matter was that the counterintelligence staff was an independent bureau: that is how he ran it; that is how Dulles, and later Helms, agreed he should run it.

People on the intelligence collection side of the Agency could be frustrated by Angleton's efforts to ensure the security of their operations: "We never had a successful Soviet operation that Angleton and his crowd didn't cast some doubt on," complained John Maury, one-time chief of the Soviet Union Division. "In house it was all right to raise doubts, but Jim and a few of his close colleagues allowed his suspicions to be widely known around the Hill."[8] A most serious, if somewhat inexplicable, charge. David Wise thought that "to Angleton . . . it made perfect sense to assume that the KGB had succeeded in planting a mole or moles inside the CIA . . .

> [T]he CI Staff argued that the intelligence services of other nations—notably the British—had been penetrated by the Soviets. Why should the CIA be exempt? . . . Angleton also had personal reasons to press the search for penetrations with such ferocity. He had been taken in by the supreme mole of the century, Kim Philby, and he was not about to make the same mistake twice."[9]

Ex-CIA officer Victor Marchetti wrote that the "counterintelligence staff operates on the assumption that the agency—as well as other elements of the United States Government—is penetrated by the K.G.B. . . .

> [Angleton] is said to keep a list of the 50 or so key positions in the C.I.A. which are most likely to have been infiltrated by the opposition, and he reportedly keeps the persons in those positions under constant surveillance."[10]

According to Rhodri Jeffreys-Jones, "To some, Angleton's obsession with compartmentalization and his suspicion of the Soviet Union's every move smacked of paranoia, but chronic skepticism is no fault in a counterintelligence chief. Angleton helped to ensure that—as far as is known—the CIA was not penetrated."[11]

Under DCI Dulles the counterintelligence staff of the Agency was given wide latitude for its work and grew accordingly. By 1959 it contained "96 [people who were] professionals, 75 clerical and four staff agents. The Staff also had one Headquarters contract agent, and several agents under [other] projects,"[12] perhaps including in this accounting Jay Lovestone and Louise Page Morris. According to a CIA historian, "As of the early 1960s Angleton did not know for sure that the Soviets currently had penetrated the CIA, but to him the absence of evidence was not evidence of absence . . .

> Angleton had become ever more aware throughout the 1950s that he had unwittingly divulged secrets to his friend 'Kim' Philby . . . If Philby had deceived Angleton—the most perceptive counterintelligence officer at the CIA—far less discerning minds could be tricked

all the easier . . . Angleton believed the Agency should err on the side of security by presuming penetration and trying to prove it had not occurred. Present lack of proof proved nothing."[13]

Angleton's counterintelligence philosophy "comprised three fundamental tenets: The Soviets will exploit Western vulnerabilities to penetration . . . Espionage and covert action operations cannot work without strong counterintelligence support . . . Counterintelligence operations and analysis must be centralized . . ."[14] The CIA Historian David Robarge also found that "Angleton's counterintelligence world was largely based on . . . a substantial empirical base on which to ground his 'wilderness of mirrors' idea . . .

> From his vantage point in X-2, Angleton saw firsthand how a strategic deception worked. The process used in the Double Cross and FORTITUDE operations followed his model almost precisely . . . Angleton knew that the Soviets had badly tricked Western services twice in sophisticated, very similar 'false flag' operations run thirty years apart: the Trust and WiN . . . Angleton's measure of the intelligence threat Moscow posed to the West also derived from his knowledge of extensive Soviet espionage operations in Europe and America before and during World War II, and in the early years of the Cold War . . . From VENONA, he found out that the Soviets had placed over 200 agents and sources inside the U.S. Government, the Manhattan Project, defense industries and the media . . ."[15]

In the early 1960s, just as Philby's careers in Beirut were coming to their conclusion, an unusually large number of defectors began to arrive in the West, each with his or her story of penetrations of Western secret security services.[16] At a meeting in a Washington, D.C., Chinese restaurant, Angleton and Peter Wright "talked until 4 a.m. . . . Who was true, and who was false? Who defected, and who was sent? . . . 'This is Kim's work,' [Angleton] muttered.'"[17] Robarge calls the "Years of the Spies" from 1959 to 1963, "one of the bleakest periods in Cold War counterintelligence history—

> [It] showed to Angleton that the Soviets had badly penetrated several Western services and gained crucial knowledge of their HUMINT [human intelligence] and SIGINT [signal intelligence] capabilities.

For several years, one intelligence disaster compounded another: 1959, Pyotr Popov (CIA source in the GRU, Soviet military intelligence) arrested; 1960, Martin and Mitchell (NSA officers) defect to USSR; 1961, George Blake (KGB mole in MI-6) arrested, Portland Ring in United Kingdom rolled up; 1962, Heinz Felfe (KGB mole in BND) arrested; Oleg Penkovsky (CIA source in GRU) arrested; 1963, Philby (MI-6) and Hamilton (NSA) defect to USSR, Jack Dunlap (GRU source in NSA) commits suicide before arrest; Stig Wennerstrom (GRU spy in Swedish military) arrested; Profumo Affair (involving GRU 'honey trap') in UK disclosed."

When Raymond Rocca testified to the Rockefeller Commission in 1975, he attempted to argue that the glass was half full, as it were: "This taken together with the six or seven defectors that came out in the '50s, who gave us living examples and identifications, and the three penetrations that we had going in the '50s of the Soviets, they were Popov, and Penkovsky, and Goyeneveski [Goleniewski], three people working inside those services over a period of time from '53 to '61.

> We had the foundation of a strategy response to the Soviet threat and all you have to do is to read the '60s and you read the results because at no time in the history of Soviet intelligence and counterintelligence have they been hit so hard as in the decade of the '60s. We got Blake in '61. We got Philby in '63. We got Pak [Georges Pâques], these are two UK fellows, Vassil [sic], another UK one, in '64. Pak in France in '64. Felfe, the Chief of German Counterintelligence, West German, about the same time. There are a number of NATO cases that grew out, all of them, of this combination of what I call strategic CI weaponry. Defectors, penetrations . . ."

"unfortunately all of these penetrations were compromised. Penkovsky was tried and shot, Popov was tried and shot. Only one got away, and this is Guyenevsky [Goleniewski],"[18] who thought he was the Tsarevich.

On 20 April 1960, *femme de letters* Mary McCarthy wrote to Carmen Angleton advising her not to marry "Bobbie": "I was terrified I might get your father on the phone if I telephoned Milan;

I thought he might cross-question me about Bobbie (having possibly heard something via Jim) and what would I have said? Knowing me, I shudder to think. 'Yes, Colonel, that bird's a homosexual.' Oh, dear. But luckily he was at the office."[19]

Which shows us that Angleton's father was still working at his National Cash Register franchise in 1960, that he and the rest of the family were well known to such literary-society figures as Mary McCarthy, and that "Jim" Angleton was part of that world as well. The correspondence of Mary McCarthy and Carmen Angleton in the Vassar College archives has many references to "Colonel" James Hugh Angleton, his wife and younger son and daughter, as well as to Cicely Angleton. References to James Angleton are conspicuously absent, with the possible exception of that to "Jim" in the quotation above. It is, however, very unlikely that he was not in contact with his sister's set, considering his frequent visits to Europe and his devotion to his parents, resident as they were in Italy.

James Angleton's sister Carmen, who had at one point substituted for him at *Furioso*, was from at least 1955 part of an international group of intellectuals and socialites, many of whom were participants in the CIA-funded Congress for Cultural Freedom (CCF). The center of this group was the friendship between Mary McCarthy and Hannah Arendt, with the Rome-based Carmen Angleton acting as a European hostess and linking agent, as it were, passing around news and gossip. (They were all particularly close to Nicola and Miriam Chiaromonte. Nicola Chiaromonte was part of the anti-communist left, editor of the CCF's Italian analogue to *Encounter*: *Tempo Presente*.) The extensive correspondence among Carmen Angleton, Mary McCarthy, and Hannah Arendt is filled with accounts of art exhibitions, museums, and Italian country churches visited; encounters with such as Bernard Berenson and Peggy Guggenheim; books read, written, and translated; love affairs and marriages begun and ended. Carmen Angleton kept open house at her apartments and her father's villa in the diplomatic district of Rome, lavishing flowers, antiques, linens, opera tickets, auto and sea trips on her friends. An obituary of Miriam Chiaromonte includes this anecdote: "Carmen Angleton, the beautiful sister of the legendary James Jesus Angleton, used often to be in the Chiaromonte home . . . The Angletons had spent part of their childhood in Italy and were very cultured people. When I [Emilia Benghi, author of the obituary] left for Milan, Carmen said to me, "Oh, Sant 'Ambrogio is my brother's favorite Romanesque church,"[20] which places James Angleton's sensibility in the same context.

In 1960, while Kim Philby was still in Beirut reporting for his two newspapers and at least two secret intelligence services, James Angleton was in a Virginia sanatorium for treatment of tuberculosis.[21] J. Edgar Hoover's deputy, Alan H. Belmont, reported to Hoover: "You will recall that in May of this year Angleton was confined to a sanitarium because of a tubercular ailment.

> For your information, Angleton returned to his home on November 4, 1960, where he will continue his convalescence. The lung infection has been cleared but he will be required to rest and continue some drug treatments for several more weeks. He very likely will not return to active duty before April 1, 1961."[22]

Once a death sentence, by 1960 tuberculosis was treated with increasing success by drug therapy. However, some of the drugs used at that time had severe side-effects and treatment times, as noted by Belmont, extended to many months.

On 26 January 1961, while Angleton was convalescing at home, his agent Jay Lovestone testified to Congress concerning a recent secret Moscow conference of communist parties. "This threat is very serious," Lovestone said. "The Communists have recovered much of the ground they lost in the Polish revolt and the Hungarian revolution." The Moscow meeting, he said, came up with "an extremist, adventurous program for world conquest" and war against the United States, deemed "an enemy of the peoples of the whole world."[23]

When Angleton returned to Washington, about a month earlier than anticipated,[24] he found the new administration preoccupied with the Bay of Pigs operation, the effort to overthrow Fidel Castro's government, which had been planned during the Eisenhower administration. Opinion in the CIA itself was divided on the Cuban invasion scheme. Richard Bissell, head of the Clandestine Services, allied himself with his predecessor Wisner's covert warriors, including Tracy Barnes and Desmond FitzGerald, in favor of the project.

Richard Helms, now chief of operations for the Clandestine Services under Bissell, was more skeptical, Helms withdrawing from discussions about Cuba, or being excluded from those discussions by Bissell.[25] Angleton sided with Helms: "Through Mario Brod* in New York, Angleton had some Mafia sources who knew Cuba, and they all told Brod that it would never work."[26] The plans for the Cuba project were similar to those for the Albania debacle, those in Poland, the Baltic states, and the Ukraine: refugee groups trained by intelligence operatives, hopes for anti-communist uprisings, information leaks alerting the local authorities. Mafia advice should not have been necessary.

In the days immediately before the invasion the Cuban police arrested virtually every CIA "asset" on the island.[27] More than a decade later, Angleton commented: "Now, what struck me, not having had any part of the Bay of Pigs, because of differences with Bissell, was that it seemed to me that both the Cubans and the Soviets knew everything that was being planned. In other words, they had the thing penetrated, and it was foredoomed."[28] Angleton thought "the whole Bay of Pigs failure was because of that penetration:

> In other words, I think that when your running operation is as massive as the Bay of Pigs, where journalists like Tad Szulc can learn the secrets and publish them in the New York Times, and where everybody and his mother down in Miami knew something was going on and given the looseness of it, I mean there's no question that the opposition doesn't find it hard to work in sources, and also because, obviously, they sent provocateurs and agents into the United States."[29]

The Bay of Pigs only confirmed Angleton's belief in the existence and efficacy of penetration as a secret intelligence tactic and the need to defend against it.

After the failure of the Bay of Pigs operation, it appears that the Kennedy administration considered a drastic plan to repair this damage to its prestige: nuclear war. Aleksandr Fursenko and

---

* Brod "was a long time agent (recruited in Italy in 1944 by Jim Angleton) who had operational involvements for us in Haiti and other places," who in 1975 was "an Agency Mafia penetration" agent. JFK Assassination File 104-10096-10112.

Timothy Naftali tell us that "According to two reports from a well-placed (GRU) source in the US national security bureaucracy,

> [B]etween 6 and 12 June 1961, the United States had decided to launch a nuclear strike on the USSR in September 1961. It was due only to the Soviet announcement of the new series of atomic tests that the United States reversed its decision. According to the GRU's informant, the tests convinced the United States that the Soviet nuclear arsenal was more powerful than previously assumed.[30]

Aside from the sensational report of a planned pre-emptive strike by the United States on the Soviet Union, we are left with a tantalizing reference to a "well-placed [GRU] source in the US national security bureaucracy." That does not necessarily mean that Soviet military secret intelligence had an agent in the CIA. A GRU employee under cover as a TASS journalist might have lunch with an official of any one of the very many organizations in the US national security bureaucracy, making that American official "a source." Or there might have been a briefing "on background." Or, it could mean that there was a GRU double agent, a mole, in the CIA.

The Bay of Pigs failure ended the careers of Allen Dulles and Richard Bissell. A new Director of Central Intelligence, John McCone, an outsider, was appointed and Angleton's friend Richard Helms was promoted, which only enhanced Angleton's own power. Within two weeks of the failed invasion, a covert annex to a policy paper prepared for the National Security Council on 4 May 1961 tasked Angleton's counterintelligence staff to cooperate with the exiled Cuban Revolutionary Council to "create, train and support a highly motivated and professionally competent apolitical and career security service which will be dedicated to the preservation of the democratic form of government."[31] In other words, to create a secret intelligence agency for the Cuban exile groups. Angleton was to "assign carefully selected and qualified Agency personnel to work with the service during the current and *post-Castro* eras."[32] [Emphasis added.] Implicit in this order to Angleton was the assumption that the "post-Castro" era would begin in the not-too-distant future. This last was not only a prediction, it was also a "tasking," but not for Angleton.

The CIA called the project to bring about a "post-Castro era"

Operation Mongoose, which, under General Edward Landsdale, was to be the instrument that would accomplish what the Bay of Pigs invasion had failed to achieve: not only the liberation of the Cuban people from totalitarian Communism, but the murder of Fidel Castro himself. The CIA officer in charge of Operation Mongoose under Landsdale was William King Harvey, Angleton's longtime colleague, the man who was said to have been the most emphatic about Philby's role in the defection of Burgess and Maclean. Angleton was involved in Operation Mongoose to the extent of placing an agent in Havana to provide the counterintelligence support for Harvey's work that had been lacking for the Bay of Pigs invasion. Angleton told the Church Committee, in a secret session only declassified much later, the following story about that agent:

> So when Bill took over in the Cuban business, then I decided that since we were very close friends that I would try to help him out by getting him a source totally unknown to everybody. And I went to the Israelis. And I had them assign a man to Havana, whom I happened to know very well. He was born in Bulgaria. He can speak Russian and the Balkan countries' languages. He is today their senior man on Soviet intelligence. He was a young officer in the days I am speaking of. And he was sent to Havana, which meant that here he was—and the communications were from him in a one time pattern,* I mean total security, from Havana to Tel Aviv, to me, and from me to Bill. And no one knew of his existence or his identify, except Harvey and myself, and of course, Dick Helms.[33]

Angleton went to Mossad, as if to another department in the CIA, and had them place an agent in Havana (who no doubt knew Spanish as well as Bulgarian), something that no one else in the CIA had been able to do. So intimate were Angleton's relations with Israel's secret intelligence organizations, so competent in these matters he thought the latter.

Operation Mongoose landed small raiding parties, printed propaganda leaflets, sabotaged factories, enlisted Mafia assassins, all to no avail.[34] It was a repetition of the failures a decade earlier with

---

* Angleton probably meant using one-time pads of codes.

similar operations directed at Albania, Poland, the Baltic states, the Ukraine . . .

James Angleton in 1975 told the Church Committee that "In December 1961 a member of the KGB in Helsinki defected to us. His name is Golitsyn . . . his is probably without any question the most major defection since World War II as far as Soviet intentions, Soviet organization, and Soviet operations are concerned."[35] He was, in a manner of speaking, the second coming of the defector from Stalin, Walter Krivitsky, who had spoken of Soviet double agents to deaf ears at the beginning of World War II. Anatoliy Golitsyn, and his stories, were better received.

Golitsyn's defection took place shortly after "the secret gathering in Moscow of eighty-one Communist parties" that Jay Lovestone testified had determined on what amounted to a secret declaration of war against the West. Golitsyn had been serving in Helsinki as "Klimov," vice-consul in the Soviet embassy, with the actual rank and duties of a major in the KGB.[36] He had attended a Soviet intelligence school from 1948 to 1952, at the time of the climax of Philby's activities in MI-6, while Angleton was establishing himself in the CIA, then spent two years in Vienna in the mid-1950s before returning to Moscow for more studies in the KGB's higher education system, earning a law degree, spending a year or two on a desk as an analyst in the Anglo-American and NATO sections of the KGB, then moving on to Finland for his second overseas tour. He was a highly educated intelligence analyst, not an operations officer. In the CIA order of things he would have been in the Directorate of Intelligence, not Plans.

Golitsyn was at first interrogated by members of the Soviet Russia division of the CIA, as was standard practice. The Soviet Russia counterintelligence section routinely "set [defectors] up in offices with assistants and, to stimulate their imaginations, did not hesitate to put into their hands, for the first time, information that came from others.

What did they think might be done? What ideas did they have to do it? . . . These people were . . . instinctively aware of how the enemy lived, worked, reasoned, and planned."[37]

Tennent Bagley recalled that what Golitsyn "told in the first months after his defection proved to be accurate and priceless. Those of us who worked with those leads came to call them 'vintage Golitsyn,' in contrast to his later, more speculative pointers and notions."[38]

The KGB itself took Golitsyn's defection very seriously, effectively suspending all foreign activities.[39] Angleton told the Church Committee that after Golitsyn's defection "the Soviets rapidly transferred 300 of their people . . .

> And as is normal in a case of this kind, the big problem is to write a damage report, which means the whole service would come to a standstill. And the objective would be to review all paper files and everything that showed his initials. And you usually would have three categories of information: you would have information which he definitely had knowledge of, and information which he did not have knowledge of, and information which you are not certain about . . . Now, when we did a similar operation on the Sergeant Dunlop who was working in the National Security Agency . . . we came to approximately 400,000 documents that he could have had access to . . . and out of this [Golitsyn] case came the finalization of the case of Philby, Burgess, and all that . . ."[40]

In 1962 British newspapers ran stories that a Soviet defector had moved from the US to UK.[41] According to Jefferson Morley, Golitsyn received "a stipend of ten thousand pounds a month from the British officials."[42] It may have been the information from Golitsyn that sent Nicholas Elliott on his way to Beirut and Philby, then, on his way to Moscow.

Beyond such specific information, including the KGB's Helsinki order of battle (organization chart) and, presumably, the names of local agents and such, Golitsyn's value to the CIA was his knowledge of the KGB gathered over fifteen years of experience.[43] Golitsyn worked with Western counterintelligence for more than a decade, causing havoc according to one interpretation, saving the West from the massive Soviet campaign planned at Lovestone's "secret gathering in Moscow of eighty-one Communist parties," according to another. As time passed, Golitsyn increasingly relied on reviewing CIA (and MI-5) files to trigger memories of what he had read in Moscow. This sort of thing is standard in police interrogations: witnesses are shown, say, photographs to jog their memories of persons of interest. However, as the KGB files faded from Golitsyn's memory, his reactions became less reliable.

When Golitsyn first began to talk with American and British intelligence officers it had been only a decade since Burgess and Maclean had gone to Moscow and Philby had fallen under suspicion. Philby was still in Beirut, reporting to and under surveillance by various intelligence services. Golitsyn's most sensational claim, and the claim that most worried Angleton, was that the Western intelligence services and governments had been penetrated by the KGB, as, of course, some of them had been. A KGB report to Khrushchev recorded that in 1960 alone, "375 foreign agents were recruited, and 32 officers of the State Security were transferred abroad and legalized."[44] And there was the plan presented to the Central Committee by KGB chairman Alexander Shelepin in March 1961, in which the KGB proposed "to carry out disinformation measures on the information that American intelligence obtains about the Soviet Union;

> to pass along the channels of American intelligence disinformation on economic, defense, and scientific-technical issues; to disinform the USA intelligence regarding real intentions of Soviet intelligence services, achieving thereby the dispersion of forces and means of the enemy's intelligence services."[45]

This is close to the description of the plan reported by Golitsyn to his CIA interrogators. Golitsyn claimed that the lack of success of Western efforts in the Cold War was attributable to the KGB's penetration of Western secret intelligence services; he believed that the deception operations he posited required for their success such penetrations, as FUSAG/FORTITUDE had depended on British intelligence's control of German agents.[46] Golitsyn argued that in this way the Western view of Soviet bloc events at the height of the Cold War was based on a projection (misinformation) emanating from Moscow itself, an effort to present—through press reports, diplomatic cocktail conversations, controlled defectors—a view of the Soviet bloc as divided, weak, reasonable, peace-loving, etc.* Cave Brown wrote that "Many suspected [Philby], then and later, of being the mastermind behind what became known as the KGB's 'grand scheme,' 'the monster plot' to disrupt and destroy the 'special relationship' between Whitehall and the White House."[47] "Many," of course, included James Angleton.

Golitsyn, and Angleton, notoriously considered the Sino-Soviet split of the 1960s as another deception operation. Recently, Ross Johnson has commented on "the broader background of looking at communism that could have brought Angleton to the conclusion that the Sino-Soviet split[48] was all a hoax . . .

> The closer you go back to 1960, the more voices you would've found wondering, 'This can't be for real,' the Sino-Soviet dispute . . . When you get ten years out, it's kind of absurd to doubt the Sino-Soviet split. But, at the time, the closer you are to the '60s, the realer it seemed. And it's not the only case. There's an NIE [National Intelligence Estimate] from the early '50s on Yugoslavia, and in there you can find a footnote from at least two of the agencies that the Tito-Stalin dispute isn't for real. So, there is that sort of mindset that over the years affected thinking . . . maybe this helps us understand some of the background that could have led Angleton or others to that kind of conclusion."[49]

As we have seen, the Soviet and Russian secret intelligence agencies had a history of large-scale deception operations, a history of which Angleton had made a close study and which he taught his staff to study as well. The outstanding operation of this kind—that of projected interpretation, as it were—was not, as it happens, a Soviet campaign, but the invention by the Western Powers of FUSAG, the notional World War II Allied invasion force created by Allied intelligence. This had been coordinated out of MI-6 with the knowledge of Angleton and the participation of Kim Philby

In October 1962, the month of the Cuban Missile Crisis,

---

* For an interesting take on Soviet/Russian strategic deception, see: "A Lesson in Russian Strategic Deception, How Moscow tries to throw us off the trail," by John Sipher, *Slate*, 3 November 2017, http://www.slate.com/articles/news_and_politics/jurisprudence/2017/11/ the_mueller_probe_and_a_lesson_in_russian_strategic_deception.html.

responsibility for Golitsyn was taken over by the CIA's counter-intelligence staff. Angleton became preoccupied with Golitsyn, telling the Church Committee staff that "for a year or so" he had worked on the case "full time," seven days a week.[50] The elegance of Golitsyn's intellectual constructs appealed to Angleton; their text-centered method of interpretation was familiar. Angleton had, after all, once been to school with teachers who had worked on a similar basis. According to David Wise, "The real danger [feared by Angleton] would be a mole high enough up in the Clandestine Services to have access to a wide array of CIA operations and plans,"[51] as had Philby, as had been Angleton's nightmare for a decade by the time Golitsyn appeared in Washington, as would in fact be the case some years later when the counterintelligence officer on the CIA's Soviet desk was Aldrich Ames. During his interrogations, Golitsyn "said he had seen some material at KGB headquarters that could only have come from a very sensitive area of the agency. From someplace high inside the CIA. The implication was plain, and frightening. If Golitsyn was right, the KGB had an agent inside the CIA."[52]

The CIA historian David Robarge believes that "Angleton's real-life experiences as a young, starting out intelligence officer really shaped his perspective on the world . . .

Here you have what Angleton was seeing as a twenty-six/twenty-seven-year-old intelligence officer, an exact duplicate of the strategic deception cycle that he fancied the Soviets were using . . . consider the success of British Intelligence at doubling German agents sent to the U.K. during World War II, then using these agents to send back disinformation to the Wehrmacht. This is what he lived through as a young officer. He has to think, 'That's us doing it. Can they do it to us? They sure can. Twice.' Knowing what Angleton knew at the time . . . The Trust, and then . . . the WiN operation . . . cooked up by the Russians and the Poles in the late '40s and early '50s to run essentially the same kind of deception operation. We're not talking about just an agent sent out to trick us on a particular report. This is a large-scale operation that cost the West and the U.S., in the case of WiN, dearly."[53]

Len Parkinson, writing in the CIA's in-house journal, *Studies in Intelligence,* stated that "we have concluded that most Soviet

Military practices and strategic theories are slow to change.

> We have, therefore, found it useful to identify as many of these practices and concepts as possible, because this helps us in analyzing genuinely new Soviet strategic doctrines, and in evaluating how the Soviets are reacting or might react to particular political and military events."[54]

Concerning Angleton's investigations based on information—and suspicions—from Golitsyn, David Wise found that, in the 1960s, "As the investigation [of possible Soviet double agents in the CIA] grew . . . to include literally dozens of suspects, the demands on Angleton's staff, and that of the Office of Security, were overwhelming." Angleton brought Newton S. Miler from his position as CIA Chief of Station in Ethiopia to help. "The work was carried out by a unit of the Counterintelligence Staff known as the Special Intelligence Group, or SIG."[55] More than a decade later Angleton said, "There was literally a panic when Golitsin said there was a mole. We were under so much pressure after Burgess and Maclean."[56] And Philby: the most intense period of the molehunt took place when MI-6 and the CIA were finally convinced that Kim Philby had always been a Soviet agent. Eventually Miler and his staff investigated more than 120 CIA officers. Tennent Bagley, who had been one of the first to interrogate Golitsyn, believed "That some such specific pointers to possible moles might turn out to be unfounded or misleading, or that they might be wrongly interpreted—and that as a result some innocent officers might unjustly suffer harm to their careers—was an inevitable hazard of our profession to be recognized and accepted by anyone entering it."[57]

Robarge wrote in 2003 that "Angleton's notorious [molehunt] combined methodological and psychological elements that proved incompatible and destructive.

> First was the fundamental dilemma in counterintelligence of proving the negative: just because a mole has not been found does not mean one is not there. Added to that insoluble quandary were Angleton's obsessive personality, intense animosity toward the Soviet Union, and feeling of betrayal by Philby. Given that the KGB had the means, motive, and opportunity to run a strategic

deception using penetration agents and disinformers, Angleton—
once Golitsyn provided him the leads he needed—would not be
deterred from finding one of them inside the CIA . . ."[58]

Angleton's search for a double agent within the CIA followed the
pattern used by the British services, with some participation by
Kim Philby, during the search for "Homer" a decade earlier. No one
was ruled out as a suspect as a matter of principle; every lead and
anomaly, as far as possible, was followed up; attention on one or
another suspect intensified as indications accumulated. The CIA's
counterespionage effort of the early sixties did not, however, follow
the course of the panic in the administration of President Truman:
there were no mass firings, no public shaming, no revocation of
passports or blacklisting from civilian employment. Some careers
were harmed, some secret intelligence operations were called into
question or terminated, which angered those who had hoped to
pursue those careers or operations. They took their revenge in interviews, ghosted articles, memoirs, "authoritative" histories.

As to how things seemed at the time, beyond Angleton's counterintelligence staff, John M. Maury, then Chief, Soviet Russian
Division, on 29 March 1963, recommended that Golitsyn, his wife,
and daughter be granted permanent residence in the United States,
as Golitsyn "has already made an outstanding contribution to the
intelligence and counterintelligence mission of the United States
Government

> by furnishing valuable information of first priority concern to the
> National Security. This Agency and the Federal Bureau of Investiga-
> tion continue to exploit his knowledgeability on Soviet intelligence
> operations in many parts of the world . . ."[59]

There is, among the vast JFK Assassination files, a document dated
23 May 1963; i.e., between Philby's disappearance from Beirut
and his surfacing in Moscow. It is labeled as a "Working Paper on
Cuban Control and Action Capabilities." Angleton described it as
"a description of the techniques used to set up a Communist control system in Cuba, and the means by which such techniques are
implemented."[60] Jefferson Morley commented that "The 'Cuban
Capabilities' memo is one of the most important documents

bearing Angleton's name to ever surface. It confirms his leading role in US-Cuba policy in 1963 while also demonstrating his intellectual power. Angleton's analysis of the strengths of Castro's government was lucid, historical and comprehensive."[61] While the paper is interesting in itself, it also has other implications. The distribution list is extensive: the Joint Chiefs of Staff, the Defense Intelligence Agency, the FBI, and the intelligence or research sections of the Department of State, USAF, Army, Navy, Coast Guard, NSA, Office of Security USIA, AID, INS, Department of Justice, and Treasury. That is, quite broadly, every office in the federal government with an interest in intelligence matters or Cuba. The formality and extent of the document (marked Top Secret), together with this distribution list, implies that it was probably not a singular production, but one of a series of similar area and subject studies produced by Angleton and his colleagues.* And that the paper was not focused on counterintelligence demonstrates James Angleton's broad influence in the CIA, beyond his formal responsibilities.

Angleton continued to see Allen Dulles after Dulles's forced retirement, their meetings and telephone calls recorded in the appointment diaries of Dulles's secretaries. It appears that Dulles turned to Angleton for literary advice, vetting a proposed biographer, helping with speeches and articles, and apparently writing, or at least drafting, the section on counterintelligence in *The Craft of Intelligence*, a book published under Dulles's name in 1963 and revised in 1965. The counterintelligence section of what is elsewhere essentially a propaganda publication has more of an air of an encyclopedia article: clear, concise, fairly comprehensive, and objective. Kim Philby is mentioned a few times in *The Craft of Intelligence*, most interestingly in the section on the communist intelligence services. "In retrospect," writes Dulles, or, more probably, Angleton,

[I]t is Philby, less well known to the general public than his close friends, the notorious Burgess and Maclean, who deserves the closest scrutiny as perhaps the outstanding example of Soviet success in achieving high-level penetration through men who belonged to

---

* There were apparently precedents to work of this sort by Angleton and his staff; e.g., the study *The Rote Kapelle: the CIA's history of Soviet intelligence and espionage networks in Western Europe, 1936–1945*.

the generation of pro-Communist intellectuals of the twenties and thirties. Philby was not only a diplomat, useful as he and Burgess and Maclean may have been to the Soviets in this capacity; he was also a high-ranking intelligence officer."[62]

This last fact was perhaps not generally known in 1965, at the height of the molehunt.

There is an often-reproduced photograph of James Angleton, a few years later, carrying from a church the small box containing the ashes of Allen Dulles.

President Kennedy was assassinated on 22 November 1963, apparently by Lee Harvey Oswald, an American, who, when serving in the Marine Corps, had been stationed at an airbase in Japan used by the U-2 aircraft. There are few, if any, political events that have generated as much controversy and sheer amount of paper, and the digital equivalent, as the Kennedy assassination. The well-known questions include whether the assassin was indeed Oswald; if so, whether he acted alone; if not, who was (or were) the assassin(s) and in either case whether there were state actors or private groups behind the assassination. Kennedy's successor, Lyndon Johnson, later said, "What raced through my mind was that if they had shot our President, driving down there, who would they shoot next? And what was going on in Washington? And when would the missiles be coming? I thought it was a conspiracy and I raised that question, and nearly everybody that was with me raised it."[63]

Oswald had defected to the Soviet Union in 1959, married a Russian, returned to the United States in 1962, becoming active in the pro-Castro Fair Play to Cuba Committee. Oswald's connections with the Soviet Union and Cuba were well known to the CIA, in part through Angleton's mail surveillance program.[64] There was a "file bearing Oswald's name, and the handwritten words 'SECRET EYES ONLY.' This notation put Oswald in a rather select group. The former Marine Corps radio operator was . . . one of three hundred Americans whose international mail was opened, copied, and filed for future use."[65] The CIA's attention having been attracted by Oswald's defection, return, and attempted redefection.

The FBI's liaison officer to the CIA, Sam Papich, "had driven to

Langley and was in Angleton's office by 10:30 a.m. on the day after the assassination, where

> the CI chief apprised him of certain "sinister implications." Angleton was bothered by [a] 1961 warning about the KGB's plotting to kill a "Western political leader," by the mystery of Oswald's travels in the USSR, and by other unresolved questions."[66]

In 1975, during the Church Committee investigations of the CIA's own assassination efforts, Senator Baker asked Angleton: "'Do you have an opinion as to whether or not Oswald was in fact a Soviet agent?' Mr. Angleton: 'I don't think that the Oswald case is dead. There are too many leads that were never followed up. There's too much information that has been developed later.'"[67] And again:

> Senator Baker: "Do you have any opinion as to whether Oswald was a Soviet Agent?"
>
> Mr. Angleton: "Yes, I have a very strong opinion . . . given the fact that the Soviet Government has a Department 13, which is under the Central Committee, who is tasked with the assassination of Western Leaders, that the door is open, and that is for future generations to speculate."[68]

At another point in his testimony, Angleton said: "Personally I would never say the Soviets did this act. On the other hand, there's an awful lot of doubts in my mind regarding the whole assassination."[69] Which presented the Committee with a sufficient depth of ambiguity.

President Johnson immediately appointed a group to investigate the assassination of his predecessor: the Warren Commission, named after its chairman, Supreme Court Chief Justice Earl Warren. (Allen Dulles, as a former Director of Central Intelligence, was a member of the Commission, as was John McCone, the then current director.) The CIA's counterintelligence staff was the point of contact between the Agency and the Warren Commission, because "It was the CI Staff that had the counterintelligence files which would support the extensive investigation which was [to be] conducted."[70] The CIA's initial file search on Oswald was conducted by the counterintelligence staff of the Soviet Russia Division, headed by Tennent

Bagley.*[71] There turned out to be a considerable amount of material in the files, especially concerning Oswald's time in Mexico City, his attempts to contact Cuban and Soviet officials there, and his earlier time in the Soviet Union. More than ten years later Raymond Rocca, Angleton's assistant since OSS days, testified to the United States President's Commission on CIA Activities within the United States (the Rockefeller Commission): "In response to why the Agency was not involved in the investigation of Oswald in the pre-assassination period,

> Mr. Rocca stated that there existed guide lines under the Delimitation Agreement with regard to military defectors which limited jurisdiction of these cases to the FBI and to the responsible military arm. In this instance it was the Navy and the FBI to the exclusion of CIA . . ."

So far, so conventional. Then: "Mr. Rocca's comments were that there are areas which the Warren Commission did not fully investigate and which, in retrospect, suggested to him that the question that Oswald may have been under KGB control was never resolved."[72] And also not quite true. The CIA did not "investigate" Oswald, in particular, before the assassination, but it did have files on him, as was routine for a defector who returned, then apparently attempted to redefect through Mexico City. According to CIA Historian Robarge: "the US government did not have actionable [sic] information that Oswald was a clear threat to the president before 22 November 1963.

> Angleton (assuming he was personally engaged) and a few members of the Counterintelligence Staff . . . concluded that a disgruntled and estranged Oswald was up to something comparatively mundane: trying to re-defect after his attempt to start another life in the United States had failed."[73]

Nonetheless, the summary among the JFK Assassination Files of what the CIA knew about Oswald's time in Mexico, dated 13

---

* It would be interesting to know the balance of effort in the Soviet Russia Division's counterintelligence staff between the molehunt and the investigation of Oswald.

December 1963, runs for twenty-one pages. It begins: "We discover Lee OSWALD in Mexico City: CIA did produce one very significant piece of information on Lee OSWALD before he shot President Kennedy.

On 1 October 1963, our Mexico City Station intercepted a telephone call Lee OSWALD made from someplace in Mexico City to the Soviet Embassy there, using his own name . . . A very sensitive operation in Mexico City provides us with secretly taken photographs of many but not all visitors to the Soviet Embassy there, taken with telephoto lenses . . ."[74]

The memorandum then becomes dramatic: "When word of the shooting of President Kennedy reached the offices of our operating divisions and staffs on the afternoon of Friday 22 November 1963, transistor radios were turned on everywhere to follow the tragedy.

When the name of Lee OSWALD was heard, the effect was electric. A phone message from the FBI came at about the same time, naming OSWALD as the possible assassin and asking for traces. The message was passed on at once by the Chief CI, Mr. Angleton, to Mr. Birch O'Neal of his Special Investigations Unit. Mrs. Betty Egeter of this Unit immediately recognized the name of Lee OSWALD and went for his file . . . Within a week, 27 cabled reports had gone out to the White House, the State Department, and the FBI . . . Many conferences were held with the FBI liaison officer who asked us for certain actions and passed us information from the FBI investigation . . ."

President Johnson had the CIA undertake an investigation of Oswald's history of contacts with Cuba and his stay in the Soviet Union. Raymond Rocca was at first put in charge of coordinating the operation. "Rocca places the beginning of the Warren Commission phase around 23 January 1964, when J. Lee Rankin contacted Helms and asked for CIA assistance for the Commission.

Helms delegated Rocca to be the 'point of contact' of the CIA with the Warren Commission. Rocca's own Counterintelligence staff involved in research matters for the Commission included

Tom Dooley, Paul Hartman and Thomas Hall. Other CIA personnel involved with the Commission were Jack Whitten, [Charles]
Murphy . . . J. C. King, Wigren . . . and [Tennent] Bagley."[75]

All of this—what the CIA and Angleton, in particular, knew about
Oswald; whether there was a relationship between Oswald and
the Agency; and darker suspicions—is part of the tar-baby of the
Kennedy assassination literature. It appears at the moment, from
a reading of the JFK Assassination Files, that the CIA knew much
about Oswald, if having materials in files is knowledge, and that
aside from maintaining the files there was no relationship between
the Agency and Oswald—he was not an agent of the CIA—and that
darker suspicions are not provable.

The CIA's "Field Double Agent Guide" counsels that "A provocation
agent establishing initial contact as a walk-in must have direct contact with the target service [e.g., CIA] at least once. And the target
service, if interested in the bait, is likely to try to arrange for future
meetings on territory under its jurisdiction (or that of a cooperative
service)."[76] The Field Guide goes on to advise that "before a decision
is reached on accepting or rejecting a DA opportunity, asking the
following four key questions will help us to strike the balance.

a. Has the potential DA told us everything? Or are there any indications of withholding? In particular, is there reason to suspect that
   he has withheld a communications channel to the opposition?
b. Does the prospective DA have stayability [sic]? That is, is he
   emotionally and psychologically stable, and are there good prospects of conducting the operation on a long-term basis? Can he
   sustain the anticipated stresses indefinitely?
c. Does the opposition trust him? Some indication of degree of
   adversary trust may be found in his length of service, the nature
   and level of his assignments, level of pay, and quality of communications systems provided him."[77]

It might be observed that from the point of view of the KGB Kim
Philby had repeatedly met all these criteria.
   In 1962 the CIA received a "walk-in" called Yuri Nosenko.
   Nosenko came from the heart of the Nomenklatura. His father

had been a Soviet Minister, a member of the Communist Party's Central Committee, a deputy to the Supreme Soviet, and close to members of the Politburo.[78] Nosenko himself had joined the GRU, Soviet military intelligence, in 1949, transferring to the KGB in 1953, where he worked in counterintelligence (the Second Chief Director- ate), first in the American Department, then, in 1955, transferring to the Tourist Department, where, after an intervening tour back in the American Department, he became deputy chief. In June 1962 (that is, before the Kennedy assassination), Nosenko was again an officer in the counterintelligence branch of the KGB. While attending a disarmament conference in Geneva, he contacted the CIA, asking for money to pay debts and offering in return to provide information about KGB operations against the United States and Great Britain. He said he would not defect, but would contact the CIA again when he was next in the West.[79] He returned to Geneva in early Febru- ary 1964 (that is, just after the Kennedy assassination and a year after Philby went to Moscow), saying that now he wished to defect. He interested his CIA interlocutors in his "bait" by saying he had seen Oswald's KGB files and that they indicated that the KGB had thought Oswald unstable and had left him to his own devices. In other words, he claimed that there was no Soviet involvement in the assassination.

The CIA brought Nosenko to Washington for evaluation of his bona fides, at first in the custody of the Soviet Russia division, which put him through the standard process for evaluation of "walk-ins" to determine whether he was in fact a defector or was instead a provo- cation or a double agent. Golitsyn said that Nosenko was lying, that he was a double or provocation agent.[80] Others defended him. This process, in which Angleton increasingly interested himself, but did not direct, went on for years. Angleton maintained a characteristic stance of studied ambiguity. Many years later, in 1978, he testified to the House Select Committee on Assassinations that: "I have never made a statement that Nosenko is a dispatched agent . . .

I have pointed out the contradictions, and the things that are not right, that have never been resolved regarding Nosenko, which raised doubt as to his bona fides. But I never came to a conclusion that Nosenko is a dispatched agent."[81]

Angleton was paid to be "the most suspicious man in the Agency": the role of counterintelligence is to see anyone coming to its attention as a potential threat.[82] But during the early 1960s the usual efforts began to appear to Angleton to be insufficient. The Soviet and their allied secret intelligence services had become increasingly aggressive. For example, General Gehlen's West German foreign intelligence apparatus (once a CIA proprietorial, as it were) was penetrated at the highest levels. In June 1960 two cryptanalysts employed by NSA defected to the Soviet Union, via Havana, just after Gary Powers' U-2 was shot down. Their work for the Soviets overlapped with and was replaced by that of an army driver, Staff Sergeant Jack E. Dunlop, who had stayed in place for five years, chauffeuring generals and secret documents to and fro, until his suicide in 1963.[83] There were probably others.

After the CIA decided that nothing decisive could be learned from Nosenko concerning the assassination, the attention of the counterintelligence staff turned to a theory that the CIA's reception of Nosenko's "message" (that Oswald had not been a Soviet agent), as a matter of espionage tradecraft, would be monitored by a "penetration agent" at a high level within the CIA itself.[84] Philby had been a double agent in place in a rival secret intelligence organization, an agent who might undertake worthwhile actions, or prevent those that were potential threats, but was more important to the KGB as reporting on the reactions of MI-6 (and the CIA) to the initiatives of the KGB. Edward Jay Epstein, as usual no doubt reflecting Angleton's own views, wrote that "What Philby provided was feedback about the CIA's [reactions] . . .

> with Philby in place, [Soviet deception planners] could continually [modify] their messages to keep them credible . . . they could accurately determine whether or not reports fed to the CIA were believed or not, and what additions or revisions would make them credible. They could also find out the preconceived picture that the CIA had and then fit their messages to it."[85]

The counterintelligence assumption that had to be made on the basis of the penetration of US and British intelligence by Philby and his Cambridge friends and their American peers was that if this had happened once, it could happen again. Indeed, prudence dictated that it had to be assumed that it was, at each moment, happening again. Hence Angleton's "molehunt," hence the suspicion of Nosenko. Defending Angleton, Robarge wrote that: "The molehunt gained momentum from mid-1963 to late 1964 for what in retrospect seem justifiable reasons.

> First, during that period Philby defected and at least five cases of Soviet espionage by U.S. military personnel and a defense contractor had resulted in arrests or were under investigation. Second, and the most unexplored or underemphasized factor, was the possible connection between the Kennedy assassination, Nosenko's defection, and the mole."[86]

Eventually Nosenko himself became in a way irrelevant. He was released, "rehabilitated," and "On January 30, 1964, Dick Helms approved a $50,000 payment to Nosenko, with an annual contract of $25,000 a year for an indefinite period, along with provisions for retirement and benefits."[87] In this way Nosenko became a paid CIA consultant by way of amends, or by way of an effort to bring closure to the controversy.[88] One would have thought that would be the end of the matter. It was not. Even Angleton's retirement did not stop the debate about Nosenko's bona fides, a debate which has continued into the following century.[89] Some retired CIA officials, and some scholars and journalists who agree with them, continue to argue that Angleton's counterintelligence efforts in the 1960s and those of his associates, such as David Murphy, "paralyzed" the Agency, or at least the efforts to recruit agents in the Soviet Union and the other communist countries. Others argue the contrary case, notably Tennant Bagley, who wrote in a book published in 2007: "the caution that Murphy . . . introduced into CIA's efforts to recruit Soviets was never allowed to hinder the acceptance of a single Soviet volunteer, nor did it preclude a well-considered recruitment approach."[90]

Neither party could prove its case, as to do so those arguing against Angleton's actions would have to prove that none of the prospective agents were tainted, while those defending him would have to prove that all those suspected were guilty. Or could have been.

Christopher Andrew tells this story: "The place is London; it's early in the morning of March 14, 1966.

Angleton and Anatoly Golitsyn . . . have just arrived without warning in London probably on the overnight flight from Washington. Angleton rings his friend, Maurice Oldfield, recently SIS representative in Washington . . . Angleton then asks for an urgent meeting with the Chief of SIS, Sir Dick White . . . and also a meeting with the Director General of MI-5, Sir Martin Furnival Jones, and some of their senior officers . . . White and Jones immediately clear their diaries, immediately cancel all their other appointments, and this is at nine o'clock in the morning . . . When the meeting begins, they agree to Angleton's proposals, which, they understand, have the support of the DCI, to set up a new and highly secret transatlantic intelligence forum, later known as CAZAB, to consider evidence of Soviet penetration and disinformation."[91]

And why not? James Angleton's position as chief of the counterintelligence staff of the Central Intelligence Agency made him the de facto leader of his counterintelligence colleagues in allied countries who were attempting to resist the KGB offensive. In the late 1960s, as Andrew's story illustrates, he institutionalized this relationship through a series of conferences with the representatives of the Canadian, Australian, New Zealand, and British (CAZAB) counterintelligence services. The first CAZAB conference took place in summer 1967 in Melbourne. It was attended by representatives from the CIA, the FBI, MI-5, MI-6, New Zealand's Secret Service, and the Australian Security Intelligence Organisation and Australian Secret Intelligence Service.[92] That raconteur of the intelligence business, Peter Wright, called the CAZAB conferences Angleton's "outstanding achievement." "The best, the brightest, and the most senior officers in Western intelligence came together once every eighteen months to discuss his agenda—the Soviet threat, the role of counterintelligence—and to conduct doom-laden future scenarios."[93] CAZAB was, and is, the alliance between the English-speaking countries' secret intelligence services. Its creation indeed may have been Angleton's greatest counterintelligence achievement.

The usual depictions of James Angleton include frequent references to his trout and bass fishing, his greenhouse full of orchids. To these should be added his literary friends, Cicely's artist friends, Carmen's café society set. He was not, only, the dark-suited man chain-smoking at his desk in Langley, brooding on the deceptions of the enemies of the West. Kim Philby's colleague Nicholas Elliott, writing after both Philby and Angleton were dead, summed up his view of James Angleton as follows: "Beneath the rather sinister mystique that Jim created around himself he was a very likeable man; and a good friend to those he could bring himself to trust . . . Jim was a patriot, a flawed but at times brilliant professional with a formidable personality and breadth of vision."[94]

PHILBY IN MOSCOW

"The British subject Philby, who occupies a leading position in British Intelligence, has applied to the Soviet authorities for political asylum and Soviet citizenship. It is learned that the USSR Supreme Soviet has complied with Philby's request." *Izvestia*, Moscow, 30 July 1963.[1]

It was not unexpected. It was, in certain circles, expected, perhaps facilitated. Most of those in the Anglo-American secret worlds who knew, or knew of, Philby had believed, with varying degrees of conviction, since the summer of 1951 that if he had not been a Soviet agent he was close enough to that as to make no difference. Only a few of his contemporaries in MI-6 had not quite been convinced. But believing something is different from knowing it. Now they knew. Knightley: "Philby was at the centre of the early CIA operations and when we assess what he was able to do for the Russians during his two years in Washington, we have to think . . . of . . . political will, of the lack of it, long-term military intentions, divisions in decision-making bodies, and relations between allies—the West's grand strategy." Even during his six years in Beirut, he would have learned, and passed to Moscow then or later, much about the people in the various security services and diplomatic posts whom he met—all those alcohol-lubricated parties. Miles Copeland, who knew Philby in Beirut as well as in Washington, offered this judgment: "What it comes to, is that when you look at that whole period from 1944 to 1951—leaving out anything [Philby] picked up other times—the entire Western intelligence effort, which was pretty big, was what you might call minus advantage. We'd have been better off doing nothing."[2]

Philby's "first months in Russia were a concentrated period of 'debriefing' getting down on paper and on tape just about everything he knew about the West which might have an intelligence value."[3]

Knightley brought out the implications of this: "Philby was empty-ing his mind of *everything* he knew about the workings of British and American intelligence . . .

> [W]hen an intelligence officer as senior as Philby defects there is not a lot that <u>can</u> be done. Intelligence agencies are big, bureaucratic organizations employing thousands of highly trained people, many with specialist skills. The way these organizations work cannot be changed overnight; the people they employ cannot be quickly replaced; operations under way for years cannot be immediately aborted."[4]

"Since Philby had knowledge of hundreds of SIS staff, their cover was blown for life, and would have been recognized by the RIS [Russian Intelligence Service] upon arriving at any foreign posting."[5]

The FBI's Robert Lamphere, once close enough to Philby to have been a guest at his dinner parties, took these matters personally. "[I]t occurred to me that the KGB must know about my work, and, in fact, about me personally. In a sense, I had been violated because they had penetrated my office in the person of Philby . . . [T]hey probably knew my idiosyncrasies, and looked for ways to counter my every move."[6] And not only Lamphere. Every high-ranking official in the FBI, perhaps even Hoover himself, had provided Philby with material for a personal file in Moscow. Also a significant number of officials of the Atomic Energy Commission and the State Department. All senior career officers in the CIA as well: named, appraised, traceable for as long as they were associated with the Agency, perhaps well into the 1970s. Also many of the higher ranking officers of the French and German services and those of the Middle Eastern countries; the Mossad and other Israeli secret intelligence organizations. Beyond personnel, there were procedures: the "methods" part of the phrase "sources and methods." People come and go, change posts, transfer from one part of an organization to another, but the ways in which the organization goes about its activities remain similar for decades. How are appraisal and performance criteria to be changed? Codes can be replaced, but the fact that certain kinds of codes are used cannot. Decisions can be altered, but altering the decision process is less possible. Positive vetting can be implemented, but the matters vetted, as it were, will change with glacial slowness.

The damage to the British services was the worst of all. It was little short of what had happened to the Italian and German secret intelligence services at the end of World War II: nearly everything they had wished to keep secret unveiled. Philby had had a decade to read files, document "order of battle" arrangements, consider the strengths and weaknesses of personnel and operations, the relationship between MI-5 and MI-6 and Special Branch and GCHQ, and the relationship of each of these to their "masters" in Whitehall; how SIS and CIA would cooperate in the event of war with the Soviet Union.[7] An indication of the magnitude of the damage can be found in the German Democratic Republic (GDR) Operations "Arrow" and "Blitz" in the fall of 1954 and the spring of 1955 during the first of which, acting on information from George Blake and Philby, the Stasi arrested 277 agents belonging to the [CIA-controlled] Gehlen Organization, 176 belonging to the US secret services and 94 French agents; while "Blitz" accounted for "521 spies and subversives," destroying the MI-6 and CIA networks in Germany.[8]

As a sample of what Philby was able to tell the KGB, we have this 1971 interview with him concerning British Intelligence Service (BIS) personnel and operations in the Near East. Here follows a representative, if somewhat lengthy, extract:

My good friend Peter Lunn, English espionage resident in Beirut from 1962–68, told [me about] a whole row of English espionage operators and Agents and contacts in BND and other of West Germany's State Departments. Lunn, who rose to a leading position in the BIS in the fifties, worked as a BIS resident in Bonn during the years of 1957–61. Lunn told me that the anti-Brandt material published in West German magazines during the fifties and sixties was inspired by BIS . . . The British Espionage and Intelligence Center located in Beirut is active practically against all Arabian states. After Peter Lunn, the leader of English espionage there was Womerthly (sic), and currently it is Derbyshire who works in the disguise of a secretary in the British Embassy. In the Embassy and in other English representative organizations the following have worked as Agents: McKnot (sic), Roderick Clube (He was recently expelled from Baghdad because of espionage activities), Randel (sic), Clifford, Vitol (sic), Howard, Newman, Temple, Rowly (sic), Noel-Clark (sic), Steel (sic), Chalmers and others. Presently such

BIS representatives as Witbread (sic), Golty (sic), Speadding (sic) are working there; people who [have] hidden themselves behind various diplomatic positions. Lebanon's British Embassy's First Secretaries Sindal (sic) and Joy are also currently active on behalf of the British espionage system. Reliable sources report that it was in Beirut that the SPA service group for the BIS was organized, that is the service who deals with falsifications and provocations and if necessary with terror. . . . Beginning in 1959 BIS in Lebanon organized, through its Agents, several armed groups for acts of terror against unwanted activists in Lebanon. BIS established direct contact with the ultra-rightest party leaders and in the early sixties prepared the overthrow of the lawful government of Lebanon and helped strengthen the military dictatorship. Scores of names of Lebanon's citizens whom the BIS has engaged in espionage activities speak of the widespread activities of the English espionage system in Lebanon. . . . The British espionage system is also carrying out undermining activities in other Arabian states. Special activities by the Great Britain espionage system are present in Amman, where the BIS resident is British First Secretary Spierce (sic), and in Aden where the BIS resident is the British Embassy First Secretary Brekhony (sic) who exchanged the known English spy K. Harden.

Question: Could you say a few words concerning the so-called psychological operations of BIS in the Near East?

K.P.: Such operations have poisoned the atmosphere of the Near East for decades and are organized by the BIS in practically all states. For example, the BIS residents prepared and distributed two anti-government brochures in Iraq in 1966 [after Philby was in Moscow]. The BIS residency in Baghdad received much help from the BIS in Beirut where the skilled master of such operations, Peter Lunn, with the help of BIS agent D. Kujamdzan, gave the final touch to the brochures and printed them on Arabian presses, procured through third parties, in the BIS headquarters. BIS also used one of its other agents, formerly Iraq's oil chief Abdulla Ismal, for undermining activities. Presently, BIS is activating a whole series of undermining activities in Egypt and Syria. Using its position in Syrian emigration circles and the closeness of the former Syrian politician Salehh Dzeddi, the BIS has during recent months alone published over fifteen [editions? of] "Al-Samar". The editorial staff of all of these contains BIS paid Agents who are in the English espionage Near East 'psychological warfare' operations. Finally I would like to add that the main purpose of this work in this area, headed by the BIS, is the organization and carrying through of psychological operations under the banner of anti-Sovietism. As far as the British espionage activities as a whole are concerned, I would like to emphasize that in many states the major part of an embassy personnel consists of special service [Secret Intelligence] workers. In some states, the British delegates are professional employees of the BIS. And one more specific remark. In my youth and during my later years, I invariably saw the inner pretence and cleverness of the British Conservatives who in their blind rage against the Soviet Union, are not for the first time, working against the best interests of the English people. That is why I am now in Moscow.[9]

In 1965, Kim Philby received recognition from the Soviet intelligence services for his great services to their cause: the Order of Lenin and the Order of the Red Banner.

It is difficult to get a clear idea of Philby's nearly twenty years in Moscow. Soviet, and of late, Russian sources tend toward the mythologizing. His image is on postage stamps; there are memorials, films, and heroic biographies of "the spy of the century." Western sources tend to picture a life of depression, isolation, and alcoholism. Picking our way through these dueling narratives, it is reasonable to assume that the first few years, until, say, the publication of the autobiographical *My Silent War* in 1967/8 (no doubt heavily directed and edited),* were occupied by the process of transferring to KGB files all that was in his memory concerning intelligence matters, as above. He was, for reasons that are not yet clear, prevented from seeing Guy Burgess,[10] but he saw much of Donald and Melinda Maclean, soon beginning an affair with the latter, which ended his marriage to Eleanor Philby, who had joined him in Moscow. Melinda Maclean returned to Donald Maclean, or set up with her children without him, then went to the United States, under somewhat mysterious circumstances, in the early 1970s, leaving Philby without sympathetic companionship.

---

* Philby was encouraged to play up differences between CIA and SIS and within SIS in his *My Silent War*. Lyubimov, Mikhail. "A Martyr to Dogma." In Philby, Rufina. *The Private Life of Kim Philby*, p. 284.

Then George Blake, who had escaped from a British prison and gone to Moscow, and his Russian wife introduced Philby to their friend Rufina, who was to be Philby's fourth, and final, wife. During the first year or two of this marriage he was subject to nightly blackout drinking episodes.[11] (It seems that Cecily Angleton left James Angleton during the same period, perhaps due to Angleton's alcoholism.) An article in the *Telegraph* reviewing Dolgopolov's biography of Philby asserts that: "The book acknowledges that Philby had a drinking problem, with his widow saying that in early years there were 'terrible moments that I struggled with.' She said he later got the problem under control, only allowing himself two drinks of cognac or whisky with water at 6pm each night." A less dramatic view came from a KGB official, Mikhail Lyubimov: "I met Philby quite a lot and drank more than one bottle of whisky with him, although all the talk about him being a terrible drinker are exaggerated." Perhaps it can be said that Philby drank too much for his own good, but was not "a terrible drinker" by late Soviet standards.[12]

Lyubimov wrote that "in about 1968, after Andropov became chairman of the KGB, Philby became one of his advisers;

> and it was accepted widely that through Philby's advice the KGB stereotype of the Moscow hood vanished. Philby met with Andropov, not at headquarters, which would have given him great status, but at a special mansion in a side street just off Derzhinsky Square . . . of course he had power. It was very nice for our chiefs to be able to say that they had been to Kim's flat, and that he had said, 'We must take these, and these, and these measures against England.'"[13]

Sometime shortly after January 1975, Lyubimov and Philby thought of a course for spies who were to be posted to England.[14] Circa 1970, according to Yuri Modin, Philby wrote an extensive report on the CIA, which included organization charts, with analyses, lists of names with comments, and a biographical directory of the upper echelons of Britain's SIS.[15]

Philby married Rufina in December 1971. They had a large apartment in a building reserved for high-ranking government officials.

(Philby's pension was the same as the salary of a KGB general.) Rufina had her own chauffeur-driven car.[16] Yuri Modin has it that Philby then stopped drinking and resumed his consulting activities that he had stopped when Melinda left him in 1966. His consulting for the Center mainly dealt with Near Eastern matters. He also was asked to look at photographs of suspected agents. Added to this, he became a trainer of new agents at the KGB's school for spies. Modin said that Philby loved doing this and was an excellent teacher.[17]

According to Rufina Philby, "A year or two after we were married, Kim began to be asked to do an occasional job for the KGB . . . A little later the nature of Kim's work changed and became rather more methodical and systematic."* Circa 1974 Philby became a mentor to young KGB officers, when he was used to "put some life into work on the British target" after the expulsion in 1971 of 105 Soviet diplomats from the UK.[18]

By the late 1970s Kim Philby had become something of a pet of the KGB. Officers would visit him to partake of his aura, bring him presents—"a bottle of whiskey for Kim" (who had apparently actually not stopped drinking)—and send him things from abroad. The archives of the Georgetown University library in Washington happen to hold what is probably a typical correspondence, that between Philby and Lyubimov, then a midlevel KGB officer stationed in Denmark. The first letter in the file, from Philby to Lyubimov, dated 14 April 1977, thanks Lyubimov for a present of tea, spices and snails. Philby says he will be going to Leningrad (where Vladimir Putin was just beginning his KGB career) for business and then to the Crimea for vacation. Similar letters about packages sent and received, a bout with bronchitis, travel, a Philby speech to a hockey team, go back and forth for the rest of the year. A letter of 2 May 1978, from Philby to Lyubimov, thanks him for sending a parcel full of presents and indicates that he will go to the Crimea for six to seven weeks, and provides a list of more items for Lyubimov to send. A letter toward the end of January 1979, thanking Lyubimov for sending the usual items, mentions that there will be a party for Philby's sixteenth anniversary in the Soviet Union, describes a trip from Leningrad to

---

* The dates here do not quite line up. Perhaps Rufina Philby had an interest in emphasizing her role in "rescuing" her husband.

Havana to Odessa and his health regimen.[19] The usual sort of correspondence between a retiree and a younger admirer. "But he still hated his golden cage, ending up as an agent run by a case officer . . . he once snapped at me [Lyubimov], 'Aren't you just being a bit too polite? Do you think I don't know I'm an agent with whom you are in operational contact? Just an agent . . .'"[20]

There is a somewhat different tone to a story told by Ben Macintyre in his biography of Oleg Gordievsky. In 1979 a long-serving Soviet agent in Norway had been arrested. "Philby received a request from the Centre, asking him to evaluate the Gunvor Haavik case and assess what had gone wrong.

> Why had the veteran Norwegian spy been arrested? For weeks Philby pored over the Haavik files and then as he had done so many times in his long career, arrived at the correct conclusion: 'The leak which betrayed the agent could only have come from inside the KGB.'"[21]

Rufina Philby recalled that "On 26 November 1977, Kim [Philby] wrote to his old friend, Erik de Mauny, for many years the B.B.C. Moscow correspondent, describing what by then had become our routine of life in Moscow with annual trips to faraway sanatoriums . . . 'my year can be said to start somewhere around the middle of September, when all my colleagues are back from summer leave.

> I work steadily until mid-May, with a two-week break in Jan. or Feb. spent in a more southerly clime, in or out of the SU. Then, in mid-May we regularly spend the standard 24 days at a sanatorium in the Crimea. I'm afraid we occupy deluxe quarters (surely at my age that is permissible?), and the doctors now know that we are a couple of crazies who dislike medical attention. So they leave us alone to swan around in the gunboats of our Frontier Guard colleagues. Then back to Moscow for a few weeks of more sporadic work, depending on the presence or absence of colleagues. The late summer is spent in some friendly country, half by the waterside (sea, lake or river), half in the mountains . . .'"[22]

The Soviet authorities at first had been unsure how to use Philby's skills after his defection, his recent Russian biographer Dolgopolov acknowledged, although he argues that Philby's work training Soviet agents with seminars given in English was valuable. Gordievsky wrote in his autobiography that the KGB "had established a routine of sending four or five young English-speaking officers to seminars which he conducted in a safe flat, a spacious apartment in Gorky Street.

> There, once a year, Philby would address the young hopefuls on various aspects of British life, explaining how different types of people would speak to each other. Then he would create little scenarios: 'Imagine I'm your contact, and I'm a lawyer. Let's have a conversation, and you ask the questions.' Then he would act as a businessman, journalist, intelligence officer, and afterwards he would write secret reports on his pupils' performance . . . Philby was a shrewd judge of character, with a perceptive understanding of other people."[23]

According to a 2004 article in the Russian publication *Sputnik*, "Intelligence officer Mikhail Bogdanov, who knew Philby, recalls such meetings.

> Philby's Seminars were held with small gaps from 1976 almost up to his death. About 15 young people specialising in British studies attended the seminars. Two or three hours would pass in no time at all. After a brief introduction, Philby (who insisted that his students call him by his first name – Kim, or at least Comrade Kim) was followed by a lively discussion. Naturally they spoke English. Then the most interesting thing began. Philby offered various intelligence situations that were followed by detailed analysis. In one situation, a British counterintelligence agent was trying to get out of a Soviet diplomat who had just arrived from the USSR what his other job really was. In another situation, the teacher became an official communications agent, who during a talk would randomly throw up a precious piece of information, which an intelligence agent had to notice and develop. At the end of each session, the students were dripping with sweat. It is hard to overestimate the value of Philby's seminars for his students. He not only showed a 'hunter's intuition', but great wisdom and an ABC of free communication with different kinds of Englishmen. It was a unique opportunity to

loosen the tongue, and train people in the habits of conversing with a 'real Englishman'. In contrast to a widespread stereotype about Kim Philby in the West, he taught them to work not against Britain, the US but how to study them."[24]

According to Rufina Philby, "In the last years of his life Kim was a happy man.

> He was honoured and respected and had been awarded many state decorations—The Order of Lenin, The Order of the Military Red Star, The Order of the Friendship of the Peoples, The Order of the Patriotic (Second World) War First Class, as well as Hungarian, Bulgarian and Cuban awards. The pupils of whom he was so fond came to see him. And he even realized his great wish: 'to have Graham Greene opposite me and a bottle of wine on a table between us'."[25]

Sir Robert Mackenzie, who had worked with Philby in the initial stages of the search for "Homer," said in 1967: "Make it clear—and this is important—that Philby didn't sell his country's secrets. He gave them away. He didn't do it for money. He never got a penny. He did it for his ideals."[26]

ANGLETON:
A DECADE OF INVESTIGATIONS

Kim Philby's career in MI-6 had ended in a blaze of headlines about "the missing diplomats." As we have seen, after he went to Moscow in 1963—perhaps in order to save MI-6 more headlines of that kind—he eventually settled into a role not unlike that of Anatoliy Golitsyn in the United States: a consultant to the country's secret intelligence agencies; well paid, comfortably accommodated, visited by some admiring patrons, and watched by some officials who were not so admiring. James Angleton's later career did not follow this pattern. He remained within his agency, as chief of the counterintelligence staff, until 1973, only retiring when forced to do so by the then Director of Central Intelligence, William Colby, with whom he had been in conflict for twenty years. Angleton told Joseph Trento that he "came to believe that the events that would lead to my own downfall at the CIA and the successful cover-up of the Soviets' involvement in the Kennedy murder were orchestrated by Philby."[1] It was all Kim's work.

> From "[19]64 to [19]70, roughly, is the heyday of the mole hunt, but it's beginning to peter out even before 1970. You have the reorganization of Soviet Bloc Division, and that's when, as I've seen from internal documentation, the level of activity really starts to go back up . . . But the basic point here is that Golitsyn was right, but the wrong people got nailed initially. Eventually, for various reasons, the real culprits were found, and, by the way, they happened to fit the suspicions that Golitsyn had advanced."[2]

This statement by David Robarge, speaking for the CIA *ex cathedra*, as it were, at a Wilson Center conference in 2014, may be taken as drawing a line under the great molehunt controversy. Gradually the counterintelligence activities within the Agency returned to the routine evaluation of bona fides and other more or less non-controversial matters. Outside the walls of Langley, after Kim Philby went to Moscow, James Angleton's work can be divided between domestic and international matters. Domestically, bowing to the demands of President Johnson, the CIA investigated and, working with the FBI, disrupted the anti-war movement and aspects of the civil rights movement. Angleton had a major research and analysis role in the former.* Among his international activities, those that are known include his cooperation with the Israeli secret intelligence organizations and to some extent the Israeli state itself, the creation of a worldwide alliance of anti-communist secret intelligence organizations, and an abortive effort in Vietnam.

The concentration on personalities in the literature on secret intelligence tends to obscure the magnitude of the Cold War secret intelligence effort on both sides. It was not a matter of Smiley and a few of his friends (and Karla and a few of his friends). It was on an industrial scale, with hundreds, eventually thousands, of governmental employees and even more "agents," "contacts," and "sources." The basic economic impact in, say, Germany, must have been significant. The KGB, like most bureaucratic organizations, issued annual reports to higher authority. One that is well known was that sent in May 1968 from then Chairman of the Committee of State Security Andropov to Brezhnev.[3] "In the period under review, special attention was given to the organization of active counter-measures against the enemy's ideological diversions . . .

> In view of the developing situation, the intelligence service of the KGB carried out a number of measures to help promotion of foreign policy and other initiatives of the Soviet Union, to unmask aggressive plans of imperialist states, to compromise policies of the American government . . . The intelligence service of the KGB . . . took measures to develop agents' access, primarily in the USA . . . During 1967 [the KGB] recruited 218 foreigners, among whom 64 possess operational capacities for work against the USA.

---

* See my *James Jesus Angleton: The CIA, and The Craft of Counterintelligence.* Amherst: University of Massachusetts Press, 2008, p. 227ff.

A passage in the report that would have been of particular interest to James Angleton stated that: "the counterintelligence branches directed their efforts at carrying out measures to gain agents' access to intelligence and other special services of imperialist states.

> During 1967 to this end the KGB arranged the planting of 31 agents in the enemy's intelligence; of them 12 were located by the enemy's special services and subjected to their intense scrutiny, which creates preconditions for the accomplishment of these 'plants' in the future."

In other words, in just that year nineteen agents were not located by "the enemy's intelligence," and presumably continued in their efforts. And then there were double agent "games:" "In order to intercept and control channels of penetration by the enemy [the KGB] into our country, continued working on successful accomplishment of operational games.

> Currently, 9 such games are being conducted, including 4 games with the intelligence of the USA, 8 games with the center of the [Russian émigré organization] NTS and 2 games with the centers of Ukrainian nationalists abroad."

Like any good bureaucracy, the KGB continually recruited new staff. From the figure of 24,952 new agents, constituting 15 percent of the total, claimed in the 1968 report, it appears that the total number of KGB agents was in excess of 160,000. The report concludes with an extensive and quite frank account of self-criticism, including complaints about the difficulties in getting and retaining good help.

As the report explicitly states that the total number of KGB agents in 1967 was approximately the same as in 1966, and does not refer to any other significant year-to-year changes, it would not be imprudent to infer that during the years of the CIA's molehunt, there were something in the order of thirty agents in "the enemy's" intelligence organizations, some, perhaps, in the British services, some in the American. That does not mean that there were KGB agents within the CIA; it does mean that the search for them was not baseless.

*

The CIA focused much of its foreign operations in the early 1960s on the contest with the KGB and its German Democratic Republic allies in Germany. There were literally hundreds of intelligence operatives on both sides, perhaps thousands of agents. Gradually, as the decade went on, however, the attention of the Central Intelligence Agency, like that of other parts of the government of the United States, began to shift to Southeast Asia.

James Angleton spent "considerable time in the Far East at the height of the Agency's effort there."[4] He proposed to establish special counterintelligence (SCI) units for Vietnam, modeled on Philby's SCI units in MI-6, the OSS version of which that Angleton had commanded in Italy during his career in X-2.[5] This proposal fell victim to a classic conflict between the operators in Saigon, employing large numbers of Vietnamese and other agents, and the counterintelligence staff, seeing it as their urgent task to separate those Vietnamese loyal to the US-backed government and those owing allegiance to the opposition. Angleton thought that the Saigon government, its military, intelligence services, and the very agents employed by the CIA were heavily infiltrated by the opposition. It was in Vietnam, over this issue, that he came into conflict, not for the first time, with William Colby.

The story of the struggle between Colby and Angleton, which was, at one level, the struggle between the CIA's "operators" and counterintelligence staff, was traced by Colby to a disagreement over policy, and more importantly, over methods, in Cold War Italy. Colby was a classic secret intelligence operator. Having parachuted into Nazi-occupied Europe as part of a Jedburgh team, and becoming bored in law practice after the war, Colby joined the CIA. After service in Scandinavia, he was posted to Italy to lay the groundwork for American influence in the 1958 elections, working under the direction of Gerald Miller, CIA chief of station in Rome. The political situation in Italy then was that, once more, the CIA-backed Christian Democrats were faced on the right by a variety of neo-fascist and monarchist parties, and on the left by the then-allied communists and socialists. According to Colby's 1978 memoir, *Honorable Men: My Life in the CIA*, he supported an "opening to the Left," the policy of certain Christian Democrats to develop a relationship with the Socialists.[6] Be that as it may, "Most of Colby's activities . . . involved direct subsidies with CIA cash . . .

The cash amounts—$20 million to $30 million dollars per year over several years—made Colby's Italian program the largest political action effort ever carried out by the Central Intelligence Agency . . . The cash that had poured through the Rome station dwarfed what had been spent on the victory of 1948—amounting to more than five times as much—but the result was paltry, a handful of seats."[7]

Despite Colby's efforts as a relatively junior CIA officer, the 1958 election brought little change in the Italian political alignments. The "Opening to the Left" by the Christian Democrats did not occur until 1962, and then only after the US and the Vatican had lifted their vetoes.

Colby's story was that while most CIA agents in Italy in the mid-1950s were run as members of networks ultimately controlled by Miller through Colby, others were run by Angleton's counterintelligence staff, or as part of Angleton's personal network. Colby writes in his memoir that sometime before the fall of 1956, that is, before the election campaign, Miller had him meet "a very secret American contact," who Colby calls "Charlie," who had been in Italy with the OSS and returned to the United States after the war, staying in touch with his Italian contacts and former OSS colleagues, including James Angleton. When Colby met him he was again in Rome under deep cover. "I learned that the secrecy of his operation as a classic 'singleton,' an individual agent operating alone rather than as a member of a net or through a chain of intermediaries, produced the impression in Washington that it reflected the direct truth about events and personalities in Italy . . .

> The professional intelligence operators who managed him, to ensure that this direct truth reached policy levels, had arranged that his reports be forwarded in their raw form in sealed envelopes to Washington and laid on the desk of senior policy-level officials as the real story direct from the source."

And then Colby paints a dramatic scene, not necessarily contemporaneous: "I learned that he had even been picked up on a Washington street corner by a black limousine so that he could orally brief the Secretary of State, John Foster Dulles, as they drove through the city . . .

Obviously such a meeting and the dramatics of clandestinity that surrounded it enhanced the impact of Charlie's views, vastly beyond the effect of the judgments of the many other reports, also from direct conversations with Italian leaders, but passed through the careful screening and collaboration process of the corps of experts on Italian political affairs not only in the editing staffs of our station, but in the analytical components of the embassy, the State Department and the CIA."[8]

Colby objected to this violation of bureaucratic norms. A cabinet official should not secretly receive raw intelligence from an agent. That information should go to the agent's CIA handler, from him or her to the Chief of Station, from him or her to Langley, where it would be fit in to the context of other reports to add to "the product" needed by the Secretary. Colby said that he stopped this direct access of "Charlie," bringing him into the chain of command.

Colby told the story somewhat differently when interviewed in 1988 for a CIA oral history: "How about your relations with Mr. Angleton?

I had first known of him when I was in Italy. He had superb Italian contacts. He had been there in the latter part of the war and met a lot of people. He is a very opinionated guy, which is all right except the idea was that his reports should go straight to God. I remember really getting upset when I heard that he was back in Washington one time, stood on a street corner and a car drove by with Allen Dulles and the secretary of state, picked him up and they had a talk in the car. I said, 'My God! Is this a serious intelligence agency?' Having this guy with his strong opinions directly at the policy level without any analysis, any comparison with the other factors going on. It just violates my sense of what intelligence is all about."[9]

It was not some "Charlie" being picked up on a street corner by Secretary of State John Foster Dulles's black limousine; it was James Angleton, getting into a car with Allen Dulles and his brother, the Secretary of State. This may have been unusual, but only because it was Angleton who routinely picked up Allen Dulles after work and drove him home—in Angleton's black Mercedes. It would seem that in his 1978 memoir, published when Angleton was still alive, Colby told a story that was somewhat confused. Perhaps his "Charlie" in that story was, in fact, James Angleton himself, or, perhaps, a conflation of James Angleton and his father. A decade later he no longer bothered to conceal his disapproval, or jealousy, of Angleton's high-level access behind the fictional "Charlie."

In 1959 Colby was sent to Saigon as Deputy Chief of the CIA's operation there, becoming chief of station in June 1960. During his years in Saigon Colby became well known for his opposition to CIA spying on Diem's government, police, or military. This again brought him into conflict with Angleton, who eventually proposed in 1965 "to develop special counterintelligence units in Vietnam [which]

> displayed certain parallels with his conduct of counterintelligence abroad as Chief of the CI Staff in the way in which the local station would be effectively cut out and command channel and communications would run direct to counterintelligence headquarters in Washington."[10]

Angleton's Vietnam CIA counterintelligence staff were not pleased by Colby's approach to security matters, going so far as to deny him access to their part of the CIA's Saigon headquarters.[11] Their skepticism at his trust in Diem's security measures was confirmed when it turned out that Diem's government in fact had been infiltrated by tens of thousands of Viet Cong agents.

Colby was brought back to Washington in 1962 as head of the Agency's Far East Division, in spite of the doubts of the counterintelligence staff. Early in 1965 Angleton's friend Richard Helms became head of the Clandestine Services and then moved up to Deputy Director of the Agency, giving Helms for the first time direct control over Colby's career. There were three candidates to replace Helms as head of the Clandestine Service—Desmond FitzGerald, Thomas Karamessines, and Colby. Helms gave the job to FitzGerald. When FitzGerald died in the fall of 1967, Helms put Karamessines in his place, passing over Colby a second time and offering him the Soviet Bloc Division, the senior division in the Clandestine Services, as a consolation prize. The year 1967, just after one of the most intense periods of counterintelligence activity within CIA itself, was not a good time to be head of the Soviet Bloc Division, which had been the main focus of that activity. It would have been a tough assignment for Colby. Given the close relationship between Helms and Angleton, placing Colby in the Soviet Bloc Division might have been a way for them to determine if Colby was in fact a mole. (As placing Philby in Beirut may have been a way for the British secret intelligence services to finally determine whether he was a Soviet agent.)

Colby recalled in his 1988 interview that when he was appointed to the Soviet Division, "I began the briefing and it was pretty clear that the Soviet Division in the Agency had been all tied up the last several years in this whole series of Nosenko and Golitsyn and all that crap.

> Every time they tried to move an inch, the CI people said, 'No, it's a fake.' I think that's why Helms was going to send me there to try to straighten the goddamn thing out. Let Angleton do his thing, but get something going there that made sense . . . I never thought that the object of CIA was to protect itself against the KGB. The object of the CIA is to get into the Kremlin; that's what our function is. Sure, you protect yourself, but you goddamn well better have the offensive mission. So, I had doubts about that."

However, Helms himself observed that Colby's "lack of under-standing of counterintelligence . . . would not have been compatible with the Soviet responsibilities, and would surely have put him at loggerheads with Jim Angleton." Angleton's basic assumption, which he shared with his peers in other secret intelligence service organizations, was that it must be assumed that the CIA might at any moment contain an official who was passing its secrets to a foreign intelligence agency. He defended the CIA against that possibility through a continuous investigation of everyone within the CIA who might be in a position to be seriously damaging if they were indeed a foreign agent. In practice the burden of proof was placed on the suspect, a situation that had been envisioned in the Agency's charter, which gave the Director the power to dismiss any of its employees without cause. This is not an absurd approach, as an approach, to the job at hand. Better safe than sorry. It also appears to have worked. The CIA staff was not infiltrated—as far as is known—on Angleton's watch. After Colby fired him and dismantled the system, it was infiltrated by Ames and his like. QED—possibly.

*

James Angleton was taken to the George Washington University
Medical Center on the evening of 11 September 1968, where he
was diagnosed with a bleeding ulcer. The next day FBI official D. J.
Brennan sent William Sullivan a memorandum on the subject: "The
purpose of this memorandum is to recommend a get-well letter be
written to Angleton, a valuable liaison contact, who has been hos-
pitalized with a bleeding ulcer . . . He is in Room 6224 South [of the
medical center]. He can receive no visitors and no telephone calls.
Angleton has been an extremely valuable liaison contact at CIA for
many years and is well known to a number of Bureau officials."[12]
A get-well note was duly sent in Hoover's name on 13 September.
The cause of the ulcer, or an aggravating condition, was Angleton's
long-standing alcoholism. He decided to stop drinking. "The CIA
veteran David Blee said: 'I wouldn't have written an insurance policy
on Jim, but then he quit drinking cold turkey and went on Anabuse.
He went to the other extreme and would ask, "Any sherry in that
soup?"'"[13] The effects of the wide-spread alcoholism of people of
Angleton's and the preceding generation are difficult to gauge. We
cannot arrange a counter-factual experiment. Would Churchill's
decisions have been different if he had not nearly always had alcohol in his system? Would Stalin's? Angleton's? Philby's? In any case,
Angleton's decisions, after the last few months of 1968, were made
without the benefit of alcohol.

Colby soon extracted himself from Langley by securing an assignment in Vietnam as deputy head of CORDS (Civil Operations
and Revolutionary Development Support Staff), a "pacification"
program intended to secure the regime in the south of the country. Colby, in his own account of the incident in his autobiography
Honorable Men, says that he was surprised and "stunned" by the
appointment. Helms notes in his memoir that he himself was "irri-
tated" by it, seeing Colby as an intriguer, pursing personal ambition
without regard to the needs of the Agency. In any case, Colby went
back to Vietnam, only to unexpectedly return to Washington and
the CIA in June 1971. Helms offered him the Executive Director-
ship of the Agency, the consolation prize that had been given to
Lyman Kirkpatrick nearly twenty years earlier when Kirkpatrick
was eliminated by illness from his ambition to become DCI. The
message was probably clear to both the sender and the recipient:

it was to be a terminal, pre-retirement position. According to John Prados, in late 1970 Colby had been the subject of a formal counterintelligence inquiry by Angleton's top lieutenants. The very fact that it was considered necessary to interrogate Colby would have in practice blotted his record, no matter what the outcome of the investigation. Colby met the Angletonian criteria for a presumption of *possible* guilt: his actions were "consistent with those of a man who was a Russian agent." That did not mean that Angleton—or Helms—thought Colby was actually a Soviet agent. It did mean that, in the end, they were unsure and that therefore, rather than risk it, he should be eased into early retirement, which is what Helms may have been preparing to do with the Executive Director appointment. In 1965 Angleton had "pointed out that although there had been no legal proof against Kim Philby in 1951, MI-6 had still fired him because of the excessive anomalies in his record."[14] A security problem, Colby had been moved away from the operational center of the CIA on the way to being moved out entirely.

But then Helms was fired by President Nixon for not cooperating on the Watergate cover-up. An outsider, James Schlesinger, was moved into Langley from the Budget Office to reorganize the Agency. Colby became head of the Plans division, renaming it Operations. He also became the chair of the Agency's new management committee, implementing the 10 percent reduction in force Schlesinger had ordered; firing hundreds of employees—many times the number whose careers had been affected by the molehunt. Colby also tried to fire Angleton, but Angleton secured the support of Schlesinger himself and stayed in place. In May 1973 Colby began the Schlesinger-ordered collection of the "Family Jewels" list of the Agency's hitherto secret operations.

On 7 March 1973 the *New York Times* ran an article, datelined Boise, Idaho, reporting "James H. Angleton Dead at 84; National Cash Register Officer." "James Hugh Angleton, a soldier and former executive of the National Cash Register Company, died Sunday at St. Luke's Hospital. He was 84 years old.

> He leaves his wife, the former Carmen Mercedes; two daughters, Carmen of Rome and Mrs. Luciano Guarniere of Florence, Italy; two sons, James and Hugh, and six grandchildren."

The *Times* noted that James H. Angleton had "spent many years in Italy as a soldier and as a businessman . . .

> After [the Second World War] he returned to Italy and worked for the restoration of Italian business and industry and for a stable, democratic government . . . After the repurchase of the N.C.R. Italian agency by the company in the nineteen-sixties, Mr. Angleton retired with his family to Boise."

With *some* of his family, not including three of his four children.

On 17 December 1974 William Colby told James Angleton that he was relieving him of his duties as chief of the counterintelligence staff and as the official in charge of liaison with Israeli intelligence. Colby said Angleton could remain with the Agency as a consultant or retire. He gave Angleton two days to consider. On 20 December Colby met with *New York Times* reporter Seymour M. Hersh and confirmed Hersh's reporting concerning the Agency's illegal domestic activities and other items on the "Family Jewels" list, emphasizing Angleton's involvement. Colby then met with Angleton, told him about the conversation with Hersh, and insisted that Angleton make a decision whether to continue at the Agency as a consultant or retire. Angleton agreed to retire. On 22 December 1974 the *New York Times* published a front-page article by Hersh: "Huge C.I.A. Operation Reported in U.S. Against Antiwar Forces, Other Dissidents in Nixon Years," based in part on interviews with Colby. Deep in the article Hersh wrote: "The C.I.A. domestic activities during the Nixon Administration were directed . . . by James Angleton, who is still in charge of the Counterintelligence Department, the agency's most powerful and mysterious unit. As head of counterintelligence, Mr. Angleton is in charge of maintaining the C.I.A.'s 'sources and methods of intelligence,' which means that he and his men must ensure that foreign intelligence agents do not penetrate the C.I.A." Hersh was incorrect on one point. James Angleton was no longer in charge of the counterintelligence staff. Colby had fired him.

Among those James Angleton talked with in the next few days was his former agent Louise Page Morris. He told Morris that he believed that Colby was a mole: "I can't understand how a Catholic who confesses to a priest can be a 'sleeper [agent].'"[15] In this interpretation if William Colby had been a Soviet agent he had achieved what Kim Philby had perhaps just missed achieving: to become his nation's highest foreign secret intelligence official. However, there was never any question that Colby had worked in the same way as Philby, that is, steadily sending information to Moscow about his organization's structure and activities. Instead, Angleton thought Colby was "a sleeper," an agent who remains quiescent and hidden until he is in a position to act. The actions William Colby took in the days following the firing of James Angleton that dismayed Angleton were two-fold: he dismantled the counterintelligence staff of the CIA and he offered public testimony concerning many of the Agency's closest-held secrets. Richard Helms charged Colby with contributing to "a wanton breach of . . . secrecy" by his cooperation in the mid-1970s with the US Senate's Church and the House of Representative's Pike committees investigating the CIA. He went on to say that Colby "effectively smashed the existing system of checks and balances protecting the national intelligence service" by his "single-handed thrusting of highly sensitive, classified data upon the Rockefeller Commission and subsequent congressional investigating committees." Helms also implied that the very fact that Colby rose to the top of the Agency was suspect, in the same way, in some accounts, that Philby's shining career in MI-6 was part of the case against him: Philby rose so effortlessly, it was said, because he had help from the other side. Helms' similar implication concerning Colby was clear.

Kim Philby, who was then in his senior adviser phase for the KGB, must have followed these events with interest.

James Angleton and his chief aides, Raymond Rocca, William Hood, and Newton Miler, retired on 31 December 1974, but were contract employees of the Agency through the end of March 1975, and consultants through the end of the following September.[16] In a June 1975 report to the Rockefeller Commission, Angleton and his associates wrote that the leadership of the CIA, that is, Colby, "is almost totally uninformed and inexperienced in the specialty of counterintelligence . . .

In our view the DCI is not exercising under NSCID/5 responsible centralized direction of counterintelligence clandestine activity . . .

The result of the 1973 changes was a decentralization of counter-intelligence, a retrogression to the inadequacies of the period 1949 to 1955 . . . counterintelligence is [now] left with a growing threat, undiminished responsibilities, a sharp reduction in capabilities and no effective access to the Agency's top managerial level on substantive issues."[17]

The report impressed Vice President Rockefeller, who sent it on to President Ford. William Colby was fired at the end of January 1976.

James Angleton's time of testifying to various congressional committees gradually came to an end. He joined the American Security Council, a descendant of the Committee on the Present Danger. He was co-editor of the American Security Council's journal and a member of its board, which included Richard Bissell, Ray Cline, and other retired CIA colleagues. Angleton also exercised the privileges of the retired public figure by attempting to influence the writing of the history of his time. He became a favorite source for journalists working on espionage matters, not unlike Kim Philby in the same years. James Angleton died of lung cancer on 11 May 1987.

Markus Wolf, long-serving head of the foreign intelligence service of the German Democratic Republic, heir to the tradition of the interwar Comintern "great illegal" agents, wrote that "betrayal is poison for every intelligence service . . . a poison of distrust enters the system.

Agents in the field, even if their work is unconnected to the area where the betrayal has occurred, suffer a cold chill of vulnerability when they next approach a dead-letter drop or tune in to coded instruction from headquarters. A traitor within an intelligence service betrays much more than the men or women whose names he gives away. He betrays the whole integrity of his service."[18]

Angleton had learned this lesson early on. For him, it had a poetic name, "the wilderness of mirrors," and a human face, that of Kim Philby.

David Robarge has given what might be taken as the official CIA summing up of Angleton's career: "A fair assessment of Angleton's career might note the following on the "credit" side:

- While he was running CIA counterintelligence, there were no known Soviet penetrations of the CIA besides "Sasha."*
- Information from, or assistance by, him and his CI Staff helped uncover, or prepared the way for later discovery of, significant Soviet espionage operations in several Western countries.
- He maintained good relations with the FBI at the working level, helping mitigate longstanding interagency hostility fostered mostly by J. Edgar Hoover.
- He contributed to the establishment of counterintelligence as a separate discipline.

On the "debit" side of the ledger would fall the following:

- By fixing on the Soviets, he largely ignored the threat that the Chinese, Czechs, East Germans, and Cubans posed. During his tenure, they either had agents in the CIA or doubled all the spies the Agency thought it was running against them.
- His operational staff was so deeply involved with defensive CI (molehunting) that it did not run enough offensive (counter-espionage) operations.
- He became far too dependent on Golitsyn and consequently mis-handled some cases either by wrongly accusing suspected enemy agents based on scant evidence, or by suppressing information he believed was sham because it contradicted his special source.
- He became too isolated later in his career, insisting on maintaining his autonomy beyond the time it was useful and defensible . . . He did not delegate enough, his recordkeeping was chaotic, he had no rapport with his subordinates, he did not encourage them to think beyond his paradigms, and his insistence on monopolizing counterintelligence prevented a proper awareness of it from being encouraged inside the CIA through training programs."[19]

Personally, according to Robarge, Angleton "was very close to a small circle of friends.

He was very considerate. He took interest in peoples' lives and families. He was a compassionate person in many ways, which

---

* Golitsyn's "mole."

strikes us as exceptionally odd when we consider the ruthlessness
and bloodlessness of the counterintelligence profession, which
adds, I think, to the fascination and the appeal of the man, to have
that kind of bifurcated personality, in a sense, the way he had the
bifurcated career."[20]

As James Angleton was dying he told Joseph Trento: "'You know,
the CIA got tens of thousands of brave people killed . . .

We played with lives as if we owned them. We gave false hope.
We—I—so misjudged what happened . . . Fundamentally, the
founding fathers of U.S. intelligence were liars . . . the only thing
they had in common was a desire for absolute power. I did things
that . . . I regret. But I was part of it and loved being in it . . . Allen
Dulles, Richard Helms, Carmel Offie, and Frank Wisner were the
grand masters. If you were in a room with them you were in a room
full of people that you had to believe would deservedly end up in
hell.' Angleton slowly sipped his tea and then said, 'I guess I will see
them there soon.'"[21]

CONCLUSION

Let us pull back for a moment from the claustrophobic world of counterintelligence. James Angleton was active in the secret world, from, say, 1944, when he joined the US Army, until a year or two before his death in 1987; Kim Philby from ten years earlier until about the same time. Neither was a mere technician of secret intelligence. Both were highly intelligent and ideologically committed. Angleton's commitment was to "the West," as he saw it, meaning in the main the replacement of the British empire as the dominant power in the world with the power of the United States, the substitution of the ideology of democratic capitalism for that of imperialist capitalism, always in opposition to Communism. This informal American empire was an expression of the enormous energy of the great coiled spring of industrializing post-Civil War America, suddenly expanding from, say, Boise, Idaho, across the three continents of the old world. Philby's commitment was to Communism, against both components of imperialist capitalism, the domination by a small class over the subject populations of empire, and over the working class of Britain itself. His motivation came out of highly specific historical and biographical circumstances: the collapse of capitalism in Britain during the early years of the Depression and his father's lifelong orientation against the Raj, for the colonized inhabitants of India, the dominated inhabitants of the Near East.

This was what they saw as being at stake in the wider world as they toiled in their chosen corners of it.

Kim Philby's expertise in counterintelligence was more or less accidental. The path of action he had chosen was that of the secret agent, the acquirer of foreign intelligence materials for "the fight against fascism." He happened to make his way into Section V of MI-6. It could have been another branch of that organization, or another secret organization, or the Foreign Office or the Treasury (like Maclean and Cairncross). But once embedded in that organization he made the best of it. Both Philby and his student James Angleton used counterintelligence as a generalizable skill, employing it first against Nazi and Italian fascist secret intelligence organizations, and then against Soviet secret intelligence organizations. Of course Philby also used the closely related skills of espionage, per se, against his American and British targets. Having taught the art of counterintelligence to Angleton, Philby had little to fear from him, or from his British peers. As Philby wrote, in the end, "I knew the SIS and MI-5 archives in great detail. I knew the sort of evidence they could bring against me . . . I knew British security procedures inside out . . ." Not to mention American security procedures.

Philby, during his time in MI-6, was a charismatic leader of small teams. Angleton, without himself being an efficient bureaucrat, built up a large bureaucratic apparatus that eventually became the center of a worldwide network of secret intelligence services. There is no indication that Philby thought often about Angleton, beyond their routine interactions in the late 1940s and very early 1950s. Angleton, it seems, thought about Philby a great deal, perhaps increasingly as time went on. Part of this was personalized—penetrations were "Kim's work." Part, the more important part, was Philby's heuristic function: Angleton subjected each counterintelligence initiative to that test: Would it defeat another Philby?

The Cold War is over. James Angleton lies buried in Boise, Kim Philby in Moscow. Their careers continue to interest a broader public than those specializing in intelligence studies. Philby's image is on postage stamps of the Russian Federation; Angleton's monument is the very design of Western counterintelligence.

PHILBY'S ARTICLES IN THE *OBSERVER* AND THE *ECONOMIST*

A 16 December 1956 front-page article in the *Observer* on "America's Middle East Aims" by "A Diplomatic Correspondent, quotes "our Beirut Correspondent, H. A. R. Philby," providing "an unofficial summary of the new American directives to her Ambassadors in the area." In the same issue of the *Observer,* an article by Philby was headlined "'Further Left' Moves in Syria." It concerns a possible governmental alliance of the Ba'ath Party and communists. These articles are what contemporary readers of the *Observer* and the *Economist* would expect from those newspapers' Middle East correspondent: factual, informed, well-written. They were all datelined from Beirut or from nearby Amman. None give a prominent place to either Saudi Arabia or Israel. They were, no doubt, read with care in London and Washington and in Moscow as well. Remarkably, for those British readers who did not restrict themselves to *The Times*, understanding of Middle Eastern events after Suez was generally based on reports in the *Observer* and the *Economist* by Kim Philby. This would continue to be the case for the remainder of the decade.

The same pattern continued in 1957: two or three articles a month in the *Observer* (except in August, when there were five and February, March and November, when there were none), three or four a month in the *Economist* (except in December, when there were none). An article in the 12 January 1957 *Economist*, datelined Amman, concerned "The Arab Mood" in regard to the Palestine question, while one published the following day in the *Observer* discussed talks between Egypt and Syria in regard to a federal union between the two countries. A front-page article in the *Observer,* datelined Beirut, on 19 January described the signing of a treaty for Arab financial aid to Jordan. Philby also saw "no sign of any weakening of Arab resolve in respect of the boycott of Israel. On the contrary, the boycott conference now being held in Beirut is studying methods of tightening the boycott." There were three articles by Philby in the *Economist* in March 1957, on the 16th, 23rd and 30th. The first, from Riyadh, "King Saud, Nasser and the West," reported Saud's support for Nasser at that moment and his neutrality in respect to the Soviet Union. The second, noting that Philby had been "lately in Riyadh," concerned Saudi finances and ambitious development plans, while the last for the month, datelined Baghdad, reported on "Development Week" in Iraq, how oil revenues were being spent on infrastructural investments.*

Continuing March's weekly run, the *Economist* ran an article by Philby on 6 April datelined Basra: "Jordan as a Yardstick," discussing the value of the Jordanian pound as a measure of Egyptian influence in the region as Arab subsidies to Jordan replaced those from Britain. Philby had simultaneous articles in the *Economist* and the *Observer* datelined 13 April. The *Observer* article, on the "Deep Roots of Jordan Struggle," was an assertion and demonstration of his area expertise, while that in the *Economist* described internal Syrian politics and that country's fear of Israel. Philby considered that there had been no major changes in the government of Jordan after a coup by the King in a 20 April article in the *Economist*. However, on the first page of the 28 April edition of the *Observer,* "H. A. R. Philby cables from Amman: Suluman Toukan has ordered the dissolution of the national steering committees throughout the country . . . It was the higher steering committee of all parties represented in the Chamber that recently met at Nablus and formulated the demands which led to the dissolution of parties and establishment of martial law."

Philby continued to appraise King Hussein's political fortunes in a 4 May *Economist* article, "King Hussein's Balancing Act," in which he also described the arrival of the US Sixth Fleet in Beirut harbor. Philby's *Observer* articles were datelined Beirut or Amman through the beginning of May, at which point he began to file them from Damascus and Baghdad. Some of these were presented as front-page news by the *Observer.* Philby's page four article "More Power

---

* This may have been the two-week period when Philby accompanied Middle East expert and his father's biographer, Elizabeth Monroe, as they both reported from Iraq.

for Syrian Left Wing," filed from Damascus on 11 May, analyzed the results of recent elections there—a victory for the Left. Philby commented that "Perhaps the strongest single factor in the success of the Left is the prestige of the Soviet Union among the Syrian masses—a natural sequel to the effective Soviet aid during the Suez crisis when the Syrians certainly expected a Western attack. It has been raised by the scrupulous care with which the Russians and the satellites have avoided any appearance of interfering in Syrian politics . . . At the moment, on no reasonable interpretation of words can Syria be described as either a Soviet satellite or a Soviet base." On the same day, the paper included an article datelined Bagdad: "The tumultuous welcome accorded King Saud on his arrival in Bagdad for his state visit to-day bears witness to the great importance attached to the visit by the Iraq Government *(cables H. A. R. Philby)*." A quite similar article was published in the *Economist* the same day. Two weeks later, Philby filed a story from Beirut, "Syria Moves Troops Out of Jordan," lessening tensions between the left-wing group of Arab countries, led by Egypt, and those on the right, such as Jordan and Saudi Arabia. A 1 June story, "Refugee Funds Short," concerned "The urgent need for more funds to keep going relief and rehabilitation services for Palestinian refugees."

Four of Philby's stories appeared in the *Economist* in June. That on the 8th reported King Saud's meeting with Hussein and worsening relations between Jordan and Syria. On 15 June Philby was recorded as having been "Lately in Ankara," reporting on problems of development in Turkey and on the 22nd there was an article headlined "Democracy in Trouble" about Turkish politics as well as one, "Can Saud Play Peacemaker," chiefly about Jordanian political matters. And a story filed from Damascus on 29 June gave *Observer* readers a briefing on the Syrian political and economic situation. There was only one article by Philby in each of the newspapers in July. An article in the 6 July 1957 edition of the *Economist,* analyzing politics in Syria, where, he reported, the pro-Soviet tendency of the government had little effect on development or daily life. The following weekend, back in Beirut, Philby summarized the conflict between Egypt, Syria, and Saudi Arabia, on the one hand, and, on the other, the conservative new government the King Hussein had installed in Jordan in an article in the *Observer.*

On 15 July, the *Guardian* published a long letter to the editor from

"H. St. J. B. Philby, 18 Grove Court Drayton Gardens, London," entitled: "Israel and the Gulf of Aqaba: The Legal Position." St. John Philby argues for the right of Egypt to close the Suez Canal and the Gulf of Aqaba to Israeli shipping on the basis of the Constantinople Convention of 1888, devised by Lord Salisbury "as the representative of the dominant Power in Egypt," and the state of war still existing in theory between Egypt and Israel. His readers would recall that the Convention concerned the British Empire, then controlling Egypt, and the Ottoman Empire, then controlling Palestine and adjacent areas. St. John Philby giving London, rather than Beirut, as his address, implicitly asserts his British, as opposed to his Arabian, persona. Two days later, the *Guardian* published a response from Norman Bentwich (former attorney-general of Mandatory Palestine), pointing out legal and historical flaws in St. John Philby's argument. Bentwich and St. John Philby had probably known one another when the former was a British colonial official in Palestine, the latter in Transjordan. St. John Philby responded in the *Guardian's* edition of 30 July, as one Middle Eastern legal expert to another, and again on 16 August, calling for arbitration "by the International Court. President Nasser agrees to be bound by its verdict. Israel does not."

In the meantime, the *Observer* of 28 July 1957 carried an article by H. A. R. Philby: "The Crisis in Oman: Role of British Troops," datelined Sharjah (Oman). He commented: "The situation in Oman is, in fact, exceedingly obscure." It was, he explained, the manifestation of a long-standing conflict between the Imam of Oman and the Sultan of Muscat, involving the Saudis and the British to some extent, the latter having troops in the area. All this complicated by the increasingly rich oil discoveries in the area.

In August Philby reported in a series of articles from Oman, where Britain had intervened in a civil war, and from a looking post in Bahrein, then he was back in Beirut and Damascus for the remainder of the year.

The first of the articles on the war in Oman appeared on 3 August in the *Economist,* detailing skirmishes, local politics, and oil exploration. On 4 August, the *Observer*'s gossip columnist "Pendennis," under the headline "Oman Bank Holiday," wrote: "We asked our far-flung correspondent, H. A. R. Philby, how he was getting on this Bank Holiday week-end, trying to report the war in Oman.

He cables a most dejected reply. 'Fort Sharjah, where all the great newsmen gathered at the start of the campaign, was bad enough.

> The fort is, in fact, a resthouse, attached to the R.A.F. base, and the air-conditioning broke down, prices were high, and the beer was as hot as the Indian Ocean. There was nothing to do except listen to an R.A.F. spokesman contributing neither to the volume nor to the accuracy of the news put out, and to worry about whether it wouldn't be better to move to Bahrein. Outside, wandering among the sand and scrub, a poor lunatic cried out endlessly that it was he who commanded the R.A.F. station . . . Bahrein is equally depressing and even further away from the scene of action. Reporting the Muscat war from there is like covering Rome from Leeds. The hotel has the feel of an elderly P. and O. liner. Fans whirr in all the rooms, moving the semi-conditioned air. Haddock with bubble and squeak is offered for breakfast."

The following week Philby, in Bahrein, was back to straight reporting in the *Observer*: "R.A.F. Bombers Attack in Oman." This was in support of what was, in effect, a British invasion of the country in response to a dispute between the Sultan and the imam over oil. On the 10th, "Our Special Correspondent" reported for the *Economist* on the situation in Yemen and the Aden Protectorates: "The idea of Mr Khrushchev, in his role of defender of the free, extending his podgy paw of friendship on that personification of ancient regimes, the Imam of Yemen, is a cynical absurdity . . . By turning the tribal protectorate territories into a tribal free-for-all with modern weapons, Russia hopes to unseat the security of the colony and has dreams of installing a satellite Yemen on the straits . . . In the long run, however, the willing co-operation of paramount chiefs in the protectorates and of political leaders in Aden will be as important as guns in resisting the aggressors."

In the meantime, a letter from St. John Philby had been published in the *Guardian* on 9 August, questioning the legal basis of British intervention on behalf of the Sultan of Muscat. H. A. R. Philby then explicated "The Lesson of Oman" in an *Observer* piece on 18 August and in "Next Steps for the Sultan," datelined Bahrain, in the *Economist* the same day. In the *Observer* he wrote that "the fact that there may be oil in Oman has turned an obscure ancient tribal quarrel into an international issue . . . That issue arose because of Egyptian interest, Saudi support for the Imam, and British counter-action in favour of the Sultan." He recommends funds for the Sultan for national development. Philby was soon back in Damascus where a crisis was beginning. The government of the United States was concerned that Syria was aligning itself with the Soviet Union in the Cold War. In a front-page article in the *Observer* on 25 August, "Russia Offers Syria Long Cheap Loan: Minister Says West's Rates Were Unfavourable, Purge Expected," Philby concluded: "The over-all picture would seem to be that the Soviet *bloc* share in Syria's trade is certainly growing, but that the share of Syria's exports taken by Western countries remains far too substantial to make unilateral dependence on the Soviets either necessary or desirable for her." Philby's article in the *Economist* the same day, "Syrian Chessboard," reported on closer Soviet-Syrian relations and political maneuvering in Damascus, notably the rise of Ba'ath Socialists. Philby rounded off August with an article in the *Economist* on "Syria's Russian Deal," datelined Damascus. "Assuming that the arrangements can be satisfactorily worked out in detail, then for some years to come the Syrian economy will be geared primarily (but not wholly) to that of the eastern block," balanced by traditional arrangements by Aleppo merchants with the West.

Reporting on a visit to the Middle East by US State Department official Loy Henderson in the 1 September 1957 *Observer,* Philby wrote that "His arrival in the Middle East during the Syrian crisis has by now practically convinced the Arabs of Western hostility."

While much of the British domestic news in the *Observer* in mid-September of 1957 was about the Wolfenden Report, Philby continued to report from Beirut about internal developments in Syria. On 14 September, in the *Observer*, he described the position of the Communist Party (negligible) and of the related Ba'athist Social-ists (significant), and trade and armaments relations with the Soviet Union (very significant). "In short, it can be said that the danger of an internal Communist coup in Syria is negligible, but that . . . relations between the Syrian and Soviet Governments are likely to be friendly to the point of cordiality in the foreseeable future." And in the non-foreseeable future of the situation in 1957, if we might sub-stitute "Russian" for "Soviet." Philby advertised his entrée to Syrian political circles: "More than one Syrian official has expressed to me in confidence the view . . ." And in this lengthy piece, spread over two pages, Philby identified himself with his presumed audience in Whitehall: "Consideration of the problem in its local context suggest that little can be done by direct means until Western relations with Egypt are satisfactorily regulated. President Nasser is still the outstanding leader of the Arab world . . . Once his own quarrel with the West is forgotten, there is every likelihood that he will try to lead the Arabs back towards a more neutral form of 'positive neutrality' than is now fashionable. More one cannot expect." An article in the *Economist,* "Wrong Foot on the Jordan," also published on 14 September 1957, Philby wrote that the US arms airlift to Jordan was seen there as an effort to split the Arab states into two groupings: Saudi Arabia, Jordan, and the gulf states as against Nasserite Egypt and Syria as part of a strategy to counter Soviet influence. A week later we have "Syria Welcomes Soviet Navy," filed to the *Observer* from Damascus on 21 September: "The head of the Syrian Foreign Office told me that there would be little difficulty in tearing to shreds Mr. Dulles's analysis of the Middle Eastern crisis which in the Arab view was due to the domination of the area by Turks, British, French and to the creation of Israel rather than to abortive schemes pursued by Russia . . . The Russians here are seeking not satellites but allies." At the end of the month, the *Observer* printed an article by Philby asking "Will Dulles Accept Arab Neutralism?" From Beirut, Philby wrote that: "It is pointed out here that renewed discussions on the basis of Arab neutralism would mean in effect jettisoning the core of the Eisenhower Doctrine, which promised the Middle Eastern States American military and economic aid provided they undertook to resist international Communism."

On 6 October, Philby reported for the *Observer* from Beirut on an appeal for funds by the United Nations for Palestinian refugees. Philby's comment was critical of the Soviet Union: "About 90 per cent of U.N.R.W.A. funds are provided by the United States and Britain. The Communist bloc supplies nothing. Yet the indifference of the Communist countries to the fate of the refugees evokes surprisingly little Arab criticism. Britain and America, it is argued, were primarily responsible for the creation of Israel and therefore for the creation of the refugee problem, so the least they can do is to pay for it." This was balanced by an article, "Who Lined Up the Arabs?" for the *Economist* the same weekend: "While the United

States government has clearly failed in its efforts to isolate Egypt and Syria,

> it has fared little better in its primary aim: that of barring the Middle East to Soviet penetration. The Soviet government has more friends in the Arab world than ever before; they are entrenching themselves skillfully in Syria; and, as the results of Soviet economic aid begin to show, the Russians will have an increasingly attractive shop-window to display in the rest of the Arab states. It is hardly surprising that pro-western Arabs are anxious to see the revision of a doctrine which after reasonable trial, obviously appeals to the benefactors rather than to the intended beneficiaries."

The *Economist* carried Philby's article about a visit to Damascus by Egyptian army officers on 19 October, "Syria's Egyptian Visitors," with comments about internal Syrian politics. At the end of the month Philby filed a story for the *Observer* from Damascus, date-lined 26 October, that shared the front page of the *Observer* with the major event of the day, the replacement of Zhukov as Soviet Defense Minister. Philby's report was about a "Big Soviet Loan Going to Syria," for the most part for irrigation projects. The *Economist* ran a similar article by Philby that weekend.

The *Economist* published three articles by Philby in November: "Syria's Chosen Course" on the 2nd, "Jumpiness in Lebanon" on the 23rd, and "Pressures on Jordan" on the 30th. The first reported on Soviet aid to Syria, the second on terrorism in Jordon, the third about UN Secretary General Hammarskjold's visit to Jordan in an effort to defuse three-way tension there, between Jordan, Egypt, and Israel. There were no news stories by H. A. R. Philby in the *Observer* in November 1957 or in either paper in December 1957 and January 1958. "In December [1957] Aileen died . . . Kim came back for the funeral . . . He stayed in England a few weeks, clearing up family affairs."[1]

There were articles in both newspapers on 15 February 1958. "Behind Syria's Decision" in the *Economist* described Syria's union with Egypt as a Ba'athist coup. The *Observer* article, "Seeds of Arab Conflict," was from Beirut. Philby described the situation arising from the union of Egypt and Syria, on the one hand, and "the proc-lamation of the Hashemite Arab Federation" of Jordan and Iraq, on the other: "Few doubt that the confrontation of the republican union with the monarchical federation contains the seeds of conflict." The *Observer* printed another analytical piece by "H. A. R. Philby, Our Correspondent in Beirut," "The New Arab Scene," across four columns on 2 March 1958, again on the issues raised by the various alignments among Arab countries. In "The New Arab Scene," he reviews the interests of Egypt and Saudi Arabia in respect to the two alliances described in his February report: "Now that the movement has begun, it may be expected to feed on itself and develop new impulses. The union of Egypt and Syria and the federation of the Hashemite kings are both committed to pursue policies towards still larger unions, though each in its own way." In articles in the *Economist* on 15, 22, and 29 March 1958, "Our Special Correspondent In Cairo" (not necessarily Philby) were critical of Nasser: "President Nasser is entrenched by western ineptness, by the power of his personality and by his weapons for advertisement. His strength can prop up his administrative house of cards. But it might collapse if ambition carries him too far and too fast towards an Arab empire that he has not the machinery to administer."

Following this pattern of fewer, but larger, articles, Philby's next appearance in the *Observer* was on 30 March (from Beirut), "New Broom in the House of Saud": "Prince Faisal has assumed power in Saudi Arabia to a chorus of approval from the Egyptian Press." Philby displayed his, or his father's entrée to the Saudi government: "The great 'Red Palace' in the centre of Riyadh, where the Cabinet has its offices, is stirring to new life . . . Prince Faisal is one of the ablest and most engaging personalities in Saudi Arabia: poised and articulate, with a thin mouth twitching sardonically and sombre, sunken eyes . . . It is commonly said there is no public opinion in Saudi Arabia. I can say from recent personal experience that that is quite untrue. Throughout the crisis the King was subject to outspoken discussion over the coffee cups. Opinion is there and plenty of it. All that is lacking are the means of public expression." Philby's analysis is that the United States had attempted to set up King Saud as a counterpoise to Nasser, and that the latter decided he would rather hand over power to his brother, who, Philby predicts, would seek a larger share of the profits of Aramco. The *Observer* carried a letter to the editor on 6 April 1958, from Alan Thompson, Edinburgh (perhaps the professor of Economics and Labour MP): "It is to be hoped that somebody in the Middle Eastern Department of our Foreign Office has read Mr. H. A. R. Philby's article on Saudi Arabia . . ."

Philby's pro-King Hussein article, "A Year of Strong Rule in Jordan" was published by the *Observer* on 13 April, datelined Amman. "Authoritarian rule in Jordan celebrates its first birthday on Monday. A dangerous year has passed since King Hussein rode to Zerka, quelled Army disturbances and scattered the friends of Egypt." He foresaw trouble if Iraq, with which Jordan was federated at the time, did not provide sufficient financing for Jordan's needs from its oil revenues. A similar article appeared in the *Economist* the same weekend. This was followed by articles in that newspaper on the 10th, 17th and 24th concerning events in Lebanon as it appeared to be sliding toward civil war. On 24 May Philby wrote in the *Observer*: "President of Lebanon Loses Grip." Philby's explanation of the crisis facing President Chamoun is very much an insider's account. The roots of the crisis, as with most in Lebanon, had to do with conflicts within the complicated sectarian governmental structure of the country, calling, inter alia, for a Christian president and Muslim prime minister. A week later, on the 31st, Philby reported in the *Observer* that a "Compromise on Lebanon Likely": "Barring accidents, it is becoming increasingly likely that a political solution will be found for the Lebanese crisis, now entering its fourth week," while in the *Economist* article, "Lebanon's Struggle," he wrote that President Chamoun had agreed not to run again. On 7 June, his article in the *Economist* described international negotiation's over Lebanese charges of Egyptian interference in its internal affairs.

Running next to an article conveying the Kenyan colonial government's denial of charges of mistreatments of Mau-Mau prisoners, H. A. R. Philby contributed a short article for the front page of the *Observer* on 14 June 1958 concerning "Worst Fighting in Beirut:" "The most serious fighting Beirut has seen since the Lebanese disturbances began broke out this morning, and vigorous exchanges of fire were still going on this afternoon, but later only occasional shots were heard." In a longer article, on page eight, about "Confusion in Beirut," Philby concluded that "For the time being mediators have exhausted themselves. Both Government and opposition are standing firm on their position, and neither can now afford to budge without hopeless loss of faith . . . The public is developing a fatalistic attitude. Bomb outrages and sporadic firing continue, with little loss of life." The *Observer* then gave Philby five columns and half a page on 22 June for "Crisis-Country Background: The Lebanon," in which he described for his readers the complexities of the country's politics, the state of play between the government and opposition at the moment, which was increasingly violent, and concluding that "A Western Power has nothing to offer this country. The Lebanese must help themselves."

Three weeks later, on 13 July, the *Observer* published a shorter piece by H. A. R. Philby, "Lebanon Looks to Iraq and Turkey." He ends on a pessimistic note: "Are we looking at the beginning of the disintegration and failure of this complex experiment in nationhood? There seem to be three possibilities." These are, a long civil war; a division of the country, and, "Thirdly, it is possible— just—that both sides will agree to the formation of a Government headed by some national figure who has so far held aloof from the present conflict." A similar article, "Chagrin in Beirut," was published in the *Economist*. King Faisal of Iraq was murdered the next day. On the following day, believing that the Syrian government was about to become dominated by communists, President Eisenhower authorized an invasion of Lebanon to stabilize the situation there. Philby, in the *Economist,* wrote on 26 July: "Muddling Through in Beirut and Amman." "Ten thousand American troops have landed in Lebanon; two thousand British parachute troops are sitting on and around the Amman military airfield." There was a coup in Iraq with repercussions in Jordan.

Writing from Beirut for the *Observer* on 9 August, Philby speculated that "Nasser and Saud May Revive Pact." This was occasioned by a visit to Riyadh by the Minister of Defence of the United Arab Republic, which Philby thought might lead to a renewed alliance between Egypt and Saudi Arabia and a revival of the Arab League, which had been "moribund in the last few years because of rivalry between Cairo and Bagdad." In the *Economist* on 16 and 30 August Philby informed his readers that "Syria Settles Down" due to its union with Egypt and friendship with the new regime in Iraq and commented on "The Arabs' Precarious Peace" as matters in Lebanon and Jordan were still unsettled.

H.A.R. Philby's byline did not again appear in the pages of the

Observer or the *Economist* until 5 October 1958, when he wrote for the former from Amman about the withdrawal of British troops from Jordan. They had arrived to help King Hussein control the country in the face of pressure from Egypt. He concludes this increasingly typical analytical piece: "Having nursed the seeds of political discontent, President Nasser may yet reap the whirlwind in the shape of Jordanian mobs clamouring for absorption" to the United Arab Republic, that is, Egypt. A similar article appeared under his byline that weekend in the *Economist*. Two articles were published in October in the *Economist* as by "Our Special Correspondent in Baghdad," one on 25 October 1958, the other on 1 November about developments in post-coup Iraq. The second stated that "If words mean anything, the trade agreements newly concluded with the United Arab Republic and the Communist block are intended to supplement, rather than replace, the older links with the West." These may have been by Philby. Be that as it may, back in Beirut, Philby reported in the *Observer*, also on 1 November 1958, that "The Lebanon Snaps Back to Normal," with the withdrawal of American forces and the formation of a new government and efforts to remove arms from the streets and prospects for an American loan to make up for the losses in the previous five months' civil strife. Just one week later, Philby was in Amman, reporting on tension in Bagdad between the Ba'athists, wanting immediate merger with the UAR, and the communists and National Democrats, who wished to wait. Philby's final report for the year in the *Observer* was a front-page article datelined Amman, 8 November: "Hussein Going to Europe." Philby speculated about the background and significance of King Hussein's planned three-week vacation, concluding that it reflected a calming of internal opposition to the regime and an agreement with Egypt that the latter would not attempt to absorb Jordan. His final article for the year in the *Economist* was on 15 November, from Amman: "Holiday in Jordan."

On 3 January 1959, the *Economist* published Philby's summary of "Nasser's Year of Wonders," concerning Nasser's anti-communist actions, his achievements and prospects. It was not until February that H. A. R. Philby again had a story in the *Observer*. On 8 February 1959, the newspaper published an article from Beirut "Nasser Puzzles the Nationalists." The article primarily concerned the conflict in Iraq between the Nationalist government of Prime

Minister Kassem and the Communist Party, but then turned to a consideration of the situation in Jordan: "King Hussein's more far-sighted friends have long thought his best chance of survival lies in an accommodation with Nasser." Perhaps a reference to St. John Philby's table talk. The following week the *Observer* published an article, datelined Beirut, 14 February: "Choice for Russia," again about the struggle for power in Iraq, this time in the context of potential Soviet influence in Iran. Simultaneously, the *Economist* published "New Faces in Baghdad," about Iraqi cabinet changes, waxing of communist influence, waning of that of the Nasserites. In his third article in the *Observer,* in February 1959, "Arab Fears of Jewish Influx," Philby reported rumors of "an new massive wave of Jewish immigrants into Israel, largely from Communist countries," which was "arousing alarm in the Arab States . . . The Arab alarm is reflected in highly coloured estimates of the extent of the immigration now contemplated. Semi-official sources speak of a first installment of a quarter of a million, rising in due course to three million." The Arab governments were blaming the Soviets for allowing the immigration and the British and Americans for funding it with public and private support. He summarized the situation by stating that "The immediate outcome of the dispute is likely to be a heightening of Nationalist-Communist tension in the Arab world . . . The long-term result of the immigration—if it takes place—will be to confirm Arab fears of a world-wide conspiracy against them, with the usual concomitant of alarms, and excursions throughout the region." On 28 February 1959 the *Economist* published his article on "King Saud's Domestic Economies," a detailed economic analysis of the situation in Saudi Arabia.

The *Economist* ran an article "Revolt at Mosul" on 14 March 1959, concerning the failed attempt by an army faction in Iraq to stage a *coup d'état*. The *Observer* published a major article by Philby under the heading: Commonwealth and Foreign Affairs: "Kassem Wins but Power Is Shaken, Inter-Party Balance Gone." He reports that the Iraqi Prime Minister's victory in an attempted coup had destabilized Kassem's balancing act between the Nationalists, that is Nasserists, and the Communists, in favor of the latter: ". . . it is difficult to see how he can continue to carry the Communists on his side without making further concessions to them . . . The alternative would be a showdown, resulting either in a Communist victory or in the establishment of pure military dictatorship with little or no pretence of popular support."

A month later, on 12 April 1959, Philby reported from Beirut to the *Observer* that the "U.A.R. Fails to Place Kassem in the Dock." Nasser had attempted to arrange an Arab League condemnation of the Iraq government's tilt toward Communism, but had achieved only a banal final communiqué. However, "The news from Baghdad points clearly to a further deterioration of the situation in Iraq. A purge of the Army and Civil Service is still in full swing and it is a matter for some doubt how long the State machine can continue to operate in view of the loss of so many experienced officials." Philby's article in the *Observer* on 18 April, published on 19 April 1959, recalled that it had been exactly two years since King Hussein "dismissed the pro-Nasser Cabinet of Suliman Nabuisi, proclaimed martial law and accepted United States aid in place of the abrogated British subsidy." On this anniversary, "The Lebanese Foreign Ministry to-day confirmed reports from Amman that the Lebanon is seeking to mediate in the prolonged dispute between Jordan and the United Arab Republic." On 25 April 1959, the *Economist* published "The Deadlock of Arabism," concerning the conflict between Qasim and Nasser, communist gains in Iraq, Nasserites in Jordan and Lebanon: "the Arab world presents a sad spectacle of disunity verging on despair." On 9 May Philby in the *Economist* wrote of "Lebanon One Year After," concerning Lebanese politics after the civil conflict.

The *Observer* published a major story by Philby that weekend, "Power Bid by Iraq Communists." After enumerating various conflicts between the Iraqi communists and the government of Prime Minister Kassem, Philby comments that "The Communist demand for participation in the Government is well-timed, since five new Ministries are to be formed soon and it seems reasonable that the Communists, as the strongest single political force in the country, should have a portfolio or two." He concludes with a balanced forecast: "Optimists place their hope in the gradual habituation of the workers to trade union disciplines and in the building up of the Popular Resistance Force, which seems more effective in controlling the streets than either the Army or the police. Pessimists fear that the Communist hold on both the unions and the P.R.F. is strong enough to ensure disorder . . . until a Communist takeover." A week later, under the headline "Communists Advance," Philby predicted that "The inclusion of Communists in the Iraqi Government seems only a matter of time." In the *Economist* that weekend Philby published an article "Towards Iraqisation," covering the Iraqi economy since the revolution with particular attention to the European-controlled Iraqi Petroleum Company.

However, it was little more than a month later, on 21 June, that the *Observer* published Philby's report that "The Communist drive for power in Iraq has suffered a sharp check, and it now seems as if the Communists and General Kassem are standing at the parting of the ways . . . Perhaps Kassem himself came to the conclusion that Communist arrogance was becoming intolerable and that he and his friends were in danger of being submerged." His article in the *Economist* that weekend, "The Saudi Scene," covered that country's "passive foreign policy and internal reform," along with its various disputes with gulf states, Oman, etc. A week after that, on 28 June 1959, the *Observer* published an article by Philby reporting that "Cairo Sees Iraqi Split." According to Philby himself, "It seems only a matter of time before General Kassem moves to suspend or suppress Communist newspapers." A page one story on 19 July in the *Observer* from Philby was headlined "15 Killed in Iraq Oil Town Riot." The riot in Kirkuk "began when pro-Communist Kurds clashed with members of the large, conservatively-inclined Turkish community which survives in Kirkuk from Ottoman times." The *Observer* printed a major article by Philby under the "Commonwealth and Foreign Affairs" heading, datelined Baghdad, also on 19 July: "Loyalty to Kassem Is the Test: Balance of Forces His Aim." Philby wrote about the proclamation that political activity would be allowed in Iraq from 6 January 1960. He wrote, wryly, that "Kassem is an idealist who believes in man's capacity for repentance, and even members of parties implicated in movements against the regime may be allowed to resume activity provided they show between now and January that they have seen the error of their ways." As was sometimes his practice, Philby supplies some local color: "My hotel is full of a breathtaking troupe of Chinese dancers who glide about the place on air. Hungary and the Soviet Union . . . also sent entertainers of high merit . . . By contrast, the political and diplomatic delegations with which most Western Powers contented themselves were less arresting, though cheerful crowns in high holiday humour gave them a good hand." (Anniversary of Kassem's revolution.) For the *Econo-mist* on 19 July 1959 he contributed "Nasser's Political Pyramid," on the UAR elections, Ba'ath losses, and Nasser's strategy.

Three weeks later, on 9 August 1959, under the Commonwealth and Foreign Affairs heading, the *Observer* ran Philby's story: "Iraq Communists Toe the Line, 'Mistakes' Admitted." Philby conclud-ed from self-criticism in Communist Party newspapers and other indications that "at present the Communists are not in a position to make a serious take-over bid." He observes that Kassem, like Nasser "draws a sharp distinction between the Soviet Government and 'international Communism'." The following week, under the *Observer's* heading "The Politics of Pasture," Philby reported from Amman concerning a "Migration Trek by 50,000 Camels." Large numbers of camels accompany Ruwalla Bedouin (or vice versa) in a migration from Syria to Saudi Arabia via the Jordanian oasis of Azraq, "a broad depression where surface and subterranean waters gather to form deep, reed-fringed pools famed for duck and sabre-toothed horseflies." Philby describes the relationship between the Bedouin tribes and the governments of the countries they pass through and one another and provides a bit of history. This "local color" article was followed by one "From Our Own Correspondent," also datelined Amman, and perhaps also by Philby, "Jordan-Nasser Breach Is Being Healed," concerning re-establishment of diplomatic relations between Jordan and Egypt. In the *Economist* on 15 August 1959, Philby published an article on "Music at Baalbeck," concern-ing a fashionable music festival.

Philby's articles three weeks later, on 6 September 1959, were "King Saud and Nasser in Accord," in the *Observer,* which reported a similar agreement between Saudi Arabia and Egypt and describes various initiatives in regard to Palestinian refugees: UN Secretary General Hammarskjold's proposal that they should be integrated into the countries were they currently reside, a counter proposal for a provisional Palestinian national government, and a comprise of an "Arab defence force for Palestine," and "Amman Courts its Palestin-ians," in the *Economist*. The latter described a tour of the West Bank by the King and issues about a putative Palestinian government. A 19 September 1959 article in the *Economist* recounts Philby's arbitrary expulsion from Damascus, which he had been visiting with his wife and children, and how "the Syrians learn from the French the secret

of carrying on with the day to day business of government, irrespec-
tive of storms in the political stratosphere." Philby published three
stories in the *Economist* in October and one in the *Observer*. The
Economist story on the 3rd, "Whose Arab Refugees," concerned
Hammarskjold's proposals for integrating Palestinian refugees in
their countries of residence; that on the 10th, "Cairo versus Peking,"
argued that "the communists are playing the Middle Eastern game
both ways. They do not want to lose the Arab nationalists as levers
to be thrown against the West whenever necessary. At the same time
they still hope to bring about a communist takeover of Arab lands
. . . It calls to mind the situation between the world wars when the
Soviet government secretly approved and publicly disavowed the
actions of the Comintern." This last being a subject on which Philly
could, but would not have, claimed some authority. The *Economist*'s contribution from Philby, "Iraq in Suspense," published on 24
October, described an attempted assassination of General Qassim
and rumors of an Iraq/UAR war. The *Observer* ran Philby's story, a
page-one item: "Mass Arrests Follow Iraq Shooting." Philby speculated that the attempted assassination of Kassem three days earlier,
was a Palestinian attempt to ignite a purge of the communist allies
of Kassem "laying the basis for a long-range *rapprochement* with
the rest of the Arab world."

There were no articles in either paper from Philby in November 1959. The *Economist* published "The Saudis Take Stock" on
12 December 1959, a detailed analysis of the Saudi economy and
finances, and then on 26 December 1959, "The Saudis Look Ahead,"
from Riyadh, a story about infrastructure projects and administrative reform. There were no articles by Philby in either newspaper in
January. There were two articles by Philby in the *Economist* in February, one on the 6th and another on the 20th. The first was about a
Syrian/Israeli border clash: "Whatever pretext sparked the battle of
Tawafiq, both sides find in it material for propagating their causes.
The danger is that appetites will grow with eating." The second was
about "Hussein's Grand Design," which was to extend Jordanian
citizenship to all Palestinian Arabs, wherever they may reside. There
were no further articles by Philby in the *Observer* until 20 March
1960, datelined Beirut the previous day, under the heading "Dead
Sea Scrolls." "Plans for Massive Jordan Search." He describes, with
some cynicism, stories of buried treasure from "the Copper Scroll"

deciphered by a scholar from Manchester University. "As many of these caves were perched high on the friable rock face, the fact that the search was conducted without loss of life or limb is remarkable. Your Correspondent recently visited the easiest of the scroll caves and found it a most shaking experience."

The *Economist* published "Sitting on the Iraqi Ltd.," on 2 April 1960, about declining communist influence in that country. On 24 April 1960, under the "Commonwealth and Foreign Affairs" heading, the *Observer* published Philby's story "Arabs to Boycott American Ships: Ultimatum for U.S. Unions." Dockers in New York had refused to unload an Egyptian ship as a protest against the Arab blacklist of US ships trading with Israel. He commented on "the forthright Syrians, who are masters of the art described by Westerners as cutting off the nose to spite the face and by Syrians as the defence of a principle without regard for material advantage." He concluded: "the episode is already troubling Arab relations with the West, as it is impossible for Arabs to grasp that President Eisenhower cannot control his trade unions in the same way as President Nasser." Then on 1 May 1960, the *Observer* ran Philby's account of the beginning of the boycott: "Angry Arabs Begin Ship Boycott, Anti-U.S. Feeling Runs High." He emphasized that the boycott was not an official Egyptian governmental action, allowing continuation of oil shipments. Another of Philby's articles on the boycott was published by the *Economist* on 7 May. On the 14th that newspaper ran his article "Lebanon's Fragile Peace," looking forward to elections in that country. Philby published nothing in June in either newspaper. In July, on the 16th, the *Economist* published two of his articles. One, "All Quiet on the Arab Front," wondered why there had been nothing newsworthy of late in the Middle East, the other concerned the Lebanese elections: "Lebanese politics are too complicated to permit reliable prophecy and it could be several months before the new government is formed."

On 7 August 1960 the *Observer* published an article by Philby, as if to demonstrate his point about the absence of news: "Girl Camels Faster than Boy Camels," a color piece datelined Beirut, 6 August. It described a race in Amman, and on 27 August the *Economist* followed suit with an article about tourism in Jordan. A month later, on 4 September, the *Observer* published "The Peacemakers Go to Jordan," datelined the previous day from Amman. The Jordanian

Prime Minister had been assassinated and tension was high between Egypt and Syria, on the one hand, and Jordan, on the other. It appeared to Philby that the assassination had been instigated from Syria. He commented that weekend in an article on the subject in the *Economist*: "In four years' experience, your correspondent has never been subject to an identity check [at the Prime Minister's office] or seen anyone else submit to one." Philby placed two more articles in the *Economist* in September, that on the 17th concerned a visit by President Nasser to the UN in New York, that on the 24th, "Cairo's Wind of Socialism," noted that with "the gathering speed of nationalization . . . [there was] a strong doctrinal wind blowing in the direction of state socialism."

Philby's next article in the *Observer* appeared on 23 October, concerning an inexperienced Syrian pilot who had gotten lost, landed in Jordan, and committed suicide. The next week there was an article about tension between Syria and Lebanon: "Syria Blames Lebanon Over Bombs," in Damascus, which caused neither damage nor injuries. This was an offshoot of continuing difficulties between Syria and Jordan. On 5 November the *Economist* carried an article by Philby, "Visas for Journalists": "The *Economist*'s Middle East correspondent has been a marked sufferer from this frontier schizophrenia. After having visited Syria regularly during 1957, he was first refused a visa in March 1958. Since then his subsequent applications have been consistently rejected and the intercessions made on his behalf by prominent Lebanese and Syrian citizens have been to no avail. In September last year he did obtain a Syrian visa in Amman, and went to Damascus on a holiday trip, with his wife and two children. When he got there he was summoned to the Sûreté and given three hours to leave the country with his family. The only reason given was that his name was 'on a list.' He was not given the opportunity to argue his case with any higher authority, then or since. Can this sort of thing serve any possible Egyptian, Syrian or United Arab interest?"

The next article, and his last for the year, in the *Observer*, was published on 11 December 1960, and once again concerned the "Renewed Search for Dead Sea Scrolls, Scientists Face High Prices and Bogus Claims." He hints that the search for the Scrolls had become a confidence game. The *Economist* noted in its issue of 31 December 1960, that "Our Middle East correspondent writes: (1) a political assessment; (2) a retrospect of the economic situation that, in part, gave rise to them." King Saud had resumed power from Prince Faisal. Philby reports that there was a business slump, but the Kingdom's finances were sound and there was much spending on infrastructure.

The *Observer* published just nine of Philby's articles in 1961. The first, on 28 January, was datelined Cairo the previous day: "A New Start in Cairo." It described the renewal of diplomatic relations between Egypt and Britain, broken during the Suez Crisis. However, according to Philby, "It is unlikely to have any immediate or appreciable effect on relations between the two countries." In an article on 4 February 1961 in the *Economist,* "Nasserism in Africa," Nasser was praised for making neutralism respectable. In an *Observer* feature article on 12 March, "Oil Village in the Desert," Philby described mechanized Aramco exploration in the Empty Quarter of Arabia that his father had explored, and he had recently visited. He reported on Saudi cabinet changes on 18 March in the *Economist* and under the title "Among Africans" on 15 April, concerning the "All-African People's Conference in Cairo, 25 March to 7 April 1961." On 29 April 1961, the *Economist* published Philby's article "Cairene Anxieties," about the "Resentment, concern and shock" expressed by Tito and Nasser about the Bay of Pigs invasion of Cuba.

The *Economist* published Philby's "Antoinette and the Arabs" on 6 May 1961 about Egyptian opposition to the marriage of King Hussein to a British citizen. On 27 May 1961 a major article, "New Approach by Persia to Soviet?" was published in the *Observer,* datelined Teheran. It began: "Dr. Amini, Prime Minister of Persia, told me to-day that he would dearly like to see better relations established with the Soviet Union." Aside from that, Philby reported that Amini's main concern was to limit corruption as a way to avert revolution. Then on 3 June 1961 the *Economist* ran his "Dr. Amini's Fifty-Fifty Chance," a leader "From Our Middle East Correspondent," datelined Teheran: "Anyone who knows what is really going on in Persia must be grossly misinformed . . . if every case of corruption were tracked down and the offender punished there would be precious few experienced people left to run the country." Still in Teheran, Philby reported on 10 June 1961, under the *Observer's* heading "Inside Persia" the next day: "Dr. Amini Starts the Long Haul." Philby lists foreign debt, land reform, the cost of living, and corruption as major issues. There is also the balancing act between Britain and the United States, on the one hand, and the Soviet Union, on the other. Philby comments that "Persians must try to live with the Soviet Union . . . This means in effect that the Russians should ease their propaganda from Moscow Radio and from the 'National Voice of Iran'—a transmitter which purports to be operating clandestinely in Persia but which is located in fact on Russian soil."

The *Economist* carried Philby's 1 July 1961 report "Baghdad Brainstorm," concerning General Qasim's declaration "last Sunday that Kuwait was a district of Basra province." The lead article on page one of the *Observer* on 2 July 1961, was by Philby, datelined Kuwait, 1 July: "Bombers Join British Forces in Kuwait, Troops awaiting any move by Iraq, Sheikhdom is not expecting war." "British troops landing in force in Kuwait to-day ready to defend the newly independent oil sheikhdom threatened by Iraq." Philby reported that the Iraqi General Kassem and his communist allies had been threatening "to enforce his claim to Kuwait by military action." On 8 July he reported in the *Economist* in an illustrated article that "Secure Behind the Shield" of British forces, "War clouds over Kuwait are disappearing almost as fast as they blew up." At the end of the month, in an article datelined Beirut, 29 July ("Hussein wants cash for Kuwait troops, Discussion with King Saud"), Philby wrote that King Hussein of Jordan had gone to Taif, King Saud's summer capital, to meet with the Saudi king. "The strangest and, from the British viewpoint, the most gratifying feature of the Kuwait incident is the reluctance of Arab States to speed the British departure by providing forces of their own to fill the gap." But two weeks later, with "Arab force will take over in Kuwait," Philby reported from Beirut on 12 August that "The early withdrawal of all British forces from Kuwait is forecast here as a result of an agreement reached between the ruler and the Arab League mission for their replacement by an Arab Defence force." In the *Economist* on 19 August 1961, Philby published a background piece on the British Arabian protectorates: "Sheikhs Seek Protection." On 16 September, reporting in the *Observer* from Cairo, Philby wrote that "Saudi-Arabian and Jordanian troops, who will constitute the bulk of the Arab defence force, have arrived in Kuwait in sufficient numbers to justify the ruler in formally requesting the British withdrawal." And on the 23rd he reported in the *Economist* on the "Grief and Realism" in Cairo on the death of Hammarskjold.

There were no articles in the *Observer* by Philby in October 1961. The *Economist* published two: "Nasser Battles On," on the 7th, about the revolt against Egypt in Syria, and "New Patters in Syria," on the 14th: "This in fact was a typically Syrian coup, with a handful of officers playing their traditional part as breakers and makers of governments." On 5 November 1961, the *Observer* published a story by Philby, with no dateline, "'Purge' to safeguard Cairo regime." Following Syria's revolt against Egypt, Nasser launched a purge in Egypt of similar "reactionary" elements. On the 11th, the *Economist* carried his story "Pyramid in the Fog," about political "reform" in Egypt. On the last day of the year, the *Observer* published two articles by Philby, datelined Beirut, 30 December. A short notice, "Kuwaitis go to first poll," on page two and then a long editorial piece, "Kuwait Today from H. A. R. Philby," some pages further into the paper. "Invisible deterrents to Kessim" provides the context for Philby's assessment that Britain's commitment to the defense of Kuwait would be enough to deter General Kessim from attempting an invasion: "General Kessim, therefore, has nothing to gain by such an adventure, and much to lose. A disaster on that scale might well lead to revolution in Baghdad with General Kessim himself this time cast for the role of Nuri as-Said."

The *Economist* carried a story by Philby in its 6 January 1962 edition, "Greater Syria, Pocket Edition," mentioning an abortive *coup d'état* on 31 December 1961. There were few other articles from "Our Middle East Correspondent" in the *Economist* in 1962. On the other hand, the number of his articles in the *Observer* increased in 1962. There were eighteen from March to December. "Film offends Lebanon," on 4 March 1963, datelined Beirut, stated that "Great offence has been caused in Beirut by a film entitled 'Summer in Lebanon,' recently shown on BBC television. Although nobody here has seen it, plenty has been heard from indignant Lebanese citizens living in Britain who have." It is mildly satirical. More seriously, an article published on 18 March, analyzed the "Cause of fighting" between Syria and Israel, attributing it to Arab concerns about real and imagined Israeli irrigation plans for the Jordan River valley. A second article, on the same date, "Saudi Arabia turns Right," reports the return of Crown Prince Faisal as a member of the Cabinet. The *Economist* ran an article by "Our Middle East Correspondent" on 31 March 1962 under the headline "Syria Back to Barracks," beginning "The Syrian army has done it again. After four months of parliamentary life its patience was exhausted and in the early hours of Wednesday morning the high command dissolved the Chamber of Deputies on the grounds that it had failed in its mission." The article concluded: "Syria has emerged again as a factor of instability in the Arab world." An article in the *Economist,* "Two Cities of Syria," without a byline, discussed the unstable post-coup situation in Syria. Another Syrian article was published in the *Economist* on 14 April 1962, this attributed to "Our Special Correspondent," datelined Damascus, giving a summary of the situation—highly unstable—as the army sought to establish a government. On 27 May, the *Observer* published an article "From H.A.R. Philby," "Syrian Cabinet suppresses its own newspaper." He uses this unusual action as an indicator of the instability of the Syrian government eight months after Syria broke from Egypt. Later in the article he describes difficulties between Egypt and Saudi Arabia and Egypt and Iraq.

An article dated 15 July from Cairo, "Call to pool world aid funds," reported on a conference on development problems. "The feeling of the conference is clearly against any attempt to form a new economic bloc of developing countries. The emphasis is rather on getting together with advanced countries to discuss means of increasing and redistributing the volume of investment and trade to the better advantage of all." A week later the *Observer* published a major article across four columns on one page, three on another "By H.A.R. Philby," about: "Nasser's Pride and Glory." On the occasion of the tenth anniversary of the Egyptian Revolution, Philby reviews the condition of the country. "If Socialism means nothing more than Government control, then Egypt is one of the most Socialist countries in the world. With the very important exception of land, the Government now runs all the basic enterprises of the country . . . There is a minimum wage . . . There is no right to strike in Egypt . . . Nobody in Egypt seriously pretends that the country is already a democracy . . . The Muslim Brotherhood and Communists were crushed and all party activity was banned . . . the Soviet Union remains the chief outside beneficiary of the squalls which beset the Egyptian revolution." "It is now as difficult to conceive an Egypt without Nasser as a Yugoslavia without Tito or an India without Nehru—and Nasser is still a young man."

The *Observer* published a straight news piece "From H.A.R. Philby," datelined Beirut, 25 August, on the following day: "Arabs may form new league," as a result of a conflict between Egypt and Syria. This was followed by "Syria has three choices" on 2 September, recording the defeat of Syrian initiatives against Egypt in the Arab League. The *Observer* newspaper published a piece by Philby on 23 September, "Policy of new Imam distrusted," concerning British reactions in regard to relations between the Aden Protectorate and the new ruler of Yemen. This was followed by a major piece that ran on 30 September, "Yemeni rebels follow same lines as Nasser," datelined Beirut, 29 September: "Latest reports from the Yemen suggest that a genuinely revolutionary situation is developing as a result of the Army coup this week," while another on 7 October, now datelined Aden on the 6th, was headlined "Why many believe tribesmen are hiding the Imam." "The fate of the Imam of the Yemen, Muhammad Badr, is a deepening mystery. The nine-man Jordanian military mission in the Yemen, which was asked by the revolutionary Government to leave the country, has arrived in Aden apparently convinced that the Imam is still alive." That weekend the *Economist* ran a piece, "Yemen Makes History," as "From Our Middle East Correspondent," datelined Aden, concerning the revolution in Yemen on 27 September 1962, that was "the first attempt [on the Arabian peninsula] that comes to mind to destroy the monarchy and replace it by a republic. The situation is very confused and the country is inaccessible to correspondents."

"As is his custom when he runs into trouble, King Saud of Saudi Arabia has called on his brother, Crown Prince Faisal, to take over responsibility for the Saudi Government," Philby wrote on 20 October 1962 for the *Observer* for the following Sunday. A feature article under the heading "Inside the Yemen by H.A.R. Philby" was published in the same issue of the paper: "Backward nation that looks for miracles," datelined Aden. He presents the situation of the day, the rebellion against the traditional rulers by an Egyptian backed "republic," the former supported by the Saudis, Jordanians, and traditional rulers in the Aden protectorate. "Meanwhile, British officialdom in Aden maintains an enigmatic silence on all matters affecting the Yemen. It seems that, for fear of provoking renewed outcries against colonialism, it is suffering from self-inflicted lingual paralysis, ignoring the fact that many neuroses tend to disappear if freely discussed." He criticizes the US and Britain for not recognizing the revolutionary government, and portrays the Imam in dark colors and concludes: "Given reasonably stable and enlightened government and two or three decades of constructive work, the Yemen could again become Arabia Felix. But those tribesmen will have to be tamed first." Also on 20 October 1962, the *Economist* ran an anonymous piece in the Opinion section, "Arabia Felix: With the Yemeni revolution, all Arabia may have come to the end of a long sleep." It began: "Until something is done about the lacework of British protected states that festoon the eastern and southern coasts of the Arabian peninsula, the Arab portrait of Britain is indelibly adorned with the horn and tails of an old-fashioned proconsul," which sounds like Philby. The article posits that change in Yemen will result in progress elsewhere in the peninsula.

The following week there was another major feature, with photographs, in the *Observer*: "Unshackling the Yemen," from H. A. R. Philby, datelined Beirut, 27 October. He criticizes official British policy in Aden and the protectorates, in the spirit of his father, but also writes that "the ability of the revolutionaries to fashion a modern State on the ruins of the old must remain in serious doubt . . . The rudiments of administration scarcely exist. Without trying, I saw 20 tanks in Sanaa alone, but despite hours spent in Republican headquarters not one typewriter." The tone seems more anti-establishment, more critical—in both senses of the word—than before. The same day saw the publication of a short piece on Yemen, without a byline, in the *Economist,* which appears to be by Philby, concerning a press conference by the new prime minister of Yemen, Brigadier Sallal. On 3 November 1962, Philby reported to the *Observer* from Beirut "Republicans control in Yemen" with "British recognition of the Yemeni Republican Government now appears imminent." On 17 November Philby was back in Aden, filing "Tension rises over Aden Merger" for publication in the *Observer* on the following day. "Arab crises have a habit of snowballing, and the upheaval in the Yemen is no exception." "Tension in Aden is growing as a result of the British Government's decision to press ahead with its plan for merging the Aden colony with the South Arabian Federation . . . most of Aden's inhabitants do not want it."

In its "Comment" the paper's editors agreed with Philby: "The Government's decision to force through a merger between Aden Colony and the Federation of South Arabia . . . without securing the consent of the people of Aden is astonishing, dangerous and unwise." On 9 December the paper published an article from Philby, "Arab Kings oppose US on Yemen." "There are persistent reports that the American Ambassadors in Amman and Jeddah have been told that if the United States recognizes the Yemeni Republic, Jordan and Saudi Arabia will immediately establish diplomatic relations with the Soviet Union . . . American and British officials here [Beirut] are getting tired of King Hussein's habit of striking gallant attitudes without first consulting those who foot the bill." And then on 23 December, "The odds against the Imam," after the US recognized the Republican Government of the Yemen. The Jordanian Prime Minister stated that "the Imam's forces are 'at the gates of Sanaa,' . . . When that tired claim was first made, I was in Sanaa myself, and could certainly have driven at least 50 miles in any direction without any risk beyond that of a jarred spine." "The oddest feature of the situation is Australian recognition of the revolutionary Government. There is speculation whether this foreshadows Australians chewing *qat* or Yemenis playing cricket."

Philby's contributions to the *Observer* continued in 1963 with a 13 January article, again on Yemen, from Beirut on the 12th, "New Yemen clashes widen Arab rift." "American hopes that recognition of the Republican Government in the Yemen would lead to an early withdrawal of foreign troops are being steadily disappointed. If anything, the situation has grown uglier. Fighting continues and it is thought that British non-recognition stems from a desire to re-establish diplomatic relations with Saudi Arabia." A week later, in the *Observer*'s number of 20 January 1963, there was a story from Philby in Beirut on the 19th "League abandons Kuwait." "The Arab League is evidently dying on its feet." Withdrawing even token forces protecting Kuwait from Iraq. "No official reason for the decision [to withdraw Saudi and Jordanian forces from Kuwait] has been given, but the deplorable increase in tension between the Arab monarchies and republics after the revolution in the Yemen doubtless swayed both King Hussein and Prince Faisal to bring back units which they can ill spare."

BIBLIOGRAPHY

SOURCES

Kim and Jim: Kim Philby and James Angleton, Friends and Enemies in the Cold War is based on primary sources while also taking into account the secondary literature and the wider issues of the times in which Philby and Angleton lived and worked.

The research for this book began more than a quarter of a century ago with that for the first complete biography of long-serving chief of the counterintelligence staff of the Central Intelligence Agency, *James Jesus Angleton, The CIA and the Craft of Counterintelligence.* Additional relevant research, especially for the life and career of H. A. R. Philby, was previously conducted in connection with my biographies of Guy Burgess and Donald and Melinda Maclean.

Work on this project has entailed remaining current with the secondary literature, including the biographies of Angleton and Philby, as they have appeared, and for the latter the most recent Russian biography with its newly released KGB materials, as well as work on Philby's associates: British, American, and Soviet. I have often referred to the papers in the ever-expanding Wilson Center Cold War International History Project, to articles in the relevant scholarly journals, to the Foreign Relations of the United States and the series of Documents on British Policy Overseas, and to more general histories of World War II and the Cold War.

Primary sources for Angleton include family letters, especially those of his wife, Cicely, her mother, Helen d'Autremont, and Angleton's sister, Carmen Angleton Hauser. I believe the last of these have not been read by other researchers interested in these issues. The archives of the National Cash Register company, the *New York Times*, and that of *Corriere della Sera* have been useful in reconstructing the business career of his father.

I have also revisited and reinterpreted Angleton's formative intellectual experience at Yale University for this book.

This brings us to government archives. The immense JFK Assassination files, extending back to World War II, contain much more of interest than matters directly relating to the assassination. I do not believe that others conducting research on Angleton's career have consulted these.

The National Archives in College Park, Maryland, hold the day-by-day and sometimes hour-by-hour record of the Office of Special Services, in which Angleton was first trained as a counterintelligence officer, in large part by Kim Philby. Both the CIA and FBI have been recently releasing important records, for example, the daily meeting logs of the Directors of Central Intelligence in the early 1950s, filling gaps in our understanding of Angleton's career. The Louise Page Morris papers at the Hoover Institution, Stanford University, throw some light on what was in effect Angleton's private network of agents. Various in-house CIA histories and studies have also now become available, such as studies of Dulles and others as directors of Central Intelligence and histories of the counterintelligence staff of CIA itself. As Angleton was classified as a "confidential informant" in the CIA for the FBI, the records of the latter have also been consulted.

James Angleton's career ended in a series of Congressional investigations. Here, again, the transcripts of the underlying interviews add significantly to our understanding of his actions and motivations. The Foreign Affairs Oral History Collection, of the Association for Diplomatic Studies and Training, provides informal recollections of senior American officials, such as James McCargar and William Colby, sometimes differing in crucial ways from their official memoirs. The transcript of a Wilson Center conference about Angleton, "Moles, Defectors, and Deceptions," has been useful for both sources and methods.

There is, of course, an entire international Kim Philby industry, beginning with the extraordinary story of his father, the well-known explorer St. John Philby. The primary source for St. John Philby remains Elizabeth Monroe's masterful biography. Less often-used sources include Aramco newsletters, MI-6 files, and the articles and reviews by and concerning St. John Philby in *The Times* (London), running for half a century, as well as the obituaries in *The Times*, the *Observer*, the *Guardian*, and elsewhere.

Concerning H. A. R. Philby himself, there are now at least half a dozen biographies, the most interesting including one of the earlier, that of *The Times* group (Page, Knightley, and Leitch); Knightley's later book, based on interviews with Philby in Moscow; that published under the name of Philby's Russian widow, Rufina Philby; and Timothy Milne's rueful posthumously published memoir of his friend—as he thought him. The recent short Russian biography, *Kim Filbi* by N. M. Dolgopolov adds certain information, as does other material made available by the Foreign Intelligence Service of the Russian Federation. There are also the authorized histories of MI-5 and MI-6, and I have found useful as well the multi-volume documentary history of the KGB, which includes some crucial materials provided to the KGB by Kim Philby and his associates. Of course such authorized documents, whether from British, American, Soviet, or Russian sources, must be used with caution. Concerning Philby's later life in Moscow, the materials in the Georgetown University Library give a view of the aging retired spy as something like an ordinary pensioner, who, however, from time to time counsels apprentice spies on best practice.

Other relevant British government materials released to the National Archives, Kew, I have used include those of the Foreign, War, and Cabinet offices, and the two secret intelligence services. Recent releases organized around "the Hunt for Homer," the eventually successful effort to identify Donald Maclean as a Soviet agent codenamed "Homer" (or in Russian, "Gomer"), are replete with information about, and in some cases by, Philby. Foreign Office remarks among the latter materials showing that British officials were misleading their American counterparts are a reminder that a Top Secret classification is no guarantee of historical reliability.

Kim Philby spent approximately the same amount of his life employed as a journalist as he did employed by MI-6 (sometimes simultaneously). I have read the archive of *The Times* to trace his reporting from the Nationalist side during the Spanish Civil War and from his time with the British Expeditionary Force early in World War II. I have read the archives of the *Observer,* the *Guardian,* the *Economist,* and the *New Republic* for his extensive reporting from the Middle East between 1956 and 1963. It is notable that for members of the British newspaper-reading public, information about the Middle East during those years that did not come from *The Times* in large part came from Kim Philby.

Archives

Central Intelligence Agency
Federal Bureau of Investigation
Georgetown University Library: Philby–Lyubimov Collection
Harvard University, Houghton Library
Hoover Institution: Louise Page Morris Papers
The National Archives, Kew, United Kingdom
The National Archives, Washington, D.C., United States
Utah State University, Merrill–Cazier Library
Vassar College Archives, Mary McCarthy Papers

Collections

Association for Diplomatic Service and Training: Oral Histories
Documents on British Policy Overseas
Foreign Intelligence Service of the Russian Federation
Foreign Relations of the United States

Newspapers and Magazines

Corriere della Serra
London Review of Books
Economist
Guardian
The Times (London)
New Republic
New York Times
NCR
Observer

Conference Proceedings

Moles, Defectors, and Deceptions: James Angleton and His Influence on US Counterintelligence. Edited by Bruce Hoffman and Christian Ostermann. A Wilson Center and Georgetown University Center for Security Studies Joint Conference, 2014.

Publications

Aburish, Said K. *Beirut Spy: The St. George Hotel Bar*. London: Bloomsbury, 1989.

Aburish, Said K. "Lost Victories, The CIA in the Middle East." http://www.iiwds.com/said_aburish/a_lostvictories.htm

Aldrich, Richard J. "American intelligence and the British Raj: The OSS, the SSU and India, 1942–1947." *Intelligence and National Security*, 13:1, 132–164, 1998. DOI: 10.1080/02684529808432466.

Alvarez, David J. *Spying through a Glass Darkly: American espionage against the Soviet Union, 1954–1946*. Lawrence, Kansas: University of Kansas Press, 2016.

Ambrose, Stephen E. *Ike's Spies*. New York: Doubleday, 1981.

Andrew, Christopher and Gordievsky, Oleg. *KGB: The Inside Story of its Foreign Operations from Lenin to Gorbachev*. New York: HarperCollins, 1992.

Andrew, Christopher and Mitrokhin, Vasili. *The Sword and the Shield: The Mitrokhin Archive and the Secret History of the KGB*. New York: Basic Books, 1999.

Anonymous. "A Fixation on Moles: James J. Angleton, Anatoliy Golitsyn, and the 'Monster Plot': Their Impact on CIA Personnel and Operations." *Studies in Intelligence*, Vol. 55, No. 4 (December 2011). Central Intelligence Agency.

Bagley, Tennent H. *Spy Wars: Moles, Mysteries, and Deadly Games*. New Haven & London: Yale University Press, 2007.

Beeston, Richard. *Looking for Trouble: The Life and Times of a Foreign Correspondent*. London: Tauris, 1997/2006.

Benghi, Emilia. "Intellettuali antifascisti in America." *La Repubblica*, 3 June 2008.

Bennett, Gill. "From World War to Cold War: the records of the Foreign Office Permanent UnderSecretary's Department, 1939–51."

Bennett, Gill. "The CORBY case: the defection of Igor Gouzenko, September 1945, in From World War to Cold War: the records of the Foreign Office Permanent UnderSecretary's Department, 1939–51."

Benson, Robert Louis and Warner, Michael. Venona: *Soviet Espionage and the American Response 1939–1957*. Washington, D.C. Central Intelligence Agency, 1996.

Beschloss, Michael R. *Taking Charge: Johnson White House Tapes, 1963–1964*. New York: Simon & Schuster, 1997.

Borovik, Genrikh. *The Philby Files: The Secret Life of the Master Spy—KGB Archives Revealed*. London: Little, Brown and Company, 1995.

Bower, Tom. *The Perfect English Spy: Sir Dick White and the Secret War 1935–90*. New York: St. Martin's Press, 1995.

Breiman, et al. *U.S. Intelligence and the Nazis*. Cambridge: Cambridge University Press, 2005.

Brooks, Cleanth and Warren, Robert Penn. *Understanding Poetry*. New York: Holt, Rinehart and Winston, 1960.

Brown, Anthony Cave. *Treason in the Blood: H. St. John Philby, Kim Philby, and the Spy Case of the Century*. Boston: Houghton Mifflin Company, 1994.

Buckle, Richard. "A Traveller in the Lebanon." *Observer*, 18 March 1956.

Cecil, Robert. *A Divided Life: A Personal Portrait of the Spy Donald Maclean*. New York: William Morrow & Co., 1989.

Central Intelligence Agency, CI SIG History.

Central Intelligence Agency, DCI Logs.

Central Intelligence Agency. "Counterintelligence Operations, Soviet Russia Division, 1946–56," The Clandestine Service Historical Series, CS HP 334, Historical Staff, August 1972.

Central Intelligence Agency. DCI Diary, January–April 1950.

Central Intelligence Agency, Field Double Agent Guide, August 1960, JFK Assassination files, 104-10213-10058.

Chalou, George C. *The Secrets War: The Office of Strategic Services in World War II*. Washington, D.C.: The National Archives and Records Service, 1992.

Citino, Nathan J. *Envisioning the Arab Future: Modernization in US-Arab Relations, 1945–1967*. Cambridge University Press, 2017.

Cockburn, Alexander. *The Golden Age Is in Us: Journeys and Encounters*. London: Verso, 1995.

Colby, William. "Oral History: Reflections of DCI Colby and Helms on the CIA's 'Time of Troubles' From the CIA Oral History Archives." https://www.cia.gov/library/center-for-the-study-of-intelligence/csi-publications/csi-studies/studies/vol51no3/reflections-of-dci-colby-and-helms-on-the-cia2019s-201ctime-of-troubles201d.html

Colby, William and Forbath, Peter. *Honorable Men: My Life in the CIA*. New York: Simon & Schuster, 1978.

Colville, John. *The Fringes of Power: 10 Downing Street Diaries, 1939–1955*. New York: W. W. Norton & Company, 1985.

Comrade Philby (KGB Spy Documentary) Timeline: World History Documentaries. https://www.youtube.com/watch?v=htukqTEeNaQ

Connelly, Mathew. *A Diplomatic Revolution: Algeria's Fight for Independence*. Oxford: Oxford University Press, 2003.

Cookridge, E. H. *The Third Man: The Full Story of Kim Philby*. New York: Putnam's, 1968.

Corke, Sarah-Jane. *US Covert Operations and Cold War Strategy: Truman, Secret Warfare and the CIA, 1945–53*. London: Routledge, 2008.

Corson, William R. *The Armies of Ignorance: The Rise of the American Intelligence Empire*. New York: Dial Press, 1977.

Costello, John. *Mask of Treachery*, New York: William Morrow & Co., 1988.

Daily Telegraph. "Kim Philby Hailed as 'Great Spy' in Russia." 12 December 2011. https://www.telegraph.co.uk/news/worldnews/europe/russia/8951921/Kim-Philby-hailed-as-great-spy-in-Russia.html

Darling, Arthur B. *The Central Intelligence Agency*. State College: Penn State University Press, 2007.

Davenport-Hines, Richard. *Enemies Within: Communists, the Cambridge Spies and the Making of Modern Britain*. London: William Collins, 2018.

Davidson, Donald. "Preface to Decision." *Sewannee Review*, LIII, 3 (Summer 1945).

Dolgopolov, N. M. *Kim Filbi*. Moscow: Moloda'ja Gvardi'ja, 2012.

Dorril, Stephen. *MI-6: Inside the Covert World of Her Majesty's Secret Intelligence Service*. New York: Free Press, 2002.

Dulles, Allen. *The Craft of Intelligence*. New York: Harper and Row, 1965.

Dupee, F. W. and Stade, George, eds. *Selected Letters of E. E. Cummings*. New York: Harcourt, Brace & World, 1969.

Elliott, Nicholas. *With My Little Eye: Observations Along the Way*. Norwich: Michael Russell, 1993.

Empson, William. *Seven Types of Ambiguity*. London: Chatto and Windus, 1930.

Encyclopaedia Britannica, Eleventh edition, 1910–11, Volume VI, "Civil Service."

Epstein, Edward Jay. *Legend: The Secret World of Lee Harvey Oswald*. New York: McGraw-Hill, 1978.

Epstein, Edward Jay. *Deception: The Invisible War Between the KGB and CIA*. New York: Simon & Schuster, 1989.

Even, Yair. "Two Squadrons and their Pilots: The First Syrian Request for the Deployment of Soviet Military Forces on its Territory, 1956." Cold War International History Project Working Paper #77 (February 2016).

Favretto, Ilaria. "The 'Opening to the Left.'" Jones, Erik and Gianfranco Pasquino. *The Oxford Book of Italian Politics*. 2015, Abstract. http://www.oxfordhandbooks.com/view/10.1093/oxfordhb/9780199669745.001.0001/oxfordhb-9780199669745-e-21

Felix, Christopher (James McCargar). *A Short Course in the Secret War*. New York: Dell, 1963.

Ford, Harold P. Colby interview, 15 March 1988, in *William E. Colby as Director of Central Intelligence, 1973–1976*. CIA History Staff, Center for the Study of Intelligence, Central Intelligence Agency, Washington, D.C., 1993.

Foreign Intelligence Service of the Russian Federation, Newsletter, 25 January 2004. http://svr.gov.ru/smi/2004/bratishka20040125.htm

Foreign Intelligence Service, Russian Federation, Newsletter, 8 September 2006. http://svr.gov.ru/smi/2006/krzv20060809-11.htm

Foreign Intelligence Service, Russian Federation. "Returning to the 'Cambridge Five'—Triumph or Failure?" Newsletter, 3 April 2008. http://svr.gov.ru/smi/2008/argned20080403.htm

Foreign Relations of the United States. Memorandum for the Record by the Director of Central Intelligence's Executive Assistant (Kirkpatrick), Washington, 14 February 1951. SUBJECT: Meeting on Integration of O/SO and O/PC. https://history.state.gov/historicaldocuments/frus1950-55Intel/d50

Fursenko, Aleksandr and Naftali, Timothy. "Soviet intelligence and the Cuban missile crisis." *Intelligence and National Security*, 13:3, 1998. https://www.belfercenter.org/sites/default/files/legacy/files/CMC50/SovietIntelligenceAndTheCubanMissileCrisis.pdf

Gardiner, Muriel. *Code Name "Mary": Memoirs of an American Woman in the Austrian Underground*. New Haven and London: Yale University Press, 1983.

Gehlen, Reinhard. David Irving (trans.) *The Service: The Memoirs of General Reinhard Gehlen*. New York: World Publishing, 1972.

Golitsyn, Anatoliy. *New Lies for Old*. London: The Bodley Head, Ltd, 1984.

Goodman, M. S. *MI-6's Atomic Man: The Rise and Fall of Commander Eric Welsh*. 2016. DOI: 10.1177/0968344515572503.

Gordievsky, Oleg. *Next Stop Execution*. London: Macmillan, 1995.

Grose, Peter. *Gentleman Spy: The Life of Allen Dulles*. New York: Houghton Mifflin, 1994.

Hamrick, S. J. *Deceiving the Deceivers: Kim Philby, Donald Maclean, and Guy Burgess*. New Haven: Yale University Press, 2004.

Harris, Charles H. III. *The Great Call-Up: The Guard, the Border, and the Mexican Revolution*. Norman: The University of Oklahoma Press, 2015.

"Hello, Comrade Philby." 18 December 1967. The interview, first published in the Russian daily newspaper *Izvestia* on 19 December 1967, was translated into English for publication in FBIS supplement "Materials On 50th Anniversary of Soviet State Security Organs, Fbis-Frb-68-007-S on 1968-01-10. Supplement number 2" titled "Hello, Comrade Philby."

Herken, Gregg. *The Georgetown Set: Friends and Rivals in Cold War Washington*. New York: Alfred A. Knopf, 2014.

Hersh, Burton. *The Old Boys: The American Elite and the Origins of the CIA*. New York: Charles Scribner's Sons, 1992.

Historical Encyclopedia of Illinois. 1901. http://genealogytrails. com/ill/christian/christianhistories.html

Hoffman, Bruce and Ostermann, Christian, eds. *Moles Defectors, and Deceptions: James Angleton and His Influence on US Counterintelligence*. A Wilson Center and Georgetown University Center for Security Studies Joint Conference, 2014.

Holzman, Michael. "Café CIA Roma: Mary McCarthy's Cold War." *Prospects*, 25, 2000.

Honigmann, Barbara. *A Chapter from My Life*. An extract translated by John S. Barrett from *Ein Kapitel aus meinem Leben*. Munich: Carl Hanser Verlag, 2004. http://www.litrix.de/apps/litrix_publications/ data/pdf1/Honigmann_Ein_Kapitel_Leseprobe_EN.pdf

Hood, William. "Angleton's World." In *Myths Surrounding James Angleton: Lessons for American Counterintelligence*, ed. William Hood et al. Washington, D.C.: Consortium for the Study of Intelligence, 1994.

Ireland, Eleanor. *First-Hand: Bletchley Park, Station X- Memories of a Colossus Operator*. https://ethw.org/First-Hand:Bletchley_Park,_Station_X_-_Memories_of_a_Colossus_Operator

Jackson, Wayne G. *Allen Welsh Dulles As Director of Central Intelligence, 26 February 1953 to 29 November 1961, Volume I, Allen Dulles, The Man*. Historical Staff, Central Intelligence Agency, 1973.

Jackson, Wayne G. *Allen Welsh Dulles As Director of Central Intelligence, 26 February 1953 to 29 November 1961, Volume IV, Allen Dulles, The Man*. Historical Staff, Central Intelligence Agency, 1973.

Jeffery, Keith. *The Secret History of MI-6*. New York: The Penguin Press, 2010.

Jeffreys-Jones, Rhodri. *The CIA and American Democracy*. New Haven: Yale University Press, 1989.

Johnson, Loch. *Spy Watching: Intelligence Accountability in the United States*. Oxford: Oxford University Press, 2018.

Kent, Sherman. *Strategic Intelligence for American World Policy*. Princeton: Princeton University Press, 1966.

Kessler, Ronald. *Inside the CIA: Revealing the Secrets of the World's Most Powerful Spy Agency*. New York: Pocket Books, 1994.

Knightley, Phillip. *The Master Spy: The Story of Kim Philby*. New York: Alfred A. Knopf, 1989.

Kuzmarov, Jeremy. *Modernizing Repression: Police Training and Nation-Building in the American Century*. Massachusetts: University of Massachusetts Press, 2012.

Kwang-On Yoo, http://koreanstudies.com/pipermail/koreanstudies_koreanstudies.com/2010-June/020342.html

La Salle, Peter. "An Encounter with *Furioso*." *Raritan*, Volume 12, Number 4.

Lamphere, Robert J. and Shachtman, Tom. *The FBI–KGB War: A Special Agent's Story*. New York: Random House, 1986.

Leigh, David. *The Wilson Plot*. New York: Pantheon Books, 1988.

Lobster as "Philby naming names." *Lobster*, 16. http://www.8bitmode.com/rogerdog/lobster/lobster16.pdf

Lyubimov, Mikhail. "A Martyr to Dogma." In Philby, Rufina. *The Private Life of Kim Philby*.

Maclean, Donald. *British Foreign Policy Since Suez*. London: Hodder and Stoughton, Ltd, 1970.

Maddrell, Paul. "Exploiting and Securing the Open Border in Berlin: the Western Secret Services, the Stasi, and the Second Berlin Crisis, 1958–1961." Cold War International History Project Working Paper #58, February 2009. https://www.wilsoncenter.org/sites/default/files/CWIHPWP58_maddrell.pdf

Maddrell, Paul. *Spying on Science: Western Intelligence in Divided Germany, 1945–1961*. Oxford University Press, 2006.

Makins, Roger. "Minute to Mr. Bevin," Top secret, Foreign Office, 17 April 1950, Documents on British Policy Overseas. London: Her Majesty's Stationery Office, Series II, Volume II, No. 19.

Manchester, William. *American Caesar: Douglas MacArthur 1880–1964*. New York: Dell, 1983.

Mangold, Tom. *Cold Warrior: James Jesus Angleton: The CIA's Master Spy Hunter*. New York: Simon and Schuster, 1991.

Marchetti, Victor. *The CIA and the Cult of Intelligence*. New York, Alfred A. Knopf, 1974.

Martin, David C. *Wilderness of Mirrors: Intrigue, Deception, and the Secrets that Destroyed Two of the Cold War's Most Important Agents*. New York: HarperCollins.

McCargar, James. Interviewed by: Charles Stuart Kennedy, Initial interview date: 18 April 1995.

McCargar, James. Interviewed by: Charles Stuart Kennedy, Initial interview date: 18 April 1995. The Association for Diplomatic Studies and Training, Foreign Affairs Oral History Project. http://www.adst.org/OH%20TOCs/McCargar,%20James.toc.pdf

McMeekin, Sean. *The Red Millionaire: A Political Biography of Willi Münzenberg, Moscow's Secret Propaganda Tsar in the West*. New Haven: Yale University Press, 2003.

Milne, Tim. *Kim Philby: The Unknown Story of the KGB's Master Spy*. London: Biteback Publishing, 2014.

Mistry, Kaeten. *The United States, Italy and the Origins of Cold War: waging political warfare: 1945–1950*. Cambridge: Cambridge University Press, 2014.

Modin, Yuri. *My Five Cambridge Friends: Burgess, Maclean, Philby, Blunt, and Cairncross*. New York: Farrar Straus Giroux, 1994.

Monroe, Elizabeth. *Philby of Arabia*. Reading: Garner Publishing Company, 1973.

Morgan, Ted. *A Covert Life: Jay Lovestone: Communist, Anti-Communist, and Spymaster*. New York: Random House, 1999.

Morley, Jefferson. *The Ghost: The Secret Life of CIA Spymaster James Jesus Angleton*. New York: St. Martin's Press, 2017.

Murphy, Charles J. V. "The Making of a Master Spy." *Time*, 24 February 1975. http://jfk.hood.edu/Collection/Weisberg%20Subject%20Index%20Files/C%20Disk/CIA%20Domestic%20Intelligence%20Part%202/Item%20016.pdf

Naftali, Timothy J. "ARTIFICE: James Angleton and X-2 Operations in Italy." In *The Secrets War: The Office of Strategic Services in World War II*, ed. George C. Chalou, 218–245. Washington DC: National Archives and Records Administration, 1992.

Naftali, Timothy. "The CIA and Eichmann's Associates." In Breiman, et al. *U.S. Intelligence and the Nazis*. Cambridge: Cambridge University Press, 2005.

NCR News, July 1927 and *The NCR*, 25 August 1928, courtesy of Gwen Goodnight Haney, Community Collections Manager, Dayton History, Dayton, Ohio.

Newton, Verne W. *The Cambridge Spies: The Untold Story of Maclean, Philby, and Burgess in America*. Lanham, Maryland: Madison Books, 1991

Office of the Director of National Intelligence, CI Reader, Volume III.

Orlov, Alexander. *Handbook of Intelligence and Guerrilla Warfare*. Ann Arbor: The University of Michigan Press, 1963.

Page, Bruce, Leitch, David, and Knightley, Phillip. *Philby: The Spy Who Betrayed a Generation*. London: Andre Deutsch, 1968.

Peake, Hayden. "The Philby Literature." In Philby, Rufina. *The Private Life of Kim Philby*.

Penrose, Barrie and Freeman, Simon. *Conspiracy of Silence*. London: Grafton, 1987.

Philby, H. A. R. *My Silent War*. New York: Grove Press, 1968.

Philby, Kim. "Autobiographical Reminiscences." In Philby, Rufina. *The Private Life of Kim Philby*.

Philby, Kim. "Lecture to the KGB, July 1977." In Philby, Rufina. *The Private Life of Kim Philby*.

Philby, Kim. "Should Agents Confess?" In Philby, Rufina. *The Private Life of Kim Philby*.

Philby, Rufina, Lyubimov, Mikhail and Peake, Hayden. *The Private Life of Kim Philby: The Moscow Years*. New York: Fromm International, 1999.

Philby, Rufina. "The Moscow Years." In Philby, Rufina. *The Private Life of Kim Philby*.

Pincher, Chapman. *Treachery: Betrayals, Blunders, and Cover-ups: Six Decades of Espionage Against America and Great Britain*. New York: Random House, 2009.

Powers, Thomas. "The Ghost: The Secret Life of CIA Spymaster James Jesus Angleton by Jefferson Morley." *London Review of Books*, Volume 40, Number 9, 10 May 2018.

Powers, Thomas. *The Man Who Kept the Secrets: Richard Helms and the CIA*. New York: Knopf, 1979.

Prados, John. *Lost Crusader: The Secret Wars of CIA Director William Colby*. Oxford: Oxford University Press, 2003.

Raviv, Dan and Melman, Yossi. *Every Spy a Prince: The Complete History of Israel's Intelligence Community*. New York: Houghton Mifflin Harcourt, 1990.

Riebling, Mark. *Wedge: The Secret War Between the FBI and CIA*. New York: Knopf, 1994.

Riley, Morris. *Philby: The Hidden Years*. London: Janus Publishing Company, 1999.

Robarge, David. "DCI John McCone and the Assassination of President John F. Kennedy." *Studies in Intelligence*, Central Intelligence Agency, September, 2013.

Roosevelt, Kermit. *War Report of the O.S.S.* New York: Walker & Co., 1976.

Ruffner, Kevin Conley. *Eagle and Swastika: CIA and NAZI War Criminals and Collaborators*. History Staff. Central Intelligence Agency. Washington, DC. April, 2003.

Russian Foreign Intelligence Service. *Sketches of History*. Moscow: International Relations, 1997.

Salter, Michael. *Nazi War Crimes, US Intelligence and Selective Prosecution at Nuremberg: controversies regarding the role of the Office of Strategic Services*. Abingdon, Rutledge-Cavendish, 2007.

Seale, Patrick and Maureen McConville. *Philby: The Long Road to Moscow*. Harmondsworth: Penguin, 1978.

Simpson, Christopher. *Blowback*. London: Crowell-Collier, 1989.

Tate, Allen. "A View of the White South." *The American Review*, 2:4, February 1934.

Thomas, Evan. *The Very Best Men*. New York: Simon & Schuster, 1995.

Trento, Joseph J. *The Secret History of the CIA*. New York: MJF Books, 2001.

Trevor Roper, Hugh. "The Philby Affair." *Encounter*, April, 1968.

Trotter, Mel. "The King's Man—Oil and Death." Alaela. Aramco Overseas Company. 13 May 2013. https://www.aramcoexpats.com/articles/the-kings-man-oil-and-death/

United States Holocaust Memorial Museum, *Holocaust Encyclopedia*, Ardeatine Caves Massacre. https://www.ushmm.org/wlc/en/article.php?ModuleId=10007940

United States House of Representatives. House Select Committee on Assassinations, James Angleton Interview, 15 June 1978.

United States Office of the Director of National Intelligence, CI [Counterintelligence] Reader, Volume III.

United States Senate Select Committee to Study Governmental Operations with Respect to Intelligence Activities, Assassination Transcripts of the Church Committee, Angleton, 19 June 1975.

United States Senate Select Committee to Study Governmental Operations with Respect to Intelligence Activities, Assassination Transcripts of the Church Committee, Angleton, 6 February 1976. NARA Record Number 157-10014-10003.

United States Senate Select Committee to Study Governmental Operations with Respect to Intelligence Activities, Assassination Transcripts of the Church Committee, Angleton, 17 September 1975.

United States Senate, Final Report of the Select Committee to Study Governmental Operations with Respect to Intelligence Activities Together with Additional Supplemental and Separate Views, Book IV, Supplementary Detailed Staff Reports on Foreign and Military Intelligence.

United States War Department. Strategic Services Unit History Project. War Report of the Office of Strategic Services. Walker & Co., 1976.

Ventresca, Robert A. *From Fascism to Democracy: Culture and*

Politics in The Italian Election of 1948. Toronto: University of Toronto Press, 2004.

Warner, Michael, ed. *CIA Cold War Records: The CIA Under Harry Truman*. Washington, D.C., History Staff, Center for the Study of Intelligence, Central Intelligence Agency, 1994.

Weinberg, Gerhard L. *A World at Arms: A Global History of World War II*. Cambridge: Cambridge University Press, 2005.

West, Nigel and Tsarev, Oleg. *The Crown Jewels: The British Secrets at the Heart of the KGB Archives*. New Haven: Yale University Press, 1999.

Wilson, Jeremy. *Lawrence of Arabia: The Authorized Biography of T. E. Lawrence*. New York: Atheneum, 1990.

Winks, Robin W. *Cloak and Gown: Scholars in the Secret War, 1939–1961*. New York: William Morrow and Company, 1987.

Wise, David. *Molehunt: The Secret Search for Traitors that Shattered the CIA*. New York: Random House, 1992.

Wolf, Markus and McElvoy, Anne. *Man Without a Face: The Autobiography of Communism's Greatest Spymaster*. New York: PublicAffairs, 1997.

Wong, Dong. "The Quarrelling Brothers: New Chinese Archives and a Reappraisal of the Sino-Soviet Split, 1959–1962." Cold War International History Project, Working Paper #49.

Wright, Peter. *Spycatcher: The Candid Autobiography of a Senior Intelligence Officer*. New York, Dell, 1988.

Zubok, Vladislav M. "Spy vs. Spy: The KGB vs. the CIA." Cold War International History Project, CWIHP Bulletin 4 (Fall 1994).

Zubok, Vladislav. Trans. "The KGB's 1967 Annual Report," 6 May 1968, History and Public Policy Program Digital Archive, TsKhSD f. 89, op. 5, d. 3, ll. 1–14. Translated for CWIHP by Vladislav Zubok. http://digitalarchive.wilsoncenter.org/document/110403

NOTES

OSS AND MI-6

1 There were similar organizations in Hong Kong, South Africa, Egypt and other parts of the Empire.

2 Aldrich, Richard J. "American intelligence and the British Raj: The O.S.S., the SSU and India, 1942–1947." *Intelligence and National Security*, 13:1, 132–164, 1998. DOI: 10.1080/02684529808432466.

3 The literature on these organizations is quite large and of varying quality. Some of it emanates from the organizations themselves, some from their retirees, some from people "close to" the organizations, some from otherwise respectable scholars who signed the Official Secrets Act and are therefore to some extent under the control of the agencies. There are, in addition, excellent independent scholars, such as Richard Aldrich.

4 This was, in effect, tantamount to having MI-6 operate in the United States.

5 Philby, H. A. R. *My Silent War*. New York: Grove Press, 1968, p. 90.

6 https://www.cia.gov/library/readingroom/docs/CIA

7 Seale, Patrick and McConville, Maureen. *Philby: The Long Road to Moscow*. Harmondsworth: Penguin, 1978, pp. 174–5.

8 Roosevelt, Kermit. "The Overseas Targets." In War Report of the O.S.S., 2:5.

9 Kent, Sherman. *Strategic Intelligence for American World Policy*. Princeton: Princeton University Press, 1966, pp. 140–41. That final question sounds as if it had the names of Philby, Maclean, and Burgess on it.

10 Darling, Arthur B. *The Central Intelligence Agency*. State College: Penn State University Press, 2007, p.18.

11 The Secret War Report of the O.S.S., pp. 49–50.

12 Milne, Timothy. *Kim Philby: The Unknown Story of the KGB's Master Spy*. London: Biteback Publishing, 2014, p. 95.

13 https://www.cia.gov/library/readingroom/docs/CIA-RDP78-04007A000100010011-7.pdf

14 Milne, p. 121

15 Milne, p. 123.

16 Records of the Office of Strategic Services (Record Group 226) 1940–1947 Entry 210. Boxes 1–538. Location: 250 64/21/1. CIA Accession: 79-00332A. Box # Subject/Record/Information. 307 Memo regarding X-2 history, 4 March 1946, ca. 20 pp. [WN#12929]

17 Costello, John. *Mask of Treachery*. New York: William Morrow & Co., 1988, pp. 423–6.

FATHERS AND SONS

1 Monroe, Elizabeth. *Philby of Arabia*. Reading: Garner Publishing Company, 1973, p. 4.

2 Monroe, p. 7.

3 "Civil Service." In *The Encyclopaedia Britannica*, Eleventh edition, 1910–11, Volume VI, pp. 412–13.

4 Monroe, p.18.

5 Monroe, p. 22.

6 Monroe, p. 25.

7 Monroe, p. 28. About $50,000 in 2015. See: http://www.historical-statistics.org/Currencyconverter.html

8 Monroe, p. 33.

9 Cave Brown, Anthony. *Treason in the Blood, H. St. John Philby, Kim Philby, and the Spy Case of the Century*. Boston: Houghton Mifflin Company, 1994, p. 24. *Treason in the Blood* is a rather curious book, apparently unedited, dependent on anonymous sources, and often inaccurate. It will be cited here under caution and only when confirmable from other sources. This citation depends on Monroe's life of St. John Philby.

10 Makin, William J. *Red Sea Nights*. London: National Travel Club, 1933, pp. 234–5.

11 Monroe, p. 54.

12 National Archives, UK, 15 December 1917, telegram from Cox, Baghdad to High Commissioner, Cairo, FO 882/8, IS/17/26.

13 Page, Bruce, Leitch, David, and Knightley, Phillip. *Philby: The Spy Who Betrayed a Generation*. London: Andre Deutsch, 1968, p. 38.

14 Monroe, p. 78.

15 Unless otherwise indicated, notices of this type are from contemporaneous numbers of *The Times*.

16 Wilson, Jeremy. *Lawrence of Arabia: The Authorized Biography of T. E. Lawr*ence. New York: Atheneum, 1990, p. 613.

17 *The Times*, 31 October 1919, p. 15.

18 Monroe, p. 95.

19 Wilson, pp. 654–5.

20 *The Times*, 14 November 1922.

21 Monroe, p. 119.

22 Monroe, p. 125.

23 In regard to Palestine, St. Philby advocated a "one-state solution" in all of Mandate Palestine, including what is now the Kingdom of Jordan, with an Arab majority and a protected Jewish minority.

24 Kim Philby received his school certificate from Westminster in January 1928.

25 Monroe, p. 156.

26 Monroe, p. 160.

27 Monroe, p. 174.

28 On 7 July the annual dinner of the Royal Central Asian Society took place with Field-Marshall Viscount Allenby in the chair. Those present included various other Marshals, Viscounts, Major-Generals, and Mr. and Mrs. H. J. Philby and Mr. Kim Philby.

29 Monroe, p. 189.

30 *Historical Encyclopedia of Illinois*, 1901. http://genealogytrails.com/ill/christian/christianhistories.html

31 James Hugh Angleton OSS Personnel File.

32 Utah State University, Merrill–Cazier Library. https://beta.worldcat.org/archivegrid/collection/data/51571797

33 Harris, Charles H. III. *The Great Call-Up: The Guard, the Border, and the Mexican Revolution*. Norman: The University of Oklahoma Press, 2015, p. 424. Jefferson Morley located this reference. Morley, Jefferson. *The Ghost: The Secret Life of CIA Spymaster James Jesus Angleton*. New York: St. Martin's Press, 2017, p. 4.

34 *The NCR* (National Cash Register newsletter), 25 August 1928.

35 *NCR News*, July 1927 and *The NCR*, 25 August 1928, courtesy of Gwen Goodnight Haney, Community Collections Manager, Dayton History, Dayton, Ohio.

36 Winks, Robin W. *Cloak and Gown: Scholars in the Secret War,*

1939–1961. New York: William Morrow and Company, 1987, p. 329. Anyone doing research concerning James Angleton must start with Winks's elegant and sympathetic chapter, "The Theorist."

37 Winks, p. 329.

38 Under "Foreign Countries Visited" in his OSS Personnel File, Hugh Angleton lists most European countries. *The Times* includes Mr. J. H. Angleton among the guests at a Canadian Dominion Day Dinner in London on 4 July 1933 (reported on 5 July). The period of intensive travel for NCR ends in 1933, when Angleton took over the franchise for Italy.

39 Winks, pp. 328–30; Mangold, Tom. *Cold Warror: James Jesus Angleton: The CIA's Master Spy Hunter*. New York: Simon and Schuster, 1991, pp. 31–3; Hood, William. "Angleton's World." In *Myths Surrounding James Angleton: Lessons for American Counterintelligence*, ed. William Hood et al. Washington, D.C.: Consortium for the Study of Intelligence, 1994, p. 2.

YOUNG MEN

1 Philby, Kim. "Autobiographical Reminiscenses." In Philby, Rufina, Lyubimov, Mikhail and Peake, Hayden. *The Private Life of Kim Philby*. New York: Fromm International, 2000, p. 205ff. According to Michael Bogdanov in the foreword to the volume, the memoir was written in 1971 (p. 9).

2 Milne, p. 20.

3 Page, Leitch and Knightley, p. 30.

4 Cockburn, Alexander. *The Golden Age Is in Us: Journeys and Encounters*. London: Verso, 1995, p. 37.

5 Cave Brown, p. 136. Typically, Cave Brown cites a lost letter remembered by an Aramco official. István Szegedi-Szüts was a Hungarian painter and illustrator, much older than Philby. There were Szüts brothers, of approximately the correct age, who were Hungarian Communists, dying horribly in the post-WWII purges.

6 Milne, pp. 13–14.

7 Milne, p. 20.

8 Seale and McConville, pp. 42–3.

9 Seale and McConville, p. 46.

10 *Sketches of History, the Russian Foreign Intelligence Service*. Moscow: International Relations, 1997, p. 41.

11   Seale and McConville, p. 75.

12   Seale and McConville, p. 63. Sprott was a psychologist and one of the lovers of John Maynard Keynes, et al.

13   Milne, pp. 21–8.

14   Milne, p. 35.

15   The phrasing here is characteristic: "the Communists," not the Soviet Union.

16   Borovik, Genrikh. *The Philby Files: The Secret Life of the Master Spy—KGB Archives Revealed*. London: Little, Brown and Company, 1995, p. 12.

17   Seale and McConville, p. 69.

18   Milne, p. 33.

19   In the summer of 1933, "In reward for his work on the index and proofs of *The Empty Quarter*, the book published by Constable in 1934 which established St. John's reputation as an explorer, Kim was given £50 by his father and the freedom to spend it as he liked. He chose to go to Vienna, and to get himself and his knapsack there he bought a motorcycle." Seale and McConville, p. 76.

20   McMeekin, Sean. *The Red Millionaire: A Political Biography of Willi Münzenberg, Moscow's Secret Propaganda Tsar in the West*. New Haven: Yale University Press, 2003, p. 165ff.

21   Cave Brown, p. 158.

22   "The Official KGB History, Volume No. 3 . . . states that Philby worked for [International Organization for Aid to Revolutionaries] MOPR in Vienna. Since MOPR was an organization run out of Moscow . . . the putative link with Munzenberg . . . is incorrect." Peake in Philby, Rufina, p. 383.

23   Cookridge, E. H. *The Third Man: The Full Story of Kim Philby*. New York: Putnam's, 1968, p. 25. Philby himself spelled the name "Lizzy" in his Beirut confession (KV 2/4428, 38z).

24   Cookridge, pp. 25–6.

25   Cookridge, p. 27.

26   Cookridge, pp. 31–4.

27   Gardiner, Muriel. *Code Name "Mary": Memoirs of an American Woman in the Austrian Underground*. New Haven and London: Yale University Press, 1983, p. 50ff.

28   Cookridge, p. 35.

29   Teddy Kollek, longtime mayor of Jerusalem and spy, may have been part of the wedding party. Cave Brown, p. 160.

30 Page, Leitch and Knightley, p. 64. Philby says that he later renewed his acquaintance with Gaitskell when seeking advice about his role in the SOE. Philby, p. 33.

31 Monroe, pp. 196–7.

32 Milne, p. 38; p. 51.

33 TNA, FCO-158–28, Milmo appendix, p. 208.

34 TNA, FCO-158–28, pp. 186–8.

35 Knightley, Phillip. *The Master Spy: The Story of Kim Philby*. New York: Alfred A. Knopf, 1989, p. 53.

36 Monroe, pp. 196–7. Confusingly, there were two Robertsons involved.

37 Philby, Kim. "Autobiographical Reminiscenses." In Philby, Rufina, p. 219ff.

38 Borovik, p. 31.

39 Borovik, p. 26.

40 Orlov, Alexander. *Handbook of Intelligence and Guerrilla Warfare*. Ann Arbor: The University of Michigan Press, 1963, pp. 108–9.

41 The SVR biography of Philby states that it was Edith Tudor-Hart, not Friedmann, who contacted Deutsch about Kim Philby.

42 Borovik, p. 28.

43 Cecil, Robert. *A Divided Life: A Personal Portrait of the Spy Donald Maclean*. New York: William Morrow & Co., 1989, p. 33.

44 Milne, pp. 44–5.

45 Philby, Kim, "Autobiographical Reminiscences." In Philby, Rufina, p. 219ff. Perhaps also editor *Germany Today*, the magazine of the Anglo-German Fellowship: Cave Brown, p.181. This may be true.

46 Page, Leitch and Knightley, p. 87.

47 Monroe, p. 192.

48 Trotter, Mel. "The King's Man: Oil and Death." Alaela. Aramco Overseas Company. 13 May 2013. https://www.aramcoexpats.com/articles/the-kings-man-oil-and-death/

49 Philby, Kim. "Autobiographical Reminiscences." In Philby, Rufina, p. 243.

50 TNA, FCO-158–28, pp. 238–40. This seems an improbably large amount of money. Perhaps the account was a pass-through for payments to her from Moscow.

51 Milne, p. 45.

52 Foreign Intelligence Service of the Russian Federation, Newsletter, 25 January 2004. http://svr.gov.ru/smi/2004/bratishka20040125.htm

53 Foreign Intelligence Service, Russian Federation, Newsletter, 8 September 2006. http://svr.gov.ru/smi/2006/krzv20060809-11.htm. It is puzzling how Burgess would have traveled, under the conditions then pertaining, from London to Gibraltar and back over, say, a long weekend.

54 TNA, FCO-158–28. Third interrogation of Philby, p. 238.

55 Monroe, pp. 205–6.

56 Milne, p. 46.

57 Honigmann, Barbara. *A Chapter from My Life*. An extract translated by John S. Barrett from *Ein Kapitel aus meinem Leben*. Munich: Carl Hanser Verlag, 2004, pp. 75–93. http://www.litrix.de/apps/litrix_publications/data/pdf1/Honigmann_Ein_Kapitel_Leseprobe_EN.pdf

58 Borovik, p. 93.

59 Page, Leitch and Knightley, p. 90.

60 Borovik, p. 106.

61 Monroe, p. 207. Monroe does not give their route from Bayonne to Cairo.

62 Borovik, p. 100.

63 *The Times* for 4 March 1938, datelined Burgos, 3 March.

64 Redgrave, Corin. *Blunt Speaking*. Radio play, p. 6.

65 *The Times* for 5 December 1938, datelined Burgos, 4 December: "Third Winter of War: Spain Facing Privation: Troop Trains on the Move."

66 *The Times*, datelined Barcelona, 27 January 1939. "Barcelona's New Regime: Republican Laws Void."

67 Borovik, p. 131.

68 *The Times*, 3 March 1939, datelined 2 March, Burgos. "Madrid Awaiting Its Fate. Franco's Troops Massing."

69 *The Times*, 19 May 1939. "General Franco in Madrid. Symbolic Ending of the War. 200,000 Troops in City. From Our Special Correspondent. Madrid, 18 May."

70 *The Times*, 20 May 1939.

71 *The Times*, 24 January 1938.

72 *The Times*, 4 July 1939. *The Times*, 21 July 1939. Hythe By-Election Result: Unionist (Tory) 12,016; Labour 9,577, People's Party (Philby) 576. "Mr. Philby forfeits his deposit."

73 The younger brother, Hugh, was sent to Harrow, the daughters to finishing schools.

74 Murphy, Charles J. V. "The Making of a Master Spy." *Time,* 24 February 1975, p. 19. http://jfk.hood.edu/Collection/Weisberg%20 Subject%20Index%20Files/C%20Disk/CIA%20Domestic%20 Intelligence%20Part%202/Item%20016.pdf

75 It is unclear why James Angleton went to Yale rather than Harvard, or Cambridge, for that matter. There are no obvious connections among his father's colleagues.

76 Davidson, Donald. "Preface to Decision." *Sewannee Review*, LIII, 3 (Summer 1945), pp. 394–412. A rather ironic statement, given the elaborate Southern classifications of mixed-race residents.

77 Tate, Allen. "A View of the White South." *The American Review*, 2:4 (February 1934).

78 Brooks and Warren, pp. xiv–xv.

79 Brooks and Warren, p. ix.

80 Powers, Thomas. "The Ghost: The Secret Life of CIA Spymaster James Jesus Angleton by Jefferson Morley." *London Review of Books*, Volume 40, Number 9, 10 May 2018, p. 19.

81 La Salle, Peter "An Encounter with *Furioso*." *Raritan*, Volume 12, Number 4, p. 110.

82 Empson, William. *Seven Types of Ambiguity*. London: Chatto and Windus, 1930, pp. 6–7.

83 JJA to E. E. Cummings, unsigned, undated, upper left corner torn off; envelope postmarked Milano 30.viii.39/NY 21 September 1939. Harvard, Houghton Library, bMS 1823 (35).

84 Harvard, Houghton Library, bMS AM 1892 (31).

85 Holzman, Michael. "Café CIA Roma: Mary McCarthy's Cold War." *Prospects*, 25, 2000.

86 Dupee and Stade, 157, 16 November 1939. There are indications that Marion Morehouse was committed to Lindbergh's America First campaign and similar right-wing views.

87 Morley, p. 11, quoting from Letter from Angleton to Pound, 28 December 1939, Ezra Pound Papers, YCAL MSS 43, Series I: Correspondence, box 2, folder 63, Beinecke Rare Book and Manuscript Library, Yale University Library.

88 Mangold, p. 37.

89 Yale, Beinecke Rare Book and Manuscript Library, Pearson Papers, Letters, Box H, 1941. Draft, no date, no addressee, no signature, reverse of letterhead paper. The University of Chicago, Department of Surgery.

90   James Hugh Angleton had begun to spend time with the US naval attaché Rome around 1940. The attaché was, in effect, the representative of the Office of Naval Intelligence, and the elder Angleton became something of an unofficial agent. He remained in Rome until 1941, arriving in New York the day of the attack on Pearl Harbor. Winks, pp. 328–30; Mangold, pp. 31–3.

WAR AND SECRET INTELLIGENCE

1   Borovik, p. 143.
2   Cookridge, E. H. *The Third Man: The Full Story of Kim Philby*. New York: Putnam's, 1968, pp. 66–7. This story may not be entirely reliable. The references to McAlmon in these stories is odd, as he does not appear to have been in Paris at the time. Perhaps Cookridge was misinformed.
3   Colville, John. *The Fringes of Power: 10 Downing Street Diaries, 1939–1955*. New York: W. W. Norton & Company, 1985, p. 40.
4   Borovik, pp. 145–6.
5   Page, Leitch and Knightley, pp. 107–8.
6   TNA, KV-2-1119, p.119.
7   This is an interesting way of describing cooperation with a government minister.
8   TNA, Letter from Valentine Vivian to Guy Liddell, KV 2/1118 33/34 dated 24.9.40.
9   Morrison, a Labour Party colleague of Dalton, was then Home Secretary.
10   TNA, KV-2-1119, p. 115.
11   Philby says that the transfer was a project of Tomas Harris. Philby, pp. 43–5.
12   The apposite quotation from Kipling was identified by *The Sunday Times* reporters.
13   Borovik, p. 153.
14   Borovik, p. 167.
15   Borovik, p. 183.
16   Dolgopolov, N. M. *Kim Filbi*. Moscow: Moloda'ja Gvardi'ja, 2012.
17   Recorded in Moscow, 22 May 1941. Dolgopolov, p. 238. I have edited Google Translate versions of these documents.
18   Newsletter, 25 September 2000, Foreign Intelligence Service, Russian Federation, http://svr.gov.ru/smi/2004/bratishka20040125.htm

19 Dolgopolov, pp. 56–7.

20 Dolgopolov, p. 240.

21 Page, Leitch and Knightley, p. 140. The curriculum vitae provided by SIS in 1951, in a typical gesture of bureaucratic malice, does not mention Philby's service in SOE, claiming him as spending the entire period in Section D.

22 As well as in regard to the American services, according to Aldrich, and, no doubt those services of many other countries.

23 Milne, pp. 54–5.

24 Milne, pp. 65–6.

25 See, for example, TNA KV 3/269.

26 Trevor Roper, Hugh. "The Philby Affair." *Encounter*, April 1968, p. 10.

27 Milne, p. 157; pp. 110–15. Milne wrote MI-5 here.

28 Jeffery, Keith. *The Secret History of MI-6*. New York: The Penguin Press, 2010, p. 490. No reference.

29 Borovik, p. 206.

30 BBC Radio 4, Monday, 4 April 2016. http://www.BBC.co.uk/programmes/b076v1zq

31 Modin, Yuri. *My Five Cambridge Friends: Burgess, Maclean, Philby, Blunt, and Cairncross*. New York: Farrar Straus Giroux, 1994, p. 61.

32 Borovik, p. 191. The extent of British penetration of American intelligence services is an interesting, if inadequately explored, topic.

33 Cave Brown, p. 296.

34 Felix, Christopher (James McCargar). *A Short Course in the Secret War*. New York: Dell, 1963, p. 121. Quoted in Cave Brown, p. 236.

35 An additional issue for the Soviet intelligence services was the contradiction between Philby's assurances that there were few, if any, British agents in the Soviet Union and the fact that thousands of people had been convicted of being British agents during the Great Purges.

36 Borovik, p. 219.

37 Borovik, pp. 221–2.

38 NARA Records of the Office of Strategic Services (Record Group 226) 1940–1947 Entry 210. Boxes 1–538. Location: 250 64/21/1. CIA Accession: 79-00332A. Box #406 Biographical and personal appraisal information, including information relating to James Hugh Angleton, 12 August 1943, 4 pp. [WN#15436].

39   Hood, "Angleton's World," p. 2.

40   Mangold, p. 38.

41   It may or may not have mattered that H.D. had been Ezra Pound's lover in their Pennsylvania youth.

42   This quotation, from *The Secret History of the CIA* by Joseph Trento, is not further traceable. It may be from one of Trento's many interviews with Angleton.

43   Cave Brown, pp. 298–9.

44   Seale and McConville, p. 214.

45   Martin, p. 13.

46   Milne, p. 108.

47   War Report, p. 338.

48   Robarge, David. "Moles, Defectors, and Deceptions: James Angleton and CIA Counterintelligence." *The Journal of Intelligence History*, 3 (Winter 2003), pp. 28–9.

49   "A Fixation on Moles: James J. Angleton, Anatoliy Golitsyn, and the 'Monster Plot': Their Impact on CIA Personnel and Operations." *Studies in Intelligence*, Vol. 55, No. 4 (December 2011). Central Intelligence Agency, pp. 40-1.

50   Bower, Tom. *The Perfect English Spy: Sir Dick White and the Secret War 1935–90*. New York: St. Martin's Press, 1995, p. 47.

51   Bower, pp. 58–9.

52   Martin, p.15.

53   Bower, p. 66.

54   Borovik, p. 237. Davenport-Hines has this as November. Davenport-Hines, Richard. *Enemies Within: Communists, the Cambridge Spies and the Making of Modern Britain*. London: William Collins, 2018, p. 314.

55   Borovik, p. 247.

56   NARA. Records of the Office of Strategic Services (Record Group 263 Entry 17 Box 5. 314 SSU/X-2 counter-intelligence summary, 1 July 1946, 16 pp. [WN#10844] SSU counter-intelligence summary, 1 August 1946, 16 pp. [WN#10844].

57   Winks, p. 350.

58   War Report, p. 502.

59   This resulted in memoranda from Angleton being preserved in both the American and British National Archives.

60   War Report, p. 339.

61   Naftali, Timothy J. "ARTIFICE: James Angleton and X-2 Operations

in Italy." In *The Secrets War: The Office of Strategic Services in World War II*, ed. George C. Chalou. Washington DC: National Archives and Records Administration, 1992, p. 220.

62   Weinberg, Gerhard L. *A World at Arms: A Global History of World War II*. Cambridge: Cambridge University Press, 2005, pp. 726–7.

63   Alvarez, David J. *Spying through a Glass Darkly: American Espionage Against the Soviet Union, 1954–1946*. Lawrence, Kansas: University of Kansas Press, 2016, p. 246.

64   NARA Records of the Office of Strategic Services (Record Group 226) 1940–1947 Entry 210. Boxes 1–538. Location: 250 64/21/1. CIA Accession: 79-00332A.

65   Cave Brown, p. 353.

66   Milne, p. 145.

67   OSS War report, p. 221.

68   Naftali, pp. 222–3.

69   Naftali, p. 220.

70   Naftali, p. 501.

71   NARA Records of the Office of Strategic Services (Record Group 226) 1940- 1947 Entry 210. Boxes 1–538. Location: 250 64/21/1. CIA Accession: 79-00332A.

72   Mangold, p. 42.

73   NARA Records of the Office of Strategic Services (Record Group 226) 1940–1947 Entry 210. Box 366 WN#14577.

74   Naftali, p. 223.

75   Naftali, pp. 225–6.

76   Some sources indicate that Angleton dropped the issue with Washington, but continued working along these lines in Italy. See Grose, *Gentleman Spy*, p. 253.

77   TNA, WO 204/12918.

78   Naftali, p. 229.

79   Naftali, p. 234.

80   Milne, p. 167; p. 163.

81   Philby, p. 148.

82   West, Nigel and Tsarev, Oleg. *The Crown Jewels: The British Secrets at the Heart of the KGB Archives*. New Haven: Yale University Press, 1999, pp. 173–4. The colorful details might be taken with a grain of salt.

83   Modin, pp. 124–5. This provides the necessary confirmation of the account given by West and Tsarev.

84   Philby, p. 160. Knightley in *The Master Spy* adds that Volkov gave a twenty-one day deadline for an answer to his offer, p. 136.

85   Jeffery, pp. 656–8; Bennett, Gill. "The CORBY case: the defection of Igor Gouzenko, September 1945." In: *From World War to Cold War: the records of the Foreign Office Permanent Under Secretary's Department, 1939–51*, p. 81.

86   West and Tsarev, pp. 238–9.

87   Philby, Kim. "Should Agents Confess?" In Philby, Rufina, p. 262ff.

88   Jeffery, p. 623.

89   Borovik, p. 241. Philby does not mention meeting Angleton in Rome on this trip in his memoir.

90   Modin, pp. 126–7.

91   Milne, pp. 150–4.

92   http://svr.gov.ru/history/stage07.htm. Machine translation, my edits.

93   Borovik, p. 249.

94   Knightley, p. 141.

95   United States Holocaust Memorial Museum, *Holocaust Encyclopedia*, Ardeatine Caves Massacre. https://www.ushmm.org/wlc/en/article.php?ModuleId=10007940.

96   Salter, Michael. *Nazi War Crimes, US Intelligence and Selective Prosecution at Nuremberg: controversies regarding the role of the Office of Strategic Services*. Abingdon, Routledge-Cavendish, 2007, p. 66; p. 80.

97   Salter, p. 80.

98   Salter, pp. 211–12. "After reviewing Zimmer's notebooks, O.S.S. and SSU officials concluded that Operation Wool preceded Operation Sunrise—in other words, the bargain was as much a German initiative as it was an American intelligence coup." RG 263. Detailed Report, Guido Zimmer, Records of the Directorate of Operations, Analysis of the Name File of Guido Zimmer by Professor Richard Breitman, American University, IWG Director of Historical Research https://www.archives.gov/iwg/declassified-records/rg-263-cia-records/rg-263-zimmer.html

99   Salter, pp. 205–6, citing JXX 6113[partly illegible], SCI/Z to AC S02 CI, AFHQ, 11 February 1946, Dollmann (?Zimmer) Name File, NA RG 263. Zimmer was an SS officer in Italy. "O.S.S. officials noted that, as well as working for O.S.S. Germany, Zimmer was, by the mid-summer of 1945, also secretary to Parilli and a paid agent of ODEUM [the Vatican's Sovereign Order of Malta]." Salter, p. 212.

100 Ruffner, Kevin Conley. "Eagle and Swastika: CIA and NAZI War Criminals and Collaborators." History Staff. Central Intelligence Agency. Washington, D.C., April 2003. Chapter 1–10, Draft Working Paper. p. 27, footnote 64. https://www.cia.gov/library/readingroom/docs/CIA%20AND%20NAZI%20WAR%20CRIM.%20AND%20COL.%20CHAP.%201-10,%20DRAFT%20WORKING%20PAPER_0001.pdf

101 Salter, pp. 216–17, citing Angleton to G-2, 13 November 1946: NA, RG 319, IRR Entry 134B, Box 40, Eugen Dollmann.

102 Salter, p. 64; p. 185.

103 Dollmann, E. *Call Me Coward*. London: Kimber and Co, 1956, p. 84.

104 Dollmann, p. 84.

105 Salter, p. 188.

106 Salter, pp. 230–1.

107 Alvarez, p. 264.

108 Alvarez, p. 242. (Vincent Scamporino to William Madox, 2 October 1944, subject: "Established Contacts in Rome Area," RG 226, Entry 210, box 386).

109 "Between 1947 and 1948, Dollmann worked for SSU/CIA in Rome and then Frankfurt in Germany." Salter, p. 190.

110 Cave Brown, pp. 343–4.

111 "It was while Dulles was in Bern in 1945 that he carried on the secret negotiations with the German military commanders in Italy that led to their surrender . . . described by him in his book, *The Secret Surrender*. What was not divulged in that book . . . was that at the same time feelers were put out by the German commanders on the Western Front. They were exploring the possibility of a German surrender to the Western Allies, while keeping up the war against the Soviet Union, so as to allow an occupation of Germany by the West. Dulles's lieutenant, the late Gero von Gaevernitz, was deeply involved in this matter . . . Dulles was instructed by Washington not to respond because it was believed that Stalin would interpret any such negotiations as a betrayal of the USSR . . ." Jackson, Wayne G. *Allen Welsh Dulles As Director of Central Intelligence, 26 February 1953 to 29 November 1961, Volume I, Allen Dulles, The Man*. Historical Staff, Central Intelligence Agency, 1973, p. 11.

112 "Returning to the 'Cambridge Five'—Triumph or Failure?"

Newsletter, 3 April 2008, Foreign Intelligence Service, Russian Federation, http://svr.gov.ru/smi/2008/argned20080403.htm.

113 Alvarez, p. 246.

114 Alvarez, p. 247.

115 Alvarez, pp. 247–8.

116 Citing SAINT, BB8 [Angleton] to SAINT, JJ1, 6 November 1945, subject: "Report of Activities of the Italian Mission from 1–31 October 1945," RG 226, Entry 108A, box 260. Alvarez, p. 255.

117 Alvarez, p. 260.

118 Alvarez, p. 262. He thought those groups were penetrated by Yugoslav intelligence.

119 Alvarez, p. 261.

120 http://svr.gov.ru/history/stage07.htm. Machine translation, my edits.

121 Alvarez, p. 267.

122 Alvarez, p. 194. (NARA, James Angleton to WASHA, 15 July 1946 RG 226, Entry 216, box 2; James Angleton to WASHA, 11 September 1946, RG 226, Entry 216, box 2.)

123 Warner, Michael. *CIA Cold War Records: The CIA Under Harry Truman*. Washington, D.C.: CIA History Staff. Center for the Study of Intelligence, 1994, pp. 24–5.

124 NARA, Records of the Office of Strategic Services (Record Group 226) 1940–1947 Entry 210. Boxes 1–538. Location: 250 64/21/1. CIA Accession: 79-00332A box 346 Status of Liaison Relations of SSU/X-2 to the Counter-Intelligence Branches of Foreign Special Services, n.d., 4 pp. [WN#03356]. [Emphasis added to call attention to another lesson Angleton had been taught by Philby, who would himself apply it during his Washington posting.]

125 NARA, Records of the Office of Strategic Services (Record Group 263) Entry 17 Box 5, 29 July 1945: Termination of an operation in Milan. 314. SSU/X-2 counter-intelligence summary, 1 July 1946, 16 pp. [WN#10844] SSU counter-intelligence summary, 1 August 1946, 16 pp. [WN#10844], p. 6; p. 19.

126 NARA, Records of the Office of Strategic Services (Record Group 263) Entry 17 Box 5, 29 July 1945: Termination of an operation in Milan. 314. SSU/X-2 counter-intelligence summary, 1 July 1946, 16 pp. [WN#10844] SSU counter-intelligence summary, 1 August 1946, 16 pp. [WN#10844], p. 20.

127 Warner, pp. 87–8

128 Morley, p. 36.

129 Mistry, Kaeten. *The United States, Italy and the origins of Cold War: waging political warfare: 1945–1950*. Cambridge: Cambridge University Press, 2014, p. 11.

130 Mistry, p. 44.

131 Mistry, pp. 44–5.

132 Mistry, p. 68

133 Mistry, p. 60.

134 Ventresca, Robert A. *From Fascism to Democracy: Culture and Politics in The Italian Election of 1948*. Toronto: University of Toronto Press, 2004, pp. 93–6.

135 Mistry, p. 47.

136 Ventresca, pp. 93–6.

137 Ventresca, pp. 93–6.

138 Mistry, pp. 115–16.

139 "Common Cause was a prototype of, and a sister organization to, the CIA-sponsored National Committee for a Free Europe." Simpson, Christopher. *Blowback*. London: Crowell-Collier, 1989, p. 222.

140 Mistry, p. 48.

141 Mistry, pp. 150–1.

142 Herken, Gregg. *The Georgetown Set: Friends and Rivals in Cold War Washington*. New York: Alfred A. Knopf, 2014, p. 69, citing JWA [Joseph Alsop] to Angleton, 9 April, "1948" folder, box 3, JWAP, Library of Congress? Private Collection?

143 "Eddie" Page was the brother of Louise Page Morris. The "Collection Overview" of her papers at the Hoover Institution, Stanford, reads: "Morris began her espionage career as an anti-Soviet counterintelligence agent during WWII. She spoke Russian and was recruited to work in the London analyzing information lifted from the Soviets. In 1943 she became the deputy chief of the USSR Research and Analysis Section, Office of Strategic Services (O.S.S.). After the war, Morris worked for O.S.S. chief 'Wild' Bill Donovan, who introduced her to Ray Murphy, Communist Expert for the State Department . . . It was through Ray Murphy that she met Jay Lovestone and began a romance with him that would last over thirty years. Lovestone was working closely with James Jesus Angleton, who would become the CIA's counterintelligence chief. Impressed with all he had heard about Morris's successful intelligence work, he propositioned [sic] that she be his personal agent, functioning

outside the CIA, going on assignments for him to collect intelligence around the world. Her cover was that she worked for Lovestone and the FTUC, operating the 'Gompers Research Library' in New York City. Louise Page Morris worked for Mr Angleton until 1974. She died in 2002."

144 McCargar, James. The Association for Diplomatic Studies and Training, Foreign Affairs Oral History Project, JAMES McCAR-GAR, Interviewed by: Charles Stuart Kennedy, Initial interview date: 18 April 1995, p. 75. Foreign Affairs Oral History Collection, Association for Diplomatic Studies and Training, Arlington, VA. www.adst.org http://www.adst.org/OH%20TOCs/McCargar

145 Ventresca, pp. 93–6.

146 Mistry, p. 52.

147 Cicely Angleton to Marion Cummings, 26 April 1948, Houghton Library, bMS, Am1892.2 (21).

ISTANBUL AND WASHINGTON

1   Borovik, p. 251.

2   See, for example, "Crisis and Imminent Possibility of Collapse in Greece," Memorandum by the Under Secretary of State (Acheson) to the Secretary of State, 21 February 1947, United States Department of State / Foreign relations of the United States, 1947. The Near East and Africa, p. 29.

3   "Weekly Summary Excerpt, 28 February 1947, The Greek Crisis." https://www.cia.gov/library/center-for-the-study-of-intelligence/csi-publications/books-and-monographs/assessing-the-soviet-threat-the-early-cold-war-years/docs.html. As opposed to the years of right-wing dictatorship that followed.

4   https://history.state.gov/milestones/1945-1952/truman-doctrine

5   "Supplementary Report of the United States Ambassador Recommending Continuing Aid to Turkey." Transmitted 15 July 1947. FRUS, 1947, The Near East and Africa, pp. 259–60.

6   FRUS, 1947, The Near East and Africa, p. 257.

7   Knightley, p. 144.

8   http://www.telegraph.co.uk/news/obituaries/politics-obituaries/6077806/John-Philby.html 23 August 2009

9   Philby, p. 181.

10 Page, Leitch and Knightley, p. 148.

11 Dolgopolov, p. 243. "Metadata": To/From/Subject only.

12 http://www.telegraph.co.uk/news/obituaries/politics-obituaries/6077806/John-Philby.html 23 August 2009

13 Knightley, p. 148; Milne, p. 171. There is some confusion in the sources about the dates and order of events during this period.

14 Seale and McConville, pp. 234–6.

15 Cookridge, p. 167.

16 Mangold, pp. 43–4.

17 Harvard, Houghton Library, bMS, AM 1823, (34), Letter: Cicely Angleton to "Marion and Cummings," dated 16 March 1946, 4814 N. 33rd, Arlington, VA.

18 Powers, *The Man Who Kept the Secrets: Richard Helms and the CIA*. New York: Knopf, 1979, p. 29.

19 On Staff C, see Hersh, Burton. *The Old Boys: The American Elite and the Origins of the CIA*. New York: Charles Scribner's Sons, 1992, p. 188.

20 Memorandum from DCI Hillenkoetter for ADSO Galloway, 22 March 1948, "Additional functions of Office of Special Operations," 22 March 1948, in Warner, p. 191.

21 Morley, p. 36.

22 Epstein, Edward Jay, in *Moles, Defectors, and Deceptions: James Angleton and His Influence on US Counterintelligence*. Edited by Bruce Hoffman and Christian Ostermann. A Wilson Center and Georgetown University Center for Security Studies Joint Conference, 2014, p. 38.

23 Epstein, Edward Jay. *Deception: The Invisible War Between the KGB and CIA*. New York: Simon & Schuster, 1989, pp. 32–3.

24 It was significant that when Colby moved to fire Angleton in 1974, he first took away Angleton's responsibility for liaison with the Israelis.

25 Hersh, p. 293.

26 Hersh, p. 294.

27 Morley, pp. 39–41.

28 Cave Brown, p. 386, citing his interviews with Sir James Easton and Ray Cline.

29 Borovik, p. 254.

30 Knightley, p. 149.

31 See Dwyer's memorandum concerning the methods of counterespionage, especially telephone taps https://www.documentcloud.org/

documents/3238471-MEMO-Peter-Dwyer-Ex-MI-6-to-Cabinet-March-31-1954.html

32 Lamphere, Robert J. and Shachtman, Tom. *The FBI–KGB War: A Special Agent's Story*. New York: Random House, 1986, p. 127.

33 Seale and McConville, p. 239.

34 Wright, *Spycatcher: The Candid Autobiography of a Senior Intelligence Officer*. New York, Dell, 1988, p. 185.

35 West and Tsarev, p. 182. It would be interesting to know Alan Turing's role in this matter. Concerning the status of Tsarev's books, see: Sheila Kerr, Oleg Tsarev's "Synthetic KGB Gems." *International Journal of Intelligence and Counterintelligence*, 14, 89–116, 2001. ". . . an assessment of Tsarev's volume also leads to three major points . . . First, that new historical evidence requires careful interpretation. Second, the secrets spies gather should be evaluated within the context of national and institutional policy formulation and implementation. Third, the notion of 'damage' from Soviet espionage, has been exaggerated and misunderstood, and it is now time to investigate the impact of Soviet espionage upon national and international politics. And, most relevantly, Tsarev, a former lieutenant colonel in the Russian Foreign Intelligence Service, also serves as a consultant to the Service's press department."

36 https://www.dni.gov/files/NCSC/documents/ci/CI_Reader_Vol3.pdf, p. 77.

37 Seale and McConville, p. 248.

38 Goodman, M. S. (2016). MI-6's Atomic Man: The Rise and Fall of Commander Eric Welsh. DOI: 10.1177/0968344515572503, pp. 12ff.

39 Seale and McConville, p. 250.

40 Cookridge, p. 150.

41 TNA, CAB 126/305.

42 Leigh, David. *The Wilson Plot*. New York: Pantheon Books, 1988, p. 11.

43 Hersh, p. 262.

44 Hersh, p. 263.

45 Cave Brown, pp. 419–20.

46 McCargar, James. Interviewed by: Charles Stuart Kennedy, Initial interview date: 18 April 1995, The Association for Diplomatic Studies and Training, Foreign Affairs Oral History Project. http://www.adst.org/OH%20TOCs/McCargar, p, 80ff.

47 Modin, p. 186.

48 Dogopolov, p. 64. At this point Burgess was Philby's link to Moscow Center, as elaborated in West and Tsarov's *The Crown Jewels*.

49 Dolgopolov, p. 245. Translation processed by "Scan & Translate" and edited.

50 Seale and McConville, p. 245.

51 Philby, pp. 190–3.

52 DCI Diary, January–April 1950.

53 DCI Diary, May 1950.

54 Joseph Trento quotes Angleton as telling him, at the end of Angleton's life: "Fundamentally, the founding fathers of U.S. intelligence were liars. The better you lied and the more you betrayed, the more likely you would be promoted." Trento, Joseph P. *The Secret History of the CIA*. New York: MJF Books, 2001, p. 479.

55 https://www.cia.gov/library/readingroom/docs/CIA-RDP80R0173 1R003400100026-0.pdf

56 Memorandum for the Record by the Director of Central Intelligence's Executive Assistant (Kirkpatrick), Washington, 14 February 1951. SUBJECT: Meeting on Integration of O/SO and O/PC. https://history.state.gov/historicaldocuments/frus1950-55Intel/d50

57 Modin, pp. 188–9. Burgess was sent back to London some months later. Perhaps this was an earlier trip to England or Modin has confused the dates.

58 Newton, Verne W. *The Cambridge Spies: The Untold Story of Maclean, Philby, and Burgess in America*. Lanham, Maryland: Madison Books, 1991, p. 271. Newton's is an unusually well-documented book for the genre. Burgess's Foreign Office rank is variously given. US government records confirm that it was as a Second Secretary, a middling, but not inconsiderable, rank: "Burgess's British passport No. 1674591, issued July 20, 1950, valid to July 20, 1951; Admitted to the US at NYC on August 4, 1950, visa no. V-1016533 (Second Secretary)." Federal Bureau of Investigations. FOIA Electronic Reading Room, Philby 9a, p. 78.

59 Some authors have claimed that Philby was out of touch with Moscow for much of the time he was in Washington due to the presumed lack of a Soviet contact there. Burgess's frequent travels to New York would have made that irrelevant.

60 Kwang-On Yoo, http://koreanstudies.com/pipermail/koreanstudies_ koreanstudies.com/2010-June/007992.html

61   Manchester, William. *American Caesar: Douglas MacArthur 1880–1964*. New York: Dell, 1983, p. 712 fn.

62   Cave Brown, p. 413.

63   McCargar, James. The Association for Diplomatic Studies and Training, Foreign Affairs Oral History Project, Interviewed by: Charles Stuart Kennedy, Initial interview date: 18 April 1995. http://www.adst.org/OH%20TOCs/McCargar

64   Dorril, Stephen. *MI-6: Inside the Covert World of Her Majesty's Secret Intelligence Service*. New York: Free Press, 2002, p. 152ff.

65   Hamrick, S. J. *Deceiving the Deceivers: Kim Philby, Donald Maclean, and Guy Burgess*. New Haven: Yale University Press, 2004, p. 52.

66   Hamrick, p. 42.

67   Top Secret SUEDE BRIDE 11 October 1951. https://www.nsa.gov/news-features/declassified-documents/venona/dated/1951/assets/files/11oct_gomer.pdf

68   There were two Colossus machines, which had been developed to use against the German Lorenz system, at Eastcote. See: https://ethw.org/First-Hand:Bletchley_Park,_Station_X_-_Memories_of_a_Colossus_Operator

69   Top Secret SUEDE BRIDE 11 October 1951. https://www.nsa.gov/news-features/declassified-documents/venona/dated/1951/assets/files/11oct_gomer.pdf

70   Patterson, 31 March 1951, To Director-General (and/or Arthur Martin?) KV 6/142.

71   Benson and Warner, p. xxv.

72   TNA, R. E. Mackenzie to Carey Foster, 30 October 1951, FCO-158–27, pp. 276–8.

73   KV 6/143.

74   TNA, KV-6-143, p. 217 of pdf., Wednesday, 30 May.

75   TNA, KV-6-143, pp. 171–2.

76   TNA, KV-6-143, p. 143.

77   TNA, KV-6-143, p. 12.

78   TNA, FV6/144.

79   Minute from Sir R. Makins to Mr. Bevin, Top secret, Foreign Office, 17 April 1950, Documents on British Policy Overseas. London: Her Majesty's Stationery Office, Series II, Volume II, No. 19, pp. 52–3.

80   On the one hand, Prime Minister Attlee saw atomic weapons as a way to reduce defense expenditures—atom bombs are cheaper than

infantry divisions—and Foreign Minister Bevin saw them as giving Britain a seat at the top table, in terms of prestige. Neither trusted the United States to defend Britain against a Soviet attack.

81   This is S. J. Hamrick's thesis in *Deceiving the Deceivers*. See his p. xiii.

82   "A Fixation on Moles: James J. Angleton, Anatoliy Golitsyn, and the 'Monster Plot': Their Impact on CIA Personnel and Operations." *Studies in Intelligence*, Vol. 55, No. 4 (December 2011). Central Intelligence Agency. P. 43.

83   Hersh, p. 321.

84   Cookridge, p. 204.

85   "Maclean/Burgess Case. B.2. Investigation Plan 11.6.51. p. 18.

86   Knightley, p. 180.

87   TNA, KV 6-144.

88   Top Secret SUEDE BRIDE 11 October 1951. https://www.nsa.gov/news-features/declassified-documents/venona/dated/1951/assets/files/11oct_gomer.pdf

89   C. "Kit" Steel, Washington embassy to Patrick Reilly, Foreign Office, 17 October 1951. FCO-158-21

90   Borovik, p. 294.

91   TNA, FCO-158-27, pp. 270–2.

92   TNA, FCO-158-27.

93   TNA, FCO-158-27.

94   TNA, FCO-158-27, p. 212.

95   TNA, FCO-158-27.

96   TNA, FCO-158-28, p. 176.

97   TNA, FCO-158-28, p. 232.

98   TNA, FCO-158-27, p. 159.

99   TNA, FCO-158-27, p. 122.

100 TNA, FCO-158-27, p. 75.

101 TNA, FCO-158-28, p. 176.

102 TNA, FCO-158-28, p. 176.

103 Philby, Kim. "Lecture to the KGB, July 1977." In Philby, Rufina, p. 255ff.

104 TNA, FCO-158-27, p. 92.

105 TNA, FCO-158-28, p. 164.

106 Kent, Sherman. *Strategic Intelligence for American World Policy*. Princeton: Princeton University Press, 1966, pp. 140–1.

107 McCargar, James. The Association for Diplomatic Studies and

Training, Foreign Affairs Oral History Project, Interviewed by: Charles Stuart Kennedy, Initial interview date: 18 April 1995 http://www.adst.org/OH%20TOCs/McCargar

108 CIA, DCI Log, 14–15 September 1951.

109 CIA, DCI Log, 18 September 1951.

110 CIA, DCI Log, 25 September 1951.

111 CIA, DCI Log, 10 October 1951.

112 CIA, DCI Log, 11 October 1951.

113 CIA, DCI Log, 26 October 1951.

114 CIA, DCI Log, 29 October 1951.

115 Corke, Sarah-Jane. *US Covert Operations and Cold War Strategy: Truman, Secret Warfare and the CIA, 1945–53*. London: Routledge, 2008, p. 3.

116 Riley, Morris. *Philby: The Hidden Years*. London: Janus Publishing Company, 1999, p. 61.

117 Bagley, Tennent H. *Spy Wars: Moles, Mysteries, and Deadly Games*. New Haven & London: Yale University Press, 2007, p. 122.

118 CIA, DCI Log, 14–15 September 1951.

119 CIA, DCI Log, 19 November 1951.

120 Borovik, p. 303.

121 Borovik, p. 310. Say, four years' middle-class income in 1954.

122 Knightley, p. 192.

FOREIGN LIAISONS

1 Allen Dulles had given Lovestone's network to James Angleton, who established a Special Projects Section for his Israel and Lovestone responsibilities. Morgan, Ted. *A Covert Life: Jay Lovestone: Communist, Anti-Communist, and Spymaster*. New York: Random House, 1999, p. 247.

2 Morgan, pp. 246–7.

3 Inventory of the Louise Page Morris Papers, Online Archive of California. http://www.oac.cdlib.org/findaid/ark:/13030/kt3c6031v4/

4 Connelly, Mathew. *A Diplomatic Revolution: Algeria's Fight for Independence*. Oxford: Oxford University Press, 2003, p. 126.

5 See Morgan, pp. 265, 271–2, 278–9. Citino, Nathan J. *Envisioning the Arab Future: Modernization in US-Arab Relations, 1945–1967*. Cambridge University Press, 2017. Circa 1962 during CIA intervention in the period of the Ba'athist coup. See Morgan, p. 278.

Kuzmarov, Jeremy. *Modernizing Repression: Police Training and Nation-Building in the American Century*. Massachusetts: University of Massachusetts Press, 2012.

6   Raviv, Dan and Melman, Yossi. *Every Spy a Prince: The Complete History of Israel's Intelligence Community*. New York: Houghton Mifflin Harcourt, 1990, pp. 77–8.

7   According to one observer, Angleton's power derived from his Israeli account, which through Soviet émigrés gave some access to information from the denied area. Author interview with Burton Wides, 9 February 1998.

8   Wise, David. *Molehunt: The Secret Search for Traitors that Shattered the CIA*. New York: Random House, 1992, p. 423; Raviv and Melman, pp. 85–91. Others put in their own claims for priority. See Gehlen, *The Service*, p. 229.

9   Foreign Relations of the United States, 1955–1957, Soviet Union, Eastern Mediterranean, Volume XXIV. https://history.state.gov/historicaldocuments/frus1955-57v24/d49; https://history.state.gov/historicaldocuments/frus1955-57v24/d51 50. Circular Telegram From the Department of State to Certain Diplomatic Missions.

10 https://history.state.gov/historicaldocuments/frus1955-57v24/d50

11 Trento, p. 478.

12 CI Reader Volume III: Office of the Director of National Intelligence https://www.dni.gov/files/NCSC/documents/ci/CI_Reader_Vol3.pdf

13 http://www.matthewaid.com/post/51394955674/debacle-the-cias-failed-agent-penetration

14 Maddrell, Paul. *Spying on Science: Western Intelligence in Divided Germany: 1945–1961*. Oxford: Oxford University Press, 2006, p. 144.

15 Winks, p. 413. See also Ambrose, Stephen E. *Ike's Spies*. New York: Doubleday, 1981.

16 Corson, William. *The Armies of Ignorance: The Rise of the American Intelligence Empire*. New York: Dial Press, 1977, pp. 366–71.

17 Johnson, Loch. *Spy Watching: Intelligence Accountability in the United States*. Oxford: Oxford University Press, 2018, p. 368.

18 Morgan, pp. 283–4.

19 Knightley, pp. 187–8.

20 Milne, p. 183.

21 Milne, pp. 186–7.

22 TNA FCO 158-28. From "C," Sinclair, to P. H. Dean. p. 138.

23 Knightley, pp. 193–4.

24 Borovik, p. 314–15.

25 Knightley, pp. 192–5.

26 TNA, FCO-158-28, p. 16.

27 Seale and McConville, p. 281.

28 Knightley, p. 198.

29 Knightley, p. 198.

30 Peake, in Philby, Rufina, p. 316. *New Republic* articles listed on pp. 389–90, 1 April 1957 to 19 May 1958.

31 Jackson, Wayne G. Allen Welsh. *Dulles As Director of Central Intelligence, 26 February 1953 to 29 November 1961, Volume IV, Allen Dulles , The Man.* Historical Staff, Central Intelligence Agency. 1973, p. 46.

32 Buckle, Richard. "A Traveller In the Lebanon." *Observer*, 18 March 1956, p. 12.

33 Seale and McConville, pp. 287–8.

34 Borovik, pp. 325–6.

35 Beeston, Richard. *Looking for Trouble: The Life and Times of a Foreign Correspondent.* London: Tauris, 1997/2006, p. 30.

36 Pincher, Chapman. *Treachery: Betrayals, Blunders, and Cover-ups: Six Decades of Espionage Against America and Great Britain.* New York: Random House, 2009, p. 471.

37 Borovik, p. 327.

38 Modin, p. 234.

39 Aburish, Said K. *Beirut Spy: The St. George Hotel Bar.* London: Bloomsbury, 1989, pp. 82–3. Aburish has given vivid character sketches of these CIA operatives: "Miles Copeland was a pathological liar; many of his reports spoke of meetings with important leaders, including Nasser, which never took place. But the contents of the reports did not matter because there was no one in Washington to act on them. James Barracks was not gay, he was a twisted, sick homosexual who, despite several official warnings and one suspension, frequented bars in search of handsome Lebanese lads. Eventually he was not taken seriously, had to move to Nigeria and died there in mysterious circumstances. Eveland was an alcoholic who needed a drink for breakfast—and he talked too much when drunk—most of the time. Fistere, a former Fortune magazine public relations executive was a hollow unwholesome expression

of Madison Avenue and its buzz language. The Roosevelt cousins had serious problems with women which vitiated their effectiveness. (Archie's first wife bedded everyone including the butler and Kim couldn't speak to a pretty woman without becoming unglued.) William Eddy was an old-fashioned missionary and self-aggrandizing fool whose mind belonged to the nineteenth century and the white man's burden. Harry Kern made it difficult for local people to cooperate with him; he spoke of his hate for the Arabs openly. There was a disturbing absence of common sense and competence. So much so, James Critchfield, for years the regional CIA chief, still sees former Saudi intelligence chief Kamal Adham, the man who had to pay the defunct Bank of Credit and Commerce International (BCCI) $100 million in settlement as 'one of the great men of the Middle East'. To this day Critchfield knows very little about the Middle East . . ." and so forth. Arburish, Said K. "Lost Victories, The CIA in the Middle East." http://www.iiwds.com/said_aburish/a_lostvictories. htm

40 Cave Brown, pp. 485–7

41 *Comrade Philby* (KGB Spy Documentary) Timeline: World History Documentaries. https://www.youtube.com/watch?v=htukq TEeNaQ

42 Knightley, p. 211. "The CIA documents refer to a CIA interrogation of Eleanor Philby after Philby's defection. A report of this interrogation dated 1 November 1965 reads: '[Mrs Philby] said her husband had remarked that all he had to do was to have one evening with Bill Eveland in Beirut and before it was over he would know of all his operations' . . . Eveland denied the accuracy of the CIA documents."

43 Maclean, p. 172.

44 Knightley, p. 201.

45 Milne, p. 191.

46 For a summary of Soviet relations with Syria in this period, see Yair Even, "Two Squadrons and their Pilots: The First Syrian Request for the Deployment of Soviet Military Forces on its Territory, 1956," Cold War International History Project Working Paper 77 (February 2016), accessed at https://www.wilsoncenter.org/publication/ syrias-1956-request-for-soviet-military-intervention

47 Borovik, p. 334.

48 Cave Brown, pp. 483–5. Apparently not available.

49   Knightley, p. 206.

50   Knightley, p. 205.

51   Riley, p. 108.

52   Milne, p. 194.

53   Andrew, Christopher and Mitrokhin, Vasili. *The Sword and the Shield: The Mitrokhin Archive and the Secret History of the KGB.* New York: Basic Books, 199, p. 185.

54   Wright, p. 164.

55   Penrose, Barrie and Freeman, Simon. *Conspiracy of Silence.* London: Grafton, 1987, pp. 415–16.

56   Milne, p. 275. The usual story is that in August 1962, Victor Rothschild, the *éminence grise* of British intelligence, met Flora Solomon at a party and she told him that Philby had been a Soviet secret agent since the 1930s. She had known, according to Peter Wright, because she and Philby had been lovers in the 1930s and Philby had tried to recruit her (*Spycatcher*, p. 172). This is very difficult to believe. Flora Solomon, nearly thirty years older than Philby, was a prominent British business executive who had started the employee benefits program of Marks and Spencer and during World War II set up the British Restaurants. To suppose that Solomon and Philby had been lovers and that he thought her a good recruit for the Comintern is rather imaginative.

57   George Blake thought Elliott had been sent to Beirut to warn Philby not to return to London.

58   One story runs that Angleton instructed an agent to get the typewriter ribbon used for the confession, but the agent failed to do so. In the FBI files on Philby there is a reference to an unsuccessful attempt to read two typewriter ribbons from Philby's house.

59   Knightley, pp. 216–17.

60   *Comrade Philby* (KGB Spy Documentary) Timeline: World History Documentaries. https://www.youtube.com/watch?v=htukqTEeNaQ

61   Winks, pp. 405–6.

62   *Comrade Philby* (KGB Spy Documentary) Timeline: World History Documentaries. https://www.youtube.com/watch?v=htukqTEeNaQ

63   Orlov, pp. 90–1.

"THIS IS KIM'S WORK"

1   Morgan, pp. 245–6.
2   Riebling, Mark. *Wedge: The Secret War Between the FBI and CIA*. New York: Knopf, 1994, p. 136; Ambrose, p. 188.
3   See Jackson, *Volume I*, pp. 73–7.
4   Jackson, *Volume I*, pp. 61–2.
5   Epstein, in *Moles, Defectors, and* pp. 21–2.
6   Morgan, p. 250.
7   Epstein, *Deception*, p. 103.
8   Hersh, pp. 357–9.
9   Wise, pp. 42–3.
10 Marchetti, Victor. *The CIA and the Cult of Intelligence*, New York, Alfred A. Knopf, 1974.
11 Jeffreys-Jones, *The CIA and American Democracy*, p. 106.
12 JFK Assassination Files, Record 104-10336010003, Memorandum from T. Jeremy Gunn to Barry Harrelson, 9 January 1997, pdf, p. 16.
13 Robarge, p. 35.
14 Robarge, pp. 30-1.
15 Robarge, pp. 32–5.
16 See Wright, p. 163.
17 Wright, pp. 308–9.
18 JFK Assassinations File Number 104-10150-10011, Rockefeller Commission, Rocca Testimony, 19/890/ PDF 34. https://upload.wikimedia.org/wikipedia/commons/e/e3/104-10150-10011_%28November_9%2C_2017_Release%29.pdf
19 Mary McCarthy papers, Vassar College.
20 Benghi, Emilia. "Intellettuali antifascisti in America." *La Repubblica*, 3 June 2008. Google translation, my edits.
21 S. Herman Horton replaced Angleton as acting chief of the Counter-intelligence Staff, and therefore handled the Eichmann matter in his stead after Mossad captured Eichmann in Argentina. See Naftali, Timothy. "The CIA and Eichmann's Associates." In Breiman, et al. *U.S. Intelligence and the Nazis*. Cambridge: Cambridge University Press, 2005.
22 R. O. L'Allier to Mr. Belmont, FBI Memorandum, 9 November 1960. Freedom of Information Act request, in the possession of the author.

23 Morgan, p. 328.

24 R. O. L'Allier to Mr. Belmont, FBI Memorandum, 28 February 1961. Freedom of Information Act request, in the possession of the author. On 28 February 1961, Hoover was told that Angleton had "returned to duty" a month or so early.

25 Thomas, Evan. *The Very Best Men*. New York: Simon & Schuster, 1995, p. 205.

26 Morgan, p. 327.

27 Powers, Thomas, pp. 109–110. This was possible because the CIA's system in Cuba had been penetrated. Kessler, Ronald. *Inside the CIA: Revealing the Secrets of the World's Most Powerful Spy Agency*. New York: Pocket Books, 1994, p. 44.

28 Senate Select Committee to Study Governmental Operations with Respect to Intelligence Activities, Assassination Transcripts of the Church Committee, Angleton, 19 June 1975, pp. 83–4.

29 Senate Select Committee to Study Governmental Operations with Respect to Intelligence Activities, Assassination Transcripts of the Church Committee, Angleton, 6 February 1976, pp. 63–4. NARA Record Number 157-10014-10003. There were stories about Cuban agents traveling to the US through Canada.

30 Fursenko, Aleksandr and Naftali, Timothy. "Soviet intelligence and the Cuban missile crisis." *Intelligence and National Security*, 13:3, 1998, p. 76. Their reference is: Archives of the Main Department of the General Staff of the Russian Federation [GRU]. Of course, this is equivalent to a reference reading: United States National Archives, that is, not traceable. https://www.belfercenter.org/sites/default/files/legacy/files/CMC50/SovietIntelligenceAndTheCuban-MissileCrisis.pdf

31 Was this done? Probably. What form did it take? How long did it last? Or is it, perhaps, still in existence?

32 US Department of State, FRUS 1961–1963, vol. 10, section 223, "Paper Prepared in the Central Intelligence Agency," Washington, 19 May 1961.

33 Senate Select Committee to Study Governmental Operations with Respect to Intelligence Activities, Assassination Transcripts of the Church Committee, Angleton, 19 June 1975, p. 84.

34 See, inter alia, https://www.archives.gov/research/jfk/release?page=22&sort=desc&order=Agency.

35 Senate Select Committee to Study Governmental Operations with

Respect to Intelligence Activities, Assassination Transcripts of the Church Committee, Angleton, 19 June 1975, p. 62.

36 Wise, p. 22, citing Golitsyn, Anatoliy. *New Lies for Old*. London: The Bodley Head, Ltd, 1984.

37 Bagley, pp. 56–7.

38 Bagley, p. 58.

39 See Zubok, Vladislav M. "Spy vs. Spy: The KGB vs. the CIA." Cold War International History Project, CWIHP Bulletin 4 (Fall 1994).

40 Senate Select Committee to Study Governmental Operations with Respect to Intelligence Activities, Assassination Transcripts of the Church Committee, Angleton, 19 June 1975, pp. 63–4; p. 65.

41 JFK Assassination file: 104-10172-10227.

42 Morley, p. 134 citing *Spycatcher*.

43 Mangold, pp. 71–4.

44 Zubok, "Spy vs. Spy."

45 Zubok, "Spy vs. Spy."

46 Golitsyn, p. 70.

47 Cave Brown, p. 535.

48 Concerning the Sino-Soviet split, see: Wong, Dong. "The Quarrelling Brothers: New Chinese Archives and a Reappraisal of the Sino-Soviet Spit, 1959–1962." Cold War International History Project, Working Paper #49.

49 Johnson, Ross, in *Moles Defectors, and Deceptions: James Angleton and His Influence on US Counterintelligence*. Edited by Bruce Hoffman and Christian Ostermann. A Wilson Center and Georgetown University Center for Security Studies Joint Conference, 2014, p. 80.

50 Senate Select Committee to Study Governmental Operations with Respect to Intelligence Activities, Assassination Transcripts of the Church Committee, Angleton, 9.17.75, p. 65.

51 Wise, pp. 161–2.

52 Wise, p. 9.

53 Robarge, David, in *Moles Defectors, and Deceptions: James Angleton and His Influence on US Counterintelligence*. Edited by Bruce Hoffman and Christian Ostermann. A Wilson Center and Georgetown University Center for Security Studies Joint Conference, 2014, p. 94.

54 Studies in Intelligence, Central Intelligence Agency, Vol. 16, No. 2, Spring 1972. https://www.cia.gov/library/readingroom/docs/CIA-RDP78T03194A000300010013-8.pdf

55 Wise, pp. 25–6.

56 Wise, p. 285.

57 Bagley, p. 59.

58 Robarge, p. 40.

59 John M. Maury, Chief, SR Division, 29 March 1963, Memorandum for DCI, JFK Assassination Files, 104-10169-10125.

60 https://www.maryferrell.org/php/jfkdb.php?field=recno&subfield=202&value=202-10002&sort=recno&page=2   Record   Number 202-10002-10039.

61 Morley, pp. 130-1.

62 Dulles, Allen. *The Craft of Intelligence.* New York: Harper and Row, 1965, p. 106.

63 Beschloss, *Taking Charge*, p. 14. "The CIA had information [on 23 November 1963] on foreign connections to the alleged assassin, Lee Harvey Oswald, which suggested to LBJ that Kennedy may have been murdered by an international conspiracy." Ibid., p. 22.

64 Epstein, Edward Jay, *Legend: The Secret World of Lee Harvey Oswald.* New York: McGraw-Hill, 1978, pp. 103; pp. 168–69.

65 Morley, p. 88.

66 Riebling, p. 205.

67 Senate Select Committee to Study Governmental Operations with Respect to Intelligence Activities, Assassination Transcripts of the Church Committee, Angleton, 19 June 1975, p. 51.

68 Senate Select Committee to Study Governmental Operations with Respect to Intelligence Activities, Assassination Transcripts of the Church Committee, Angleton, 19 June 1975, pp. 49–50.

69 Senate Select Committee to Study Governmental Operations with Respect to Intelligence Activities, Assassination Transcripts of the Church Committee, Angleton, 6 February 1976, p. 43. NARA Record Number 157-10014-10003.

70 JFK Assassination System, Agency: SSCSGO; Record Number: 157-10014-10002; Thomas Karamessines, 04/14/76, p. 45.

71 Counterintelligence Operations, Soviet Russia Division, 1946–1965, The Clandestine Service Historical Series, CS HP 334, Historical Staff, Central Intelligence Agency, August 1972, p. 71ff.

72 JFK Assassination Files, 104-10419-10001, Memorandum for the Record, 13 November 1975, Subject: Meeting of Mr. Rocca with Members of the Senate Select Committee Staff.

73 http://www.washingtondecoded.com/site/2017/12/david-robarges-2nd-rejoinder.html

74 JFK Assassination System, Record Number: 104-10052-10119.

75 JFK Assassination System, Agency: SSCIA, Record Number: 157-10008-10210. Interview Summary, Interview With: Raymond Rocca . . . 3/15/76

76 JFK Assassination files, 104-10213-10058, Central Intelligence Agency, Field Double Agent Guide, August 1960, JFK Assassination files, 104-10213-10058, p. 11.

77 JFK Assassination files, 104-10213-10058, Central Intelligence Agency, Field Double Agent Guide, August 1960, JFK Assassination files, 104-10213-10058, p. 17. Fourth question redacted.

78 Heuer, p. 380.

79 Robarge, David. "DCI John McCone and the Assassination of President John F. Kennedy." As reprinted in *Studies in Intelligence*, September 2013, p. 14.

80 Robarge, "DCI John McCone and the Assassination of President John F. Kennedy," p. 18. The reference is to the Mitrokhin archive.

81 James Angleton Interview, House Select Committee on Assassinations, 15 June 1978, p. 14.

82 See Powers, p. 328.

83 Andrew and Gordievsky, *KGB*, p. 379–81.

84 See Wise, p. 232.

85 Epstein, *Deception*, p. 42.

86 Robarge, "Moles, Defectors, and Deceptions: James Angleton and CIA Counterintelligence." p. 40.

87 Morley, p. 159. Morley writes in a footnote that Helms's approval came five days before Nosenko told CIA he wanted to defect. See NARA JFK CIA RIF 104-10106-10081 Subject: BERTOTALLY, Bruce A.

88 Riebling, pp. 243–4.

89 See Heuer, pp. 380–6.

90 Bagley, pp. 213–14.

91 Andrew, Christopher, in *Moles, Defectors, and Deceptions: James Angleton and His Influence on US Counterintelligence.* Edited by Bruce Hoffman and Christian Ostermann. A Wilson Center and Georgetown University Center for Security Studies Joint Conference, 2014, pp. 45–6.

92 Leigh, p. 152.

93   Wright, pp. 307–8.
94   Elliott, Nicholas. *With My Little Eye: Observations Along the Way.*
     Norwich: Michael Russell, 1993, pp. 81–2.

PHILBY IN MOSCOW

 1   See also: 18 December 1967, *Izvestia* article under the heading,
     "Hello, Comrade Philby." The interview, first published in the Rus-
     sian daily newspaper *Izvestia* on 19 December 1967, was translated
     into English for publication in FBIS supplement "Materials on 50th
     Anniversary of Soviet State Security Organs, Fbis-Frb-68-007-S on
     1968-01-10. Supplement number 2" titled "Hello, Comrade Philby."
 2   Knightley, Philby, p. 1.
 3   Seale and McConville, pp. 320–1.
 4   Knightley, p. 226.
 5   Riley, p. 22.
 6   Lamphere and Shachtman, pp. 237–9.
 7   Knightley, p. 157.
 8   Maddrell, p. 143ff. For an interesting description and documentation
     of the secret intelligence struggle in the GDR, and double agent trade-
     craft, see: Maddrell's February 2009 Cold War International History
     Project Working Pager #58: "Exploiting and Securing the Open Border
     in Berlin: the Western Secret Services, the Stasi, and the Second Berlin
     Crisis, 1958–1961." https://www.wilsoncenter.org/sites/default/files/
     CWIHPWP58_maddrell.pdf
 9   According to the FBI, "The Wednesday, 13 October 1971, edition
     of 'Kodumaa,' Number 41, (677), contained on p. 3 an interview
     with KIM Philby." This was printed in the British magazine *Lobster*
     as "Philby naming names." *Lobster*, 16: http://www.8bitmode.com/
     rogerdog/lobster/lobster16.pdf
10   For further research: ". . . a most interesting book written by Guy
     Burgess as a secret training manual for Soviet intelligence officers."
     Lyubimov, Mikhail. "A Martyr to Dogma." In Philby, Rufina.
     p. 284.
11   Philby, Rufina, p. 59; p. 67.
12   "Mikhail Lubimov . . . A genial, relaxed fellow with a good brain,
     he had been posted to the London station in the 1960s . . . The result
     was that he fell in love with the place, and became an enthusiastic
     advocate of all things British, not least English literature and Scotch

whisky." Gordievsky, Oleg. *Next Stop Execution*. London: Macmillan, 1995, pp. 218–19.

13 Cave Brown, p. 591. "The Kim Philby–Mikhail Lyubimov Collection contains 12 letters from Kim Philby to Mikhail Lyubimov. The letters were sent from Moscow to Copenhagen. In the letters, Philby thanks Lyubimov for sending many packages with presents to Philby. Moreover, Philby touches on his travel plans, especially to the Crimea. Also, Philby makes a reference to his autobiography 'My Silent War' and to celebrating his 16th anniversary of living in the Soviet Union. In addition to the letters from Philby to Lyubimov, there are three letters from Lyubimov to Philby. The Philby–Lyubimov Collection is stored in one small archival box (0.25 linear feet)." https://findingaids.library.georgetown.edu/repositories/15/resources/10329

14 Lyubimov, Mikhail. "A Martyr to Dogma." In Philby, Rufina. p. 283.

15 Modin, p. 262.

16 Lyubimov, p. 288.

17 Modin, pp. 264–5.

18 Philby, Rufina, pp. 84–7.

19 https://findingaids.library.georgetown.edu/repositories/15/archival_objects/1241066

20 Lyubimov, p. 287.

21 Macintyre, Ben. *The Spy and the Traitor*. London: Penguin Random House UK, 2018, pp. 102–3.

22 Philby, Rufina, p. 35.

23 Gordievsky, pp. 228–9. According to Gordievsky, Mikhail Leonidovich Bogdanov, for example, "had been one of Kim Philby's brightest pupils in his little seminars." p. 310 footnote. Bogdanov, former Russian ambassador to Israel and Egypt, is currently Deputy Minister of Foreign Affairs and Special Presidential Representative for the Middle East and Africa.

24 Lashkul, Vyacheslav. "The Moscow Life of Kim Philby," *Sputnik*, 30 January 2004. https://sputniknews.com/analysis/2004013039906480/

25 Philby, Rufina, p. 202.

26 Riley, p. 159, citing Knightley, *Philby, KGB Masterspy*, p. 262.

ANGLETON: A DECADE OF INVESTIGATIONS

1 Trento, p. 277. Trento's book includes materials, such as this, from interviews with Angleton. Otherwise, it should not be used as a sole source.

2 Robarge, in *Moles, Defectors, and Deceptions: James Angleton and His Influence on US* p. 99.

3 "The KGB's 1967 Annual Report," 6 May 1968, History and Public Policy Program Digital Archive, TsKhSD f. 89, op. 5, d. 3, ll. 1-14. Translated for CWIHP by Vladislav Zubok. http://digitalarchive.wilsoncenter.org/document/110403

4 US Senate, Final Report of the Select Committee to Study Governmental Operations with Respect to Intelligence Activities Together with Additional Supplemental and Separate Views, Book IV, Supplementary Detailed Staff Reports on Foreign and Military Intelligence, p. 68.

5 "Extracts from CI History," JFK Assassination System, Agency: CIA, Record Number: 104-10301-10011, p. 22. https://history-matters.com/archive/jfk/cia/ddo_ci/104-10301-10011/html/104-10301

6 "By the mid-1950s it was evident that the centrist coalition was no longer practicable and, after a failed attempt to govern with the Movimento Sociale Italiano, the idea of involving the Socialists gained traction. This was facilitated by the growing consensus within the Democrazia Cristiana (DC) around the need for economic planning to ensure even economic development. However, party divisions meant that the 'opening to the left' was not endorsed until the 1962 party congress. The opening was made possible by the removal of Vatican and US vetoes, by the Socialists' dealignment from Communism after the Hungarian Uprising and by their acceptance of NATO. The alliance with the Socialists began in 1963 and lasted until 1968." Favretto, Ilaria. "The 'Opening to the Left.'" Jones, Erik and Gianfranco Pasquino. *The Oxford Book of Italian Politics*, 2015, Abstract. http://www.oxfordhandbooks.com/view/10.1093/oxfordhb/9780199669745.001.0001/oxfordhb-9780199669745-e-21

7 Prados, Hohn. *Lost Crusader: The Secret Wars of CIA Director William Colby*. Oxford: Oxford University Press, 2003, pp. 59–60.

8 Colby, William and Forbath, Peter. *Honorable Men: My Life in the CIA*. New York: Simon & Schuster, 1978, pp. 130–3.

9 Colby interview 15 March 1988, in *William E. Colby as Director of*

Central Intelligence, 1973-1976, by Harold P. Ford, CIA History Staff, Center for the Study of Intelligence, Central Intelligence Agency, Washington, D.C., 1993, p. 77. Oral History: Reflections of DCI Colby and Helms on the CIA's "Time of Troubles" From the CIA Oral History Archives. https://www.cia.gov/library/center-for-the-study-of-intelligence/csi-publications/csi-studies/studies/vol51no3/reflections-of-dci-colby-and-helms-on-the-cia2019s-201ctime-of-troubles201d.html

10   CIA CI SIG History, pdf, p. 22.

11   Private information.

12   D. J. Brennan, Jr., to W. C. Sullivan, FBI Memorandum, 12 September 1968. FOIA FBI file on James Angleton in the possession of the author.

13   Morgan, p. 348. Morgan was given the FBI's Angleton files by the author, who obtained them through an FOIA request.

14   Pincher, pp. 533–4.

15   Morgan, p. 350.

16   JFK Assassination Records, Miler, Newton S. Personnel File, 104-10224-10007, p. 28.

17   JFK Assassination Records, File Number 1781000410115.

18   Wolf, Markus and McElvoy, Anne. *Man Without a Face: The Autobiography of Communism's Greatest Spymaster*. New York: PublicAffairs, 1997 p. 175.

19   Robarge, "Moles, Defectors, and Deceptions: James Angleton and CIA Counterintelligence," p. 47.

20   Robarge, in *Moles, Defectors, and Deceptions: James Angleton and His Influence on US Counterintelligence*. p. 107.

21   Trento, p. 479.

PHILBY'S ARTICLES IN THE *OBSERVER* AND THE *ECONOMIST*

1   Milne, p. 191.

INDEX